Saints up and down the centuries have prayed the Psalms each day, including John Paul II, Pier Giorgio Frassati, Thérèse of Lisieux, Thomas Aquinas, Augustine, Benedict, and the first Apostles. And, of course, this is how Mary, Joseph, and Jesus prayed too. They knew, loved, and prayed the Psalms. So, you're entering into this same tradition of prayer shared by the greatest men and women in Christian history.

The Liturgy of the Hours is composed of five major "hours" or times of prayer:

Morning Prayer—also known as Lauds, prayed first thing in the morning

Daytime Prayer—prayed sometime between mid-morning and mid-afternoon

Evening Prayer—also known as Vespers, prayed in the early evening

Night Prayer—also known as Compline, offered just before bedtime

Office of Readings—the longest hour, featuring lengthy readings from the Bible, Church Fathers, or other saints, prayed at any point during the day

This booklet contains the core hours of Morning, Evening, and Night Prayer.

The word "hours" can be misleading. It doesn't refer to the time it takes to complete each prayer, but to the hours of the day. None of the liturgical hours takes anywhere close to sixty minutes. In fact, the two main hours, Morning and Evening Prayer, take around fifteen minutes each, while Night Prayer takes only five to ten minutes.

The Liturgy of the Hours is well-known among clergy and religious, who are required to pray the five major hours every day. Permanent deacons are obliged to pray Morning and Evening Prayer. Among the laity, the Liturgy of the Hours has been less popular, but that is starting to change. The Second Vatican Council taught that "the laity, too, are encouraged to recite the divine office, either with the priests, or among themselves, or even individually."[2] Recent popes have repeated this invitation. Pope St. Paul VI especially emphasized the call for families to pray the Liturgy of the Hours, saying, "No avenue should be left unexplored to ensure that this clear and practical recommendation finds within Christian families growing and joyful acceptance."[3]

[2] *Sacrosanctum Concilium* 100.
[3] Paul VI, *Marialis Cultus* 53.

10

Why Pray the Liturgy of the Hours?

There are many reasons why you should pray the Liturgy of the Hours, whether individually or with others, but here are seven.

First, it unites us to Jesus Christ. The Liturgy of the Hours joins us with Christ in singing an eternal hymn of praise to the Father. As Vatican II taught, "It is the very prayer which Christ Himself, together with His body, addresses to the Father."[4] If you want to grow deeper in your relationship with Christ, and you already frequent the sacraments, your next step should be to begin praying the Liturgy of the Hours. Few practices will draw you closer to Jesus.

Second, the Liturgy of the Hours allows you to pray with the Church. Personal prayer is good and necessary, but when the Church offers praise to God through the Liturgy of the Hours, "it unites itself with that hymn of praise sung throughout all ages in the halls of heaven."[5] We join not only people from every tribe and tongue, every people and nation, but the entire communion of saints in heaven.

Third, the Liturgy of the Hours is the highest form of prayer after the Mass. Why? Because the Liturgy of the Hours is not just the private prayer of some Christians, but the unified, sacred prayer

[4] *Sacrosanctum Concilium* 84.
[5] *General Instruction on the Liturgy of the Hours* 16. See *Sacrosanctum Concilium* 83.

of the whole Church, uniting all the faithful, from all vocations, in all countries, into one single prayer to the Father, echoing the very Word of God back to its source. (It's also the supreme way to pray as a family. Pope St. Paul VI affirmed this in *Marialis Cultus*, calling it "the high point which family prayer can reach."[6])

Fourth, *the Liturgy of the Hours is thoroughly biblical.* "Its readings are drawn from sacred Scripture, God's words in the Psalms are sung in his presence, and the intercessions, prayers, and hymns are inspired by Scripture and steeped in its spirit."[7] The more you pray the Hours, the more the Bible saturates your mind and heart. You'll begin noticing yourself memorizing large chunks of Scripture—the Canticles especially, which are repeated each morning and evening—and you'll find that biblical passages spring to mind during your own quiet, personal prayer. All of this will make your prayer more biblical.

Fifth, *the Liturgy of the Hours will mature and deepen the rest of your spiritual life.* After praying the Hours for some time, you will begin to see the world differently. You will develop a renewed spiritual vision, seeing the world as God sees it, more attuned to the dynamics of justice, love, sin, compassion, and forgiveness. You are changed as a consequence. You will also notice your

[6] Paul VI, *Marialis Cultus* 54.
[7] *General Instruction on the Liturgy of the Hours* 14. See *Sacrosanctum Concilium* 24.

times of personal prayer outside the Liturgy of the Hours becoming more elevated and intense. The Liturgy of the Hours incorporates each major dimension of Christian prayer—worship, thanksgiving, petition, and intercession—and by praying the Hours, you become more proficient in each one.

Sixth, the Liturgy of the Hours allows you to "pray without ceasing." Jesus taught about the need to "pray always and not to lose heart" (Luke 18:1), and St. Paul directed us to "pray without ceasing" (1 Thess. 5:17). But for many Christians, these directives seem unrealistic, if not impossible. How can we pray continually, especially when our days are jam-packed with duties and commitments? The Liturgy of the Hours offers a solution, allowing you to lock in times of prayer throughout the day and, more than that, combine your voice with millions of others throughout the world who are also praying the Hours. At every moment, someone somewhere is offering these prayers to God. So, while we might not be able to "pray without ceasing" as individuals, we can do so together as a Church.

Seventh, and finally, the Liturgy of the Hours makes God the center of your day. When you begin each day with Morning Prayer, close it with Evening Prayer, and offer Night Prayer before bed, you establish three fixed pillars during the day around which the rest of your activities turn. For other people, the main pillars of the day might be breakfast, lunch, and dinner, or perhaps work meetings or other activities. Everything else, including spiritual commitments, fits around those moments. But that changes when you pray the Liturgy of the Hours. Prayer becomes the new hinge of your day, reorienting your mind so that you give highest priority to the things of God.

Practical Tips for Praying

So the Liturgy of the Hours is definitely worth praying! Yet the next obvious question is: How do you do it? How do you begin? The answer used to be complicated. It required special books, personal instruction, lots of page flipping and bookmarks, and a solid familiarity with the liturgical calendar. It was confusing, expensive, and difficult.

That is no longer the case. This *Word on Fire Liturgy of the Hours* booklet, which you hold in your hands, has made it easier than ever to enter into this chorus of praise. It's simple: you just read and pray. No special expertise, no page flipping, no ribbons, no guessing which prayers to say. You can get started right away.

That said, here are some recommendations that will enhance your experience.

First, start slow. If you're new to this form of prayer, you might not want to immediately start praying all three hours included in this booklet—Morning, Evening, and Night

Prayer—every day. Instead, perhaps consider starting with just Night Prayer, the shortest and easiest hour. It repeats on a seven-day cycle. So, for example, you pray the exact same Night Prayer each Monday night throughout the year, meaning you'll quickly become familiar and comfortable with it. Start with Night Prayer, and do it consistently for a week or two. From there, add one more hour, either Morning or Evening, before finally working up to all three in this booklet.

Second, be at peace if you aren't able to pray every hour, every day. Unless you are a priest or consecrated religious, you are not required to pray all the hours each day, which means there is no pressure on you. It is, of course, ideal if you can commit to praying Morning, Evening, and Night Prayer every day, and few things will deepen your prayer life more than consistently doing that, but don't feel deflated if you miss an hour here or there or have to take a short break. Like all prayer, the Liturgy of the Hours should be a gift, not a burden. So be at peace with what you can handle.

Third, push through the initial difficulties. Sometimes, those new to the Liturgy of the Hours find it to be stilted and monotonous, especially if they're used to more spontaneous, personal prayer. After all, it follows the same pattern, day after day, repeating the same Psalms and prayers on a cyclical basis. If you feel bored by this initially, that's okay; it's common. But push through it.

The spiritual fruit of the Liturgy of the Hours typically begins to bloom only after a few months of dedicated, consistent praying. It's similar in that way to the Mass and the Rosary. Both of those prayers include formal, repetitive recitation, which can seem monotonous at first. But at some point, after regular dedication, they open up with surprising freshness and power. You learn to appreciate the repetition the same way a child delights in saying "Do it again! Do it again!" to their parents. That will eventually happen, too, with the Liturgy of the Hours, so persevere.

Fourth, get outside of yourself. The Liturgy of the Hours has been described as "the prayer of the Church with Christ and to Christ."[8] This is because you not only pray alongside Christ but, in a mystical way, you pray with him and through him. So, as you pray the Psalms, learn to pray them as if it were Christ within you offering these words to the Father. For example, when praying Psalm 86, imagine yourself as Christ on the cross, and let it be that inner Christ saying, "O give your strength to your servant, and save your handmaid's son. Show me a sign of your favor, that my foes may see to their shame, that you console me and give me your help." You can also offer these prayers on behalf of other Christians throughout the world. You might not feel that enemies "surround me all the day like a flood"

---

[8]*General Instruction on the Liturgy of the Hours* 2.

or that "my one companion is darkness," as we find in Night Prayer each Friday. But certainly there are other Christians in the world in that position, and you can give voice to their laments. Let their cries become your prayer, on their behalf. Remember, this is the prayer of the whole Church: it transcends you and your personal concerns, important as those are. Through it, you become one with Christ and his entire Body.

Fifth, and finally, learn more about the Liturgy of the Hours. A basic principle of the spiritual life is that the more you study a facet of the faith, the more impactful it becomes. For instance, if you want to heighten your experience of the Mass, read some books about it. Understand it better, and it will soon shimmer in a new light. The same applies to the Liturgy of the Hours. The better you understand its history, purpose, and logic, the more profound your experience will be. Here are some excellent books that will help toward that end:

> *The Everyday Catholic's Guide to the Liturgy of the Hours* by Daria Sockey

> *A Layman's Guide to the Liturgy of the Hours* by Fr. Timothy Gallagher

> *Praying the Liturgy of the Hours: A Personal Journey* by Fr. Timothy Gallagher

> *General Instruction on the Liturgy of the Hours*

You will find other helpful resources at **wordonfire.org/pray**. But don't wait until you become a master at the Liturgy of the Hours to start praying it. Begin now. Start with this booklet: flip to the correct day, and commence with Morning, Evening, or Night Prayer. Then find other people—in your family, your parish, your community—and invite them to pray the Liturgy of the Hours with you.

Join your voice to this great chorus of praise as you begin now to sanctify each day.

Brandon Vogt

General Editor of Word on Fire Liturgy of the Hours
Senior Publishing Director at Word on Fire

Using Alternate Melodies to Sing the Hymns

If you are unfamiliar with the hymn assigned to a particular hour and you do not read music, you can still sing most of the hymns in this book.

The great majority of Latin hymns sung in the Liturgy of the Hours over the past two millennia are written in a metrical pattern called "Long Meter." Each stanza or verse in Long Meter contains four lines, with eight syllables per line (8.8.8.8), stressing the even-numbered syllables (with some stress variation allowed on the first two and last two syllables in each line). An example of an English hymn in Long Meter is the well-known Advent hymn "Creator of the Stars of Night":

Cre - **a** - tor **of** the **stars** of **night**,
Your **peo** - ple's **ev** - er - **last** - ing **Light**,
Je - sus, Re - **deem** - er **of** us **all**,
We **pray** you **hear** us **when** we **call**.

For well over a thousand years, both in its original Latin and in translation, this particular hymn has ordinarily been set to a single Gregorian chant melody known as CONDITOR ALME SIDERUM (the melody we used in our December issue). Yet throughout the history of Christian hymnody, most tunes have been shared quite freely among multiple texts, and many texts can be sung to more than one tune. Any text and tune that share the same metrical pattern can be paired (although some melodies tend better than others to suit a given text's mood, arc, or patterns of emphasis).

In addition to "Creator of the Stars of Night," familiar Long Meter hymns include "All People That on Earth Do Dwell," "Jesus Shall Reign," "Lift Up Your Heads," "O Radiant Light," "Take Up Your Cross," "The God Whom Earth and Sea and Sky," and "When I Survey the Wondrous Cross." Many Christians know one or several of these hymns, and any Long Meter text can be set to any Long Meter melody.

Likewise, most hymn texts in other meters can also fit more than one melody. For instance, almost any text with the syllable pattern 8.7.8.7 D can be sung to Beethoven's HYMN TO JOY ("Joyful, Joyful, We Adore Thee") or to the Welsh tune HYFRYDOL ("Alleluia! Sing to Jesus!" and "Love Divine, All Loves Excelling"). To use another well-known example, almost any text with the syllables 8.6.8.6 can be sung to "Amazing Grace."

At the end of this booklet you will find an index of hymns included in this month's issue of *Word on Fire Liturgy of the Hours* with metrical information and alternate melody options for most texts. If you or your group do not know the tune we have assigned to a given hymn text, you can use these suggestions to sing the same lyrics to a more familiar melody.

August 2024

Thursday, August 1, 2024
St. Alphonsus Liguori

MORNING PRAYER——————————————————

God, + come to my assistance.
—Lord, make haste to help me.

Glory to the Father, and to the Son,
    and to the Holy Spirit:
—as it was in the beginning, is now,
    and will be for ever. Amen. Alleluia.

Hymn   *Jesus, Eternal Truth Sublime, p. 693*

Psalmody   Ant. 1 **Awake, lyre and harp, with praise let us awake the dawn.**

Psalm 57   Have mercy on me, God, have mercy
for in you my soul has taken refuge.
In the shadow of your wings I take refuge
till the storms of destruction pass by.

I call to God the Most High,
to God who has always been my help.
May he send from heaven and save me
and shame those who assail me.

May God send his truth and his love.

My soul lies down among lions,
who would devour the sons of men.
Their teeth are spears and arrows,
their tongue a sharpened sword.

O God, arise above the heavens;
may your glory shine on earth!

They laid a snare for my steps,
my soul was bowed down.
They dug a pit in my path
but fell in it themselves.

My heart is ready, O God,
my heart is ready.
I will sing, I will sing your praise.
Awake, my soul,
awake, lyre and harp,
I will awake the dawn.

I will thank you, Lord, among the peoples,
among the nations I will praise you
for your love reaches to the heavens
and your truth to the skies.

O God, arise above the heavens;
may your glory shine on earth!

Glory to the Father, and to the Son,
    and to the Holy Spirit:
—as it was in the beginning, is now,
and will be for ever. Amen.

Ant.

Awake, lyre and harp, with praise let us awake the dawn.

Ant. 2

My people, says the Lord, will be filled with my blessings.

Canticle:
Jeremiah
31:10–14

Hear the word of the Lord, O nations,
proclaim it on distant coasts, and say:
He who scattered Israel, now gathers
    them together,
he guards them as a shepherd his flock.

The Lord shall ransom Jacob,
he shall redeem him from the hand of his
    conqueror.

Shouting, they shall mount the
    heights of Zion,
they shall come streaming to the Lord's
    blessings:
the grain, the wine, and the oil,
the sheep and the oxen;
they themselves shall be like watered gardens,
never again shall they languish.

Then the virgins shall make merry and dance,
and young men and old as well.
I will turn their mourning into joy,
I will console and gladden them after
    their sorrows.
I will lavish choice portions upon the priests,
and my people shall be filled with my
    blessings,
says the Lord.

Glory to the Father, and to the Son,
    and to the Holy Spirit:
—as it was in the beginning, is now,
    and will be for ever. Amen.

Ant.   **My people, says the Lord, will be filled with my blessings.**

Ant. 3   **The Lord is great and worthy to be praised in the city of our God.**

Psalm 48   The Lord is great and worthy to be praised
in the city of our God.
His holy mountain rises in beauty,
the joy of all the earth.

Mount Zion, true pole of the earth,
the Great King's city!
God, in the midst of its citadels,
has shown himself its stronghold.

For the kings assembled together,
together they advanced.
They saw; at once they were astounded;
dismayed, they fled in fear.

A trembling seized them there,
like the pangs of birth.
By the east wind you have destroyed
the ships of Tarshish.

As we have heard, so we have seen
in the city of our God,
in the city of the Lord of hosts
which God upholds for ever.

O God, we ponder your love
within your temple.
Your praise, O God, like your name
reaches the ends of the earth.

With justice your right hand is filled.
Mount Zion rejoices;
the people of Judah rejoice
at the sight of your judgments.

Walk through Zion, walk all round it;
count the number of its towers.
Review all its ramparts,
examine its castles,

that you may tell the next generation
that such is our God,
our God for ever and always.
It is he who leads us.

Glory to the Father, and to the Son,
    and to the Holy Spirit:
—as it was in the beginning, is now,
and will be for ever. Amen.

Ant.   **The Lord is great and worthy to be praised
in the city of our God.**

Reading   Simply I learned about Wisdom, and
Wisdom 7:13-14   ungrudgingly do I share—
                her riches I do not hide away;
            For to men she is an unfailing treasure;
                those who gain this treasure win the
                    friendship of God,
                to whom the gifts they have from
                    discipline commend them.

Responsory   Let the peoples proclaim the wisdom of
    the saints.
  —Let the peoples proclaim the wisdom of
     the saints.

  With joyful praise let the Church tell forth
  —the wisdom of the saints.

  Glory to the Father, and to the Son,
    and to the Holy Spirit.
  —Let the peoples proclaim the wisdom of
     the saints.

Gospel
Canticle

Ant. **Those who are learned will be as
radiant as the sky in all its beauty; those
who instruct the people in goodness will
shine like the stars for all eternity.**

Canticle of
Zechariah
Luke 1:68–79

Blessed + be the Lord, the God of Israel;
he has come to his people and set them free.

He has raised up for us a mighty savior,
born of the house of his servant David.

Through his holy prophets he
  promised of old
that he would save us from our enemies,
from the hands of all who hate us.

He promised to show mercy to our fathers
and to remember his holy covenant.

This was the oath he swore to our
    father Abraham:
to set us free from the hands of our enemies,
free to worship him without fear,
holy and righteous in his sight
    all the days of our life.

You, my child, shall be called the prophet of
    the Most High;
for you will go before the Lord to
    prepare his way,
to give his people knowledge of salvation
by the forgiveness of their sins.

In the tender compassion of our God
the dawn from on high shall break upon us,
to shine on those who dwell in darkness and
    the shadow of death,
and to guide our feet into the way of peace.

Glory to the Father, and to the Son,
    and to the Holy Spirit:
—as it was in the beginning, is now,
and will be for ever. Amen.

Ant.

**Those who are learned will be as radiant as
the sky in all its beauty; those who instruct
the people in goodness will shine like the
stars for all eternity.**

Intercessions   Christ is the Good Shepherd who laid down
his life for his sheep. Let us praise and
thank him as we pray:
Nourish your people, Lord.

Christ, you decided to show your merciful
love through your holy shepherds,
—let your mercy always reach us through them.

Through your vicars you continue to
perform the ministry of shepherd of souls,
—direct us always through our leaders.

Through your holy ones, the leaders of your
people, you served as physician of our
bodies and our spirits,
—continue to fulfill your ministry of life and
holiness in us.

You taught your flock through the prudence
and love of your saints,
—grant us continual growth in holiness under
the direction of our pastors.

**The Lord's
Prayer**   Our Father, who art in heaven,
hallowed be thy name;
thy kingdom come,
thy will be done
on earth as it is in heaven.
Give us this day our daily bread,
and forgive us our trespasses,
as we forgive those who trespass against us;
and lead us not into temptation,
but deliver us from evil.

Pater noster, qui es in cælis:
sanctificetur nomen tuum;
adveniat regnum tuum;
fiat voluntas tua,
sicut in cælo, et in terra.
Panem nostrum cotidianum da nobis hodie;
et dimitte nobis debita nostra,
sicut et nos dimittimus debitoribus nostris;
et ne nos inducas in tentationem;
sed libera nos a malo.

Concluding Prayer

Father,
you constantly build up your Church
by the lives of your saints.
Give us the grace to follow Saint Alphonsus
in his loving concern for the salvation of men,
and so come to share his reward in heaven.
Grant this through our Lord Jesus Christ,
　　your Son,
who lives and reigns with you and
　　the Holy Spirit,
God, for ever and ever.
—Amen.

Dismissal

If praying individually, or in a group without a priest or deacon:

May the Lord + bless us,
protect us from all evil
and bring us to everlasting life.
—Amen.

If praying with a priest or deacon, he dismisses the people:

The Lord be with you.
—And with your spirit.

May almighty God bless you,
the Father, and the Son, + and the Holy Spirit.
—Amen.

Go in peace.
—Thanks be to God.

EVENING PRAYER————————————

God, + come to my assistance.
—Lord, make haste to help me.

Glory to the Father, and to the Son,
and to the Holy Spirit:
—as it was in the beginning, is now,
and will be for ever. Amen. Alleluia.

Hymn   *The Saints of God!, p. 702*

Psalmody   Ant. 1 **I cried to you, Lord, and you healed
me; I will praise you for ever.**

Psalm 30   I will praise you, Lord, you have rescued me
and have not let my enemies rejoice over me.

O Lord, I cried to you for help
and you, my God, have healed me.
O Lord, you have raised my soul
from the dead,
restored me to life from those who sink into
the grave.

Sing psalms to the Lord, you who love him,
give thanks to his holy name.
His anger lasts but a moment;
    his favor through life.
At night there are tears, but joy comes
    with dawn.

I said to myself in my good fortune:
"Nothing will ever disturb me."
Your favor had set me on a mountain fastness,
then you hid your face and I was put to
    confusion.

To you, Lord, I cried,
to my God I made appeal:
"What profit would my death be,
    my going to the grave?
Can dust give you praise or proclaim
    your truth?"

The Lord listened and had pity.
The Lord came to my help.
For me you have changed my mourning
    into dancing,
you removed my sackcloth and clothed
    me with joy.
So my soul sings psalms to you unceasingly.
O Lord my God, I will thank you for ever.

Glory to the Father, and to the Son,
    and to the Holy Spirit:
—as it was in the beginning, is now,
    and will be for ever. Amen.

Ant.   **I cried to you, Lord, and you healed me; I will praise you for ever.**

Ant. 2   **The one who is sinless in the eyes of God is blessed indeed.**

Psalm 32   Happy the man whose offense is forgiven,
whose sin is remitted.
O happy the man to whom the Lord
imputes no guilt,
in whose spirit is no guile.

I kept it secret and my frame was wasted.
I groaned all the day long
for night and day your hand
was heavy upon me.
Indeed, my strength was dried up
as by the summer's heat.

But now I have acknowledged my sins;
my guilt I did not hide.
I said: "I will confess
my offense to the Lord."
And you, Lord, have forgiven
the guilt of my sin.

So let every good man pray to you
in the time of need.
The floods of water may reach high
but him they shall not reach.
You are my hiding place, O Lord;
you save me from distress.
You surround me with cries of deliverance.

I will instruct you and teach you
the way you should go;
I will give you counsel
with my eye upon you.

Be not like horse and mule, unintelligent,
needing bridle and bit,
else they will not approach you.
Many sorrows has the wicked
but he who trusts in the Lord,
loving mercy surrounds him.

Rejoice, rejoice in the Lord,
exult, you just!
O come, ring out your joy,
all you upright of heart.

Glory to the Father, and to the Son,
    and to the Holy Spirit:
—as it was in the beginning, is now,
and will be for ever. Amen.

Ant.   **The one who is sinless in the eyes of God is
blessed indeed.**

Ant. 3   **The Father has given Christ all power, honor
and kingship; all people will obey him.**

Canticle:
Revelation
11:17–18;
12:10b–12a

We praise you, the Lord God Almighty,
who is and who was.
You have assumed your great power,
you have begun your reign.

The nations have raged in anger,
but then came your day of wrath
and the moment to judge the dead:
the time to reward your servants
    the prophets
and the holy ones who revere you,
the great and the small alike.

Now have salvation and power come,
the reign of our God and the authority
of his Anointed One.
For the accuser of our brothers is cast out,
who night and day accused them before God.

They defeated him by the blood of the Lamb
and by the word of their testimony;
love for life did not deter them from death.
So rejoice, you heavens,
and you that dwell therein!

Glory to the Father, and to the Son,
    and to the Holy Spirit:
—as it was in the beginning, is now,
and will be for ever. Amen.

Ant.   **The Father has given Christ all power, honor and kingship; all people will obey him.**

Reading
James 3:17–18

Wisdom from above is first of all innocent. It is also peaceable, lenient, docile, rich in sympathy and the kindly deeds that are its fruits, impartial and sincere. The harvest of justice is sown in peace for those who cultivate peace.

Responsory   In the midst of the Church he spoke with
                   eloquence.
              —In the midst of the Church he spoke with
                   eloquence.

              The Lord filled him with the spirit of
                  wisdom and understanding.
              —He spoke with eloquence.

              Glory to the Father, and to the Son,
                  and to the Holy Spirit.
              —In the midst of the Church he spoke with
                   eloquence.

Gospel Canticle   Ant. **O blessed doctor, Saint Alphonsus,
                   light of holy Church and lover of God's law,
                   pray to the Son of God for us.**

Canticle of Mary Luke 1:46–55

My + soul proclaims the greatness of the Lord,
my spirit rejoices in God my Savior
for he has looked with favor on his
        lowly servant.

From this day all generations will
        call me blessed:
the Almighty has done great things for me,
and holy is his Name.

He has mercy on those who fear him
in every generation.

He has shown the strength of his arm,
he has scattered the proud in their conceit.

He has cast down the mighty from
    their thrones,
and has lifted up the lowly.

He has filled the hungry with good things,
and the rich he has sent away empty.

He has come to the help of his servant Israel
for he has remembered his promise of mercy,
the promise he made to our fathers,
to Abraham and his children for ever.

Glory to the Father, and to the Son,
    and to the Holy Spirit:
—as it was in the beginning, is now,
and will be for ever. Amen.

Ant.   **O blessed doctor, Saint Alphonsus, light of
holy Church and lover of God's law, pray to
the Son of God for us.**

Intercessions   Jesus Christ is worthy of all praise, for he was
        appointed high priest among men and
        their representative before God. We honor
        him and in our weakness we pray:
Bring salvation to your people, Lord.

You marvelously illuminated your Church
        through distinguished leaders and holy
        men and women,
—let Christians rejoice always in such splendor.

You forgave the sins of your people when
their holy leaders like Moses sought your
compassion,
—through their intercession continue to purify
and sanctify your holy people.

In the midst of their brothers and sisters you
anointed your holy ones and filled them
with the Holy Spirit,
—fill all the leaders of your people with the
same Spirit.

You yourself are the only visible possession of
our holy pastors,
—let none of them, won at the price of your
blood, remain far from you.

The shepherds of your Church keep your
flock from being snatched out of your
hand. Through them you give your flock
eternal life,
—save those who have died, those for whom
you gave up your life.

**The Lord's
Prayer**

Our Father, who art in heaven,
hallowed be thy name;
thy kingdom come,
thy will be done
on earth as it is in heaven.
Give us this day our daily bread,
and forgive us our trespasses,
as we forgive those who trespass against us;
and lead us not into temptation,
but deliver us from evil.

Pater noster, qui es in cælis:
sanctificetur nomen tuum;
adveniat regnum tuum;
fiat voluntas tua,
sicut in cælo, et in terra.
Panem nostrum cotidianum da nobis hodie;
et dimitte nobis debita nostra,
sicut et nos dimittimus debitoribus nostris;
et ne nos inducas in tentationem;
sed libera nos a malo.

Concluding Prayer

Father,
you constantly build up your Church
by the lives of your saints.
Give us the grace to follow Saint Alphonsus
in his loving concern for the salvation of men,
and so come to share his reward in heaven.
Grant this through our Lord Jesus Christ,
　　your Son,
who lives and reigns with you and
　　the Holy Spirit,
God, for ever and ever.
—Amen.

Dismissal

If praying individually, or in a group without a priest or deacon:

May the Lord + bless us,
protect us from all evil
and bring us to everlasting life.
—Amen.

If praying with a priest or deacon, he dismisses the people:

The Lord be with you.
—And with your spirit.

May almighty God bless you,
the Father, and the Son, + and the Holy Spirit.
—Amen.

Go in peace.
—Thanks be to God.

NIGHT PRAYER————————————————

God, + come to my assistance.
—Lord, make haste to help me.

Glory to the Father, and to the Son,
and to the Holy Spirit:
—as it was in the beginning, is now,
and will be for ever. Amen. Alleluia.

Examen   *An optional brief examination of conscience may be made. Call to mind your sins and failings this day.*

Hymn   *O Gladsome Light, p. 696*

Psalmody   Ant. **In you, my God, my body will rest in hope.**

Psalm 16   Preserve me, God, I take refuge in you.
I say to the Lord: "You are my God.
My happiness lies in you alone."

He has put into my heart a marvelous love
for the faithful ones who dwell in his land.
Those who choose other gods increase
their sorrows.
Never will I offer their offerings of blood.
Never will I take their name upon my lips.

O Lord, it is you who are my portion and cup;
it is you yourself who are my prize.
The lot marked out for me is my delight:
welcome indeed the heritage that falls to me!

I will bless the Lord who gives me counsel,
who even at night directs my heart.
I keep the Lord ever in my sight:
since he is at my right hand, I shall
    stand firm.

And so my heart rejoices, my soul is glad;
even my body shall rest in safety.
For you will not leave my soul
    among the dead,
nor let your beloved know decay.

You will show me the path of life,
the fullness of joy in your presence,
at your right hand happiness for ever.

Glory to the Father, and to the Son,
    and to the Holy Spirit:
—as it was in the beginning, is now,
and will be for ever. Amen.

Ant.   **In you, my God, my body will rest in hope.**

Reading   May the God of peace make you perfect in
1 Thessalonians   holiness. May he preserve you whole and
5:23   entire, spirit, soul, and body, irreproachable
at the coming of our Lord Jesus Christ.

Responsory   Into your hands, Lord, I commend my spirit.
—Into your hands, Lord, I commend my spirit.

You have redeemed us, Lord God of truth.
—I commend my spirit.

Glory to the Father, and to the Son,
and to the Holy Spirit.
—Into your hands, Lord, I commend my spirit.

*Gospel
Canticle*   Ant. **Protect us, Lord, as we stay awake;
watch over us as we sleep, that awake, we
may keep watch with Christ, and asleep,
rest in his peace.**

*Canticle of
Simeon
Luke 2:29–32*   Lord, + now you let your servant go in peace;
your word has been fulfilled:
my own eyes have seen the salvation
which you have prepared in the sight of
every people:
a light to reveal you to the nations
and the glory of your people Israel.

Glory to the Father, and to the Son,
and to the Holy Spirit:
—as it was in the beginning, is now,
and will be for ever. Amen.

Ant.   **Protect us, Lord, as we stay awake; watch
over us as we sleep, that awake, we may
keep watch with Christ, and asleep, rest in
his peace.**

Concluding Prayer

Let us pray.
Lord God,
send peaceful sleep
to refresh our tired bodies.
May your help always renew us
and keep us strong in your service.
We ask this through Christ our Lord.
—Amen.

Blessing

May the all-powerful Lord
grant us a restful night
and a peaceful death.
—Amen.

Marian Antiphon

Sing the "Salve Regina," found on p. 700, or pray a Hail Mary.

Friday, August 2, 2024
Friday of the Seventeenth Week in Ordinary Time

MORNING PRAYER

God, + come to my assistance.
—Lord, make haste to help me.

Glory to the Father, and to the Son,
    and to the Holy Spirit:
—as it was in the beginning, is now,
    and will be for ever. Amen. Alleluia.

Hymn

Holy, Holy, Holy, p. 690

Ant. 1 **Lord, you will accept the true sacrifice offered on your altar.**

Psalm 51   Have mercy on me, God, in your kindness.
In your compassion blot out my offense.
O wash me more and more from my guilt
and cleanse me from my sin.

My offenses truly I know them;
my sin is always before me.
Against you, you alone, have I sinned;
what is evil in your sight I have done.

That you may be justified when you
      give sentence
and be without reproach when you judge.
O see, in guilt I was born,
a sinner was I conceived.

Indeed you love truth in the heart;
then in the secret of my heart teach
      me wisdom.
O purify me, then I shall be clean;
O wash me, I shall be whiter than snow.

Make me hear rejoicing and gladness,
that the bones you have crushed may revive.
From my sins turn away your face
and blot out all my guilt.

A pure heart create for me, O God,
put a steadfast spirit within me.
Do not cast me away from your presence,
nor deprive me of your holy spirit.

Give me again the joy of your help;
with a spirit of fervor sustain me,
that I may teach transgressors your ways
and sinners may return to you.

O rescue me, God, my helper,
and my tongue shall ring out your goodness.
O Lord, open my lips
and my mouth shall declare your praise.

For in sacrifice you take no delight,
burnt offering from me you would refuse,
my sacrifice, a contrite spirit.
A humbled, contrite heart you will not spurn.

In your goodness, show favor to Zion:
rebuild the walls of Jerusalem.
Then you will be pleased with lawful sacrifice,
holocausts offered on your altar.

Glory to the Father, and to the Son,
and to the Holy Spirit:
—as it was in the beginning, is now,
and will be for ever. Amen.

Ant.   **Lord, you will accept the true sacrifice
offered on your altar.**

Ant. 2   **All the descendants of Israel will glory in
the Lord's gift of victory.**

Canticle:
Isaiah 45:15–25

Truly with you God is hidden,
the God of Israel, the savior!
Those are put to shame and disgrace
who vent their anger against him.
Those go in disgrace
who carve images.

Israel, you are saved by the Lord,
     saved forever!
You shall never be put to shame or disgrace
in future ages.

For thus says the Lord,
the creator of the heavens,
who is God,
the designer and maker of the earth
who established it,
not creating it to be a waste,
but designing it to be lived in:

I am the Lord, and there is no other.
I have not spoken from hiding
nor from some dark place of the earth.
And I have not said to the
     descendants of Jacob,
"Look for me in an empty waste."
I, the Lord, promise justice,
I foretell what is right.

Come and assemble, gather together,
you fugitives from among the Gentiles!
They are without knowledge who bear
     wooden idols
and pray to gods that cannot save.

Come here and declare
in counsel together:
Who announced this from the beginning
and foretold it from of old?
Was it not I, the Lord,
besides whom there is no other God?
There is no just and saving God but me.

Turn to me and be safe,
all you ends of the earth,
for I am God; there is no other!

By myself I swear,
uttering my just decree
and my unalterable word:

To me every knee shall bend;
by me every tongue shall swear,
saying, "Only in the Lord
are just deeds and power.

Before him in shame shall come
all who vent their anger against him.
In the Lord shall be the vindication
        and the glory
of all the descendants of Israel."

Glory to the Father, and to the Son,
        and to the Holy Spirit:
—as it was in the beginning, is now,
and will be for ever. Amen.

Ant.   **All the descendants of Israel will glory in
the Lord's gift of victory.**

Ant. 3   **Let us go into God's presence singing for joy.**

Psalm 100   Cry out with joy to the Lord, all the earth.
Serve the Lord with gladness.
Come before him, singing for joy.

Know that he, the Lord, is God.
He made us, we belong to him,
we are his people, the sheep of his flock.

Go within his gates, giving thanks.
Enter his courts with songs of praise.
Give thanks to him and bless his name.

Indeed, how good is the Lord,
eternal his merciful love.
He is faithful from age to age.

Glory to the Father, and to the Son,
    and to the Holy Spirit:
—as it was in the beginning, is now,
and will be for ever. Amen.

Ant.   **Let us go into God's presence singing for joy.**

Reading   Never let evil talk pass your lips; say only the
Ephesians   good things men need to hear, things that
4:29–32   will really help them. Do nothing that will
sadden the Holy Spirit with whom you were
sealed against the day of redemption. Get rid
of all bitterness, all passion and anger, harsh
words, slander, and malice of every kind.
In place of these, be kind to one another,
compassionate, and mutually forgiving, just
as God has forgiven you in Christ.

Responsory

At daybreak, be merciful to me.
—At daybreak, be merciful to me.

Make known to me the path that I
    must walk.
—Be merciful to me.

Glory to the Father, and to the Son,
    and to the Holy Spirit.
—At daybreak, be merciful to me.

*Gospel
Canticle*

Ant. **The Lord has come to his people and
set them free.**

*Canticle of
Zechariah
Luke 1:68–79*

Blessed + be the Lord, the God of Israel;
he has come to his people and set them free.

He has raised up for us a mighty savior,
born of the house of his servant David.

Through his holy prophets he
    promised of old
that he would save us from our enemies,
from the hands of all who hate us.

He promised to show mercy to our fathers
and to remember his holy covenant.

This was the oath he swore to our
    father Abraham:
to set us free from the hands of our enemies,
free to worship him without fear,
holy and righteous in his sight
    all the days of our life.

You, my child, shall be called the prophet of
 the Most High;
for you will go before the Lord to
 prepare his way,
to give his people knowledge of salvation
by the forgiveness of their sins.

In the tender compassion of our God
the dawn from on high shall break upon us,
to shine on those who dwell in darkness and
 the shadow of death,
and to guide our feet into the way of peace.

Glory to the Father, and to the Son,
 and to the Holy Spirit:
—as it was in the beginning, is now,
 and will be for ever. Amen.

Ant. **The Lord has come to his people and set
them free.**

Intercessions Through his cross the Lord Jesus brought
 salvation to the human race. We adore
 him and in faith we call out to him:
Lord, pour out your mercy upon us.

Christ, Rising Sun, warm us with your rays,
—and restrain us from every evil impulse.

Keep guard over our thoughts, words
 and actions,
—and make us pleasing in your sight this day.

Turn your gaze from our sinfulness,
—and cleanse us from our iniquities.

Through your cross and resurrection,
—fill us with the consolation of the Spirit.

The Lord's Prayer

Our Father, who art in heaven,
hallowed be thy name;
thy kingdom come,
thy will be done
on earth as it is in heaven.
Give us this day our daily bread,
and forgive us our trespasses,
as we forgive those who trespass against us;
and lead us not into temptation,
but deliver us from evil.

Pater noster, qui es in cælis:
sanctificetur nomen tuum;
adveniat regnum tuum;
fiat voluntas tua,
sicut in cælo, et in terra.
Panem nostrum cotidianum da nobis hodie;
et dimitte nobis debita nostra,
sicut et nos dimittimus debitoribus nostris;
et ne nos inducas in tentationem;
sed libera nos a malo.

<table>
<tr><td>Concluding
Prayer</td><td>

God our Father,
you conquer the darkness of ignorance
by the light of your Word.
Strengthen within our hearts
the faith you have given us;
let not temptation ever quench the fire
that your love has kindled within us.
We ask this through our Lord Jesus Christ,
    your Son,
who lives and reigns with you and
    the Holy Spirit,
God, for ever and ever.
—Amen.

</td></tr>
</table>

Concluding
Prayer

God our Father,
you conquer the darkness of ignorance
by the light of your Word.
Strengthen within our hearts
the faith you have given us;
let not temptation ever quench the fire
that your love has kindled within us.
We ask this through our Lord Jesus Christ,
    your Son,
who lives and reigns with you and
    the Holy Spirit,
God, for ever and ever.
—Amen.

Dismissal   *If praying individually, or in a group without a priest or deacon:*

May the Lord + bless us,
protect us from all evil
and bring us to everlasting life.
—Amen.

If praying with a priest or deacon, he dismisses the people:

The Lord be with you.
—And with your spirit.

May almighty God bless you,
the Father, and the Son, + and the Holy Spirit.
—Amen.

Go in peace.
—Thanks be to God.

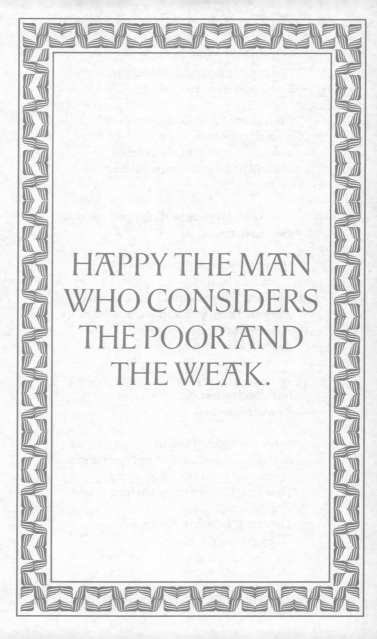

HAPPY THE MAN
WHO CONSIDERS
THE POOR AND
THE WEAK.

EVENING PRAYER————————

God, + come to my assistance.
—Lord, make haste to help me.

Glory to the Father, and to the Son,
    and to the Holy Spirit:
—as it was in the beginning, is now,
    and will be for ever. Amen. Alleluia.

Hymn   *O God, Creator of All Things, p. 697*

Psalmody   Ant. 1 **Lord, lay your healing hand upon me,
            for I have sinned.**

Psalm 41   Happy the man who considers the poor
                and the weak.
            The Lord will save him in the day of evil,
            will guard him, give him life, make him
                happy in the land
            and will not give him up to the will
                of his foes.
            The Lord will help him on his bed of pain,
            he will bring him back from sickness
                to health.

            As for me, I said: "Lord, have mercy on me,
            heal my soul for I have sinned against you."
            My foes are speaking evil against me.
            "How long before he dies and his name be
                forgotten?"
            They come to visit me and speak
                empty words,
            their hearts full of malice, they spread
                it abroad.

My enemies whisper together against me.
They all weigh up the evil which is on me:
"Some deadly thing has fastened upon him,
he will not rise again from where he lies."
Thus even my friend, in whom I trusted,
who ate my bread, has turned against me.

But you, O Lord, have mercy on me.
Let me rise once more and I will repay them.
By this I shall know that you are my friend,
if my foes do not shout in triumph over me.
If you uphold me I shall be unharmed
and set in your presence for evermore.

Blessed be the Lord, the God of Israel
from age to age. Amen. Amen.

Glory to the Father, and to the Son,
     and to the Holy Spirit:
—as it was in the beginning, is now,
and will be for ever. Amen.

Ant.   **Lord, lay your healing hand upon me,
for I have sinned.**

Ant. 2 **The mighty Lord is with us; the God of
Jacob is our stronghold.**

Psalm 46

God is for us a refuge and strength,
a helper close at hand, in time of distress:
so we shall not fear though the earth
    should rock,
though the mountains fall into the depths
    of the sea,
even though its waters rage and foam,
even though the mountains be shaken by
    its waves.

The Lord of hosts is with us:
the God of Jacob is our stronghold.

The waters of a river give joy to God's city,
the holy place where the Most High dwells.
God is within, it cannot be shaken;
God will help it at the dawning of the day.
Nations are in tumult, kingdoms are shaken:
he lifts his voice, the earth shrinks away.

The Lord of hosts is with us:
the God of Jacob is our stronghold.

Come, consider the works of the Lord,
the redoubtable deeds he has done on
    the earth.
He puts an end to wars over all the earth;
the bow he breaks, the spear he snaps.
He burns the shields with fire.
"Be still and know that I am God,
supreme among the nations, supreme on
    the earth!"

The Lord of hosts is with us:
the God of Jacob is our stronghold.

Glory to the Father, and to the Son,
  and to the Holy Spirit:
—as it was in the beginning, is now,
  and will be for ever. Amen.

Ant.   **The mighty Lord is with us; the God of
        Jacob is our stronghold.**

Ant. 3 **All nations will come and worship before
        you, O Lord.**

Canticle: Mighty and wonderful are your works,
Revelation   Lord God Almighty!
15:3–4   Righteous and true are your ways,
            O King of the nations!

Who would dare refuse you honor,
  or the glory due your name, O Lord?

Since you alone are holy,
  all nations shall come
  and worship in your presence.
Your mighty deeds are clearly seen.

Glory to the Father, and to the Son,
  and to the Holy Spirit:
—as it was in the beginning, is now,
  and will be for ever. Amen.

Ant.   **All nations will come and worship before
        you, O Lord.**

Reading
Romans 15:1–3

We who are strong in faith should be patient with the scruples of those whose faith is weak; we must not be selfish. Each should please his neighbor so as to do him good by building up his spirit. Thus, in accord with Scripture, Christ did not please himself: "The reproaches they uttered against you fell on me."

Responsory

Christ loved us and washed away our sins,
     in his own blood.
—Christ loved us and washed away our sins,
     in his own blood.

He made us a nation of kings and priests,
—in his own blood.

Glory to the Father, and to the Son,
     and to the Holy Spirit.
—Christ loved us and washed away our sins,
     in his own blood.

Gospel Canticle

Ant. **The Lord has come to the help of his servants, for he has remembered his promise of mercy.**

Canticle of Mary
Luke 1:46–55

My + soul proclaims the greatness of the Lord,
my spirit rejoices in God my Savior
for he has looked with favor on his
     lowly servant.

From this day all generations will
     call me blessed:
the Almighty has done great things for me,
and holy is his Name.

He has mercy on those who fear him
in every generation.

He has shown the strength of his arm,
he has scattered the proud in their conceit.

He has cast down the mighty from
     their thrones,
and has lifted up the lowly.

He has filled the hungry with good things,
and the rich he has sent away empty.

He has come to the help of his servant Israel
for he has remembered his promise of mercy,
the promise he made to our fathers,
to Abraham and his children for ever.

Glory to the Father, and to the Son,
     and to the Holy Spirit:
—as it was in the beginning, is now,
and will be for ever. Amen.

Ant.
**The Lord has come to the help of his
servants, for he has remembered his
promise of mercy.**

Intercessions   Blessed be God, who hears the prayers of the
needy, and fills the hungry with good
things. Let us pray to him in confidence:
Lord, *show us your mercy.*

Merciful Father, upon the cross Jesus offered
you the perfect evening sacrifice,
—we pray now for all the suffering members of
his Church.

Release those in bondage, give sight to
the blind,
—shelter the widow and the orphan.

Clothe your faithful people in the armor of
salvation,
—and shield them from the deceptions of
the devil.

Let your merciful presence be with us, Lord,
at the hour of our death,
—may we be found faithful and leave this
world in your peace.

Lead the departed into the light of your
dwelling place,
—that they may gaze upon you for all eternity.

The Lord's Prayer

Our Father, who art in heaven,
hallowed be thy name;
thy kingdom come,
thy will be done
on earth as it is in heaven.
Give us this day our daily bread,
and forgive us our trespasses,
as we forgive those who trespass against us;
and lead us not into temptation,
but deliver us from evil.

Pater noster, qui es in cælis:
sanctificetur nomen tuum;
adveniat regnum tuum;
fiat voluntas tua,
sicut in cælo, et in terra.
Panem nostrum cotidianum da nobis hodie;
et dimitte nobis debita nostra,
sicut et nos dimittimus debitoribus nostris;
et ne nos inducas in tentationem;
sed libera nos a malo.

Concluding Prayer

God our Father,
help us to follow the example
of your Son's patience in suffering.
By sharing the burden he carries,
may we come to share his glory
in the kingdom where he lives with you and
the Holy Spirit,
God, for ever and ever.
—Amen.

Dismissal *If praying individually, or in a group without a priest or deacon:*

May the Lord + bless us,
protect us from all evil
and bring us to everlasting life.
—Amen.

If praying with a priest or deacon, he dismisses the people:

The Lord be with you.
—And with your spirit.

May almighty God bless you,
the Father, and the Son, + and the Holy Spirit.
—Amen.

Go in peace.
—Thanks be to God.

NIGHT PRAYER ———————————

God, + come to my assistance.
—Lord, make haste to help me.

Glory to the Father, and to the Son,
   and to the Holy Spirit:
—as it was in the beginning, is now,
and will be for ever. Amen. Alleluia.

Examen *An optional brief examination of conscience may be made. Call to mind your
sins and failings this day.*

Hymn *O Gladsome Light, p. 696*

Psalmody Ant. **Day and night I cry to you, my God.**

Psalm 88

Lord my God, I call for help by day;
I cry at night before you.
Let my prayer come into your presence.
O turn your ear to my cry.

For my soul is filled with evils;
my life is on the brink of the grave.
I am reckoned as one in the tomb:
I have reached the end of my strength,

like one alone among the dead;
like the slain lying in their graves;
like those you remember no more,
cut off, as they are, from your hand.

You have laid me in the depths of the tomb,
in places that are dark, in the depths.
Your anger weighs down upon me:
I am drowned beneath your waves.

You have taken away my friends
and made me hateful in their sight.
Imprisoned, I cannot escape;
my eyes are sunken with grief.

I call to you, Lord, all the day long;
to you I stretch out my hands.
Will you work your wonders for the dead?
Will the shades stand and praise you?

Will your love be told in the grave
or your faithfulness among the dead?
Will your wonders be known in the dark
or your justice in the land of oblivion?

As for me, Lord, I call to you for help:
in the morning my prayer comes before you.
Lord, why do you reject me?
Why do you hide your face?

Wretched, close to death from my youth,
I have borne your trials; I am numb.
Your fury has swept down upon me;
your terrors have utterly destroyed me.

They surround me all the day like a flood,
they assail me all together.
Friend and neighbor you have taken away:
my one companion is darkness.

Glory to the Father, and to the Son,
    and to the Holy Spirit:
—as it was in the beginning, is now,
and will be for ever. Amen.

Ant.   **Day and night I cry to you, my God.**

Reading   You are in our midst, O Lord,
Jeremiah 14:9a   your name we bear:
        do not forsake us, O Lord, our God!

Responsory   Into your hands, Lord, I commend my spirit.
—Into your hands, Lord, I commend my spirit.

You have redeemed us, Lord God of truth.
—I commend my spirit.

Glory to the Father, and to the Son,
> and to the Holy Spirit.
—Into your hands, Lord, I commend my spirit.

Gospel Canticle

Ant. **Protect us, Lord, as we stay awake; watch over us as we sleep, that awake, we may keep watch with Christ, and asleep, rest in his peace.**

Canticle of Simeon Luke 2:29–32

Lord, + now you let your servant go in peace;
your word has been fulfilled:
my own eyes have seen the salvation
which you have prepared in the sight of
> every people:
a light to reveal you to the nations
and the glory of your people Israel.

Glory to the Father, and to the Son,
> and to the Holy Spirit:
—as it was in the beginning, is now,
> and will be for ever. Amen.

Ant.

Protect us, Lord, as we stay awake; watch over us as we sleep, that awake, we may keep watch with Christ, and asleep, rest in his peace.

Concluding Prayer

Let us pray.
All-powerful God,
keep us united with your Son
in his death and burial
so that we may rise to new life with him,
who lives and reigns for ever and ever.
—Amen.

Blessing May the all-powerful Lord
grant us a restful night
and a peaceful death.
—Amen.

Marian
Antiphon   *Sing the "Salve Regina," found on p. 700, or pray a Hail Mary.*

Saturday, August 3, 2024
Saturday of the Seventeenth Week in Ordinary Time

MORNING PRAYER——————

God, + come to my assistance.
—Lord, make haste to help me.

Glory to the Father, and to the Son,
and to the Holy Spirit:
—as it was in the beginning, is now,
and will be for ever. Amen. Alleluia.

Hymn *Holy, Holy, Holy, p. 690*

Psalmody Ant. 1 **Dawn finds me ready to welcome you, my God.**

Psalm
119:145–152   I call with all my heart; Lord, hear me,
I will keep your commands.
I call upon you, save me
and I will do your will.

I rise before dawn and cry for help,
I hope in your word.
My eyes watch through the night
to ponder your promise.

In your love hear my voice, O Lord;
give me life by your decrees.
Those who harm me unjustly draw near:
they are far from your law.

But you, O Lord, are close:
your commands are truth.
Long have I known that your will
is established for ever.

Glory to the Father, and to the Son,
    and to the Holy Spirit:
as it was in the beginning, is now,
and will be for ever. Amen.

Ant.   **Dawn finds me ready to welcome you,
my God.**

Ant. 2   **The Lord is my strength, and I shall sing
his praise, for he has become my Savior.**

Canticle:
Exodus 15:1–4a,
8–13, 17–18

I will sing to the Lord, for he is gloriously
    triumphant;
horse and chariot he has cast into the sea.

My strength and my courage is the Lord,
and he has been my savior.
He is my God, I praise him;
the God of my father, I extol him.

The Lord is a warrior,
Lord is his name!
Pharaoh's chariots and army he hurled
    into the sea.
At a breath of your anger the waters piled up,
the flowing waters stood like a mound,
the flood waters congealed in the midst
    of the sea.

The enemy boasted, "I will pursue and
    overtake them;
I will divide the spoils and have my
    fill of them;
I will draw my sword; my hand shall
    despoil them!"
When your wind blew, the sea covered them;
like lead they sank in the mighty waters.

Who is like to you among the gods, O Lord?
Who is like to you, magnificent in holiness?
O terrible in renown, worker of wonders,
when you stretched out your right hand, the
    earth swallowed them!

In your mercy you led the people
    you redeemed;
in your strength you guided them to your
    holy dwelling.

And you brought them in and planted them
    on the mountain of your inheritance—
the place where you made your seat, O Lord,
the sanctuary, O Lord, which your hands
    established.
The Lord shall reign forever and ever.

Glory to the Father, and to the Son,
    and to the Holy Spirit:
—as it was in the beginning, is now,
    and will be for ever. Amen.

Ant. **The Lord is my strength, and I shall sing his praise, for he has become my Savior.**

Ant. 3 **O praise the Lord, all you nations.**

Psalm 117 O praise the Lord, all you nations,
    acclaim him, all you peoples!

Strong is his love for us;
he is faithful for ever.

Glory to the Father, and to the Son,
    and to the Holy Spirit:
—as it was in the beginning, is now,
    and will be for ever. Amen.

Ant. **O praise the Lord, all you nations.**

Reading
2 Peter 1:10–11
Be solicitous to make your call and election permanent, brothers; surely those who do so will never be lost. On the contrary, your entry into the everlasting kingdom of our Lord and Savior Jesus Christ will be richly provided for.

Responsory I cry to you, O Lord, for you are my refuge.
—I cry to you, O Lord, for you are my refuge.

You are all I desire in the land of the living,
—for you are my refuge.

69

Glory to the Father, and to the Son,
    and to the Holy Spirit.
—I cry to you, O Lord, for you are my refuge.

**Gospel
Canticle**   Ant. **Lord, shine on those who dwell in
darkness and the shadow of death.**

*Canticle of
Zechariah
Luke 1:68–79*   Blessed + be the Lord, the God of Israel;
he has come to his people and set them free.

He has raised up for us a mighty savior,
born of the house of his servant David.

Through his holy prophets he
    promised of old
that he would save us from our enemies,
from the hands of all who hate us.

He promised to show mercy to our fathers
and to remember his holy covenant.

This was the oath he swore to our
    father Abraham:
to set us free from the hands of our enemies,
free to worship him without fear,
holy and righteous in his sight
    all the days of our life.

You, my child, shall be called the prophet of
    the Most High;
for you will go before the Lord to
    prepare his way,
to give his people knowledge of salvation
by the forgiveness of their sins.

In the tender compassion of our God
the dawn from on high shall break upon us,
to shine on those who dwell in darkness and
    the shadow of death,
and to guide our feet into the way of peace.

Glory to the Father, and to the Son,
    and to the Holy Spirit:
—as it was in the beginning, is now,
and will be for ever. Amen.

Ant. **Lord, shine on those who dwell in darkness
and the shadow of death.**

Intercessions Let us all praise Christ. In order to become
our faithful and merciful high priest
before the Father's throne, he chose to
become one of us, a brother in all things.
In prayer we ask of him:
Lord, share with us the treasure of your love.

Sun of Justice, you filled us with light at
    our baptism,
—we dedicate this day to you.

At every hour of the day, we give you glory,
—in all our deeds, we offer you praise.

Mary, your mother, was obedient to your word,
—direct our lives in accordance with that word.

Our lives are surrounded with passing
    things; set our hearts on things of heaven,
—so that through faith, hope and charity we
    may come to enjoy the vision of your glory.

The Lord's
Prayer

Our Father, who art in heaven,
hallowed be thy name;
thy kingdom come,
thy will be done
on earth as it is in heaven.
Give us this day our daily bread,
and forgive us our trespasses,
as we forgive those who trespass against us;
and lead us not into temptation,
but deliver us from evil.

Pater noster, qui es in cælis:
sanctificetur nomen tuum;
adveniat regnum tuum;
fiat voluntas tua,
sicut in cælo, et in terra.
Panem nostrum cotidianum da nobis hodie;
et dimitte nobis debita nostra,
sicut et nos dimittimus debitoribus nostris;
et ne nos inducas in tentationem;
sed libera nos a malo.

Concluding
Prayer

Lord,
free us from the dark night of death.
Let the light of resurrection
dawn within our hearts
to bring us to the radiance of eternal life.
We ask this through our Lord Jesus Christ,
your Son,
who lives and reigns with you and
the Holy Spirit,
God, for ever and ever.
—Amen.

Dismissal   *If praying individually, or in a group without a priest or deacon:*

May the Lord + bless us,
protect us from all evil
and bring us to everlasting life.
—Amen.

If praying with a priest or deacon, he dismisses the people:

The Lord be with you.
—And with your spirit.

May almighty God bless you,
the Father, and the Son, + and the Holy Spirit.
—Amen.

Go in peace.
—Thanks be to God.

EVENING PRAYER ——————————————

BEGINS THE EIGHTEENTH SUNDAY IN ORDINARY TIME

God, + come to my assistance.
—Lord, make haste to help me.

Glory to the Father, and to the Son,
    and to the Holy Spirit:
—as it was in the beginning, is now,
and will be for ever. Amen. Alleluia.

Hymn   *O God, Creator of All Things, p. 697*

Psalmody   Ant. 1 **Your word, O Lord, is the lantern to
light our way, alleluia.**

Psalm
119:105–112

Your word is a lamp for my steps
and a light for my path.
I have sworn and have made up my mind
to obey your decrees.

Lord, I am deeply afflicted:
by your word give me life.
Accept, Lord, the homage of my lips
and teach me your decrees.

Though I carry my life in my hands,
I remember your law.
Though the wicked try to ensnare me
I do not stray from your precepts.

Your will is my heritage for ever,
the joy of my heart.
I set myself to carry out your will
in fullness, for ever.

Glory to the Father, and to the Son,
    and to the Holy Spirit:
—as it was in the beginning, is now,
and will be for ever. Amen.

Ant.   **Your word, O Lord, is the lantern to light
our way, alleluia.**

Ant. 2   **When I see your face, O Lord, I shall know
the fullness of joy, alleluia.**

Psalm 16   Preserve me, God, I take refuge in you.
I say to the Lord: "You are my God.
My happiness lies in you alone."

He has put into my heart a marvelous love
for the faithful ones who dwell in his land.
Those who choose other gods increase
    their sorrows.
Never will I offer their offerings of blood.
Never will I take their name upon my lips.

O Lord, it is you who are my portion and cup;
it is you yourself who are my prize.
The lot marked out for me is my delight:
welcome indeed the heritage that falls to me!

I will bless the Lord who gives me counsel,
who even at night directs my heart.
I keep the Lord ever in my sight:
since he is at my right hand,
    I shall stand firm.

And so my heart rejoices, my soul is glad;
even my body shall rest in safety.
For you will not leave my soul
    among the dead,
nor let your beloved know decay.

You will show me the path of life,
the fullness of joy in your presence,
at your right hand happiness for ever.

Glory to the Father, and to the Son,
    and to the Holy Spirit:
—as it was in the beginning, is now,
and will be for ever. Amen.

Ant.   **When I see your face, O Lord, I shall know
the fullness of joy, alleluia.**

Ant. 3   **Let everything in heaven and on earth bend
              the knee at the name of Jesus, alleluia.**

Canticle: Though he was in the form of God,
Philippians   Jesus did not deem equality with God
2:6–11   something to be grasped at.

              Rather, he emptied himself
              and took the form of a slave,
              being born in the likeness of men.

              He was known to be of human estate,
              and it was thus that he humbled himself,
              obediently accepting even death,
              death on a cross!

              Because of this,
              God highly exalted him
              and bestowed on him the name
              above every other name,

              So that at Jesus' name
              every knee must bend
              in the heavens, on the earth,
              and under the earth,
              and every tongue proclaim
              to the glory of God the Father:
              JESUS CHRIST IS LORD!

              Glory to the Father, and to the Son,
                  and to the Holy Spirit:
              —as it was in the beginning, is now,
              and will be for ever. Amen.

Ant.   **Let everything in heaven and on earth bend the knee at the name of Jesus, alleluia.**

Reading
Colossians
1:2b–6a
May God our Father give you grace and peace. We always give thanks to God, the Father of our Lord Jesus Christ, in our prayers for you because we have heard of your faith in Christ Jesus and the love you bear toward all the saints—moved as you are by the hope held in store for you in heaven. You heard of this hope through the message of truth, the gospel, which has come to you, has borne fruit, and has continued to grow in your midst, as it has everywhere in the world.

Responsory
From the rising of the sun to its setting,
may the name of the Lord be praised.
—From the rising of the sun to its setting,
may the name of the Lord be praised.

His splendor reaches far beyond the heavens;
—may the name of the Lord be praised.

Glory to the Father, and to the Son,
and to the Holy Spirit.
—From the rising of the sun to its setting,
may the name of the Lord be praised.

Gospel
Canticle
Ant. **A great crowd gathered around Jesus, and they had nothing to eat. He called his disciples and said: I have compassion on all these people.**

*Canticle of
Mary
Luke 1:46–55*

My + soul proclaims the greatness of the Lord,
my spirit rejoices in God my Savior
for he has looked with favor on his
      lowly servant.

From this day all generations will
      call me blessed:
the Almighty has done great things for me,
and holy is his Name.

He has mercy on those who fear him
in every generation.

He has shown the strength of his arm,
he has scattered the proud in their conceit.

He has cast down the mighty from
      their thrones,
and has lifted up the lowly.

He has filled the hungry with good things,
and the rich he has sent away empty.

He has come to the help of his servant Israel
for he has remembered his promise of mercy,
the promise he made to our fathers,
to Abraham and his children for ever.

Glory to the Father, and to the Son,
      and to the Holy Spirit:
—as it was in the beginning, is now,
      and will be for ever. Amen.

Ant.   **A great crowd gathered around Jesus, and they had nothing to eat. He called his disciples and said: I have compassion on all these people.**

Intercessions   God aids and protects the people he has chosen for his inheritance. Let us give thanks to him and proclaim his goodness:
Lord, *we trust in you.*

We pray for N., our Pope, and N., our bishop,
—protect them and in your goodness make them holy.

May the sick feel their companionship with the suffering Christ,
—and know that they will enjoy his eternal consolation.

In your goodness have compassion on the homeless,
—help them to find proper housing.

In your goodness give and preserve the fruits of the earth,
—so that each day there may be bread enough for all.

Lord, you attend the dying with great mercy,
—grant them an eternal dwelling.

The Lord's
Prayer

Our Father, who art in heaven,
hallowed be thy name;
thy kingdom come,
thy will be done
on earth as it is in heaven.
Give us this day our daily bread,
and forgive us our trespasses,
as we forgive those who trespass against us;
and lead us not into temptation,
but deliver us from evil.

Pater noster, qui es in cælis:
sanctificetur nomen tuum;
adveniat regnum tuum;
fiat voluntas tua,
sicut in cælo, et in terra.
Panem nostrum cotidianum da nobis hodie;
et dimitte nobis debita nostra,
sicut et nos dimittimus debitoribus nostris;
et ne nos inducas in tentationem;
sed libera nos a malo.

Concluding
Prayer

Father of everlasting goodness,
our origin and guide,
be close to us
and hear the prayers of all who praise you.
Forgive our sins and restore us to life.
Keep us safe in your love.
Grant this through our Lord Jesus Christ,
     your Son,
who lives and reigns with you and
     the Holy Spirit,
God, for ever and ever.
—Amen.

Dismissal   *If praying individually, or in a group without a priest or deacon:*

May the Lord + bless us,
protect us from all evil
and bring us to everlasting life.
—Amen.

If praying with a priest or deacon, he dismisses the people:

The Lord be with you.
—And with your spirit.

May almighty God bless you,
the Father, and the Son, + and the Holy Spirit.
—Amen.

Go in peace.
—Thanks be to God.

NIGHT PRAYER

God, + come to my assistance.
—Lord, make haste to help me.

Glory to the Father, and to the Son,
    and to the Holy Spirit:
—as it was in the beginning, is now,
and will be for ever. Amen. Alleluia.

Examen   *An optional brief examination of conscience may be made. Call to mind your
sins and failings this day.*

Hymn   *O Gladsome Light, p. 696*

Psalmody   Ant. 1 **Have mercy, Lord, and hear my prayer.**

Psalm 4

When I call, answer me, O God of justice;
from anguish you released me; have mercy
    and hear me!

O men, how long will your hearts be closed,
will you love what is futile and seek
    what is false?

It is the Lord who grants favors to those
    whom he loves;
the Lord hears me whenever I call him.

Fear him; do not sin: ponder on your bed
    and be still.
Make justice your sacrifice and trust
    in the Lord.

"What can bring us happiness?" many say.
Let the light of your face shine on us, O Lord.

You have put into my heart a greater joy
than they have from abundance of corn
    and new wine.

I will lie down in peace and sleep
    comes at once
for you alone, Lord, make me dwell in safety.

Glory to the Father, and to the Son,
    and to the Holy Spirit:
—as it was in the beginning, is now,
    and will be for ever. Amen.

Ant.   **Have mercy, Lord, and hear my prayer.**

Ant. 2   **In the silent hours of night, bless the Lord.**

Psalm 134

O come, bless the Lord,
all you who serve the Lord,
who stand in the house of the Lord,
in the courts of the house of our God.

Lift up your hands to the holy place
and bless the Lord through the night.

May the Lord bless you from Zion,
he who made both heaven and earth.

Glory to the Father, and to the Son,
      and to the Holy Spirit:
as it was in the beginning, is now,
and will be for ever. Amen.

Ant.   **In the silent hours of night, bless the Lord.**

Reading
Deuteronomy
6:4–7

Hear, O Israel! The Lord is our God, the Lord
alone! Therefore, you shall love the Lord,
your God, with all your heart, and with all
your soul, and with all your strength. Take
to heart these words which I enjoin on you
today. Drill them into your children. Speak
of them at home and abroad, whether you
are busy or at rest.

Responsory   Into your hands, Lord, I commend my spirit.
—Into your hands, Lord, I commend my spirit.

You have redeemed us, Lord God of truth.
—I commend my spirit.

Glory to the Father, and to the Son,
   and to the Holy Spirit.
—Into your hands, Lord, I commend my spirit.

Gospel
Canticle   Ant. **Protect us, Lord, as we stay awake;
watch over us as we sleep, that awake, we
may keep watch with Christ, and asleep,
rest in his peace.**

*Canticle of
Simeon
Luke 2:29–32*   Lord, + now you let your servant go in peace;
your word has been fulfilled:
my own eyes have seen the salvation
which you have prepared in the sight of
   every people:
a light to reveal you to the nations
and the glory of your people Israel.

Glory to the Father, and to the Son,
   and to the Holy Spirit:
—as it was in the beginning, is now,
   and will be for ever. Amen.

Ant.   **Protect us, Lord, as we stay awake; watch
over us as we sleep, that awake, we may
keep watch with Christ, and asleep, rest in
his peace.**

Concluding Prayer
Let us pray.
Lord,
be with us throughout this night.
When day comes may we rise from sleep
to rejoice in the resurrection of your Christ,
who lives and reigns for ever and ever.
—Amen.

Blessing
May the all-powerful Lord
grant us a restful night
and a peaceful death.
—Amen.

Marian Antiphon
Sing the "Salve Regina," found on p. 700, or pray a Hail Mary.

GIVE THANKS
TO THE LORD
FOR HE IS GOOD,
FOR HIS LOVE
ENDURES
FOREVER.

Sunday, August 4, 2024
Eighteenth Sunday in Ordinary Time

MORNING PRAYER——————————————

God, + come to my assistance.
—Lord, make haste to help me.

Glory to the Father, and to the Son,
    and to the Holy Spirit:
—as it was in the beginning, is now,
    and will be for ever. Amen. Alleluia.

Hymn   *Holy, Holy, Holy, p. 690*

Psalmody   Ant. 1 **Blessed is he who comes in the name of the Lord, alleluia.**

Psalm 118   Give thanks to the Lord for he is good,
    for his love endures forever.

Let the sons of Israel say:
"His love endures for ever."
Let the sons of Aaron say:
"His love endures for ever."
Let those who fear the Lord say:
"His love endures for ever."

I called to the Lord in my distress;
he answered and freed me.
The Lord is at my side; I do not fear.
What can man do against me?
The Lord is at my side as my helper:
I shall look down on my foes.

It is better to take refuge in the Lord
than to trust in men:
it is better to take refuge in the Lord
than to trust in princes.

The nations all encompassed me;
in the Lord's name I crushed them.
They compassed me, compassed me about;
in the Lord's name I crushed them.
They compassed me about like bees;
they blazed like a fire among thorns.
In the Lord's name I crushed them.

I was hard-pressed and was falling
but the Lord came to help me.
The Lord is my strength and my song;
he is my savior.
There are shouts of joy and victory
in the tents of the just.

The Lord's right hand has triumphed;
his right hand raised me.
The Lord's right hand has triumphed;
I shall not die, I shall live
and recount his deeds.
I was punished, I was punished by the Lord,
but not doomed to die.

Open to me the gates of holiness:
I will enter and give thanks.
This is the Lord's own gate
where the just may enter.
I will thank you for you have answered
and you are my savior.

The stone which the builders rejected
has become the corner stone.
This is the work of the Lord,
a marvel in our eyes.
This day was made by the Lord;
we rejoice and are glad.

O Lord, grant us salvation;
O Lord, grant success.
Blessed in the name of the Lord
is he who comes.
We bless you from the house of the Lord;
the Lord God is our light.

Go forward in procession with branches
even to the altar.
You are my God, I thank you.
My God, I praise you.
Give thanks to the Lord for he is good;
for his love endures for ever.

Glory to the Father, and to the Son,
    and to the Holy Spirit:
—as it was in the beginning, is now,
and will be for ever. Amen.

Ant.   **Blessed is he who comes in the name of
the Lord, alleluia.**

Ant. 2   **Let us sing a hymn of praise to our God,
alleluia.**

Canticle:
Daniel 3:52–57

Blessed are you, O Lord, the God of our fathers,
praiseworthy and exalted above all forever.

And blessed is your holy and glorious name,
praiseworthy and exalted above all
    for all ages.

Blessed are you in the temple of your
    holy glory,
praiseworthy and glorious above all forever.

Blessed are you on the throne of
    your kingdom,
praiseworthy and exalted above all forever.

Blessed are you who look into the depths
from your throne upon the cherubim,
praiseworthy and exalted above all forever.

Blessed are you in the firmament of heaven,
praiseworthy and glorious forever.

Bless the Lord, all you works of the Lord,
praise and exalt him above all forever.

Glory to the Father, and to the Son,
    and to the Holy Spirit:
—as it was in the beginning, is now,
and will be for ever. Amen.

Ant.

**Let us sing a hymn of praise to our God,
alleluia.**

Ant. 3

Praise the Lord for his infinite greatness, alleluia.

Psalm 150

Praise God in his holy place,
   praise him in his mighty heavens.
Praise him for his powerful deeds,
   praise his surpassing greatness.

O praise him with sound of trumpet,
   praise him with lute and harp.
Praise him with timbrel and dance,
   praise him with strings and pipes.

O praise him with resounding cymbals,
   praise him with clashing of cymbals.
Let everything that lives and that breathes
   give praise to the Lord.

Glory to the Father, and to the Son,
   and to the Holy Spirit:
—as it was in the beginning, is now,
   and will be for ever. Amen.

Ant.

Praise the Lord for his infinite greatness, alleluia.

Reading
Ezekiel
36:25–27

I will sprinkle clean water upon you to cleanse you from all your impurities, and from all your idols I will cleanse you. I will give you a new heart and place a new spirit within you, taking from your bodies your stony hearts and giving you natural hearts. I will put my spirit within you and make you live by my statutes, careful to observe my decrees.

Responsory   We give thanks to you, O God,
              as we call upon your name.
      —We give thanks to you, O God,
              as we call upon your name.

              We cry aloud how marvelous you are,
      —as we call upon your name.

              Glory to the Father, and to the Son,
              and to the Holy Spirit.
      —We give thanks to you, O God,
              as we call upon your name.

*Gospel
Canticle*   Ant. **Do not work for food that will perish,
            but for food that lasts to eternal life.**

*Canticle of
Zechariah
Luke 1:68–79*   Blessed + be the Lord, the God of Israel;
               he has come to his people and set them free.

               He has raised up for us a mighty savior,
               born of the house of his servant David.

               Through his holy prophets he
                   promised of old
               that he would save us from our enemies,
               from the hands of all who hate us.

               He promised to show mercy to our fathers
               and to remember his holy covenant.

This was the oath he swore to our
    father Abraham:
to set us free from the hands of our enemies,
free to worship him without fear,
holy and righteous in his sight
    all the days of our life.

You, my child, shall be called the prophet of
    the Most High;
for you will go before the Lord to
    prepare his way,
to give his people knowledge of salvation
by the forgiveness of their sins.

In the tender compassion of our God
the dawn from on high shall break upon us,
to shine on those who dwell in darkness and
    the shadow of death,
and to guide our feet into the way of peace.

Glory to the Father, and to the Son,
    and to the Holy Spirit:
—as it was in the beginning, is now,
and will be for ever. Amen.

Ant. **Do not work for food that will perish, but
for food that lasts to eternal life.**

Intercessions Let us give thanks to our Savior who came
into this world as God's presence among
us. Let us call upon him:
Christ, King of Glory, be our light and our joy.

Lord Jesus, you are the rising Sun, the
firstfruits of the future resurrection,
—grant that we may not sit in the shadow of
death but walk in the light of life.

Show us your goodness, present in
every creature,
—that we may contemplate your glory
everywhere.

Do not allow us to be overcome by evil today,
—but grant that we may overcome evil
through the power of good.

You were baptized in the Jordan and
anointed by the Holy Spirit,
—grant that we may this day give thanks to
your Holy Spirit.

The Lord's   Our Father, who art in heaven,
Prayer   hallowed be thy name;
thy kingdom come,
thy will be done
on earth as it is in heaven.
Give us this day our daily bread,
and forgive us our trespasses,
as we forgive those who trespass against us;
and lead us not into temptation,
but deliver us from evil.

Pater noster, qui es in cælis:
sanctificetur nomen tuum;
adveniat regnum tuum;
fiat voluntas tua,
sicut in cælo, et in terra.
Panem nostrum cotidianum da nobis hodie;
et dimitte nobis debita nostra,
sicut et nos dimittimus debitoribus nostris;
et ne nos inducas in tentationem;
sed libera nos a malo.

Concluding Prayer

Father of everlasting goodness,
our origin and guide,
be close to us
and hear the prayers of all who praise you.
Forgive our sins and restore us to life.
Keep us safe in your love.
Grant this through our Lord Jesus Christ,
        your Son,
who lives and reigns with you and
        the Holy Spirit,
God, for ever and ever.
—Amen.

Dismissal

If praying individually, or in a group without a priest or deacon:

May the Lord + bless us,
protect us from all evil
and bring us to everlasting life.
—Amen.

If praying with a priest or deacon, he dismisses the people:

The Lord be with you.
—And with your spirit.

May almighty God bless you,
the Father, and the Son, + and the Holy Spirit.
—Amen.

Go in peace.
—Thanks be to God.

EVENING PRAYER

God, + come to my assistance.
—Lord, make haste to help me.

Glory to the Father, and to the Son,
and to the Holy Spirit:
—as it was in the beginning, is now,
and will be for ever. Amen. Alleluia.

Hymn   *O God, Creator of All Things, p. 697*

Psalmody   Ant. 1 **Christ our Lord is a priest for ever,
like Melchizedek of old, alleluia.**

Psalm 110:1–5, 7 The Lord's revelation to my Master:
"Sit on my right:
your foes I will put beneath your feet."

The Lord will wield from Zion
your scepter of power:
rule in the midst of all your foes.

A prince from the day of your birth
on the holy mountains;
from the womb before the dawn I begot you.

The Lord has sworn an oath he will
    not change.
"You are a priest for ever,
  a priest like Melchizedek of old."

The Master standing at your right hand
will shatter kings in the day of his
    great wrath.

He shall drink from the stream by
    the wayside
and therefore he shall lift up his head.

Glory to the Father, and to the Son,
    and to the Holy Spirit:
—as it was in the beginning, is now,
and will be for ever. Amen.

Ant.   **Christ our Lord is a priest for ever, like
Melchizedek of old, alleluia.**

Ant. 2   **God dwells in highest heaven; he has
power to do all he wills, alleluia.**

Psalm 115   Not to us, Lord, not to us,
but to your name give the glory
for the sake of your love and your truth,
lest the heathen say: "Where is their God?"

But our God is in the heavens;
he does whatever he wills.
Their idols are silver and gold,
the work of human hands.

They have mouths but they cannot speak;
they have eyes but they cannot see;
they have ears but they cannot hear;
they have nostrils but they cannot smell.

With their hands they cannot feel;
with their feet they cannot walk.
No sound comes from their throats.
Their makers will come to be like them
and so will all who trust in them.

Sons of Israel, trust in the Lord;
he is their help and their shield.
Sons of Aaron, trust in the Lord;
he is their help and their shield.

You who fear him, trust in the Lord;
he is their help and their shield.
He remembers us, and he will bless us;
he will bless the sons of Israel.
He will bless the sons of Aaron.

The Lord will bless those who fear him,
the little no less than the great:
to you may the Lord grant increase,
to you and all your children.

May you be blessed by the Lord,
the maker of heaven and earth.
The heavens belong to the Lord
but the earth he has given to men.

The dead shall not praise the Lord,
nor those who go down into the silence.
But we who live bless the Lord
now and for ever. Amen.

Glory to the Father, and to the Son,
and to the Holy Spirit:
as it was in the beginning, is now,
and will be for ever. Amen.

Ant.   **God dwells in highest heaven; he has
power to do all he wills, alleluia.**

Ant. 3   **Praise God, all you who serve him, both
great and small, alleluia.**

*Canticle: See
Revelation
19:1–7*

Alleluia.
Salvation, glory, and power to our God:
his judgments are honest and true.
Alleluia.

Alleluia.
Sing praise to our God, all you his servants,
all who worship him reverently,
great and small.
Alleluia.

Alleluia.
The Lord our all-powerful God is King;
let us rejoice, sing praise, and give him glory.
Alleluia.

Alleluia.
The wedding feast of the Lamb has begun,
and his bride is prepared to welcome him.
Alleluia.

Alleluia.
Glory to the Father, and to the Son,
and to the Holy Spirit:
Alleluia.

Alleluia.
as it was in the beginning, is now,
and will be for ever. Amen.
Alleluia.

Ant. **Praise God, all you who serve him, both great and small, alleluia.**

Reading
2 Thessalonians
2:13–14

We are bound to thank God for you always, beloved brothers in the Lord, because you are the first fruits of those whom God has chosen for salvation, in holiness of spirit and fidelity to truth. He called you through our preaching of the good news so that you might achieve the glory of our Lord Jesus Christ.

Responsory   Our Lord is great, mighty is his power.
—Our Lord is great, mighty is his power.

His wisdom is beyond compare,
—mighty is his power.

Glory to the Father, and to the Son,
and to the Holy Spirit.
—Our Lord is great, mighty is his power.

**Gospel
Canticle**

Ant. **Brothers, if you desire to be truly rich,
set your heart on true riches.**

*Canticle of
Mary
Luke 1:46–55*

My + soul proclaims the greatness of the Lord,
my spirit rejoices in God my Savior
for he has looked with favor on his
    lowly servant.

From this day all generations will
    call me blessed:
the Almighty has done great things for me,
and holy is his Name.

He has mercy on those who fear him
in every generation.

He has shown the strength of his arm,
he has scattered the proud in their conceit.

He has cast down the mighty from
    their thrones,
and has lifted up the lowly.

He has filled the hungry with good things,
and the rich he has sent away empty.

He has come to the help of his servant Israel
for he has remembered his promise of mercy,
the promise he made to our fathers,
to Abraham and his children for ever.

Glory to the Father, and to the Son,
    and to the Holy Spirit:
—as it was in the beginning, is now,
and will be for ever. Amen.

Ant.   **Brothers, if you desire to be truly rich, set
         your heart on true riches.**

Intercessions   All praise and honor to Christ! He lives for
         ever to intercede for us, and he is able to
         save those who approach the Father in
         his name. Sustained by our faith, let us
         call upon him:
         Remember your people, Lord.

         As the day draws to a close, Sun of Justice,
         we invoke your name upon the whole
         human race,
         — so that all men may enjoy your never
         failing light.

         Preserve the covenant which you have
         ratified in your blood,
         — cleanse and sanctify your Church.

         Remember your assembly, Lord,
         — your dwelling place.

         Guide travelers along the path of peace and
         prosperity,
         — so that they may reach their destinations in
         safety and joy.

         Receive the souls of the dead, Lord,
         — grant them your favor and the gift of
         eternal glory.

The Lord's Prayer

Our Father, who art in heaven,
hallowed be thy name;
thy kingdom come,
thy will be done
on earth as it is in heaven.
Give us this day our daily bread,
and forgive us our trespasses,
as we forgive those who trespass against us;
and lead us not into temptation,
but deliver us from evil.

Pater noster, qui es in cælis:
sanctificetur nomen tuum;
adveniat regnum tuum;
fiat voluntas tua,
sicut in cælo, et in terra.
Panem nostrum cotidianum da nobis hodie;
et dimitte nobis debita nostra,
sicut et nos dimittimus debitoribus nostris;
et ne nos inducas in tentationem;
sed libera nos a malo.

Concluding Prayer

Father of everlasting goodness,
our origin and guide,
be close to us
and hear the prayers of all who praise you.
Forgive our sins and restore us to life.
Keep us safe in your love.
Grant this through our Lord Jesus Christ,
    your Son,
who lives and reigns with you and
    the Holy Spirit,
God, for ever and ever.
—Amen.

Dismissal   *If praying individually, or in a group without a priest or deacon:*

May the Lord + bless us,
protect us from all evil
and bring us to everlasting life.
—Amen.

If praying with a priest or deacon, he dismisses the people:

The Lord be with you.
—And with your spirit.

May almighty God bless you,
the Father, and the Son, + and the Holy Spirit.
—Amen.

Go in peace.
—Thanks be to God.

NIGHT PRAYER ─────────────

God, + come to my assistance.
—Lord, make haste to help me.

Glory to the Father, and to the Son,
    and to the Holy Spirit:
—as it was in the beginning, is now,
and will be for ever. Amen. Alleluia.

Examen   *An optional brief examination of conscience may be made. Call to mind your
sins and failings this day.*

Hymn   *O Gladsome Light, p. 696*

Psalmody   Ant. **Night holds no terrors for me sleeping
under God's wings.**

Psalm 91   He who dwells in the shelter of the Most High
and abides in the shade of the Almighty
says to the Lord: "My refuge,
my stronghold, my God in whom I trust!"

It is he who will free you from the snare
of the fowler who seeks to destroy you;
he will conceal you with his pinions
and under his wings you will find refuge.

You will not fear the terror of the night
nor the arrow that flies by day,
nor the plague that prowls in the darkness
nor the scourge that lays waste at noon.

A thousand may fall at your side,
ten thousand fall at your right,
you, it will never approach;
his faithfulness is buckler and shield.

Your eyes have only to look
to see how the wicked are repaid,
you who have said: "Lord, my refuge!"
and have made the Most High your dwelling.

Upon you no evil shall fall,
no plague approach where you dwell.
For you has he commanded his angels,
to keep you in all your ways.

They shall bear you upon their hands
lest you strike your foot against a stone.
On the lion and the viper you will tread
and trample the young lion and the dragon.

Since he clings to me in love, I will free him;
protect him for he knows my name.
When he calls I shall answer: "I am with you."
I will save him in distress and give him glory.

With length of life I will content him;
I shall let him see my saving power.

Glory to the Father, and to the Son,
    and to the Holy Spirit:
—as it was in the beginning, is now,
and will be for ever. Amen.

Ant.   **Night holds no terrors for me sleeping
under God's wings.**

Reading
Revelation
22:4–5

They shall see the Lord face to face and bear
his name on their foreheads. The night shall
be no more. They will need no light from
lamps or the sun, for the Lord God shall give
them light, and they shall reign forever.

Responsory   Into your hands, Lord, I commend my spirit.
—Into your hands, Lord, I commend my spirit.

You have redeemed us, Lord God of truth.
—I commend my spirit.

Glory to the Father, and to the Son,
    and to the Holy Spirit.
—Into your hands, Lord, I commend my spirit.

Gospel Canticle

Ant. **Protect us, Lord, as we stay awake; watch over us as we sleep, that awake, we may keep watch with Christ, and asleep, rest in his peace.**

Canticle of Simeon
Luke 2:29–32

Lord, + now you let your servant go in peace;
your word has been fulfilled:
my own eyes have seen the salvation
which you have prepared in the sight of
   every people:
a light to reveal you to the nations
and the glory of your people Israel.

Glory to the Father, and to the Son,
   and to the Holy Spirit:
—as it was in the beginning, is now,
   and will be for ever. Amen.

Ant. **Protect us, Lord, as we stay awake; watch over us as we sleep, that awake, we may keep watch with Christ, and asleep, rest in his peace.**

Concluding Prayer

Let us pray.
Lord,
we have celebrated today
the mystery of the rising of Christ to new life.
May we now rest in your peace,
safe from all that could harm us,
and rise again refreshed and joyful,
to praise you throughout another day.
We ask this through Christ our Lord.
—Amen.

Blessing   May the all-powerful Lord
            grant us a restful night
            and a peaceful death.
            —Amen.

Marian   *Sing the "Salve Regina," found on p. 700, or pray a Hail Mary.*
Antiphon

Monday, August 5, 2024
Monday of the Eighteenth Week in Ordinary Time

MORNING PRAYER

God, + come to my assistance.
—Lord, make haste to help me.

Glory to the Father, and to the Son,
    and to the Holy Spirit:
—as it was in the beginning, is now,
    and will be for ever. Amen. Alleluia.

Hymn   *Holy, Holy, Holy, p. 690*

Psalmody   Ant. 1 **When will I come to the end of my
            pilgrimage and enter the presence of God?**

Psalm 42   Like the deer that yearns
            for running streams,
            so my soul is yearning
            for you, my God.

My soul is thirsting for God,
the God of my life;
when can I enter and see
the face of God?

My tears have become my bread,
by night, by day,
as I hear it said all the day long:
"Where is your God?"

These things will I remember
as I pour out my soul:
how I would lead the rejoicing crowd
into the house of God,
amid cries of gladness and thanksgiving,
the throng wild with joy.

Why are you cast down, my soul,
why groan within me?
Hope in God; I will praise him still,
my savior and my God.

My soul is cast down within me
as I think of you,
from the country of Jordan and
    Mount Hermon,
from the Hill of Mizar.

Deep is calling on deep,
in the roar of waters:
your torrents and all your waves
swept over me.

By day the Lord will send
his loving kindness;
by night I will sing to him,
praise the God of my life.

I will say to God, my rock:
"Why have you forgotten me?
Why do I go mourning,
oppressed by the foe?"

With cries that pierce me to the heart,
my enemies revile me,
saying to me all the day long:
"Where is your God?"

Why are you cast down, my soul,
why groan within me?
Hope in God; I will praise him still,
my savior and my God.

Glory to the Father, and to the Son,
    and to the Holy Spirit:
as it was in the beginning, is now,
and will be for ever. Amen.

Ant.   **When will I come to the end of my
pilgrimage and enter the presence of God?**

Ant. 2   **Lord, show us the radiance of your mercy.**

Canticle:
Sirach 36:1–5,
10–13

Come to our aid, O God of the universe,
and put all the nations in dread of you!
Raise your hand against the heathen,
that they may realize your power.

As you have used us to show them
    your holiness,
so now use them to show us your glory.
Thus they will know, as we know,
that there is no God but you.

Give new signs and work new wonders;
show forth the splendor of your right
    hand and arm.

Gather all the tribes of Jacob,
that they may inherit the land as of old.
Show mercy to the people called by
    your name;
Israel, whom you named your first-born.

Take pity on your holy city,
Jerusalem, your dwelling place.
Fill Zion with your majesty,
your temple with your glory.

Glory to the Father, and to the Son,
    and to the Holy Spirit:
—as it was in the beginning, is now,
and will be for ever. Amen.

Ant.   **Lord, show us the radiance of your mercy.**

Ant. 3   **The vaults of heaven ring with your praise,
          O Lord.**

Psalm 19a The heavens proclaim the glory of God
           and the firmament shows forth the work of
               his hands.
           Day unto day takes up the story
           and night unto night makes known
               the message.

           No speech, no word, no voice is heard
           yet their span extends through all the earth,
           their words to the utmost bounds of
               the world.

           There he has placed a tent for the sun;
           it comes forth like a bridegroom coming
               from his tent,
           rejoices like a champion to run its course.

           At the end of the sky is the rising of the sun;
           to the furthest end of the sky is its course.
           There is nothing concealed from its
               burning heat.

           Glory to the Father, and to the Son,
               and to the Holy Spirit:
           —as it was in the beginning, is now,
               and will be for ever. Amen.

Ant.   **The vaults of heaven ring with your praise,
          O Lord.**

Reading
Jeremiah 15:16

When I found your words, I devoured them;
    they became my joy and the happiness
        of my heart,
Because I bore your name,
    O Lord, God of hosts.

Responsory

Sing for joy, God's chosen ones, give him the
    praise that is due.
—Sing for joy, God's chosen ones, give him the
    praise that is due.

Sing a new song to the Lord;
—give him the praise that is due.

Glory to the Father, and to the Son,
    and to the Holy Spirit.
—Sing for joy, God's chosen ones, give him the
    praise that is due.

Gospel
Canticle

Ant. **Blessed be the Lord, for he has come to
his people and set them free.**

*Canticle of
Zechariah
Luke 1:68–79*

Blessed + be the Lord, the God of Israel;
he has come to his people and set them free.

He has raised up for us a mighty savior,
born of the house of his servant David.

Through his holy prophets he
    promised of old
that he would save us from our enemies,
from the hands of all who hate us.

He promised to show mercy to our fathers
and to remember his holy covenant.

This was the oath he swore to our
    father Abraham:
to set us free from the hands of our enemies,
free to worship him without fear,
holy and righteous in his sight
    all the days of our life.

You, my child, shall be called the prophet of
    the Most High;
for you will go before the Lord to
    prepare his way,
to give his people knowledge of salvation
by the forgiveness of their sins.

In the tender compassion of our God
the dawn from on high shall break upon us,
to shine on those who dwell in darkness and
    the shadow of death,
and to guide our feet into the way of peace.

Glory to the Father, and to the Son,
    and to the Holy Spirit:
—as it was in the beginning, is now,
    and will be for ever. Amen.

Ant.   **Blessed be the Lord, for he has come to his
people and set them free.**

Intercessions Our Savior has made us a nation of priests to
              offer acceptable sacrifice to the Father. Let
              us call upon him in gratitude:
              Preserve us in your ministry, Lord.

              Christ, eternal priest, you conferred the holy
                   priesthood on your people,
              —grant that we may offer spiritual sacrifices
                   acceptable to the Father.

              In your goodness pour out on us the fruits of
                   your Spirit,
              —patience, kindness and gentleness.

              May we love you and possess you,
                   for you are love,
              —and may every action of our lives praise you.

              May we seek those things which are
                   beneficial to our brothers, without
                   counting the cost,
              —to help them on the way to salvation.

The Lord's   Our Father, who art in heaven,
Prayer   hallowed be thy name;
              thy kingdom come,
              thy will be done
              on earth as it is in heaven.
              Give us this day our daily bread,
              and forgive us our trespasses,
              as we forgive those who trespass against us;
              and lead us not into temptation,
              but deliver us from evil.

Pater noster, qui es in cælis:
sanctificetur nomen tuum;
adveniat regnum tuum;
fiat voluntas tua,
sicut in cælo, et in terra.
Panem nostrum cotidianum da nobis hodie;
et dimitte nobis debita nostra,
sicut et nos dimittimus debitoribus nostris;
et ne nos inducas in tentationem;
sed libera nos a malo.

Concluding Prayer

Almighty Father,
you have brought us to the light of a new day:
keep us safe the whole day through
from every sinful inclination.
May all our thoughts, words and actions
aim at doing what is pleasing in your sight.
We ask this through our Lord Jesus Christ,
    your Son,
who lives and reigns with you and
    the Holy Spirit,
God, for ever and ever.
—Amen.

Dismissal   *If praying individually, or in a group without a priest or deacon:*

May the Lord + bless us,
protect us from all evil
and bring us to everlasting life.
—Amen.

If praying with a priest or deacon, he dismisses the people:

The Lord be with you.
—And with your spirit.

May almighty God bless you,
the Father, and the Son, + and the Holy Spirit.
—Amen.

Go in peace.
—Thanks be to God.

EVENING PRAYER————————————

God, + come to my assistance.
—Lord, make haste to help me.

Glory to the Father, and to the Son,
and to the Holy Spirit:
—as it was in the beginning, is now,
and will be for ever. Amen. Alleluia.

Hymn   *O God, Creator of All Things, p. 697*

Psalmody   Ant. 1 **Yours is more than mortal beauty;
every word you speak is full of grace.**

Psalm 45   My heart overflows with noble words.
To the king I must speak the song I
have made;
my tongue as nimble as the pen of a scribe.

You are the fairest of the children of men
and graciousness is poured upon your lips:
because God has blessed you for evermore.

O mighty one, gird your sword upon
your thigh;
in splendor and state, ride on in triumph
for the cause of truth and goodness and right.

Take aim with your bow in your dread
    right hand.
Your arrows are sharp: peoples fall
    beneath you.
The foes of the king fall down and lose heart.

Your throne, O God, shall endure for ever.
A scepter of justice is the scepter of
    your kingdom.
Your love is for justice; your hatred for evil.

Therefore God, your God, has anointed you
with the oil of gladness above other kings:
your robes are fragrant with aloes and myrrh.

From the ivory palace you are greeted
    with music.
The daughters of kings are among your
    loved ones.
On your right stands the queen in
    gold of Ophir.

Glory to the Father, and to the Son,
    and to the Holy Spirit:
—as it was in the beginning, is now,
    and will be for ever. Amen.

Ant. **Yours is more than mortal beauty; every
word you speak is full of grace.**

Ant. 2 **The Bridegroom is here; go out and
welcome him.**

Psalm 45
(continued)

Listen, O daughter, give ear to my words:
forget your own people and your
        father's house.
So will the king desire your beauty:
he is your lord, pay homage to him.

And the people of Tyre shall come with gifts,
the richest of the people shall seek your favor.
The daughter of the king is clothed
        with splendor,
her robes embroidered with pearls
        set in gold.

She is led to the king with her maiden
        companions.
They are escorted amid gladness and joy;
they pass within the palace of the king.

Sons shall be yours in place of your fathers:
you will make them princes over all the earth.
May this song make your name for ever
        remembered.
May the peoples praise you from age to age.

Glory to the Father, and to the Son,
        and to the Holy Spirit:
—as it was in the beginning, is now,
and will be for ever. Amen.

Ant.

**The Bridegroom is here; go out and
welcome him.**

Ant. 3

**God planned in the fullness of time to
restore all things in Christ.**

Canticle:
Ephesians
1:3–10

Praised be the God and Father
of our Lord Jesus Christ,
who has bestowed on us in Christ
every spiritual blessing in the heavens.

God chose us in him
before the world began
to be holy
and blameless in his sight.

He predestined us
to be his adopted sons through Jesus Christ,
such was his will and pleasure,
that all might praise the glorious favor
he has bestowed on us in his beloved.

In him and through his blood, we have
    been redeemed,
and our sins forgiven,
so immeasurably generous
is God's favor to us.

God has given us the wisdom
to understand fully the mystery,
the plan he was pleased
to decree in Christ.

A plan to be carried out
in Christ, in the fullness of time,
to bring all things into one in him,
in the heavens and on earth.

Glory to the Father, and to the Son,
    and to the Holy Spirit:
—as it was in the beginning, is now,
    and will be for ever. Amen.

Ant. **God planned in the fullness of time to restore all things in Christ.**

Reading
1 Thessalonians
2:13

We thank God constantly that in receiving his message from us you took it, not as the word of men, but as it truly is, the word of God at work within you who believe.

Responsory

Accept my prayer, O Lord, which rises
    up to you.
—Accept my prayer, O Lord, which rises
    up to you.

Like burning incense in your sight,
—which rises up to you.

Glory to the Father, and to the Son,
    and to the Holy Spirit.
—Accept my prayer, O Lord, which rises
    up to you.

Gospel
Canticle

Ant. **For ever will my soul proclaim the greatness of the Lord.**

Canticle of
Mary
Luke 1:46–55

My + soul proclaims the greatness of the Lord,
my spirit rejoices in God my Savior
for he has looked with favor on his
        lowly servant.

From this day all generations will
        call me blessed:
the Almighty has done great things for me,
and holy is his Name.

He has mercy on those who fear him
in every generation.

He has shown the strength of his arm,
he has scattered the proud in their conceit.

He has cast down the mighty from
        their thrones,
and has lifted up the lowly.

He has filled the hungry with good things,
and the rich he has sent away empty.

He has come to the help of his servant Israel
for he has remembered his promise of mercy,
the promise he made to our fathers,
to Abraham and his children for ever.

Glory to the Father, and to the Son,
        and to the Holy Spirit:
—as it was in the beginning, is now,
        and will be for ever. Amen.

Ant.   **For ever will my soul proclaim the
          greatness of the Lord.**

Intercessions Let us praise Christ, who loves, nourishes and
supports his Church. With faith let us cry
out to him:
Answer the prayers of your people, Lord.

Lord Jesus, grant that all men be saved,
—and come to the knowledge of truth.

Preserve our holy father, Pope N., and N.,
our bishop,
—come with your power to help them.

Remember those who long for honest work,
—so that they may lead a life of
peaceful security.

Lord, be the refuge of the poor,
—their help in distress.

We commend to your care all bishops, priests
and deacons who have died,
—may they sing your praises for ever around
your heavenly throne.

The Lord's
Prayer   Our Father, who art in heaven,
hallowed be thy name;
thy kingdom come,
thy will be done
on earth as it is in heaven.
Give us this day our daily bread,
and forgive us our trespasses,
as we forgive those who trespass against us;
and lead us not into temptation,
but deliver us from evil.

Pater noster, qui es in cælis:
sanctificetur nomen tuum;
adveniat regnum tuum;
fiat voluntas tua,
sicut in cælo, et in terra.
Panem nostrum cotidianum da nobis hodie;
et dimitte nobis debita nostra,
sicut et nos dimittimus debitoribus nostris;
et ne nos inducas in tentationem;
sed libera nos a malo.

Concluding Prayer

Almighty Father,
you have given us the strength
to work throughout this day.
Receive our evening sacrifice of praise
in thanksgiving for your countless gifts.
We ask this through our Lord Jesus Christ,
    your Son,
who lives and reigns with you and
    the Holy Spirit,
God, for ever and ever.
—Amen.

Dismissal

If praying individually, or in a group without a priest or deacon:

May the Lord + bless us,
protect us from all evil
and bring us to everlasting life.
—Amen.

If praying with a priest or deacon, he dismisses the people:

The Lord be with you.
—And with your spirit.

May almighty God bless you,
the Father, and the Son, + and the Holy Spirit.
—Amen.

Go in peace.
—Thanks be to God.

NIGHT PRAYER

God, + come to my assistance.
—Lord, make haste to help me.

Glory to the Father, and to the Son,
and to the Holy Spirit:
—as it was in the beginning, is now,
and will be for ever. Amen. Alleluia.

Examen   *An optional brief examination of conscience may be made. Call to mind your sins and failings this day.*

Hymn   *O Gladsome Light, p. 696*

Psalmody   Ant. **O Lord, our God, unwearied is your love for us.**

Psalm 86   Turn your ear, O Lord, and give answer
for I am poor and needy.
Preserve my life, for I am faithful:
save the servant who trusts in you.

You are my God; have mercy on me, Lord,
for I cry to you all the day long.
Give joy to your servant, O Lord,
for to you I lift up my soul.

O Lord, you are good and forgiving,
full of love to all who call.

Give heed, O Lord, to my prayer
and attend to the sound of my voice.

In the day of distress I will call
and surely you will reply.
Among the gods there is none like you,
    O Lord;
nor work to compare with yours.

All the nations shall come to adore you
and glorify your name, O Lord:
for you are great and do marvelous deeds,
you who alone are God.

Show me, Lord, your way
so that I may walk in your truth.
Guide my heart to fear your name.

I will praise you, Lord my God, with
    all my heart
and glorify your name for ever;
for your love to me has been great:
you have saved me from the depths of
    the grave.

The proud have risen against me;
ruthless men seek my life:
to you they pay no heed.

But you, God of mercy and compassion,
slow to anger, O Lord,
abounding in love and truth,
turn and take pity on me.

O give your strength to your servant
and save your handmaid's son.
Show me a sign of your favor
that my foes may see to their shame
that you console me and give me your help.

Glory to the Father, and to the Son,
   and to the Holy Spirit:
—as it was in the beginning, is now,
and will be for ever. Amen.

Ant. **O Lord, our God, unwearied is your love for us.**

Reading
1 Thessalonians 5:9–10

God has destined us for acquiring salvation through our Lord Jesus Christ. He died for us, that all of us, whether awake or asleep, together might live with him.

Responsory

Into your hands, Lord, I commend my spirit.
—Into your hands, Lord, I commend my spirit.

You have redeemed us, Lord God of truth.
—I commend my spirit.

Glory to the Father, and to the Son,
   and to the Holy Spirit.
—Into your hands, Lord, I commend my spirit.

Gospel Canticle

Ant. **Protect us, Lord, as we stay awake; watch over us as we sleep, that awake, we may keep watch with Christ, and asleep, rest in his peace.**

Canticle of
Simeon
Luke 2:29–32

Lord, + now you let your servant go in peace;
your word has been fulfilled:
my own eyes have seen the salvation
which you have prepared in the sight of
    every people:
a light to reveal you to the nations
and the glory of your people Israel.

Glory to the Father, and to the Son,
    and to the Holy Spirit:
as it was in the beginning, is now,
and will be for ever. Amen.

Ant.

**Protect us, Lord, as we stay awake; watch
over us as we sleep, that awake, we may
keep watch with Christ, and asleep, rest in
his peace.**

Concluding
Prayer

Let us pray.
Lord,
give our bodies restful sleep
and let the work we have done today
bear fruit in eternal life.
We ask this through Christ our Lord.
—Amen.

Blessing

May the all-powerful Lord
grant us a restful night
and a peaceful death.
—Amen.

Marian
Antiphon

Sing the "Salve Regina," found on p. 700, or pray a Hail Mary.

O GOD, YOU ARE
MY GOD, FOR
YOU I LONG;
FOR YOU MY
SOUL IS
THIRSTING.

Tuesday, August 6, 2024
Transfiguration of the Lord

MORNING PRAYER——————————————————

God, + come to my assistance.
—Lord, make haste to help me.

Glory to the Father, and to the Son,
    and to the Holy Spirit:
—as it was in the beginning, is now,
and will be for ever. Amen. Alleluia.

Hymn   *O Light of Light, by Love Inclined, p. 698*

Psalmody   Ant. 1 **Today the Lord Jesus Christ shone
with splendor on the mountain, his face
like the sun and his clothes white as snow.**

Psalm 63:2–9   O God, you are my God, for you I long;
for you my soul is thirsting.
My body pines for you
like a dry, weary land without water.
So I gaze on you in the sanctuary
to see your strength and your glory.

For your love is better than life,
my lips will speak your praise.
So I will bless you all my life,
in your name I will lift up my hands.
My soul shall be filled as with a banquet,
my mouth shall praise you with joy.

On my bed I remember you.
On you I muse through the night
for you have been my help;
in the shadow of your wings I rejoice.
My soul clings to you;
your right hand holds me fast.

Glory to the Father, and to the Son,
    and to the Holy Spirit:
—as it was in the beginning, is now,
and will be for ever. Amen.

Ant.   **Today the Lord Jesus Christ shone with splendor on the mountain, his face like the sun and his clothes white as snow.**

Ant. 2   **Today the Lord was transfigured and the voice of the Father bore witness to him; Moses and Elijah appeared with him in glory and spoke with him about the death he was to undergo.**

Canticle:
Daniel
3:57–88, 56

Bless the Lord, all you works of the Lord.
Praise and exalt him above all forever.
Angels of the Lord, bless the Lord.
You heavens, bless the Lord.
All you waters above the heavens,
    bless the Lord.
All you hosts of the Lord, bless the Lord.
Sun and moon, bless the Lord.
Stars of heaven, bless the Lord.

Every shower and dew, bless the Lord.
All you winds, bless the Lord.
Fire and heat, bless the Lord.
Cold and chill, bless the Lord.
Dew and rain, bless the Lord.
Frost and chill, bless the Lord.
Ice and snow, bless the Lord.
Nights and days, bless the Lord.
Light and darkness, bless the Lord.
Lightnings and clouds, bless the Lord.

Let the earth bless the Lord.
Praise and exalt him above all forever.
Mountains and hills, bless the Lord.
Everything growing from the earth,
    bless the Lord.
You springs, bless the Lord.
Seas and rivers, bless the Lord.
You dolphins and all water creatures,
    bless the Lord.
All you birds of the air, bless the Lord.
All you beasts, wild and tame, bless the Lord.
You sons of men, bless the Lord.

O Israel, bless the Lord.
Praise and exalt him above all forever.
Priests of the Lord, bless the Lord.
Servants of the Lord, bless the Lord.
Spirits and souls of the just, bless the Lord.
Holy men of humble heart, bless the Lord.
Hananiah, Azariah, Mishael, bless the Lord.
Praise and exalt him above all forever.

Let us bless the Father, and the Son,
    and the Holy Spirit.
Let us praise and exalt him above all forever.
Blessed are you, Lord, in the firmament
    of heaven.
Praiseworthy and glorious and exalted above
    all forever.

Ant. **Today the Lord was transfigured and the
voice of the Father bore witness to him;
Moses and Elijah appeared with him in
glory and spoke with him about the death
he was to undergo.**

Ant. 3 **The law was given through Moses and
prophecy through Elijah. Radiant in the
divine majesty, they were seen speaking
with the Lord.**

Psalm 149

Sing a new song to the Lord,
his praise in the assembly of the faithful.
Let Israel rejoice in its maker,
let Zion's sons exult in their king.
Let them praise his name with dancing
and make music with timbrel and harp.

For the Lord takes delight in his people.
He crowns the poor with salvation.
Let the faithful rejoice in their glory,
shout for joy and take their rest.
Let the praise of God be on their lips
and a two-edged sword in their hand,

to deal out vengeance to the nations
and punishment on all the peoples;
to bind their kings in chains
and their nobles in fetters of iron;
to carry out the sentence pre-ordained;
this honor is for all his faithful.

Glory to the Father, and to the Son,
    and to the Holy Spirit:
— as it was in the beginning, is now,
and will be for ever. Amen.

Ant.   **The law was given through Moses and
          prophecy through Elijah. Radiant in the
          divine majesty, they were seen speaking
          with the Lord.**

Reading   The angel carried me away in spirit to the
Revelation top of a very high mountain and showed me
21:10, 23 the holy city Jerusalem coming down out
          of heaven from God. The city had no need
          of sun or moon, for the glory of God gave it
          light, and its lamp was the Lamb.

Responsory With glory and honor, Lord,
              you have crowned him.
          — With glory and honor, Lord,
              you have crowned him.

          You set him over the works of your hands.
          — Lord, you have crowned him.

Glory to the Father, and to the Son,
and to the Holy Spirit.
—With glory and honor, Lord, you have
crowned him.

*Gospel
Canticle*

Ant. **A voice spoke from the cloud: This
is my beloved Son in whom I am well
pleased; listen to him.**

*Canticle of
Zechariah
Luke 1:68–79*

Blessed + be the Lord, the God of Israel;
he has come to his people and set them free.

He has raised up for us a mighty savior,
born of the house of his servant David.

Through his holy prophets he
promised of old
that he would save us from our enemies,
from the hands of all who hate us.

He promised to show mercy to our fathers
and to remember his holy covenant.

This was the oath he swore to our
father Abraham:
to set us free from the hands of our enemies,
free to worship him without fear,
holy and righteous in his sight
all the days of our life.

You, my child, shall be called the prophet of
    the Most High;
for you will go before the Lord to
    prepare his way,
to give his people knowledge of salvation
by the forgiveness of their sins.

In the tender compassion of our God
the dawn from on high shall break upon us,
to shine on those who dwell in darkness and
    the shadow of death,
and to guide our feet into the way of peace.

Glory to the Father, and to the Son,
    and to the Holy Spirit:
—as it was in the beginning, is now,
    and will be for ever. Amen.

Ant.   **A voice spoke from the cloud: This is my
beloved Son in whom I am well pleased;
listen to him.**

Intercessions   In the presence of his disciples our Savior
    was wonderfully transfigured on Mount
    Tabor. Let us pray to him with confidence:
Lord, in your light may we see light.

Father of mercies, you glorified your
    heavenly Son and revealed yourself in the
    bright cloud,
—grant that we may listen in faith to the word
    of Christ.

O God, you have filled your chosen people
with the bounty of your house,
—grant that we may always find the source of
our life in the body of Christ.

O God, you have scattered the darkness with
your light and have poured your light
into our hearts so that we might look
upon the radiant face of Jesus Christ,
—nourish in us the desire to contemplate your
beloved Son.

O God, according to your plan, you have
called us to holiness by your grace which
you have revealed in Jesus Christ,
—through your Gospel show to all mankind
the glorious splendor of unending life.

Loving Father, you have so loved us that we
have been called to be sons of God,
—when Christ comes grant that we may
be like him.

The Lord's
Prayer

Our Father, who art in heaven,
hallowed be thy name;
thy kingdom come,
thy will be done
on earth as it is in heaven.
Give us this day our daily bread,
and forgive us our trespasses,
as we forgive those who trespass against us;
and lead us not into temptation,
but deliver us from evil.

Pater noster, qui es in cælis:
sanctificetur nomen tuum;
adveniat regnum tuum;
fiat voluntas tua,
sicut in cælo, et in terra.
Panem nostrum cotidianum da nobis hodie;
et dimitte nobis debita nostra,
sicut et nos dimittimus debitoribus nostris;
et ne nos inducas in tentationem;
sed libera nos a malo.

Concluding Prayer

God our Father,
in the transfigured glory of Christ your Son,
you strengthen our faith
by confirming the witness of your prophets,
and show us the splendor of your beloved
        sons and daughters.
As we listen to the voice of your Son,
help us to become heirs to eternal
        life with him
who lives and reigns with you and
        the Holy Spirit,
God, for ever and ever.
—Amen.

Dismissal

If praying individually, or in a group without a priest or deacon:

May the Lord + bless us,
protect us from all evil
and bring us to everlasting life.
—Amen.

If praying with a priest or deacon, he dismisses the people:

The Lord be with you.
—And with your spirit.

May almighty God bless you,
the Father, and the Son,+ and the Holy Spirit.
—Amen.

Go in peace.
—Thanks be to God.

EVENING PRAYER

God,+ come to my assistance.
—Lord, make haste to help me.

Glory to the Father, and to the Son,
    and to the Holy Spirit:
—as it was in the beginning, is now,
and will be for ever. Amen. Alleluia.

Hymn   *O Wondrous Type! O Vision Fair, p. 699*

Psalmody   Ant. 1 **Jesus took Peter, James and his brother John and led them up a high mountain where they could be alone, and he was transfigured before them.**

Psalm 110:1–5, 7   The Lord's revelation to my Master:
    "Sit on my right:
    your foes I will put beneath your feet."

The Lord will wield from Zion
your scepter of power:
rule in the midst of all your foes.

A prince from the day of your birth
on the holy mountains;
from the womb before the dawn I begot you.

The Lord has sworn an oath he will
    not change.
"You are a priest for ever,
  a priest like Melchizedek of old."

The Master standing at your right hand
will shatter kings in the day of his
    great wrath.

He shall drink from the stream by
    the wayside
and therefore he shall lift up his head.

Glory to the Father, and to the Son,
    and to the Holy Spirit:
—as it was in the beginning, is now,
  and will be for ever. Amen.

Ant.   **Jesus took Peter, James and his brother
John and led them up a high mountain
where they could be alone, and he was
transfigured before them.**

Ant. 2   **A bright cloud overshadowed them and
suddenly a voice spoke from the cloud:
This is my beloved Son in whom I am well
pleased; listen to him.**

Psalm 121   I lift up my eyes to the mountains:
from where shall come my help?
My help shall come from the Lord
who made heaven and earth.

May he never allow you to stumble!
Let him sleep not, your guard.
No, he sleeps not nor slumbers,
Israel's guard.

The Lord is your guard and your shade;
at your right side he stands.
By day the sun shall not smite you
nor the moon in the night.

The Lord will guard you from evil,
he will guard your soul.
The Lord will guard your going and coming
both now and for ever.

Glory to the Father, and to the Son,
    and to the Holy Spirit:
— as it was in the beginning, is now,
and will be for ever. Amen.

Ant.   **A bright cloud overshadowed them and
suddenly a voice spoke from the cloud:
This is my beloved Son in whom I am well
pleased; listen to him.**

Ant. 3   **As they came down from the mountain
Jesus commanded them: Tell no one of
the vision until the Son of Man has risen
from the dead.**

Canticle: See
1 Timothy 3:16

Praise the Lord, all you nations.

Christ manifested in the flesh,
Christ justified in the Spirit.

Praise the Lord, all you nations.

Christ contemplated by the angels,
Christ proclaimed by the pagans.

Praise the Lord, all you nations.

Christ who is believed in the world,
Christ exalted in glory.

Praise the Lord, all you nations.

Glory to the Father, and to the Son,
    and to the Holy Spirit:
—as it was in the beginning, is now,
    and will be for ever. Amen.

Ant.

**As they came down from the mountain
Jesus commanded them: Tell no one of
the vision until the Son of Man has risen
from the dead.**

Reading
Romans
8:16–17

The Spirit himself gives witness with our
spirit that we are children of God. But if we
are children, we are heirs as well: heirs of
God, heirs with Christ, if only we suffer with
him so as to be glorified with him.

Responsory Beauty and wealth surround him,
alleluia, alleluia.
—Beauty and wealth surround him,
alleluia, alleluia.

Richness and splendor adorn his holy place.
—Alleluia, alleluia.

Glory to the Father, and to the Son,
and to the Holy Spirit.
—Beauty and wealth surround him,
alleluia, alleluia.

Gospel Canticle Ant. **When they heard the voice from the cloud, the disciples fell on their faces, overcome with fear; Jesus came up to them, touched them and said: Stand up. Do not be afraid.**

Canticle of Mary
Luke 1:46–55

My + soul proclaims the greatness of the Lord,
my spirit rejoices in God my Savior
for he has looked with favor on his
lowly servant.

From this day all generations will
call me blessed:
the Almighty has done great things for me,
and holy is his Name.

He has mercy on those who fear him
in every generation.

He has shown the strength of his arm,
he has scattered the proud in their conceit.

He has cast down the mighty from
    their thrones,
and has lifted up the lowly.

He has filled the hungry with good things,
and the rich he has sent away empty.

He has come to the help of his servant Israel
for he has remembered his promise of mercy,
the promise he made to our fathers,
to Abraham and his children for ever.

Glory to the Father, and to the Son,
    and to the Holy Spirit:
—as it was in the beginning, is now,
    and will be for ever. Amen.

Ant. **When they heard the voice from the cloud,
the disciples fell on their faces, overcome
with fear; Jesus came up to them, touched
them and said: Stand up. Do not be afraid.**

Intercessions In the presence of his disciples our Savior
        was wonderfully transfigured on Mount
        Tabor. Let us pray to him with confidence:
    Lord, in your light may we see light.

O Christ, before your passion and death you
        revealed the resurrection to your disciples
        on Mount Tabor; we pray for your
        Church which labors amid the cares and
        anxieties of this world,
—that in its trials it may always be transfigured
        by the joy of your victory.

O Christ, you took Peter, James and John
and led them up a high mountain
by themselves; we pray for our pope
and bishops,
—that they may inspire in your people the
hope of being transfigured at the last day.

O Christ, upon the mountaintop you let
the light of your face shine over Moses
and Elijah,
—we ask your blessing upon the Jewish
people; of old you called them to be your
chosen nation.

O Christ, you gave light to the world when
the glory of the Creator arose over you,
—we pray for men of good will that they may
walk in your light.

O Christ, you will reform our lowly body and
make it like your glorious one,
—we pray for our brothers and sisters who
have died that they may share in your
glory for ever.

The Lord's
Prayer

Our Father, who art in heaven,
hallowed be thy name;
thy kingdom come,
thy will be done
on earth as it is in heaven.
Give us this day our daily bread,
and forgive us our trespasses,
as we forgive those who trespass against us;
and lead us not into temptation,
but deliver us from evil.

Pater noster, qui es in cælis:
sanctificetur nomen tuum;
adveniat regnum tuum;
fiat voluntas tua,
sicut in cælo, et in terra.
Panem nostrum cotidianum da nobis hodie;
et dimitte nobis debita nostra,
sicut et nos dimittimus debitoribus nostris;
et ne nos inducas in tentationem;
sed libera nos a malo.

Concluding Prayer

God our Father,
in the transfigured glory of Christ your Son,
you strengthen our faith
by confirming the witness of your prophets,
and show us the splendor of your beloved
       sons and daughters.
As we listen to the voice of your Son,
help us to become heirs to eternal
       life with him
who lives and reigns with you and
       the Holy Spirit,
God, for ever and ever.
—Amen.

Dismissal

If praying individually, or in a group without a priest or deacon:

May the Lord + bless us,
protect us from all evil
and bring us to everlasting life.
—Amen.

If praying with a priest or deacon, he dismisses the people:

The Lord be with you.
—And with your spirit.

May almighty God bless you,
    the Father, and the Son, +and the Holy Spirit.
—Amen.

Go in peace.
—Thanks be to God.

NIGHT PRAYER

God, +come to my assistance.
—Lord, make haste to help me.

Glory to the Father, and to the Son,
    and to the Holy Spirit:
—as it was in the beginning, is now,
    and will be for ever. Amen. Alleluia.

Examen   *An optional brief examination of conscience may be made. Call to mind your*
     sins and failings this day.

Hymn   *O Gladsome Light, p. 696*

Psalmody   Ant. **Do not hide your face from me; in you
I put my trust.**

Psalm 143:1–11   Lord, listen to my prayer:
    turn your ear to my appeal.
You are faithful, you are just; give answer.
Do not call your servant to judgment
    for no one is just in your sight.

The enemy pursues my soul;
he has crushed my life to the ground;
he has made me dwell in darkness
    like the dead, long forgotten.
Therefore my spirit fails;
    my heart is numb within me.

147

I remember the days that are past:
I ponder all your works.
I muse on what your hand has wrought
and to you I stretch out my hands.
Like a parched land my soul thirsts for you.

Lord, make haste and answer;
for my spirit fails within me.
Do not hide your face
lest I become like those in the grave.

In the morning let me know your love
for I put my trust in you.
Make me know the way I should walk:
to you I lift up my soul.

Rescue me, Lord, from my enemies;
I have fled to you for refuge.
Teach me to do your will
for you, O Lord, are my God.
Let your good spirit guide me
in ways that are level and smooth.

For your name's sake, Lord, save my life;
in your justice save my soul from distress.

Glory to the Father, and to the Son,
    and to the Holy Spirit:
—as it was in the beginning, is now,
    and will be for ever. Amen.

Ant.   **Do not hide your face from me; in you I
put my trust.**

Reading
1 Peter 5:8–9a

Stay sober and alert. Your opponent the
devil is prowling like a roaring lion looking
for someone to devour. Resist him, solid in
your faith.

Responsory

Into your hands, Lord, I commend my spirit.
—Into your hands, Lord, I commend my spirit.

You have redeemed us, Lord God of truth.
—I commend my spirit.

Glory to the Father, and to the Son,
    and to the Holy Spirit.
—Into your hands, Lord, I commend my spirit.

**Gospel
Canticle**

Ant. **Protect us, Lord, as we stay awake;
watch over us as we sleep, that awake, we
may keep watch with Christ, and asleep,
rest in his peace.**

*Canticle of
Simeon
Luke 2:29–32*

Lord, +now you let your servant go in peace;
your word has been fulfilled:
my own eyes have seen the salvation
which you have prepared in the sight of
    every people:
a light to reveal you to the nations
and the glory of your people Israel.

Glory to the Father, and to the Son,
    and to the Holy Spirit:
—as it was in the beginning, is now,
    and will be for ever. Amen.

Ant.   **Protect us, Lord, as we stay awake; watch over us as we sleep, that awake, we may keep watch with Christ, and asleep, rest in his peace.**

Concluding Prayer

Let us pray.
Lord,
fill this night with your radiance.
May we sleep in peace and rise with joy
to welcome the light of a new day in
    your name.
We ask this through Christ our Lord.
—Amen.

Blessing

May the all-powerful Lord
grant us a restful night
and a peaceful death.
—Amen.

Marian Antiphon

Sing the "Salve Regina," found on p. 700, or pray a Hail Mary.

FOR YOUR
NAME'S SAKE,
LORD, SAVE
MY LIFE;
IN YOUR JUSTICE
SAVE MY SOUL
FROM DISTRESS.

Wednesday, August 7, 2024
Wednesday of the Eighteenth Week in Ordinary Time

MORNING PRAYER————————————————

God, + come to my assistance.
—Lord, make haste to help me.

Glory to the Father, and to the Son,
    and to the Holy Spirit:
—as it was in the beginning, is now,
and will be for ever. Amen. Alleluia.

Hymn   *Holy, Holy, Holy, p. 690*

Psalmody   Ant. 1 **O God, all your ways are holy; what god can compare with our God?**

Psalm 77   I cry aloud to God,
cry aloud to God that he may hear me.

In the day of my distress I sought the Lord.
My hands were raised at night
    without ceasing;
my soul refused to be consoled.
I remembered my God and I groaned.
I pondered and my spirit fainted.

You withheld sleep from my eyes.
I was troubled, I could not speak.
I thought of the days of long ago
and remembered the years long past.
At night I mused within my heart.
I pondered and my spirit questioned.

"Will the Lord reject us for ever?
Will he show us his favor no more?
Has his love vanished for ever?
Has his promise come to an end?
Does God forget his mercy
or in anger withhold his compassion?"

I said: "This is what causes my grief;
that the way of the Most High has changed."
I remember the deeds of the Lord,
I remember your wonders of old,
I muse on all your works
and ponder your mighty deeds.

Your ways, O God, are holy.
What god is great as our God?
You are the God who works wonders.
You showed your power among the peoples.
Your strong arm redeemed your people,
the sons of Jacob and Joseph.

The waters saw you, O God,
the waters saw you and trembled;
the depths were moved with terror.
The clouds poured down rain,
the skies sent forth their voice;
your arrows flashed to and fro.

Your thunder rolled round the sky,
your flashes lighted up the world.
The earth was moved and trembled
when your way led through the sea,
your path through the mighty waters,
and no one saw your footprints.

You guided your people like a flock
by the hand of Moses and Aaron.

Glory to the Father, and to the Son,
   and to the Holy Spirit:
—as it was in the beginning, is now,
and will be for ever. Amen.

Ant.   **O God, all your ways are holy; what god can
compare with our God?**

Ant. 2   **My heart leaps up with joy to the Lord, for
he humbles only to exalt us.**

Canticle: My heart exults in the Lord,
1 Samuel 2:1–10   my horn is exalted in my God.

I have swallowed up my enemies;
I rejoice in my victory.
There is no Holy One like the Lord;
there is no Rock like our God.

Speak boastfully no longer,
nor let arrogance issue from your mouths.
For an all-knowing God is the Lord,
a God who judges deeds.

The bows of the mighty are broken,
while the tottering gird on strength.
The well-fed hire themselves out for bread,
while the hungry batten on spoil.
The barren wife bears seven sons,
while the mother of many languishes.

The Lord puts to death and gives life;
he casts down to the nether world;
he raises up again.
The Lord makes poor and makes rich,
he humbles, he also exalts.

He raises the needy from the dust;
from the ash heap he lifts up the poor,
to seat them with nobles
and make a glorious throne their heritage.

For the pillars of the earth are the Lord's,
and he has set the world upon them.
He will guard the footsteps of his
    faithful ones,
but the wicked shall perish in the darkness.
For not by strength does man prevail;
the Lord's foes shall be shattered.

The Most High in heaven thunders;
the Lord judges the ends of the earth.
Now may he give strength to his king
and exalt the horn of his anointed!

Glory to the Father, and to the Son,
    and to the Holy Spirit:
—as it was in the beginning, is now,
and will be for ever. Amen.

Ant.   **My heart leaps up with joy to the Lord, for
he humbles only to exalt us.**

Ant. 3   **The Lord is king, let the earth rejoice.**

The Lord is king, let earth rejoice,
let all the coastlands be glad.
Cloud and darkness are his raiment;
his throne, justice and right.

A fire prepares his path;
it burns up his foes on every side.
His lightnings light up the world,
the earth trembles at the sight.

The mountains melt like wax
before the Lord of all the earth.
The skies proclaim his justice;
all peoples see his glory.

Let those who serve idols be ashamed,
those who boast of their worthless gods.
All you spirits, worship him.

Zion hears and is glad;
the people of Judah rejoice
because of your judgments, O Lord.

For you indeed are the Lord,
most high above all the earth,
exalted far above all spirits.

The Lord loves those who hate evil;
he guards the souls of his saints;
he sets them free from the wicked.

Light shines forth for the just
and joy for the upright of heart.
Rejoice, you just, in the Lord;
give glory to his holy name.

Glory to the Father, and to the Son,
and to the Holy Spirit:
— as it was in the beginning, is now,
and will be for ever. Amen.

Ant. **The Lord is king, let the earth rejoice.**

Reading
Romans 8:35, 37

Who will separate us from the love of Christ?
Trial, or distress, or persecution, or hunger,
or nakedness, or danger, or the sword? Yet in
all this we are more than conquerors because
of him who has loved us.

Responsory

I will bless the Lord all my life long.
— I will bless the Lord all my life long.

With a song of praise ever on my lips,
— all my life long.

Glory to the Father, and to the Son,
and to the Holy Spirit.
— I will bless the Lord all my life long.

Gospel
Canticle

Ant. **Let us serve the Lord in holiness all the
days of our life.**

Canticle of
Zechariah
Luke 1:68–79

Blessed+ be the Lord, the God of Israel;
he has come to his people and set them free.

He has raised up for us a mighty savior,
born of the house of his servant David.

Through his holy prophets he
      promised of old
that he would save us from our enemies,
from the hands of all who hate us.

He promised to show mercy to our fathers
and to remember his holy covenant.

This was the oath he swore to our
      father Abraham:
to set us free from the hands of our enemies,
free to worship him without fear,
holy and righteous in his sight
      all the days of our life.

You, my child, shall be called the prophet of
      the Most High;
for you will go before the Lord to
      prepare his way,
to give his people knowledge of salvation
by the forgiveness of their sins.

In the tender compassion of our God
the dawn from on high shall break upon us,
to shine on those who dwell in darkness and
      the shadow of death,
and to guide our feet into the way of peace.

Glory to the Father, and to the Son,
      and to the Holy Spirit:
—as it was in the beginning, is now,
      and will be for ever. Amen.

Ant.   **Let us serve the Lord in holiness all the days of our life.**

Intercessions   Blessed be God our Savior, who promised to remain with his Church all days, until the end of the world. Let us give him thanks and call out:
Remain with us, Lord.

Remain with us the whole day, Lord,
—let your grace be a sun that never sets.

We dedicate this day to you as an offering,
—do not let us offer anything that is evil.

May your gift of light pervade this whole day,
—that we may be the salt of the earth and the light of the world.

May the love of your Holy Spirit direct our hearts and our lips,
—and may we always act in accordance with your will.

The Lord's Prayer   Our Father, who art in heaven,
hallowed be thy name;
thy kingdom come,
thy will be done
on earth as it is in heaven.
Give us this day our daily bread,
and forgive us our trespasses,
as we forgive those who trespass against us;
and lead us not into temptation,
but deliver us from evil.

159

Pater noster, qui es in cælis:
sanctificetur nomen tuum;
adveniat regnum tuum;
fiat voluntas tua,
sicut in cælo, et in terra.
Panem nostrum cotidianum da nobis hodie;
et dimitte nobis debita nostra,
sicut et nos dimittimus debitoribus nostris;
et ne nos inducas in tentationem;
sed libera nos a malo.

Concluding Prayer

Lord,
as a new day dawns
send the radiance of your light
to shine in our hearts.
Make us true to your teaching;
keep us free from error and sin.
We ask this through our Lord Jesus Christ,
    your Son,
who lives and reigns with you and
    the Holy Spirit,
God, for ever and ever.
—Amen.

Dismissal

If praying individually, or in a group without a priest or deacon:

May the Lord + bless us,
protect us from all evil
and bring us to everlasting life.
—Amen.

If praying with a priest or deacon, he dismisses the people:

The Lord be with you.
—And with your spirit.

May almighty God bless you,
the Father, and the Son, + and the Holy Spirit.
—Amen.

Go in peace.
—Thanks be to God.

EVENING PRAYER ————————————

God, + come to my assistance.
—Lord, make haste to help me.

Glory to the Father, and to the Son,
    and to the Holy Spirit:
—as it was in the beginning, is now,
and will be for ever. Amen. Alleluia.

Hymn   *O God, Creator of All Things, p. 697*

Psalmody   Ant. 1 **Eagerly we await the fulfillment of our
                hope, the glorious coming of our Savior.**

Psalm 62   In God alone is my soul at rest;
                my help comes from him.
                He alone is my rock, my stronghold,
                my fortress: I stand firm.

                How long will you all attack one man
                to break him down,
                as though he were a tottering wall,
                or a tumbling fence?

                Their plan is only to destroy:
                they take pleasure in lies.
                With their mouth they utter blessing
                but in their heart they curse.

In God alone be at rest, my soul;
for my hope comes from him.
He alone is my rock, my stronghold,
my fortress: I stand firm.

In God is my safety and glory,
the rock of my strength.
Take refuge in God, all you people.
Trust him at all times.
Pour out your hearts before him
for God is our refuge.

Common folk are only a breath,
great men an illusion.
Placed in the scales, they rise;
they weigh less than a breath.

Do not put your trust in oppression
nor vain hopes on plunder.
Do not set your heart on riches
even when they increase.

For God has said only one thing:
only two do I know:
that to God alone belongs power
and to you, Lord, love;
and that you repay each man
according to his deeds.

Glory to the Father, and to the Son,
    and to the Holy Spirit:
—as it was in the beginning, is now,
and will be for ever. Amen.

Ant. **Eagerly we await the fulfillment of our hope, the glorious coming of our Savior.**

Ant. 2 **May God turn his radiant face toward us, and fill us with his blessings.**

Psalm 67

O God, be gracious and bless us
and let your face shed its light upon us.
So will your ways be known upon earth
and all nations learn your saving help.

Let the peoples praise you, O God;
let all the peoples praise you.

Let the nations be glad and exult
for you rule the world with justice.
With fairness you rule the peoples,
you guide the nations on earth.

Let the peoples praise you, O God;
let all the peoples praise you.

The earth has yielded its fruit
for God, our God, has blessed us.
May God still give us his blessing
till the ends of the earth revere him.

Glory to the Father, and to the Son,
    and to the Holy Spirit:
—as it was in the beginning, is now,
and will be for ever. Amen.

Ant. **May God turn his radiant face toward us, and fill us with his blessings.**

Ant. 3   **Through him all things were made; he
holds all creation together in himself.**

Canticle:
Colossians
1:12–20

Let us give thanks to the Father
for having made you worthy
to share the lot of the saints
in light.

He rescued us
from the power of darkness
and brought us
into the kingdom of his beloved Son.
Through him we have redemption,
the forgiveness of our sins.

He is the image of the invisible God,
the first-born of all creatures.
In him everything in heaven and on earth
    was created,
things visible and invisible.

All were created through him;
all were created for him.
He is before all else that is.
In him everything continues in being.

It is he who is head of the body, the church!
he who is the beginning,
the first-born of the dead,
so that primacy may be his in everything.

It pleased God to make absolute fullness
    reside in him
and, by means of him, to reconcile
    everything in his person,
both on earth and in the heavens,
making peace through the blood of his cross.

Glory to the Father, and to the Son,
    and to the Holy Spirit:
—as it was in the beginning, is now,
and will be for ever. Amen.

Ant. **Through him all things were made; he
holds all creation together in himself.**

Reading
1 Peter 5:5b–7

In your relations with one another, clothe
yourselves with humility, because God "is
stern with the arrogant but to the humble he
shows kindness." Bow humbly under God's
mighty hand, so that in due time he may lift
you high. Cast all your cares on him because
he cares for you.

Responsory

Keep us, O Lord, as the apple of your eye.
—Keep us, O Lord, as the apple of your eye.

Gather us under the shadow of your wings,
    and keep us,
—as the apple of your eye.

Glory to the Father, and to the Son,
    and to the Holy Spirit.
—Keep us, O Lord, as the apple of your eye.

Gospel
Canticle

Ant. **Lord, with the strength of your arm scatter the proud and lift up the lowly.**

Canticle of
Mary
Luke 1:46–55

My + soul proclaims the greatness of the Lord,
my spirit rejoices in God my Savior
for he has looked with favor on his
    lowly servant.

From this day all generations will
    call me blessed:
the Almighty has done great things for me,
and holy is his Name.

He has mercy on those who fear him
in every generation.

He has shown the strength of his arm,
he has scattered the proud in their conceit.

He has cast down the mighty from
    their thrones,
and has lifted up the lowly.

He has filled the hungry with good things,
and the rich he has sent away empty.

He has come to the help of his servant Israel
for he has remembered his promise of mercy,
the promise he made to our fathers,
to Abraham and his children for ever.

Glory to the Father, and to the Son,
    and to the Holy Spirit:
—as it was in the beginning, is now,
and will be for ever. Amen.

Ant.   **Lord, with the strength of your arm scatter the proud and lift up the lowly.**

Intercessions   Beloved brothers and sisters, let us rejoice in our God, for he takes great delight in bestowing benefits on his people. Let us fervently pray:
Increase your grace and your peace, Lord.

Eternal God, for whom a thousand years are like the passing day,
—help us to remember that life is like a flower which blossoms in the morning, but withers in the evening.

Give your people manna to satisfy their hunger,
—and living water to quench their thirst for all eternity.

Let your faithful ones seek and taste the things that are above,
—and let them direct their work and their leisure to your glory.

Grant us good weather, Lord,
—that we may reap the copious fruits of the earth.

Show the faithful departed the vision of your face,
—let them rejoice in the contemplation of your presence.

The Lord's
Prayer

Our Father, who art in heaven,
hallowed be thy name;
thy kingdom come,
thy will be done
on earth as it is in heaven.
Give us this day our daily bread,
and forgive us our trespasses,
as we forgive those who trespass against us;
and lead us not into temptation,
but deliver us from evil.

Pater noster, qui es in cælis:
sanctificetur nomen tuum;
adveniat regnum tuum;
fiat voluntas tua,
sicut in cælo, et in terra.
Panem nostrum cotidianum da nobis hodie;
et dimitte nobis debita nostra,
sicut et nos dimittimus debitoribus nostris;
et ne nos inducas in tentationem;
sed libera nos a malo.

Concluding
Prayer

Lord God,
holy is your name,
and renowned your compassion,
cherished by every generation.
Hear our evening prayer
and let us sing your praise,
and proclaim your greatness for ever.
We ask this through our Lord Jesus Christ,
    your Son,
who lives and reigns with you and
    the Holy Spirit,
God, for ever and ever.
—Amen.

Dismissal *If praying individually, or in a group without a priest or deacon:*

May the Lord + bless us,
protect us from all evil
and bring us to everlasting life.
—Amen.

If praying with a priest or deacon, he dismisses the people:

The Lord be with you.
—And with your spirit.

May almighty God bless you,
the Father, and the Son, + and the Holy Spirit.
—Amen.

Go in peace.
—Thanks be to God.

NIGHT PRAYER

God, + come to my assistance.
—Lord, make haste to help me.

Glory to the Father, and to the Son,
    and to the Holy Spirit:
—as it was in the beginning, is now,
and will be for ever. Amen. Alleluia.

Examen *An optional brief examination of conscience may be made. Call to mind your sins and failings this day.*

Hymn *O Gladsome Light, p. 696*

Psalmody Ant. 1 **Lord God, be my refuge and my strength.**

Psalm 31:1–6

In you, O Lord, I take refuge.
Let me never be put to shame.
In your justice, set me free,
hear me and speedily rescue me.

Be a rock of refuge for me,
a mighty stronghold to save me,
for you are my rock, my stronghold.
For your name's sake, lead me and guide me.

Release me from the snares they have hidden
for you are my refuge, Lord.
Into your hands I commend my spirit.
It is you who will redeem me, Lord.

Glory to the Father, and to the Son,
    and to the Holy Spirit:
—as it was in the beginning, is now,
and will be for ever. Amen.

Ant.   **Lord God, be my refuge and my strength.**

Ant. 2   **Out of the depths I cry to you, Lord.**

Psalm 130

Out of the depths I cry to you, O Lord,
Lord, hear my voice!
O let your ears be attentive
to the voice of my pleading.

If you, O Lord, should mark our guilt,
Lord, who would survive?
But with you is found forgiveness:
for this we revere you.

My soul is waiting for the Lord,
I count on his word.
My soul is longing for the Lord
more than watchman for daybreak.
Let the watchman count on daybreak
and Israel on the Lord.

Because with the Lord there is mercy
and fullness of redemption,
Israel indeed he will redeem
from all its iniquity.

Glory to the Father, and to the Son,
    and to the Holy Spirit:
— as it was in the beginning, is now,
and will be for ever. Amen.

Ant.   **Out of the depths I cry to you, Lord.**

Reading
Ephesians
4:26–27

If you are angry, let it be without sin. The sun must not go down on your wrath; do not give the devil a chance to work on you.

Responsory

Into your hands, Lord, I commend my spirit.
— Into your hands, Lord, I commend my spirit.

You have redeemed us, Lord God of truth.
— I commend my spirit.

Glory to the Father, and to the Son,
    and to the Holy Spirit.
— Into your hands, Lord, I commend my spirit.

Gospel
Canticle

Ant. **Protect us, Lord, as we stay awake;
watch over us as we sleep, that awake, we
may keep watch with Christ, and asleep,
rest in his peace.**

Canticle of
Simeon
Luke 2:29–32

Lord, + now you let your servant go in peace;
your word has been fulfilled:
my own eyes have seen the salvation
which you have prepared in the sight of
    every people:
a light to reveal you to the nations
and the glory of your people Israel.

Glory to the Father, and to the Son,
    and to the Holy Spirit:
as it was in the beginning, is now,
and will be for ever. Amen.

Ant.

**Protect us, Lord, as we stay awake; watch
over us as we sleep, that awake, we may
keep watch with Christ, and asleep, rest in
his peace.**

Concluding
Prayer

Let us pray.
Lord Jesus Christ,
you have given your followers
an example of gentleness and humility,
a task that is easy, a burden that is light.
Accept the prayers and work of this day,
and give us the rest that will strengthen us
to render more faithful service to you
who live and reign for ever and ever.
Amen.

Blessing

May the all-powerful Lord
grant us a restful night
and a peaceful death.
—Amen.

Marian
Antiphon

Sing the "Salve Regina," found on p. 700, or pray a Hail Mary.

Thursday, August 8, 2024
St. Dominic

MORNING PRAYER

God, + come to my assistance.
—Lord, make haste to help me.

Glory to the Father, and to the Son,
    and to the Holy Spirit:
—as it was in the beginning, is now,
and will be for ever. Amen. Alleluia.

Hymn

Jesus, Eternal Truth Sublime, p. 693

Psalmody

Ant. 1 **Stir up your mighty power, Lord;
come to our aid.**

Psalm 80

O shepherd of Israel, hear us,
you who lead Joseph's flock,
shine forth from your cherubim throne
upon Ephraim, Benjamin, Manasseh.
O Lord, rouse up your might,
O Lord, come to our help.

God of hosts, bring us back;
let your face shine on us and we
        shall be saved.

Lord God of hosts, how long
will you frown on your people's plea?
You have fed them with tears for their bread,
an abundance of tears for their drink.
You have made us the taunt of our neighbors,
our enemies laugh us to scorn.

God of hosts, bring us back;
let your face shine on us and we
        shall be saved.

You brought a vine out of Egypt;
to plant it you drove out the nations.
Before it you cleared the ground;
it took root and spread through the land.

The mountains were covered with its shadow,
the cedars of God with its boughs.
It stretched out its branches to the sea,
to the Great River it stretched out its shoots.

Then why have you broken down its walls?
It is plucked by all who pass by.
It is ravaged by the boar of the forest,
devoured by the beasts of the field.

God of hosts, turn again, we implore,
look down from heaven and see.

Visit this vine and protect it,
the vine your right hand has planted.
Men have burnt it with fire and destroyed it.
May they perish at the frown of your face.

May your hand be on the man you
      have chosen,
the man you have given your strength.
And we shall never forsake you again:
give us life that we may call upon your name.

God of hosts, bring us back;
let your face shine on us and we
      shall be saved.

Glory to the Father, and to the Son,
      and to the Holy Spirit:
—as it was in the beginning, is now,
and will be for ever. Amen.

Ant.   **Stir up your mighty power, Lord; come
to our aid.**

Ant. 2   **The Lord has worked marvels for us; make
it known to the ends of the world.**

Canticle: I give you thanks, O Lord;
Isaiah 12:1–6   though you have been angry with me,
your anger has abated, and you have
      consoled me.

God indeed is my savior;
I am confident and unafraid.
My strength and my courage is the Lord,
and he has been my savior.

175

With joy you will draw water
at the fountain of salvation, and say
    on that day:
Give thanks to the Lord, acclaim his name;
among the nations make known his deeds,
proclaim how exalted is his name.

Sing praise to the Lord for his glorious
    achievement;
let this be known throughout all the earth.

Shout with exultation, O city of Zion,
for great in your midst
is the Holy One of Israel!

Glory to the Father, and to the Son,
    and to the Holy Spirit:
—as it was in the beginning, is now,
and will be for ever. Amen.

Ant.   **The Lord has worked marvels for us; make
it known to the ends of the world.**

Ant. 3   **Ring out your joy to God our strength.**

Psalm 81   Ring out your joy to God our strength,
shout in triumph to the God of Jacob.

Raise a song and sound the timbrel,
the sweet-sounding harp and the lute,
blow the trumpet at the new moon,
when the moon is full, on our feast.

For this is Israel's law,
a command of the God of Jacob.
He imposed it as a rule on Joseph,
when he went out against the land of Egypt.

A voice I did not know said to me:
"I freed your shoulder from the burden;
your hands were freed from the load.
You called in distress and I saved you.

I answered, concealed in the storm cloud,
at the waters of Meribah I tested you.
Listen, my people, to my warning,
O Israel, if only you would heed!

Let there be no foreign god among you,
no worship of an alien god.
I am the Lord your God,
who brought you from the land of Egypt.
Open wide your mouth and I will fill it.

But my people did not heed my voice
and Israel would not obey,
so I left them in their stubbornness of heart
to follow their own designs.

O that my people would heed me,
that Israel would walk in my ways!
At once I would subdue their foes,
turn my hand against their enemies.

The Lord's enemies would cringe at their feet
and their subjection would last for ever.
But Israel I would feed with finest wheat
and fill them with honey from the rock."

Glory to the Father, and to the Son,
   and to the Holy Spirit:
—as it was in the beginning, is now,
   and will be for ever. Amen.

Ant.   **Ring out your joy to God our strength.**

Reading
Hebrews
13:7–9a

Remember your leaders who spoke the word
of God to you; consider how their lives ended,
and imitate their faith. Jesus Christ is the
same yesterday, today, and forever. Do not be
carried away by all kinds of strange teaching.

Responsory   On your walls, Jerusalem, I have set my
   watchmen to guard you.
—On your walls, Jerusalem, I have set my
   watchmen to guard you.

Day or night, they will not cease to proclaim
   the name of the Lord.
—I have set my watchmen to guard you.

Glory to the Father, and to the Son,
   and to the Holy Spirit.
—On your walls, Jerusalem, I have set my
   watchmen to guard you.

Gospel
Canticle

Ant. **What you say of me does not come
from yourselves; it is the Spirit of my
Father speaking in you.**

Canticle of
Zechariah
Luke 1:68–79

Blessed + be the Lord, the God of Israel;
he has come to his people and set them free.

He has raised up for us a mighty savior,
born of the house of his servant David.

Through his holy prophets he
    promised of old
that he would save us from our enemies,
from the hands of all who hate us.

He promised to show mercy to our fathers
and to remember his holy covenant.

This was the oath he swore to our
    father Abraham:
to set us free from the hands of our enemies,
free to worship him without fear,
holy and righteous in his sight
    all the days of our life.

You, my child, shall be called the prophet of
    the Most High;
for you will go before the Lord to
    prepare his way,
to give his people knowledge of salvation
by the forgiveness of their sins.

In the tender compassion of our God
the dawn from on high shall break upon us,
to shine on those who dwell in darkness and
    the shadow of death,
and to guide our feet into the way of peace.

Glory to the Father, and to the Son,
     and to the Holy Spirit:
—as it was in the beginning, is now,
     and will be for ever. Amen.

Ant. **What you say of me does not come from
yourselves; it is the Spirit of my Father
speaking in you.**

Intercessions Christ is the Good Shepherd who laid down
          his life for his sheep. Let us praise and
          thank him as we pray:
     Nourish your people, Lord.

Christ, you decided to show your merciful
     love through your holy shepherds,
—let your mercy always reach us through them.

Through your vicars you continue to
     perform the ministry of shepherd of souls,
—direct us always through our leaders.

Through your holy ones, the leaders of your
     people, you served as physician of our
     bodies and our spirits,
—continue to fulfill your ministry of life and
     holiness in us.

You taught your flock through the prudence
     and love of your saints,
—grant us continual growth in holiness under
     the direction of our pastors.

The Lord's
Prayer

Our Father, who art in heaven,
hallowed be thy name;
thy kingdom come,
thy will be done
on earth as it is in heaven.
Give us this day our daily bread,
and forgive us our trespasses,
as we forgive those who trespass against us;
and lead us not into temptation,
but deliver us from evil.

Pater noster, qui es in cælis:
sanctificetur nomen tuum;
adveniat regnum tuum;
fiat voluntas tua,
sicut in cælo, et in terra.
Panem nostrum cotidianum da nobis hodie;
et dimitte nobis debita nostra,
sicut et nos dimittimus debitoribus nostris;
et ne nos inducas in tentationem;
sed libera nos a malo.

Concluding
Prayer

Lord,
let the holiness and teaching of Saint Dominic
come to the aid of your Church.
May he help us now with his prayers
as he once inspired people by his preaching.
We ask this through our Lord Jesus Christ,
     your Son,
who lives and reigns with you and
     the Holy Spirit,
God, for ever and ever.
—Amen.

Dismissal   *If praying individually, or in a group without a priest or deacon:*

May the Lord + bless us,
protect us from all evil
and bring us to everlasting life.
—Amen.

If praying with a priest or deacon, he dismisses the people:

The Lord be with you.
—And with your spirit.

May almighty God bless you,
  the Father, and the Son, + and the Holy Spirit.
—Amen.

Go in peace.
—Thanks be to God.

EVENING PRAYER

God, + come to my assistance.
—Lord, make haste to help me.

Glory to the Father, and to the Son,
    and to the Holy Spirit:
—as it was in the beginning, is now,
  and will be for ever. Amen. Alleluia.

Hymn   *The Saints of God!, p. 702*

Psalmody   Ant. 1 **I have made you the light of all
nations to carry my salvation to the ends of
the earth.**

Psalm 72

O God, give your judgment to the king,
to a king's son your justice,
that he may judge your people in justice
and your poor in right judgment.

May the mountains bring forth peace for
    the people
and the hills, justice.
May he defend the poor of the people
and save the children of the needy
and crush the oppressor.

He shall endure like the sun and the moon
from age to age.
He shall descend like rain on the meadow,
like raindrops on the earth.

In his days justice shall flourish
and peace till the moon fails.
He shall rule from sea to sea,
from the Great River to earth's bounds.

Before him his enemies shall fall,
his foes lick the dust.
The kings of Tarshish and the sea coasts
shall pay him tribute.

The kings of Sheba and Seba
shall bring him gifts.
Before him all kings shall fall prostrate,
all nations shall serve him.

Glory to the Father, and to the Son,
    and to the Holy Spirit:
—as it was in the beginning, is now,
    and will be for ever. Amen.

Ant.   **I have made you the light of all nations to
carry my salvation to the ends of the earth.**

Ant. 2   **The Lord will save the children of the poor
and rescue them from slavery.**

Psalm 72   For he shall save the poor when they cry
(continued)   and the needy who are helpless.
He will have pity on the weak
and save the lives of the poor.

From oppression he will rescue their lives,
to him their blood is dear.
Long may he live,
may the gold of Sheba be given him.
They shall pray for him without ceasing
and bless him all the day.

May corn be abundant in the land
to the peaks of the mountains.
May its fruit rustle like Lebanon;
may men flourish in the cities
like grass on the earth.

May his name be blessed for ever
and endure like the sun.
Every tribe shall be blessed in him,
all nations bless his name.

Blessed be the Lord, God of Israel,
who alone works wonders,
ever blessed his glorious name.
Let his glory fill the earth.

Amen! Amen!

Glory to the Father, and to the Son,
    and to the Holy Spirit:
—as it was in the beginning, is now,
and will be for ever. Amen.

Ant.   **The Lord will save the children of the poor
and rescue them from slavery.**

Ant. 3   **Now the victorious reign of our God
has begun.**

Canticle:
Revelation
11:17–18;
12:10b–12a

We praise you, the Lord God Almighty,
who is and who was.
You have assumed your great power,
you have begun your reign.

The nations have raged in anger,
but then came your day of wrath
and the moment to judge the dead:
the time to reward your servants the prophets
and the holy ones who revere you,
the great and the small alike.

Now have salvation and power come,
the reign of our God and the authority
of his Anointed One.
For the accuser of our brothers is cast out,
who night and day accused them before God.

They defeated him by the blood of the Lamb
and by the word of their testimony;
love for life did not deter them from death.
So rejoice, you heavens,
and you that dwell therein!

Glory to the Father, and to the Son,
    and to the Holy Spirit:
—as it was in the beginning, is now,
and will be for ever. Amen.

Ant.   **Now the victorious reign of our God
has begun.**

Reading
1 Peter 5:1–4

To the elders among you I, a fellow elder, a
witness of Christ's sufferings and sharer in
the glory that is to be revealed, make this
appeal. God's flock is in your midst; give it
a shepherd's care. Watch over it willingly
as God would have you do, not under
constraint; and not for shameful profit
either, but generously. Be examples to the
flock, not lording it over those assigned to
you, so that when the chief Shepherd appears
you will win for yourselves the unfading
crown of glory.

Responsory

This is a man who loved his brethren and
    ever prayed for them.
—This is a man who loved his brethren and
    ever prayed for them.

He spent himself in their service,
—and ever prayed for them.

Glory to the Father, and to the Son,
  and to the Holy Spirit.
—This is a man who loved his brethren and
  ever prayed for them.

*Gospel
Canticle*

Ant. **This is a faithful and wise steward: the
Lord entrusted the care of his household
to him, so that he might give them their
portion of food at the proper season.**

*Canticle of
Mary
Luke 1:46–55*

My + soul proclaims the greatness of the Lord,
my spirit rejoices in God my Savior
for he has looked with favor on his
  lowly servant.

From this day all generations will
  call me blessed:
the Almighty has done great things for me,
and holy is his Name.

He has mercy on those who fear him
in every generation.

He has shown the strength of his arm,
he has scattered the proud in their conceit.

He has cast down the mighty from
  their thrones,
and has lifted up the lowly.

He has filled the hungry with good things,
and the rich he has sent away empty.

He has come to the help of his servant Israel
for he has remembered his promise of mercy,
the promise he made to our fathers,
to Abraham and his children for ever.

Glory to the Father, and to the Son,
    and to the Holy Spirit:
—as it was in the beginning, is now,
and will be for ever. Amen.

Ant. **This is a faithful and wise steward: the Lord
entrusted the care of his household to him,
so that he might give them their portion of
food at the proper season.**

Intercessions Jesus Christ is worthy of all praise, for he was
    appointed high priest among men and
    their representative before God. We honor
    him and in our weakness we pray:
Bring salvation to your people, Lord.

You marvelously illuminated your Church
    through distinguished leaders and holy
    men and women,
—let Christians rejoice always in such splendor.

You forgave the sins of your people when
    their holy leaders like Moses sought your
    compassion,
—through their intercession continue to purify
    and sanctify your holy people.

In the midst of their brothers and sisters you
    anointed your holy ones and filled them
    with the Holy Spirit,
—fill all the leaders of your people with the
    same Spirit.

You yourself are the only visible possession of
    our holy pastors,
—let none of them, won at the price of your
    blood, remain far from you.

The shepherds of your Church keep your
    flock from being snatched out of your
    hand. Through them you give your flock
    eternal life,
—save those who have died, those for whom
    you gave up your life.

The Lord's Prayer

Our Father, who art in heaven,
hallowed be thy name;
thy kingdom come,
thy will be done
on earth as it is in heaven.
Give us this day our daily bread,
and forgive us our trespasses,
as we forgive those who trespass against us;
and lead us not into temptation,
but deliver us from evil.

Pater noster, qui es in cælis:
sanctificetur nomen tuum;
adveniat regnum tuum;
fiat voluntas tua,
sicut in cælo, et in terra.
Panem nostrum cotidianum da nobis hodie;
et dimitte nobis debita nostra,
sicut et nos dimittimus debitoribus nostris;
et ne nos inducas in tentationem;
sed libera nos a malo.

Concluding Prayer

Lord,
let the holiness and teaching of Saint Dominic
come to the aid of your Church.
May he help us now with his prayers
as he once inspired people by his preaching.
We ask this through our Lord Jesus Christ,
    your Son,
who lives and reigns with you and
    the Holy Spirit,
God, for ever and ever.
—Amen.

Dismissal

If praying individually, or in a group without a priest or deacon:

May the Lord + bless us,
protect us from all evil
and bring us to everlasting life.
—Amen.

If praying with a priest or deacon, he dismisses the people:

The Lord be with you.
—And with your spirit.

May almighty God bless you,
the Father, and the Son, + and the Holy Spirit.
—Amen.

Go in peace.
—Thanks be to God.

NIGHT PRAYER

God, + come to my assistance.
—Lord, make haste to help me.

Glory to the Father, and to the Son,
and to the Holy Spirit:
—as it was in the beginning, is now,
and will be for ever. Amen. Alleluia.

Examen *An optional brief examination of conscience may be made. Call to mind your sins and failings this day.*

Hymn *O Gladsome Light, p. 696*

Psalmody Ant. **In you, my God, my body will rest in hope.**

Psalm 16 Preserve me, God, I take refuge in you.
I say to the Lord: "You are my God.
My happiness lies in you alone."

He has put into my heart a marvelous love
for the faithful ones who dwell in his land.
Those who choose other gods increase
their sorrows.
Never will I offer their offerings of blood.
Never will I take their name upon my lips.

O Lord, it is you who are my portion and cup;
it is you yourself who are my prize.
The lot marked out for me is my delight:
welcome indeed the heritage that falls to me!

I will bless the Lord who gives me counsel,
who even at night directs my heart.
I keep the Lord ever in my sight:
since he is at my right hand, I shall
    stand firm.

And so my heart rejoices, my soul is glad;
even my body shall rest in safety.
For you will not leave my soul
    among the dead,
nor let your beloved know decay.

You will show me the path of life,
the fullness of joy in your presence,
at your right hand happiness for ever.

Glory to the Father, and to the Son,
    and to the Holy Spirit:
—as it was in the beginning, is now,
and will be for ever. Amen.

Ant.   **In you, my God, my body will rest in hope.**

Reading
1 Thessalonians
5:23

May the God of peace make you perfect in
holiness. May he preserve you whole and
entire, spirit, soul, and body, irreproachable
at the coming of our Lord Jesus Christ.

Responsory   Into your hands, Lord, I commend my spirit.
—Into your hands, Lord, I commend my spirit.

You have redeemed us, Lord God of truth.
—I commend my spirit.

Glory to the Father, and to the Son,
and to the Holy Spirit.
—Into your hands, Lord, I commend my spirit.

Gospel   Ant. **Protect us, Lord, as we stay awake;**
Canticle   **watch over us as we sleep, that awake, we**
may keep watch with Christ, and asleep,
rest in his peace.

Canticle of   Lord, + now you let your servant go in peace;
Simeon   your word has been fulfilled:
Luke 2:29–32   my own eyes have seen the salvation
which you have prepared in the sight of
every people:
a light to reveal you to the nations
and the glory of your people Israel.

Glory to the Father, and to the Son,
and to the Holy Spirit:
—as it was in the beginning, is now,
and will be for ever. Amen.

Ant.   **Protect us, Lord, as we stay awake; watch**
over us as we sleep, that awake, we may
keep watch with Christ, and asleep, rest in
his peace.

Concluding
Prayer

Let us pray.
Lord God,
send peaceful sleep
to refresh our tired bodies.
May your help always renew us
and keep us strong in your service.
We ask this through Christ our Lord.
—Amen.

Blessing

May the all-powerful Lord
grant us a restful night
and a peaceful death.
—Amen.

Marian
Antiphon

Sing the "Salve Regina," found on p. 700, or pray a Hail Mary.

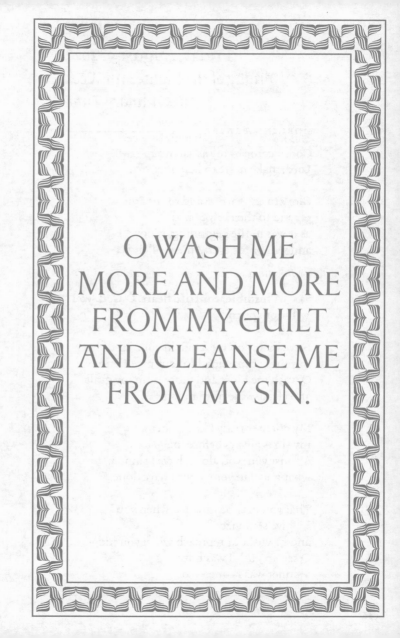

O WASH ME
MORE AND MORE
FROM MY GUILT
AND CLEANSE ME
FROM MY SIN.

Friday, August 9, 2024
Friday of the Eighteenth Week in Ordinary Time

MORNING PRAYER————————————

God, + come to my assistance.
—Lord, make haste to help me.

Glory to the Father, and to the Son,
    and to the Holy Spirit:
—as it was in the beginning, is now,
and will be for ever. Amen. Alleluia.

Hymn   *Holy, Holy, Holy, p. 690*

Psalmody   Ant. 1 **A humble, contrite heart, O God, you will not spurn.**

Psalm 51   Have mercy on me, God, in your kindness.
In your compassion blot out my offense.
O wash me more and more from my guilt
and cleanse me from my sin.

My offenses truly I know them;
my sin is always before me.
Against you, you alone, have I sinned;
what is evil in your sight I have done.

That you may be justified when you
    give sentence
and be without reproach when you judge.
O see, in guilt I was born,
a sinner was I conceived.

Indeed you love truth in the heart;
then in the secret of my heart teach
　　me wisdom.
O purify me, then I shall be clean;
O wash me, I shall be whiter than snow.

Make me hear rejoicing and gladness,
that the bones you have crushed may revive.
From my sins turn away your face
and blot out all my guilt.

A pure heart create for me, O God,
put a steadfast spirit within me.
Do not cast me away from your presence,
nor deprive me of your holy spirit.

Give me again the joy of your help;
with a spirit of fervor sustain me,
that I may teach transgressors your ways
and sinners may return to you.

O rescue me, God, my helper,
and my tongue shall ring out your goodness.
O Lord, open my lips
and my mouth shall declare your praise.

For in sacrifice you take no delight,
burnt offering from me you would refuse,
my sacrifice, a contrite spirit.
A humbled, contrite heart you will not spurn.

In your goodness, show favor to Zion:
rebuild the walls of Jerusalem.
Then you will be pleased with lawful sacrifice,
holocausts offered on your altar.

Glory to the Father, and to the Son,
    and to the Holy Spirit:
—as it was in the beginning, is now,
    and will be for ever. Amen.

Ant.   **A humble, contrite heart, O God, you will
not spurn.**

Ant. 2   **Even in your anger, Lord, you will
remember compassion.**

Canticle:
Habakkuk
3:2–4, 13a,
15–19

O Lord, I have heard your renown,
and feared, O Lord, your work.
In the course of the years revive it,
in the course of the years make it known;
in your wrath remember compassion!

God comes from Teman,
the Holy One from Mount Paran.
Covered are the heavens with his glory,
and with his praise the earth is filled.

His splendor spreads like the light;
rays shine forth from beside him,
where his power is concealed.
You come forth to save your people,
to save your anointed one.

You tread the sea with your steeds
amid the churning of the deep waters.
I hear, and my body trembles;
at the sound, my lips quiver.

Decay invades my bones,
my legs tremble beneath me.
I await the day of distress
that will come upon the people who
    attack us.

For though the fig tree blossom not
nor fruit be on the vines,
though the yield of the olive fail
and the terraces produce no nourishment,

though the flocks disappear from the fold
and there be no herd in the stalls,
yet will I rejoice in the Lord
and exult in my saving God.

God, my Lord, is my strength;
he makes my feet swift as those of hinds
and enables me to go upon the heights.

Glory to the Father, and to the Son,
    and to the Holy Spirit:
—as it was in the beginning, is now,
and will be for ever. Amen.

Ant.   **Even in your anger, Lord, you will
remember compassion.**

Ant. 3   **O praise the Lord, Jerusalem!**

Psalm 147:12-20   O praise the Lord, Jerusalem!
Zion, praise your God!

He has strengthened the bars of your gates,
he has blessed the children within you.
He established peace on your borders,
he feeds you with finest wheat.

He sends out his word to the earth
and swiftly runs his command.
He showers down snow white as wool,
he scatters hoar-frost like ashes.

He hurls down hailstones like crumbs.
The waters are frozen at his touch;
he sends forth his word and it melts them:
at the breath of his mouth the waters flow.

He makes his word known to Jacob,
to Israel his laws and decrees.
He has not dealt thus with other nations;
he has not taught them his decrees.

Glory to the Father, and to the Son,
and to the Holy Spirit:
as it was in the beginning, is now,
and will be for ever. Amen.

Ant. 3   **O praise the Lord, Jerusalem!**

Reading
Ephesians
2:13–16

Now in Christ Jesus you who once were far off have been brought near through the blood of Christ. It is he who is our peace, and who made the two of us one by breaking down the barrier of hostility that kept us apart. In his own flesh he abolished the law with its commands and precepts, to create in himself one new man from us who had been two and to make peace, reconciling both of us to God in one body through his cross, which put that enmity to death.

Responsory

The Lord, the Most High, has done good
    things for me.
In need I shall cry out to him.
—The Lord, the Most High, has done good
    things for me.
In need I shall cry out to him.

May he send his strength to rescue me.
—In need I shall cry out to him.

Glory to the Father, and to the Son,
    and to the Holy Spirit.
—The Lord, the Most High, has done good
    things for me.
In need I shall cry out to him.

Gospel
Canticle

Ant. **Through the tender compassion of our God the dawn from on high shall break upon us.**

*Canticle of
Zechariah*
Luke 1:68–79

Blessed + be the Lord, the God of Israel;
he has come to his people and set them free.

He has raised up for us a mighty savior,
born of the house of his servant David.

Through his holy prophets he
    promised of old
that he would save us from our enemies,
from the hands of all who hate us.

He promised to show mercy to our fathers
and to remember his holy covenant.

This was the oath he swore to our
    father Abraham:
to set us free from the hands of our enemies,
free to worship him without fear,
holy and righteous in his sight
    all the days of our life.

You, my child, shall be called the prophet of
    the Most High;
for you will go before the Lord to
    prepare his way,
to give his people knowledge of salvation
by the forgiveness of their sins.

In the tender compassion of our God
the dawn from on high shall break upon us,
to shine on those who dwell in darkness and
    the shadow of death,
and to guide our feet into the way of peace.

Glory to the Father, and to the Son,
   and to the Holy Spirit:
—as it was in the beginning, is now,
   and will be for ever. Amen.

Ant. **Through the tender compassion of
our God the dawn from on high shall
break upon us.**

Intercessions Let us adore Christ who offered himself to
   the Father through the Holy Spirit to
   cleanse us from the works of death. Let
   us adore him and call upon him with
   sincere hearts:
In your will is our peace, Lord.

From your generosity we have received the
   beginning of this day,
—grant us also the beginning of new life.

You created all things, and now you provide
   for their growth,
—may we always perceive your handiwork
   in creation.

With your own blood, you ratified the new
   and eternal covenant,
—may we remain faithful to that covenant by
   following your precepts.

On the cross, blood and water flowed from
   your side,
—may this saving stream wash away our sins
   and gladden the City of God.

The Lord's
Prayer

Our Father, who art in heaven,
hallowed be thy name;
thy kingdom come,
thy will be done
on earth as it is in heaven.
Give us this day our daily bread,
and forgive us our trespasses,
as we forgive those who trespass against us;
and lead us not into temptation,
but deliver us from evil.

Pater noster, qui es in cælis:
sanctificetur nomen tuum;
adveniat regnum tuum;
fiat voluntas tua,
sicut in cælo, et in terra.
Panem nostrum cotidianum da nobis hodie;
et dimitte nobis debita nostra,
sicut et nos dimittimus debitoribus nostris;
et ne nos inducas in tentationem;
sed libera nos a malo.

Concluding
Prayer

All-powerful Father,
as now we bring you our songs of praise,
so may we sing your goodness
in the company of your saints for ever.
We ask this through our Lord Jesus Christ,
    your Son,
who lives and reigns with you and
    the Holy Spirit,
God, for ever and ever.
—Amen.

Dismissal   *If praying individually, or in a group without a priest or deacon:*

May the Lord + bless us,
protect us from all evil
and bring us to everlasting life.
—Amen.

If praying with a priest or deacon, he dismisses the people:

The Lord be with you.
—And with your spirit.

May almighty God bless you,
the Father, and the Son, + and the Holy Spirit.
—Amen.

Go in peace.
—Thanks be to God.

EVENING PRAYER

God, + come to my assistance.
—Lord, make haste to help me.

Glory to the Father, and to the Son,
    and to the Holy Spirit:
—as it was in the beginning, is now,
and will be for ever. Amen. Alleluia.

Hymn   *O God, Creator of All Things, p. 697*

Psalmody   Ant. 1 **Lord, keep my soul from death, never
let me stumble.**

Psalm 116:1–9

I love the Lord for he has heard
the cry of my appeal;
for he turned his ear to me
in the day when I called him.

They surrounded me, the snares of death,
with the anguish of the tomb;
they caught me, sorrow and distress.
I called on the Lord's name.

O Lord, my God, deliver me!

How gracious is the Lord, and just;
our God has compassion.
The Lord protects the simple hearts;
I was helpless so he saved me.

Turn back, my soul, to your rest
for the Lord has been good;
he has kept my soul from death,
my eyes from tears
and my feet from stumbling.

I will walk in the presence of the Lord
in the land of the living.

Glory to the Father, and to the Son,
    and to the Holy Spirit:
—as it was in the beginning, is now,
and will be for ever. Amen.

Ant.

**Lord, keep my soul from death, never let
me stumble.**

Ant. 2   **My help comes from the Lord, who made
heaven and earth.**

Psalm 121   I lift up my eyes to the mountains:
from where shall come my help?
My help shall come from the Lord
who made heaven and earth.

May he never allow you to stumble!
Let him sleep not, your guard.
No, he sleeps not nor slumbers,
Israel's guard.

The Lord is your guard and your shade;
at your right side he stands.
By day the sun shall not smite you
nor the moon in the night.

The Lord will guard you from evil,
he will guard your soul.
The Lord will guard your going and coming
both now and for ever.

Glory to the Father, and to the Son,
    and to the Holy Spirit:
—as it was in the beginning, is now,
and will be for ever. Amen.

Ant.   **My help comes from the Lord, who made
heaven and earth.**

Ant. 3   **King of all the ages, your ways are
perfect and true.**

Canticle:
Revelation
15:3–4

Mighty and wonderful are your works,
Lord God Almighty!
Righteous and true are your ways,
O King of the nations!

Who would dare refuse you honor,
or the glory due your name, O Lord?

Since you alone are holy,
all nations shall come
and worship in your presence.
Your mighty deeds are clearly seen.

Glory to the Father, and to the Son,
    and to the Holy Spirit:
—as it was in the beginning, is now,
    and will be for ever. Amen.

Ant.   **King of all the ages, your ways are**
          perfect and true.

Reading
1 Corinthians
2:7–10a

What we utter is God's wisdom: a mysterious,
a hidden wisdom. God planned it before all
ages for our glory. None of the rulers of this
age knew the mystery; if they had known it,
they would never have crucified the Lord of
glory. Of this wisdom it is written:
    "Eye has not seen, ear has not heard,
        nor has it so much as dawned on man
            what God has prepared for those who
                love him."
Yet God has revealed this wisdom to us
through the Spirit.

Responsory   Christ died for our sins to make of us an
   offering to God.
—Christ died for our sins to make of us an
   offering to God.

He died to this world of sin, and rose in the
   power of the Spirit.
—To make of us an offering to God.

Glory to the Father, and to the Son,
   and to the Holy Spirit.
—Christ died for our sins to make of us an
   offering to God.

Gospel Canticle   Ant. **Remember your mercy, Lord, the promise of mercy you made to our fathers.**

Canticle of Mary
Luke 1:46–55

My + soul proclaims the greatness of the Lord,
my spirit rejoices in God my Savior
for he has looked with favor on his
   lowly servant.

From this day all generations will
   call me blessed:
the Almighty has done great things for me,
and holy is his Name.

He has mercy on those who fear him
in every generation.

He has shown the strength of his arm,
he has scattered the proud in their conceit.

209

He has cast down the mighty from
    their thrones,
and has lifted up the lowly.

He has filled the hungry with good things,
and the rich he has sent away empty.

He has come to the help of his servant Israel
for he has remembered his promise of mercy,
the promise he made to our fathers,
to Abraham and his children for ever.

Glory to the Father, and to the Son,
    and to the Holy Spirit:
—as it was in the beginning, is now,
    and will be for ever. Amen.

Ant. **Remember your mercy, Lord,
the promise of mercy you made to
our fathers.**

Intercessions Let us bless Christ, the compassionate and
    merciful Lord, who wipes away the tears
    of those who weep. Let us cry out to him
    in love and ask:
    Have mercy on your people, Lord.

Lord Jesus, you console the humble,
—be attentive to the tears of the poor.

Merciful God, hear the cries of the dying,
—comfort them with your presence.

Make exiles aware of your providential care,
—may they return to their home on earth and
        finally enter their home in heaven.

Be merciful to sinners who have fallen away
        from your love,
—reconcile them to yourself and to your Church.

Save our brothers who have died,
—let them share in the fullness of redemption.

The Lord's
Prayer

Our Father, who art in heaven,
hallowed be thy name;
thy kingdom come,
thy will be done
on earth as it is in heaven.
Give us this day our daily bread,
and forgive us our trespasses,
as we forgive those who trespass against us;
and lead us not into temptation,
but deliver us from evil.

Pater noster, qui es in cælis:
sanctificetur nomen tuum;
adveniat regnum tuum;
fiat voluntas tua,
sicut in cælo, et in terra.
Panem nostrum cotidianum da nobis hodie;
et dimitte nobis debita nostra,
sicut et nos dimittimus debitoribus nostris;
et ne nos inducas in tentationem;
sed libera nos a malo.

Concluding
Prayer

God our Father,
the contradiction of the cross
proclaims your infinite wisdom.
Help us to see that the glory of your Son
is revealed in the suffering he freely accepted.
Give us faith to claim as our only glory
the cross of our Lord Jesus Christ,
who lives and reigns with you and
    the Holy Spirit,
God, for ever and ever.
—Amen.

Dismissal   *If praying individually, or in a group without a priest or deacon:*

May the Lord + bless us,
protect us from all evil
and bring us to everlasting life.
—Amen.

If praying with a priest or deacon, he dismisses the people:

The Lord be with you.
—And with your spirit.

May almighty God bless you,
the Father, and the Son, + and the Holy Spirit.
—Amen.

Go in peace.
—Thanks be to God.

NIGHT PRAYER————————————————

God, + come to my assistance.
—Lord, make haste to help me.

Glory to the Father, and to the Son,
    and to the Holy Spirit:
—as it was in the beginning, is now,
    and will be for ever. Amen. Alleluia.

Examen   *An optional brief examination of conscience may be made. Call to mind your sins and failings this day.*

Hymn   *O Gladsome Light, p. 696*

Psalmody   Ant. **Day and night I cry to you, my God.**

Psalm 88   Lord my God, I call for help by day;
I cry at night before you.
Let my prayer come into your presence.
O turn your ear to my cry.

For my soul is filled with evils;
my life is on the brink of the grave.
I am reckoned as one in the tomb:
I have reached the end of my strength,

like one alone among the dead;
like the slain lying in their graves;
like those you remember no more,
cut off, as they are, from your hand.

You have laid me in the depths of the tomb,
in places that are dark, in the depths.
Your anger weighs down upon me:
I am drowned beneath your waves.

You have taken away my friends
and made me hateful in their sight.
Imprisoned, I cannot escape;
my eyes are sunken with grief.

I call to you, Lord, all the day long;
to you I stretch out my hands.
Will you work your wonders for the dead?
Will the shades stand and praise you?

Will your love be told in the grave
or your faithfulness among the dead?
Will your wonders be known in the dark
or your justice in the land of oblivion?

As for me, Lord, I call to you for help:
in the morning my prayer comes before you.
Lord, why do you reject me?
Why do you hide your face?

Wretched, close to death from my youth,
I have borne your trials; I am numb.
Your fury has swept down upon me;
your terrors have utterly destroyed me.

They surround me all the day like a flood,
they assail me all together.
Friend and neighbor you have taken away:
my one companion is darkness.

Glory to the Father, and to the Son,
     and to the Holy Spirit:
—as it was in the beginning, is now,
and will be for ever. Amen.

Ant. **Day and night I cry to you, my God.**

Reading
Jeremiah 14:9a

You are in our midst, O Lord,
    your name we bear:
    do not forsake us, O Lord, our God!

Responsory

Into your hands, Lord, I commend my spirit.
—Into your hands, Lord, I commend my spirit.

You have redeemed us, Lord God of truth.
—I commend my spirit.

Glory to the Father, and to the Son,
    and to the Holy Spirit.
—Into your hands, Lord, I commend my spirit.

Gospel
Canticle

Ant. **Protect us, Lord, as we stay awake;
watch over us as we sleep, that awake, we
may keep watch with Christ, and asleep,
rest in his peace.**

*Canticle of
Simeon
Luke 2:29–32*

Lord, + now you let your servant go in peace;
your word has been fulfilled:
my own eyes have seen the salvation
which you have prepared in the sight of
    every people:
a light to reveal you to the nations
and the glory of your people Israel.

Glory to the Father, and to the Son,
    and to the Holy Spirit:
—as it was in the beginning, is now,
    and will be for ever. Amen.

Ant.   **Protect us, Lord, as we stay awake; watch over us as we sleep, that awake, we may keep watch with Christ, and asleep, rest in his peace.**

Concluding Prayer

Let us pray.
All-powerful God,
keep us united with your Son
in his death and burial
so that we may rise to new life with him,
who lives and reigns for ever and ever.
—Amen.

Blessing

May the all-powerful Lord
grant us a restful night
and a peaceful death.
—Amen.

Marian Antiphon   *Sing the "Salve Regina," found on p. 700, or pray a Hail Mary.*

Saturday, August 10, 2024
St. Lawrence

MORNING PRAYER——————————

God, + come to my assistance.
—Lord, make haste to help me.

Glory to the Father, and to the Son,
    and to the Holy Spirit:
—as it was in the beginning, is now,
    and will be for ever. Amen. Alleluia.

Hymn   *Blessed Feasts of Blessed Martyrs, p. 682*

Psalmody   Ant. 1 **My soul clings to you, my God, because I endured death by fire for your sake.**

Psalm 63:2–9   O God, you are my God, for you I long;
for you my soul is thirsting.
My body pines for you
like a dry, weary land without water.
So I gaze on you in the sanctuary
to see your strength and your glory.

For your love is better than life,
my lips will speak your praise.
So I will bless you all my life,
in your name I will lift up my hands.
My soul shall be filled as with a banquet,
my mouth shall praise you with joy.

On my bed I remember you.
On you I muse through the night
for you have been my help;
in the shadow of your wings I rejoice.
My soul clings to you;
your right hand holds me fast.

Glory to the Father, and to the Son,
    and to the Holy Spirit:
—as it was in the beginning, is now,
    and will be for ever. Amen.

Ant. **My soul clings to you, my God, because I
endured death by fire for your sake.**

Ant. 2 **The Lord sent his angel to free me
from the fire, and I escaped the
flames unharmed.**

Canticle:
Daniel
3:57–88, 56

Bless the Lord, all you works of the Lord.
Praise and exalt him above all forever.
Angels of the Lord, bless the Lord.
You heavens, bless the Lord.
All you waters above the heavens,
    bless the Lord.
All you hosts of the Lord, bless the Lord.
Sun and moon, bless the Lord.
Stars of heaven, bless the Lord.

Every shower and dew, bless the Lord.
All you winds, bless the Lord.
Fire and heat, bless the Lord.
Cold and chill, bless the Lord.
Dew and rain, bless the Lord.
Frost and chill, bless the Lord.
Ice and snow, bless the Lord.
Nights and days, bless the Lord.
Light and darkness, bless the Lord.
Lightnings and clouds, bless the Lord.

Let the earth bless the Lord.
Praise and exalt him above all forever.
Mountains and hills, bless the Lord.
Everything growing from the earth,
     bless the Lord.
You springs, bless the Lord.
Seas and rivers, bless the Lord.
You dolphins and all water creatures,
     bless the Lord.
All you birds of the air, bless the Lord.
All you beasts, wild and tame, bless the Lord.
You sons of men, bless the Lord.

O Israel, bless the Lord.
Praise and exalt him above all forever.
Priests of the Lord, bless the Lord.
Servants of the Lord, bless the Lord.
Spirits and souls of the just, bless the Lord.
Holy men of humble heart, bless the Lord.
Hananiah, Azariah, Mishael, bless the Lord.
Praise and exalt him above all forever.

Let us bless the Father, and the Son,
    and the Holy Spirit.
Let us praise and exalt him above all forever.
Blessed are you, Lord, in the firmament
    of heaven.
Praiseworthy and glorious and exalted above
    all forever.

Ant.

The Lord sent his angel to free me from the fire, and I escaped the flames unharmed.

Ant. 3

Blessed Lawrence prayed: I thank you, Lord, for permitting me to enter the gates of your kingdom.

Psalm 149

Sing a new song to the Lord,
his praise in the assembly of the faithful.
Let Israel rejoice in its maker,
let Zion's sons exult in their king.
Let them praise his name with dancing
and make music with timbrel and harp.

For the Lord takes delight in his people.
He crowns the poor with salvation.
Let the faithful rejoice in their glory,
shout for joy and take their rest.
Let the praise of God be on their lips
and a two-edged sword in their hand,

to deal out vengeance to the nations
and punishment on all the peoples;
to bind their kings in chains
and their nobles in fetters of iron;
to carry out the sentence pre-ordained;
this honor is for all his faithful.

Glory to the Father, and to the Son,
    and to the Holy Spirit:
—as it was in the beginning, is now,
and will be for ever. Amen.

Ant.   **Blessed Lawrence prayed: I thank you, Lord,
for permitting me to enter the gates of
your kingdom.**

Reading
2 Corinthians
1:3–5

Praised be God, the Father of our Lord Jesus
Christ, the Father of mercies, and the God
of all consolation! He comforts us in all our
afflictions and thus enables us to comfort
those who are in trouble, with the same
consolation we have received from him.
As we have shared much in the suffering
of Christ, so through Christ do we share
abundantly in his consolation.

Responsory   The Lord is my strength,
I shall always praise him.
—The Lord is my strength,
I shall always praise him.

He has become my Savior.
—I shall always praise him.

Glory to the Father, and to the Son,
    and to the Holy Spirit.
—The Lord is my strength,
I shall always praise him.

Gospel
Canticle

Ant. **Do not be afraid, my son, for I am with you; if you should walk through the fire, the flames will not harm you, nor will the odor of burning cling to you.**

Canticle of
Zechariah
Luke 1:68–79

Blessed + be the Lord, the God of Israel;
he has come to his people and set them free.

He has raised up for us a mighty savior,
born of the house of his servant David.

Through his holy prophets he
    promised of old
that he would save us from our enemies,
from the hands of all who hate us.

He promised to show mercy to our fathers
and to remember his holy covenant.

This was the oath he swore to our
    father Abraham:
to set us free from the hands of our enemies,
free to worship him without fear,
holy and righteous in his sight
    all the days of our life.

You, my child, shall be called the prophet of
    the Most High;
for you will go before the Lord to
    prepare his way,
to give his people knowledge of salvation
by the forgiveness of their sins.

In the tender compassion of our God
the dawn from on high shall break upon us,
to shine on those who dwell in darkness and
    the shadow of death,
and to guide our feet into the way of peace.

Glory to the Father, and to the Son,
    and to the Holy Spirit:
—as it was in the beginning, is now,
and will be for ever. Amen.

Ant. **Do not be afraid, my son, for I am with you;
if you should walk through the fire, the
flames will not harm you, nor will the odor
of burning cling to you.**

Intercessions Our Savior's faithfulness is mirrored in the
    fidelity of his witnesses who shed their
    blood for the word of God. Let us praise
    him in remembrance of them:
You redeemed us by your blood.

Your martyrs freely embraced death in
    bearing witness to the faith,
—give us the true freedom of the Spirit, O Lord.

Your martyrs professed their faith by
    shedding their blood,
—give us a faith, O Lord, that is
    constant and pure.

Your martyrs followed in your footsteps by
    carrying the cross,
—help us to endure courageously the
    misfortunes of life.

Your martyrs washed their garments in the
　　blood of the Lamb,
—help us to avoid the weaknesses of the flesh
　　and worldly allurements.

The Lord's
Prayer

Our Father, who art in heaven,
hallowed be thy name;
thy kingdom come,
thy will be done
on earth as it is in heaven.
Give us this day our daily bread,
and forgive us our trespasses,
as we forgive those who trespass against us;
and lead us not into temptation,
but deliver us from evil.

Pater noster, qui es in cælis:
sanctificetur nomen tuum;
adveniat regnum tuum;
fiat voluntas tua,
sicut in cælo, et in terra.
Panem nostrum cotidianum da nobis hodie;
et dimitte nobis debita nostra,
sicut et nos dimittimus debitoribus nostris;
et ne nos inducas in tentationem;
sed libera nos a malo.

Concluding Prayer

Father,
you called Saint Lawrence to serve you by love
and crowned his life with glorious
    martyrdom.
Help us to be like him
in loving you and doing your work.
Grant this through our Lord Jesus Christ,
    your Son,
who lives and reigns with you and
    the Holy Spirit,
God, for ever and ever.
—Amen.

Dismissal

If praying individually, or in a group without a priest or deacon:

May the Lord + bless us,
protect us from all evil
and bring us to everlasting life.
—Amen.

If praying with a priest or deacon, he dismisses the people:

The Lord be with you.
—And with your spirit.

May almighty God bless you,
the Father, and the Son, + and the Holy Spirit.
—Amen.

Go in peace.
—Thanks be to God.

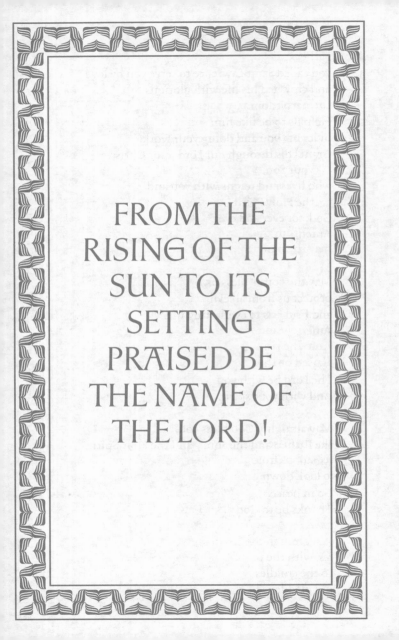

FROM THE
RISING OF THE
SUN TO ITS
SETTING
PRAISED BE
THE NAME OF
THE LORD!

EVENING PRAYER————
BEGINS THE NINETEENTH SUNDAY IN ORDINARY TIME

God, + come to my assistance.
—Lord, make haste to help me.

Glory to the Father, and to the Son,
    and to the Holy Spirit:
—as it was in the beginning, is now,
    and will be for ever. Amen. Alleluia.

Hymn   *The Saints of God!, p. 702*

Psalmody   Ant. 1 **From the rising of the sun to its setting,
    may the name of the Lord be praised.**

Psalm 113   Praise, O servants of the Lord,
    praise the name of the Lord!
    May the name of the Lord be blessed
    both now and for evermore!
    From the rising of the sun to its setting
    praised be the name of the Lord!

    High above all nations is the Lord,
    above the heavens his glory.
    Who is like the Lord, our God,
    who has risen on high to his throne
    yet stoops from the heights to look down,
    to look down upon heaven and earth?

    From the dust he lifts up the lowly,
    from his misery he raises the poor
    to set him in the company of princes,
    yes, with the princes of his people.
    To the childless wife he gives a home
    and gladdens her heart with children.

Glory to the Father, and to the Son,
    and to the Holy Spirit:
—as it was in the beginning, is now,
    and will be for ever. Amen.

Ant.   **From the rising of the sun to its setting,
         may the name of the Lord be praised.**

Ant. 2   **I shall take into my hand the saving chalice
         and invoke the name of the Lord.**

Psalm 116:10–19   I trusted, even when I said:
         "I am sorely afflicted,"
         and when I said in my alarm:
         "No man can be trusted."

         How can I repay the Lord
         for his goodness to me?
         The cup of salvation I will raise;
         I will call on the Lord's name.

         My vows to the Lord I will fulfill
         before all his people.
         O precious in the eyes of the Lord
         is the death of his faithful.

         Your servant, Lord, your servant am I;
         you have loosened my bonds.
         A thanksgiving sacrifice I make:
         I will call on the Lord's name.

         My vows to the Lord I will fulfill
         before all his people,
         in the courts of the house of the Lord,
         in your midst, O Jerusalem.

Glory to the Father, and to the Son,
and to the Holy Spirit:
as it was in the beginning, is now,
and will be for ever. Amen.

Ant.   **I shall take into my hand the saving chalice
and invoke the name of the Lord.**

Ant. 3   **The Lord Jesus humbled himself and God
exalted him for ever.**

Canticle:
Philippians
2:6–11

Though he was in the form of God,
Jesus did not deem equality with God
something to be grasped at.

Rather, he emptied himself
and took the form of a slave,
being born in the likeness of men.

He was known to be of human estate,
and it was thus that he humbled himself,
obediently accepting even death,
death on a cross!

Because of this,
God highly exalted him
and bestowed on him the name
above every other name,

So that at Jesus' name
every knee must bend
in the heavens, on the earth,
and under the earth,
and every tongue proclaim
to the glory of God the Father:
JESUS CHRIST IS LORD!

Glory to the Father, and to the Son,
    and to the Holy Spirit:
—as it was in the beginning, is now,
and will be for ever. Amen.

Ant.   **The Lord Jesus humbled himself and God
          exalted him for ever.**

Reading   May the God of peace, who brought up from
Hebrews   the dead the great Shepherd of the sheep by
13:20–21   the blood of the eternal covenant, Jesus our
          Lord, furnish you with all that is good, that
          you may do his will. Through Jesus Christ
          may he carry out in you all that is pleasing to
          him. To Christ be glory forever! Amen.

Responsory   Our hearts are filled with wonder as we
                contemplate your works, O Lord.
          —Our hearts are filled with wonder as we
                contemplate your works, O Lord.

          We praise the wisdom which
                wrought them all,
          —as we contemplate your works, O Lord.

Glory to the Father, and to the Son,
>> and to the Holy Spirit.
—Our hearts are filled with wonder as we
>> contemplate your works, O Lord.

**Gospel
Canticle**

Ant. **Lord, bid me walk across the waters.
Jesus reached out to take hold of Peter,
and said: O man of little faith, why did
you falter?**

*Canticle of
Mary
Luke 1:46–55*

My + soul proclaims the greatness of the Lord,
my spirit rejoices in God my Savior
for he has looked with favor on his
>> lowly servant.

From this day all generations will
>> call me blessed:
the Almighty has done great things for me,
and holy is his Name.

He has mercy on those who fear him
in every generation.

He has shown the strength of his arm,
he has scattered the proud in their conceit.

He has cast down the mighty from
>> their thrones,
and has lifted up the lowly.

He has filled the hungry with good things,
and the rich he has sent away empty.

He has come to the help of his servant Israel
for he has remembered his promise of mercy,
the promise he made to our fathers,
to Abraham and his children for ever.

Glory to the Father, and to the Son,
   and to the Holy Spirit:
—as it was in the beginning, is now,
and will be for ever. Amen.

Ant. **Lord, bid me walk across the waters. Jesus
reached out to take hold of Peter, and said:
O man of little faith, why did you falter?**

Intercessions Christ had compassion on the hungry and
   performed a miracle of love for them.
   Mindful of this, let us pray:
Show us your love, Lord.

Lord, we recognize that all the favors we
   have received today come through your
   generosity,
—do not let them return to you empty, but let
   them bear fruit.

Light and salvation of all nations, protect the
   missionaries you have sent into the world,
—enkindle in them the fire of your Spirit.

Grant that man may shape the world in
   keeping with human dignity,
—and respond generously to the needs
   of our time.

Healer of body and spirit, comfort the sick
  and be present to the dying,
—in your mercy visit and refresh us.

May the faithful departed be numbered
  among the saints,
—whose names are in the Book of Life.

The Lord's Prayer

Our Father, who art in heaven,
hallowed be thy name;
thy kingdom come,
thy will be done
on earth as it is in heaven.
Give us this day our daily bread,
and forgive us our trespasses,
as we forgive those who trespass against us;
and lead us not into temptation,
but deliver us from evil.

Pater noster, qui es in cælis:
sanctificetur nomen tuum;
adveniat regnum tuum;
fiat voluntas tua,
sicut in cælo, et in terra.
Panem nostrum cotidianum da nobis hodie;
et dimitte nobis debita nostra,
sicut et nos dimittimus debitoribus nostris;
et ne nos inducas in tentationem;
sed libera nos a malo.

Concluding Prayer

Almighty and ever-living God,
your Spirit made us your children,
confident to call you Father.
Increase your Spirit within us
and bring us to our promised inheritance.
Grant this through our Lord Jesus Christ,
     your Son,
who lives and reigns with you and
     the Holy Spirit,
God, for ever and ever.
—Amen.

Dismissal   *If praying individually, or in a group without a priest or deacon:*

May the Lord + bless us,
protect us from all evil
and bring us to everlasting life.
—Amen.

If praying with a priest or deacon, he dismisses the people:

The Lord be with you.
—And with your spirit.

May almighty God bless you,
the Father, and the Son, + and the Holy Spirit.
—Amen.

Go in peace.
—Thanks be to God.

NIGHT PRAYER————————————

God, + come to my assistance.
—Lord, make haste to help me.

Glory to the Father, and to the Son,
     and to the Holy Spirit:
—as it was in the beginning, is now,
     and will be for ever. Amen. Alleluia.

Examen   *An optional brief examination of conscience may be made. Call to mind your sins and failings this day.*

Hymn   *O Gladsome Light, p. 696*

Psalmody   Ant. 1 **Have mercy, Lord, and hear my prayer.**

Psalm 4   When I call, answer me, O God of justice;
     from anguish you released me; have mercy
          and hear me!

O men, how long will your hearts be closed,
will you love what is futile and seek
     what is false?

It is the Lord who grants favors to those
     whom he loves;
the Lord hears me whenever I call him.

Fear him; do not sin: ponder on your bed
     and be still.
Make justice your sacrifice and trust
     in the Lord.

"What can bring us happiness?" many say.
Let the light of your face shine on us, O Lord.

You have put into my heart a greater joy
than they have from abundance of corn
    and new wine.

I will lie down in peace and sleep
    comes at once
for you alone, Lord, make me dwell in safety.

Glory to the Father, and to the Son,
    and to the Holy Spirit:
—as it was in the beginning, is now,
    and will be for ever. Amen.

Ant.   **Have mercy, Lord, and hear my prayer.**

Ant. 2   **In the silent hours of night, bless the Lord.**

Psalm 134   O come, bless the Lord,
all you who serve the Lord,
who stand in the house of the Lord,
in the courts of the house of our God.

Lift up your hands to the holy place
and bless the Lord through the night.

May the Lord bless you from Zion,
he who made both heaven and earth.

Glory to the Father, and to the Son,
    and to the Holy Spirit:
—as it was in the beginning, is now,
    and will be for ever. Amen.

Ant.   **In the silent hours of night, bless the Lord.**

Reading
Deuteronomy
6:4–7

Hear, O Israel! The Lord is our God, the Lord alone! Therefore, you shall love the Lord, your God, with all your heart, and with all your soul, and with all your strength. Take to heart these words which I enjoin on you today. Drill them into your children. Speak of them at home and abroad, whether you are busy or at rest.

Responsory

Into your hands, Lord, I commend my spirit.
—Into your hands, Lord, I commend my spirit.

You have redeemed us, Lord God of truth.
—I commend my spirit.

Glory to the Father, and to the Son,
    and to the Holy Spirit.
—Into your hands, Lord, I commend my spirit.

Gospel
Canticle

Ant. **Protect us, Lord, as we stay awake; watch over us as we sleep, that awake, we may keep watch with Christ, and asleep, rest in his peace.**

Canticle of
Simeon
Luke 2:29–32

Lord, + now you let your servant go in peace;
your word has been fulfilled:
my own eyes have seen the salvation
which you have prepared in the sight of
        every people:
a light to reveal you to the nations
and the glory of your people Israel.

Glory to the Father, and to the Son,
    and to the Holy Spirit:
—as it was in the beginning, is now,
and will be for ever. Amen.

Ant.   **Protect us, Lord, as we stay awake; watch over us as we sleep, that awake, we may keep watch with Christ, and asleep, rest in his peace.**

Concluding Prayer

Let us pray.
Lord,
be with us throughout this night.
When day comes may we rise from sleep
to rejoice in the resurrection of your Christ,
who lives and reigns for ever and ever.
—Amen.

Blessing

May the all-powerful Lord
grant us a restful night
and a peaceful death.
—Amen.

Marian Antiphon

Sing the "Salve Regina," found on p. 700, or pray a Hail Mary.

Sunday, August 11, 2024
Nineteenth Sunday in Ordinary Time

MORNING PRAYER———————————

God, + come to my assistance.
—Lord, make haste to help me.

Glory to the Father, and to the Son,
    and to the Holy Spirit:
—as it was in the beginning, is now,
    and will be for ever. Amen. Alleluia.

Hymn   *Now That the Sun Is Gleaming Bright, p. 695*

Psalmody   Ant. 1   **Glorious is the Lord on high, alleluia.**

Psalm 93

The Lord is king, with majesty enrobed;
the Lord has robed himself with might,
he has girded himself with power.

The world you made firm, not to be moved;
your throne has stood firm from of old.
From all eternity, O Lord, you are.

The waters have lifted up, O Lord,
the waters have lifted up their voice,
the waters have lifted up their thunder.

Greater than the roar of mighty waters,
more glorious than the surgings of the sea,
the Lord is glorious on high.

Truly your decrees are to be trusted.
Holiness is fitting to your house,
O Lord, until the end of time.

Glory to the Father, and to the Son,
    and to the Holy Spirit:
—as it was in the beginning, is now,
    and will be for ever. Amen.

Ant.   **Glorious is the Lord on high, alleluia.**

Ant. 2   **To you, Lord, be highest glory and praise
for ever, alleluia.**

Canticle:
Daniel
3:57–88, 56

Bless the Lord, all you works of the Lord.
Praise and exalt him above all forever.
Angels of the Lord, bless the Lord.
You heavens, bless the Lord.
All you waters above the heavens,
    bless the Lord.
All you hosts of the Lord, bless the Lord.
Sun and moon, bless the Lord.
Stars of heaven, bless the Lord.

Every shower and dew, bless the Lord.
All you winds, bless the Lord.
Fire and heat, bless the Lord.
Cold and chill, bless the Lord.
Dew and rain, bless the Lord.
Frost and chill, bless the Lord.
Ice and snow, bless the Lord.
Nights and days, bless the Lord.
Light and darkness, bless the Lord.
Lightnings and clouds, bless the Lord.

Let the earth bless the Lord.
Praise and exalt him above all forever.
Mountains and hills, bless the Lord.
Everything growing from the earth,
      bless the Lord.
You springs, bless the Lord.
Seas and rivers, bless the Lord.
You dolphins and all water creatures,
      bless the Lord.
All you birds of the air, bless the Lord.
All you beasts, wild and tame, bless the Lord.
You sons of men, bless the Lord.

O Israel, bless the Lord.
Praise and exalt him above all forever.
Priests of the Lord, bless the Lord.
Servants of the Lord, bless the Lord.
Spirits and souls of the just, bless the Lord.
Holy men of humble heart, bless the Lord.
Hananiah, Azariah, Mishael, bless the Lord.
Praise and exalt him above all forever.

Let us bless the Father, and the Son,
      and the Holy Spirit.
Let us praise and exalt him above all forever.
Blessed are you, Lord, in the firmament
      of heaven.
Praiseworthy and glorious and exalted above
      all for ever.

Ant.   **To you, Lord, be highest glory and praise
for ever, alleluia.**

Ant. 3   **Praise the Lord from the heavens, alleluia.**

241

Psalm 148

Praise the Lord from the heavens,
 praise him in the heights.
Praise him, all his angels,
 praise him, all his host.

Praise him, sun and moon,
 praise him, shining stars.
Praise him, highest heavens
 and the waters above the heavens.

Let them praise the name of the Lord.
He commanded: they were made.
He fixed them for ever,
 gave a law which shall not pass away.

Praise the Lord from the earth,
 sea creatures and all oceans,
fire and hail, snow and mist,
 stormy winds that obey his word;

all mountains and hills,
 all fruit trees and cedars,
beasts, wild and tame,
 reptiles and birds on the wing;

all earth's kings and peoples,
 earth's princes and rulers;
young men and maidens,
 old men together with children.

Let them praise the name of the Lord
 for he alone is exalted.
The splendor of his name
 reaches beyond heaven and earth.

He exalts the strength of his people.
He is the praise of all his saints,
of the sons of Israel,
of the people to whom he comes close.

Glory to the Father, and to the Son,
    and to the Holy Spirit:
—as it was in the beginning, is now,
and will be for ever. Amen.

Ant.   **Praise the Lord from the heavens, alleluia.**

Reading   Thus says the Lord God: O my people, I will
Ezekiel   open your graves and have you rise from
37:12b–14   them, and bring you back to the land of
            Israel. Then you shall know that I am the
            Lord, when I open your graves and have you
            rise from them, O my people! I will put my
            spirit in you that you may live, and I will
            settle you upon your land; thus you shall
            know that I am the Lord. I have promised,
            and I will do it, says the Lord.

Responsory   Christ, Son of the living God,
                 have mercy on us.
            —Christ, Son of the living God,
                 have mercy on us.

            You are seated at the right hand of the Father,
            —have mercy on us.

            Glory to the Father, and to the Son,
                and to the Holy Spirit.
            —Christ, Son of the living God,
                have mercy on us.

243

Gospel
Canticle

Ant. **Amen, amen I say to you: Whoever**
believes in me will live for ever, alleluia.

Canticle of
Zechariah
Luke 1:68–79

Blessed + be the Lord, the God of Israel;
he has come to his people and set them free.

He has raised up for us a mighty savior,
born of the house of his servant David.

Through his holy prophets he
    promised of old
that he would save us from our enemies,
from the hands of all who hate us.

He promised to show mercy to our fathers
and to remember his holy covenant.

This was the oath he swore to our
    father Abraham:
to set us free from the hands of our enemies,
free to worship him without fear,
holy and righteous in his sight
    all the days of our life.

You, my child, shall be called the prophet of
    the Most High;
for you will go before the Lord to
    prepare his way,
to give his people knowledge of salvation
by the forgiveness of their sins.

In the tender compassion of our God
the dawn from on high shall break upon us,
to shine on those who dwell in darkness and
    the shadow of death,
and to guide our feet into the way of peace.

Glory to the Father, and to the Son,
    and to the Holy Spirit:
—as it was in the beginning, is now,
and will be for ever. Amen.

Ant.   **Amen, amen I say to you: Whoever believes
in me will live for ever, alleluia.**

Intercessions   Father, you sent the Holy Spirit to enlighten
        the hearts of men; hear us as we pray:
    Enlighten your people, Lord.

Blessed are you, O God, our light,
—you have given us a new day resplendent
    with your glory.

You enlightened the world through the
    resurrection of your Son,
—through your Church shed this light
    on all men.

You gave the disciples of your only-begotten
    Son the Spirit's gift of understanding,
—through the same Spirit keep the Church
    faithful to you.

Light of nations, remember those who
    remain in darkness,
—open their eyes and let them recognize you,
    the only true God.

**The Lord's
Prayer**

Our Father, who art in heaven,
hallowed be thy name;
thy kingdom come,
thy will be done
on earth as it is in heaven.
Give us this day our daily bread,
and forgive us our trespasses,
as we forgive those who trespass against us;
and lead us not into temptation,
but deliver us from evil.

Pater noster, qui es in cælis:
sanctificetur nomen tuum;
adveniat regnum tuum;
fiat voluntas tua,
sicut in cælo, et in terra.
Panem nostrum cotidianum da nobis hodie;
et dimitte nobis debita nostra,
sicut et nos dimittimus debitoribus nostris;
et ne nos inducas in tentationem;
sed libera nos a malo.

Concluding Prayer

Almighty and ever-living God,
your Spirit made us your children,
confident to call you Father.
Increase your Spirit within us
and bring us to our promised inheritance.
Grant this through our Lord Jesus Christ,
      your Son,
who lives and reigns with you and
      the Holy Spirit,
God, for ever and ever.
—Amen.

Dismissal

If praying individually, or in a group without a priest or deacon:

May the Lord + bless us,
protect us from all evil
and bring us to everlasting life.
—Amen.

If praying with a priest or deacon, he dismisses the people:

The Lord be with you.
—And with your spirit.

May almighty God bless you,
the Father, and the Son, + and the Holy Spirit.
—Amen.

Go in peace.
—Thanks be to God.

EVENING PRAYER————————

God, + come to my assistance.
—Lord, make haste to help me.

Glory to the Father, and to the Son,
    and to the Holy Spirit:
—as it was in the beginning, is now,
    and will be for ever. Amen. Alleluia.

Hymn   *From All That Dwell Below the Skies, p. 684*

Psalmody   Ant. 1 **The Lord said to my Master: Sit at my right hand, alleluia.**

Psalm 110:1–5, 7   The Lord's revelation to my Master:
    "Sit on my right:
    your foes I will put beneath your feet."

The Lord will wield from Zion
your scepter of power:
    rule in the midst of all your foes.

A prince from the day of your birth
on the holy mountains;
    from the womb before the dawn I begot you.

The Lord has sworn an oath he will
        not change.
"You are a priest for ever,
    a priest like Melchizedek of old."

The Master standing at your right hand
will shatter kings in the day of his
        great wrath.

He shall drink from the stream by
    the wayside
and therefore he shall lift up his head.

Glory to the Father, and to the Son,
    and to the Holy Spirit:
—as it was in the beginning, is now,
and will be for ever. Amen.

Ant.   **The Lord said to my Master: Sit at my right
hand, alleluia.**

Ant. 2   **Our compassionate Lord has left us a
memorial of his wonderful work, alleluia.**

Psalm 111   I will thank the Lord with all my heart
in the meeting of the just and their assembly.
Great are the works of the Lord,
to be pondered by all who love them.

Majestic and glorious his work,
his justice stands firm for ever.
He makes us remember his wonders.
The Lord is compassion and love.

He gives food to those who fear him;
keeps his covenant ever in mind.
He has shown his might to his people
by giving them the lands of the nations.

His works are justice and truth;
his precepts are all of them sure,
standing firm for ever and ever;
they are made in uprightness and truth.

He has sent deliverance to his people
and established his covenant for ever.
Holy his name, to be feared.

To fear the Lord is the first stage of wisdom;
all who do so prove themselves wise.
His praise shall last for ever!

Glory to the Father, and to the Son,
    and to the Holy Spirit:
—as it was in the beginning, is now,
and will be for ever. Amen.

Ant.   **Our compassionate Lord has left us a
memorial of his wonderful work, alleluia.**

Ant. 3   **All power is yours, Lord God, our mighty
King, alleluia.**

Canticle: See
Revelation
19:1–7

Alleluia.
Salvation, glory, and power to our God:
his judgments are honest and true.
Alleluia.

Alleluia.
Sing praise to our God, all you his servants,
all who worship him reverently, great
    and small.
Alleluia.

Alleluia.
The Lord our all-powerful God is King;
let us rejoice, sing praise, and give him glory.
Alleluia.

Alleluia.
The wedding feast of the Lamb has begun,
and his bride is prepared to welcome him.
Alleluia.

Alleluia.
Glory to the Father, and to the Son,
and to the Holy Spirit:
Alleluia.

Alleluia.
as it was in the beginning, is now,
and will be for ever. Amen.
Alleluia.

Ant. **All power is yours, Lord God, our mighty King, alleluia.**

Reading
1 Peter 1:3–5

Praised be the God and Father
of our Lord Jesus Christ,
he who in his great mercy
gave us new birth;
a birth unto hope which draws its life
from the resurrection of Jesus Christ
    from the dead;
a birth to an imperishable inheritance,
incapable of fading or defilement,
which is kept in heaven for you
who are guarded with God's power
    through faith;
a birth to a salvation which stands ready
to be revealed in the last days.

Responsory The whole creation proclaims the greatness
of your glory.
—The whole creation proclaims the greatness
of your glory.

Eternal ages praise
—the greatness of your glory.

Glory to the Father, and to the Son,
and to the Holy Spirit.
—The whole creation proclaims the greatness
of your glory.

Gospel   Ant. **Where your treasure is, there is your**
Canticle   **heart, says the Lord.**

Canticle of   My + soul proclaims the greatness of the Lord,
Mary   my spirit rejoices in God my Savior
Luke 1:46—55 for he has looked with favor on his
lowly servant.

From this day all generations will
call me blessed:
the Almighty has done great things for me,
and holy is his Name.

He has mercy on those who fear him
in every generation.

He has shown the strength of his arm,
he has scattered the proud in their conceit.

He has cast down the mighty from
their thrones,
and has lifted up the lowly.

He has filled the hungry with good things,
and the rich he has sent away empty.

He has come to the help of his servant Israel
for he has remembered his promise of mercy,
the promise he made to our fathers,
to Abraham and his children for ever.

Glory to the Father, and to the Son,
     and to the Holy Spirit:
—as it was in the beginning, is now,
and will be for ever. Amen.

Ant.   **Where your treasure is, there is your heart,
says the Lord.**

Intercessions The world was created by the Word of
God, re-created by his redemption, and
it is continually renewed by his love.
Rejoicing in him we call out:
Renew the wonders of your love, Lord.

We give thanks to God whose power is
     revealed in nature,
—and whose providence is revealed in history.

Through your Son, the herald of
     reconciliation, the victor of the cross,
—free us from empty fear and hopelessness.

May all those who love and pursue justice,
—work together without deceit to build a
     world of true peace.

Be with the oppressed, free the captives,
    console the sorrowing, feed the hungry,
    strengthen the weak,
—in all people reveal the victory of your cross.

After your Son's death and burial you raised
    him up again in glory,
—grant that the faithful departed may
    live with him.

The Lord's
Prayer

Our Father, who art in heaven,
hallowed be thy name;
thy kingdom come,
thy will be done
on earth as it is in heaven.
Give us this day our daily bread,
and forgive us our trespasses,
as we forgive those who trespass against us;
and lead us not into temptation,
but deliver us from evil.

Pater noster, qui es in cælis:
sanctificetur nomen tuum;
adveniat regnum tuum;
fiat voluntas tua,
sicut in cælo, et in terra.
Panem nostrum cotidianum da nobis hodie;
et dimitte nobis debita nostra,
sicut et nos dimittimus debitoribus nostris;
et ne nos inducas in tentationem;
sed libera nos a malo.

Concluding
Prayer

Almighty and ever-living God,
your Spirit made us your children,
confident to call you Father.
Increase your Spirit within us
and bring us to our promised inheritance.
Grant this through our Lord Jesus Christ,
    your Son,
who lives and reigns with you and
    the Holy Spirit,
God, for ever and ever.
—Amen.

Dismissal   *If praying individually, or in a group without a priest or deacon:*

May the Lord + bless us,
protect us from all evil
and bring us to everlasting life.
—Amen.

If praying with a priest or deacon, he dismisses the people:

The Lord be with you.
—And with your spirit.

May almighty God bless you,
the Father, and the Son, + and the Holy Spirit.
—Amen.

Go in peace.
—Thanks be to God.

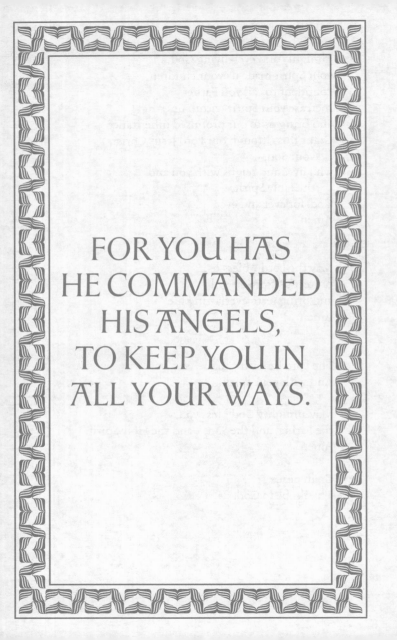

FOR YOU HAS
HE COMMANDED
HIS ANGELS,
TO KEEP YOU IN
ALL YOUR WAYS.

NIGHT PRAYER————————————

God, + come to my assistance.
—Lord, make haste to help me.

Glory to the Father, and to the Son,
    and to the Holy Spirit:
—as it was in the beginning, is now,
    and will be for ever. Amen. Alleluia.

Examen   *An optional brief examination of conscience may be made. Call to mind your*
    sins and failings this day.

Hymn   *O Gladsome Light, p. 696*

Psalmody   Ant. **Night holds no terrors for me sleeping
under God's wings.**

Psalm 91   He who dwells in the shelter of
        the Most High
and abides in the shade of the Almighty
says to the Lord: "My refuge,
my stronghold, my God in whom I trust!"

It is he who will free you from the snare
of the fowler who seeks to destroy you;
he will conceal you with his pinions
and under his wings you will find refuge.

You will not fear the terror of the night
nor the arrow that flies by day,
nor the plague that prowls in the darkness
nor the scourge that lays waste at noon.

A thousand may fall at your side,
ten thousand fall at your right,
you, it will never approach;
his faithfulness is buckler and shield.

Your eyes have only to look
to see how the wicked are repaid,
you who have said: "Lord, my refuge!"
and have made the Most High your dwelling.

Upon you no evil shall fall,
no plague approach where you dwell.
For you has he commanded his angels,
to keep you in all your ways.

They shall bear you upon their hands
lest you strike your foot against a stone.
On the lion and the viper you will tread
and trample the young lion and the dragon.

Since he clings to me in love, I will free him;
protect him for he knows my name.
When he calls I shall answer: "I am with you."
I will save him in distress and give him glory.

With length of life I will content him;
I shall let him see my saving power.

Glory to the Father, and to the Son,
    and to the Holy Spirit:
—as it was in the beginning, is now,
    and will be for ever. Amen.

Ant.   **Night holds no terrors for me sleeping
under God's wings.**

Reading
Revelation
22:4–5

They shall see the Lord face to face and bear his name on their foreheads. The night shall be no more. They will need no light from lamps or the sun, for the Lord God shall give them light, and they shall reign forever.

Responsory

Into your hands, Lord, I commend my spirit.
—Into your hands, Lord, I commend my spirit.

You have redeemed us, Lord God of truth.
—I commend my spirit.

Glory to the Father, and to the Son,
    and to the Holy Spirit.
—Into your hands, Lord, I commend my spirit.

Gospel Canticle

Ant. **Protect us, Lord, as we stay awake; watch over us as we sleep, that awake, we may keep watch with Christ, and asleep, rest in his peace.**

Canticle of Simeon
Luke 2:29–32

Lord, + now you let your servant go in peace;
your word has been fulfilled:
my own eyes have seen the salvation
which you have prepared in the sight of
    every people:
a light to reveal you to the nations
and the glory of your people Israel.

Glory to the Father, and to the Son,
    and to the Holy Spirit:
—as it was in the beginning, is now,
    and will be for ever. Amen.

Ant. **Protect us, Lord, as we stay awake; watch over us as we sleep, that awake, we may keep watch with Christ, and asleep, rest in his peace.**

Concluding Prayer

Let us pray.
Lord,
we have celebrated today
the mystery of the rising of Christ to new life.
May we now rest in your peace,
safe from all that could harm us,
and rise again refreshed and joyful,
to praise you throughout another day.
We ask this through Christ our Lord.
—Amen.

Blessing

May the all-powerful Lord
grant us a restful night
and a peaceful death.
—Amen.

Marian Antiphon

Sing the "Salve Regina," found on p. 700, or pray a Hail Mary.

Monday, August 12, 2024
Monday of the Nineteenth Week in Ordinary Time

MORNING PRAYER ————————————————

God, + come to my assistance.
—Lord, make haste to help me.

Glory to the Father, and to the Son,
    and to the Holy Spirit:
—as it was in the beginning, is now,
    and will be for ever. Amen. Alleluia.

Hymn   *Now That the Sun Is Gleaming Bright, p. 695*

Psalmody   Ant. 1 **Blessed are they who dwell in your house, O Lord.**

Psalm 84

How lovely is your dwelling place,
Lord, God of hosts.

My soul is longing and yearning,
is yearning for the courts of the Lord.
My heart and my soul ring out their joy
to God, the living God.

The sparrow herself finds a home
and the swallow a nest for her brood;
she lays her young by your altars,
Lord of hosts, my king and my God.

They are happy, who dwell in your house,
for ever singing your praise.
They are happy, whose strength is in you,
in whose hearts are the roads to Zion.

As they go through the Bitter Valley
they make it a place of springs,
the autumn rain covers it with blessings.
They walk with ever growing strength,
they will see the God of gods in Zion.

O Lord God of hosts, hear my prayer,
give ear, O God of Jacob.
Turn your eyes, O God, our shield,
look on the face of your anointed.

One day within your courts
is better than a thousand elsewhere.
The threshold of the house of God
I prefer to the dwellings of the wicked.

For the Lord God is a rampart, a shield;
he will give us his favor and glory.
The Lord will not refuse any good
to those who walk without blame.

Lord, God of hosts,
happy the man who trusts in you!

Glory to the Father, and to the Son,
    and to the Holy Spirit:
—as it was in the beginning, is now,
and will be for ever. Amen.

Ant.   **Blessed are they who dwell in your house,
O Lord.**

Ant. 2   **Come, let us climb the mountain
of the Lord.**

Canticle:
Isaiah 2:2–5

In days to come,
the mountain of the Lord's house
shall be established as the highest mountain
and raised above the hills.

All nations shall stream toward it;
many peoples shall come and say:
"Come, let us climb the Lord's mountain,
to the house of the God of Jacob,
that he may instruct us in his ways,
and we may walk in his paths."

For from Zion shall go forth instruction,
and the word of the Lord from Jerusalem.

He shall judge between the nations,
and impose terms on many peoples.
They shall beat their swords into plowshares
and their spears into pruning hooks;
one nation shall not raise the sword
        against another,
nor shall they train for war again.

O house of Jacob, come,
let us walk in the light of the Lord!

Glory to the Father, and to the Son,
        and to the Holy Spirit:
—as it was in the beginning, is now,
and will be for ever. Amen.

Ant.   **Come, let us climb the mountain
of the Lord.**

Ant. 3   **Sing to the Lord and bless his name.**

Psalm 96

O sing a new song to the Lord,
sing to the Lord, all the earth.
O sing to the Lord, bless his name.

Proclaim his help day by day,
tell among the nations his glory
and his wonders among all the peoples.

The Lord is great and worthy of praise,
to be feared above all gods;
the gods of the heathens are naught.

It was the Lord who made the heavens,
his are majesty and state and power
and splendor in his holy place.

Give the Lord, you families of peoples,
give the Lord glory and power,
give the Lord the glory of his name.

Bring an offering and enter his courts,
worship the Lord in his temple.
O earth, tremble before him.

Proclaim to the nations: "God is king."
The world he made firm in its place;
he will judge the peoples in fairness.

Let the heavens rejoice and earth be glad,
let the sea and all within it thunder praise,
let the land and all it bears rejoice,
all the trees of the wood shout for joy

at the presence of the Lord for he comes,
he comes to rule the earth.
With justice he will rule the world,
he will judge the peoples with his truth.

Glory to the Father, and to the Son,
    and to the Holy Spirit:
—as it was in the beginning, is now,
and will be for ever. Amen.

Ant.   **Sing to the Lord and bless his name.**

Reading   Always speak and act as men destined
James 2:12–13   for judgment under the law of freedom.
Merciless is the judgment on the man who
has not shown mercy; but mercy triumphs
over judgment.

Responsory   Blessed be the Lord our God, blessed from
    age to age.
—Blessed be the Lord our God, blessed from
    age to age.

His marvelous works are beyond compare,
—blessed from age to age.

Glory to the Father, and to the Son,
    and to the Holy Spirit.
—Blessed be the Lord our God, blessed from
    age to age.

Gospel   Ant. **Blessed be the Lord our God.**
Canticle

Canticle of
Zechariah
Luke 1:68–79

Blessed + be the Lord, the God of Israel;
he has come to his people and set them free.

He has raised up for us a mighty savior,
born of the house of his servant David.

Through his holy prophets he
    promised of old
that he would save us from our enemies,
from the hands of all who hate us.

He promised to show mercy to our fathers
and to remember his holy covenant.

This was the oath he swore to our
    father Abraham:
to set us free from the hands of our enemies,
free to worship him without fear,
holy and righteous in his sight
    all the days of our life.

You, my child, shall be called the prophet of
    the Most High;
for you will go before the Lord to
    prepare his way,
to give his people knowledge of salvation
by the forgiveness of their sins.

In the tender compassion of our God
the dawn from on high shall break upon us,
to shine on those who dwell in darkness and
    the shadow of death,
and to guide our feet into the way of peace.

Glory to the Father, and to the Son,
and to the Holy Spirit:
—as it was in the beginning, is now,
and will be for ever. Amen.

Ant.   **Blessed be the Lord our God.**

Intercessions   Man was created to glorify God through his
deeds. Let us earnestly pray:
May we give glory to your name, Lord.

We bless you, Creator of all things,
—for you have given us the goods of the earth
and brought us to this day.

Look with favor on us as we begin our
daily work,
—let us be fellow workers with you.

Make our work today benefit our brothers
and sisters,
—that with them and for them we may build
an earthly city, pleasing to you.

Grant joy and peace to us,
—and to all we meet this day.

The Lord's
Prayer

Our Father, who art in heaven,
hallowed be thy name;
thy kingdom come,
thy will be done
on earth as it is in heaven.
Give us this day our daily bread,
and forgive us our trespasses,
as we forgive those who trespass against us;
and lead us not into temptation,
but deliver us from evil.

Pater noster, qui es in cælis:
sanctificetur nomen tuum;
adveniat regnum tuum;
fiat voluntas tua,
sicut in cælo, et in terra.
Panem nostrum cotidianum da nobis hodie;
et dimitte nobis debita nostra,
sicut et nos dimittimus debitoribus nostris;
et ne nos inducas in tentationem;
sed libera nos a malo.

Concluding
Prayer

Lord God,
king of heaven and earth,
direct our minds and bodies throughout this day,
and make us holy.
Keep us faithful to your law in thought,
        word and deed.
Be our helper now and always,
free us from sin,
and bring us to salvation in that kingdom
where you live and reign with the Father and
        the Holy Spirit,
God, for ever and ever.
—Amen.

Dismissal   *If praying individually, or in a group without a priest or deacon:*

May the Lord + bless us,
protect us from all evil
and bring us to everlasting life.
—Amen.

If praying with a priest or deacon, he dismisses the people:

The Lord be with you.
—And with your spirit.

May almighty God bless you,
the Father, and the Son, + and the Holy Spirit.
—Amen.

Go in peace.
—Thanks be to God.

EVENING PRAYER

God, + come to my assistance.
—Lord, make haste to help me.

Glory to the Father, and to the Son,
    and to the Holy Spirit:
—as it was in the beginning, is now,
and will be for ever. Amen. Alleluia.

Hymn   *From All That Dwell Below the Skies, p. 684*

Psalmody   Ant. 1 **Our eyes are fixed intently on the
Lord, waiting for his merciful help.**

Psalm 123

To you have I lifted up my eyes,
you who dwell in the heavens;
my eyes, like the eyes of slaves
on the hand of their lords.

Like the eyes of a servant
on the hand of her mistress,
so our eyes are on the Lord our God
till he show us his mercy.

Have mercy on us, Lord, have mercy.
We are filled with contempt.
Indeed all too full is our soul
with the scorn of the rich,
with the proud man's disdain.

Glory to the Father, and to the Son,
    and to the Holy Spirit:
—as it was in the beginning, is now,
and will be for ever. Amen.

Ant.

**Our eyes are fixed intently on the Lord,
waiting for his merciful help.**

Ant. 2

**Our help is in the name of the Lord who
made heaven and earth.**

Psalm 124

"If the Lord had not been on our side,"
this is Israel's song.
"If the Lord had not been on our side
when men rose up against us,
then would they have swallowed us alive
when their anger was kindled.

Then would the waters have engulfed us,
the torrent gone over us;
over our head would have swept
the raging waters."

Blessed be the Lord who did not give us
as prey to their teeth!
Our life, like a bird, has escaped
from the snare of the fowler.

Indeed the snare has been broken
and we have escaped.
Our help is in the name of the Lord,
who made heaven and earth.

Glory to the Father, and to the Son,
    and to the Holy Spirit:
—as it was in the beginning, is now,
and will be for ever. Amen.

Ant.   **Our help is in the name of the Lord who made heaven and earth.**

Ant. 3   **God chose us in his Son to be his adopted children.**

Canticle:
Ephesians
1:3–10

Praised be the God and Father
of our Lord Jesus Christ,
who has bestowed on us in Christ
every spiritual blessing in the heavens.

God chose us in him
before the world began
to be holy
and blameless in his sight.

He predestined us
to be his adopted sons through Jesus Christ,
such was his will and pleasure,
that all might praise the glorious favor
he has bestowed on us in his beloved.

In him and through his blood,
    we have been redeemed,
and our sins forgiven,
so immeasurably generous
is God's favor to us.

God has given us the wisdom
to understand fully the mystery,
the plan he was pleased
to decree in Christ.

A plan to be carried out
in Christ, in the fullness of time,
to bring all things into one in him,
in the heavens and on earth.

Glory to the Father, and to the Son,
    and to the Holy Spirit:
—as it was in the beginning, is now,
and will be for ever. Amen.

Ant.   **God chose us in his Son to be his
adopted children.**

Reading
James 4:11–12

Do not, my brothers, speak ill of one another.
The one who speaks ill of his brother or
judges his brother is speaking against the
law. It is the law he judges. If, however, you
judge the law you are no observer of the law,
you are its judge. There is but one Lawgiver
and Judge, one who can save and destroy.
Who then are you to judge your neighbor?

Responsory

Lord, you alone can heal me, for I have
    grieved you by my sins.
—Lord, you alone can heal me, for I have
    grieved you by my sins.

Once more I say: O Lord, have mercy on me,
—for I have grieved you by my sins.

Glory to the Father, and to the Son,
    and to the Holy Spirit.
—Lord, you alone can heal me, for I have
    grieved you by my sins.

Gospel
Canticle

Ant. **My soul proclaims the greatness of the
Lord for he has looked with favor on his
lowly servant.**

*Canticle of
Mary
Luke 1:46–55*

My + soul proclaims the greatness of the Lord,
my spirit rejoices in God my Savior
for he has looked with favor on his
    lowly servant.

From this day all generations will
    call me blessed:
the Almighty has done great things for me,
and holy is his Name.

He has mercy on those who fear him
in every generation.

He has shown the strength of his arm,
he has scattered the proud in their conceit.

He has cast down the mighty from
    their thrones,
and has lifted up the lowly.

He has filled the hungry with good things,
and the rich he has sent away empty.

He has come to the help of his servant Israel
for he has remembered his promise of mercy,
the promise he made to our fathers,
to Abraham and his children for ever.

Glory to the Father, and to the Son,
    and to the Holy Spirit:
—as it was in the beginning, is now,
and will be for ever. Amen.

Ant.   **My soul proclaims the greatness of the
Lord for he has looked with favor on his
lowly servant.**

Intercessions   Christ desires to lead all men to salvation. Let
    us implore him with all our heart:
    Draw all things to yourself, Lord.

Through your precious blood, Lord, you
    redeemed us from the slavery of sin,
—grant us the freedom of the sons of God.

Bestow your grace upon our bishop N., and
    upon all bishops,
—may they administer your sacraments with
    fervent joy.

Grant that all who seek the truth may find it,
—and in finding it may they desire it
    all the more.

Be present to comfort widows, orphans and
    all the abandoned, Lord,
—may they feel close to you and cling to you.

Receive our departed brethren into the
    heavenly kingdom,
—where with the Father and the Holy Spirit
    you will be all in all.

The Lord's Prayer

Our Father, who art in heaven,
hallowed be thy name;
thy kingdom come,
thy will be done
on earth as it is in heaven.
Give us this day our daily bread,
and forgive us our trespasses,
as we forgive those who trespass against us;
and lead us not into temptation,
but deliver us from evil.

Pater noster, qui es in cælis:
sanctificetur nomen tuum;
adveniat regnum tuum;
fiat voluntas tua,
sicut in cælo, et in terra.
Panem nostrum cotidianum da nobis hodie;
et dimitte nobis debita nostra,
sicut et nos dimittimus debitoribus nostris;
et ne nos inducas in tentationem;
sed libera nos a malo.

Concluding Prayer

God our Father,
at the close of day we come to you,
the light that never fades.
Shine in the darkness of our night
and forgive our sins and failings.
We ask this through our Lord Jesus Christ,
    your Son,
who lives and reigns with you and
    the Holy Spirit,
God, for ever and ever.
—Amen.

Dismissal

If praying individually, or in a group without a priest or deacon:

May the Lord + bless us,
protect us from all evil
and bring us to everlasting life.
—Amen.

If praying with a priest or deacon, he dismisses the people:

The Lord be with you.
—And with your spirit.

May almighty God bless you,
    the Father, and the Son, + and the Holy Spirit.
—Amen.

Go in peace.
—Thanks be to God.

NIGHT PRAYER

God, + come to my assistance.
—Lord, make haste to help me.

Glory to the Father, and to the Son,
    and to the Holy Spirit:
—as it was in the beginning, is now,
    and will be for ever. Amen. Alleluia.

Examen *An optional brief examination of conscience may be made. Call to mind your sins and failings this day.*

Hymn *O Gladsome Light, p. 696*

Psalmody Ant. **O Lord, our God, unwearied is your love for us.**

Psalm 86 Turn your ear, O Lord, and give answer
for I am poor and needy.
Preserve my life, for I am faithful:
save the servant who trusts in you.

You are my God; have mercy on me, Lord,
for I cry to you all the day long.
Give joy to your servant, O Lord,
for to you I lift up my soul.

O Lord, you are good and forgiving,
full of love to all who call.
Give heed, O Lord, to my prayer
and attend to the sound of my voice.

In the day of distress I will call
and surely you will reply.
Among the gods there is none like you,
    O Lord;
nor work to compare with yours.

All the nations shall come to adore you
and glorify your name, O Lord:
for you are great and do marvelous deeds,
you who alone are God.

Show me, Lord, your way
so that I may walk in your truth.
Guide my heart to fear your name.

I will praise you, Lord my God, with
    all my heart
and glorify your name for ever;
for your love to me has been great:
you have saved me from the depths of
    the grave.

The proud have risen against me;
ruthless men seek my life:
to you they pay no heed.

But you, God of mercy and compassion,
slow to anger, O Lord,
abounding in love and truth,
turn and take pity on me.

O give your strength to your servant
and save your handmaid's son.
Show me a sign of your favor
that my foes may see to their shame
that you console me and give me your help.

Glory to the Father, and to the Son,
      and to the Holy Spirit:
—as it was in the beginning, is now,
and will be for ever. Amen.

Ant.   **O Lord, our God, unwearied is your
love for us.**

Reading
1 Thessalonians
5:9–10
God has destined us for acquiring salvation
through our Lord Jesus Christ. He died for
us, that all of us, whether awake or asleep,
together might live with him.

Responsory   Into your hands, Lord, I commend my spirit.
—Into your hands, Lord, I commend my spirit.

You have redeemed us, Lord God of truth.
—I commend my spirit.

Glory to the Father, and to the Son,
      and to the Holy Spirit.
—Into your hands, Lord, I commend my spirit.

Gospel
Canticle
Ant. **Protect us, Lord, as we stay awake;
watch over us as we sleep, that awake, we
may keep watch with Christ, and asleep,
rest in his peace.**

Canticle of
Simeon
Luke 2:29–32

Lord, + now you let your servant go in peace;
your word has been fulfilled:
my own eyes have seen the salvation
which you have prepared in the sight of
        every people:
a light to reveal you to the nations
and the glory of your people Israel.

Glory to the Father, and to the Son,
        and to the Holy Spirit:
—as it was in the beginning, is now,
and will be for ever. Amen.

Ant.   **Protect us, Lord, as we stay awake; watch
over us as we sleep, that awake, we may
keep watch with Christ, and asleep, rest in
his peace.**

Concluding   *Let us pray.*
Prayer   Lord,
              give our bodies restful sleep
              and let the work we have done today
              bear fruit in eternal life.
              We ask this through Christ our Lord.
              —Amen.

Blessing   May the all-powerful Lord
            grant us a restful night
            and a peaceful death.
            —Amen.

Marian   *Sing the "Salve Regina," found on p. 700, or pray a Hail Mary.*
Antiphon

Tuesday, August 13, 2024
Tuesday of the Nineteenth Week in Ordinary Time

God, + come to my assistance.
—Lord, make haste to help me.

Glory to the Father, and to the Son,
 and to the Holy Spirit:
—as it was in the beginning, is now,
 and will be for ever. Amen. Alleluia.

Hymn *Now That the Sun Is Gleaming Bright, p. 695*

Psalmody Ant. 1 **Lord, you have blessed your land; you have forgiven the sins of your people.**

Psalm 85 O Lord, you once favored your land
and revived the fortunes of Jacob,
you forgave the guilt of your people
and covered all their sins.
You averted all your rage,
you calmed the heat of your anger.

Revive us now, God, our helper!
Put an end to your grievance against us.
Will you be angry with us for ever,
will your anger never cease?

Will you not restore again our life
that your people may rejoice in you?
Let us see, O Lord, your mercy
and give us your saving help.

I will hear what the Lord God has to say,
a voice that speaks of peace,
peace for his people and his friends
and those who turn to him in their hearts.
His help is near for those who fear him
and his glory will dwell in our land.

Mercy and faithfulness have met;
justice and peace have embraced.
Faithfulness shall spring from the earth
and justice look down from heaven.

The Lord will make us prosper
and our earth shall yield its fruit.
Justice shall march before him
and peace shall follow his steps.

Glory to the Father, and to the Son,
    and to the Holy Spirit:
—as it was in the beginning, is now,
and will be for ever. Amen.

Ant.   **Lord, you have blessed your land; you have
forgiven the sins of your people.**

Ant. 2   **My soul has yearned for you in the
night, and as morning breaks I watch for
your coming.**

Canticle: A strong city have we;
Isaiah 26:1–4,   he sets up walls and ramparts to protect us.
7–9, 12   Open up the gates
to let in a nation that is just,
one that keeps faith.

A nation of firm purpose you keep in peace;
in peace, for its trust in you.
Trust in the Lord forever!
For the Lord is an eternal Rock.

The way of the just is smooth;
the path of the just you make level.
Yes, for your way and your
    judgments, O Lord,
we look to you;
your name and your title
are the desire of our souls.

My soul yearns for you in the night,
yes, my spirit within me keeps vigil for you;
when your judgment dawns upon the earth,
the world's inhabitants learn justice.

O Lord, you mete out peace to us,
for it is you who have accomplished all we
    have done.

Glory to the Father, and to the Son,
    and to the Holy Spirit:
—as it was in the beginning, is now,
and will be for ever. Amen.

Ant.   **My soul has yearned for you in the
night, and as morning breaks I watch for
your coming.**

Ant. 3   **Lord, let the light of your face
shine upon us.**

Psalm 67

O God, be gracious and bless us
and let your face shed its light upon us.
So will your ways be known upon earth
and all nations learn your saving help.

Let the peoples praise you, O God;
let all the peoples praise you.

Let the nations be glad and exult
for you rule the world with justice.
With fairness you rule the peoples,
you guide the nations on earth.

Let the peoples praise you, O God;
let all the peoples praise you.

The earth has yielded its fruit
for God, our God, has blessed us.
May God still give us his blessing
till the ends of the earth revere him.

Let the peoples praise you, O God;
let all the peoples praise you.

Glory to the Father, and to the Son,
    and to the Holy Spirit:
—as it was in the beginning, is now,
and will be for ever. Amen.

Ant.

**Lord, let the light of your face
shine upon us.**

Reading
1 John 4:14–15

We have seen for ourselves, and can testify,
  that the Father has sent the Son as savior of
    the world.
  When anyone acknowledges that Jesus is the
    Son of God,
  God dwells in him
  and he in God.

Responsory

My God stands by me, all my trust is in him.
—My God stands by me, all my trust is in him.

I find refuge in him, and I am truly free;
—all my trust is in him.

Glory to the Father, and to the Son,
  and to the Holy Spirit.
—My God stands by me, all my trust is in him.

Gospel
Canticle

Ant. **God has raised up for us a mighty
Savior, as he promised of old through his
holy prophets.**

Canticle of
Zechariah
Luke 1:68–79

Blessed + be the Lord, the God of Israel;
he has come to his people and set them free.

He has raised up for us a mighty savior,
born of the house of his servant David.

Through his holy prophets he
  promised of old
that he would save us from our enemies,
from the hands of all who hate us.

He promised to show mercy to our fathers
and to remember his holy covenant.

This was the oath he swore to our
    father Abraham:
to set us free from the hands of our enemies,
free to worship him without fear,
holy and righteous in his sight
    all the days of our life.

You, my child, shall be called the prophet of
    the Most High;
for you will go before the Lord to
    prepare his way,
to give his people knowledge of salvation
by the forgiveness of their sins.

In the tender compassion of our God
the dawn from on high shall break upon us,
to shine on those who dwell in darkness and
    the shadow of death,
and to guide our feet into the way of peace.

Glory to the Father, and to the Son,
    and to the Holy Spirit:
—as it was in the beginning, is now,
and will be for ever. Amen.

Ant.   **God has raised up for us a mighty Savior,
as he promised of old through his
holy prophets.**

Intercessions   Lord Jesus, by your blood you have purchased
for yourself a new people. We adore you
and beseech you:
Remember your people, Lord.

Our King and our Redeemer, hear the
praises of your Church at the beginning
of this day,
—teach her to glorify your majesty
without ceasing.

You are our hope and our strength, in
you we trust,
—may we never despair.

Look kindly upon our weakness and hasten
to our aid,
—for without you we can do nothing.

Remember the poor and the afflicted, do not
let this day be a burden to them,
—but a consolation and a joy.

The Lord's   Our Father, who art in heaven,
Prayer   hallowed be thy name;
thy kingdom come,
thy will be done
on earth as it is in heaven.
Give us this day our daily bread,
and forgive us our trespasses,
as we forgive those who trespass against us;
and lead us not into temptation,
but deliver us from evil.

Pater noster, qui es in cælis:
sanctificetur nomen tuum;
adveniat regnum tuum;
fiat voluntas tua,
sicut in cælo, et in terra.
Panem nostrum cotidianum da nobis hodie;
et dimitte nobis debita nostra,
sicut et nos dimittimus debitoribus nostris;
et ne nos inducas in tentationem;
sed libera nos a malo.

Concluding Prayer

God our Father,
yours is the beauty of creation
and the good things you have given us.
Help us to begin this day joyfully
    in your name
and to spend it in loving service
of you and our fellow man.
We ask this through our Lord Jesus Christ,
    your Son,
who lives and reigns with you and
    the Holy Spirit,
God, for ever and ever.
—Amen.

Dismissal   *If praying individually, or in a group without a priest or deacon:*

May the Lord + bless us,
protect us from all evil
and bring us to everlasting life.
—Amen.

If praying with a priest or deacon, he dismisses the people:

The Lord be with you.
—And with your spirit.

May almighty God bless you,
the Father, and the Son, + and the Holy Spirit.
—Amen.

Go in peace.
—Thanks be to God.

EVENING PRAYER ————————————

God, + come to my assistance.
—Lord, make haste to help me.

Glory to the Father, and to the Son,
and to the Holy Spirit:
—as it was in the beginning, is now,
and will be for ever. Amen. Alleluia.

Hymn   *From All That Dwell Below the Skies, p. 684*

Psalmody   Ant. 1 **The Lord surrounds his people with
his strength.**

Psalm 125   Those who put their trust in the Lord
are like Mount Zion, that cannot be shaken,
that stands for ever.

Jerusalem! The mountains surround her,
so the Lord surrounds his people
both now and for ever.

For the scepter of the wicked shall not rest
over the land of the just
for fear that the hands of the just
should turn to evil.

Do good, Lord, to those who are good,
to the upright of heart;
but the crooked and those who do evil,
drive them away!

On Israel, peace!

Glory to the Father, and to the Son,
    and to the Holy Spirit:
—as it was in the beginning, is now,
and will be for ever. Amen.

Ant.   **The Lord surrounds his people with
his strength.**

Ant. 2   **Unless you acquire the heart of a child,
you cannot enter the kingdom of God.**

Psalm 131   O Lord, my heart is not proud
nor haughty my eyes.
I have not gone after things too great
nor marvels beyond me.

Truly I have set my soul
in silence and peace.
As a child has rest in its mother's arms,
even so my soul.

O Israel, hope in the Lord
both now and for ever.

Glory to the Father, and to the Son,
    and to the Holy Spirit:
—as it was in the beginning, is now,
and will be for ever. Amen.

Ant.   **Unless you acquire the heart of a child,
         you cannot enter the kingdom of God.**

Ant. 3   **Lord, you have made us a kingdom and
         priests for God our Father.**

Canticle:
Revelation 4:11;   O Lord our God, you are worthy
5:9, 10, 12   to receive glory and honor and power.

         For you have created all things;
         by your will they came to be and were made.

         Worthy are you, O Lord,
         to receive the scroll and break open its seals.

         For you were slain;
         with your blood you purchased for God
         men of every race and tongue,
         of every people and nation.

         You made of them a kingdom,
         and priests to serve our God,
         and they shall reign on the earth.

         Worthy is the Lamb that was slain
         to receive power and riches,
         wisdom and strength,
         honor and glory and praise.

         Glory to the Father, and to the Son,
             and to the Holy Spirit:
         —as it was in the beginning, is now,
         and will be for ever. Amen.

Ant. **Lord, you have made us a kingdom and priests for God our Father.**

Reading
Romans
12:9–12

Your love must be sincere. Detest what is evil, cling to what is good. Love one another with the affection of brothers. Anticipate each other in showing respect. Do not grow slack but be fervent in spirit; he whom you serve is the Lord. Rejoice in hope, be patient under trial, persevere in prayer.

Responsory Through all eternity, O Lord, your promise
            stands unshaken.
          —Through all eternity, O Lord, your promise
            stands unshaken.

Your faithfulness will never fail;
—your promise stands unshaken.

Glory to the Father, and to the Son,
    and to the Holy Spirit.
—Through all eternity, O Lord, your promise
    stands unshaken.

Gospel
Canticle

Ant. **My spirit rejoices in God my Savior.**

Canticle of
Mary
Luke 1:46–55

My + soul proclaims the greatness of the Lord,
my spirit rejoices in God my Savior
for he has looked with favor on his
    lowly servant.

From this day all generations will
    call me blessed:
the Almighty has done great things for me,
and holy is his Name.

He has mercy on those who fear him
in every generation.

He has shown the strength of his arm,
he has scattered the proud in their conceit.

He has cast down the mighty from
    their thrones,
and has lifted up the lowly.

He has filled the hungry with good things,
and the rich he has sent away empty.

He has come to the help of his servant Israel
for he has remembered his promise of mercy,
the promise he made to our fathers,
to Abraham and his children for ever.

Glory to the Father, and to the Son,
    and to the Holy Spirit:
—as it was in the beginning, is now,
and will be for ever. Amen.

Ant.   **My spirit rejoices in God my Savior.**

Intercessions   God establishes his people in hope. Let us cry
        out to him with joy:
    You are the hope of your people, Lord.

    We thank you, Lord,
    —because in Christ you have given us all the
        treasures of wisdom and knowledge.

O God, in your hands are the hearts of the
    powerful; bestow your wisdom upon
    government leaders,
—may they draw from the fountain
    of your counsel and please you in
    thought and deed.

The talents of artists reflect your splendor,
—may their work give the world hope and joy.

You do not allow us to be tested beyond
    our ability,
—strengthen the weak and raise up the fallen.

Through your Son you promised to raise
    men up on the Last Day,
—do not forget those who have died.

The Lord's
Prayer

Our Father, who art in heaven,
hallowed be thy name;
thy kingdom come,
thy will be done
on earth as it is in heaven.
Give us this day our daily bread,
and forgive us our trespasses,
as we forgive those who trespass against us;
and lead us not into temptation,
but deliver us from evil.

Pater noster, qui es in cælis:
sanctificetur nomen tuum;
adveniat regnum tuum;
fiat voluntas tua,
sicut in cælo, et in terra.
Panem nostrum cotidianum da nobis hodie;
et dimitte nobis debita nostra,
sicut et nos dimittimus debitoribus nostris;
et ne nos inducas in tentationem;
sed libera nos a malo.

Concluding Prayer

Lord,
may our evening prayer rise up to you,
and your blessing come down upon us.
May your help and salvation be ours
now and through all eternity.
We ask this through our Lord Jesus Christ,
    your Son,
who lives and reigns with you and
    the Holy Spirit,
God, for ever and ever.
—Amen.

Dismissal

If praying individually, or in a group without a priest or deacon:

May the Lord + bless us,
protect us from all evil
and bring us to everlasting life.
—Amen.

If praying with a priest or deacon, he dismisses the people:

The Lord be with you.
—And with your spirit.

May almighty God bless you,
the Father, and the Son, + and the Holy Spirit.
—Amen.

Go in peace.
—Thanks be to God.

NIGHT PRAYER

God, + come to my assistance.
—Lord, make haste to help me.

Glory to the Father, and to the Son,
    and to the Holy Spirit:
—as it was in the beginning, is now,
    and will be for ever. Amen. Alleluia.

Examen	*An optional brief examination of conscience may be made. Call to mind your sins and failings this day.*
Hymn	*O Gladsome Light, p. 696*
Psalmody	Ant. **Do not hide your face from me; in you I put my trust.**

Psalm 143:1–11

Lord, listen to my prayer:
turn your ear to my appeal.
You are faithful, you are just; give answer.
Do not call your servant to judgment
for no one is just in your sight.

The enemy pursues my soul;
he has crushed my life to the ground;
he has made me dwell in darkness
like the dead, long forgotten.
Therefore my spirit fails;
my heart is numb within me.

I remember the days that are past:
I ponder all your works.
I muse on what your hand has wrought
and to you I stretch out my hands.
Like a parched land my soul thirsts for you.

Lord, make haste and answer;
for my spirit fails within me.
Do not hide your face
lest I become like those in the grave.

In the morning let me know your love
for I put my trust in you.
Make me know the way I should walk:
to you I lift up my soul.

Rescue me, Lord, from my enemies;
I have fled to you for refuge.
Teach me to do your will
for you, O Lord, are my God.
Let your good spirit guide me
in ways that are level and smooth.

For your name's sake, Lord, save my life;
in your justice save my soul from distress.

Glory to the Father, and to the Son,
    and to the Holy Spirit:
—as it was in the beginning, is now,
    and will be for ever. Amen.

Ant.   **Do not hide your face from me; in you I
put my trust.**

Reading
1 Peter 5:8–9a

Stay sober and alert. Your opponent the devil is prowling like a roaring lion looking for someone to devour. Resist him, solid in your faith.

Responsory

Into your hands, Lord, I commend my spirit.
—Into your hands, Lord, I commend my spirit.

You have redeemed us, Lord God of truth.
—I commend my spirit.

Glory to the Father, and to the Son,
     and to the Holy Spirit.
—Into your hands, Lord, I commend my spirit.

Gospel
Canticle

Ant. **Protect us, Lord, as we stay awake; watch over us as we sleep, that awake, we may keep watch with Christ, and asleep, rest in his peace.**

Canticle of
Simeon
Luke 2:29–32

Lord, + now you let your servant go in peace;
your word has been fulfilled:
my own eyes have seen the salvation
which you have prepared in the sight of
     every people:
a light to reveal you to the nations
and the glory of your people Israel.

Glory to the Father, and to the Son,
     and to the Holy Spirit:
—as it was in the beginning, is now,
     and will be for ever. Amen.

Ant.   **Protect us, Lord, as we stay awake; watch over us as we sleep, that awake, we may keep watch with Christ, and asleep, rest in his peace.**

Concluding
Prayer

Let us pray.
Lord,
fill this night with your radiance.
May we sleep in peace and rise with joy
to welcome the light of a new day in
    your name.
We ask this through Christ our Lord.
—Amen.

Blessing

May the all-powerful Lord
grant us a restful night
and a peaceful death.
—Amen.

Marian
Antiphon

Sing the "Salve Regina," found on p. 700, or pray a Hail Mary.

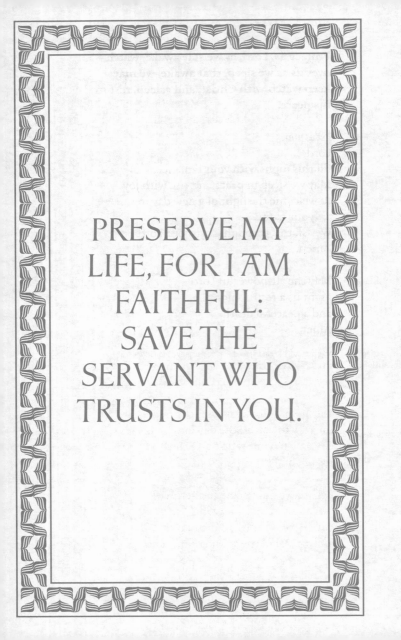

PRESERVE MY
LIFE, FOR I AM
FAITHFUL:
SAVE THE
SERVANT WHO
TRUSTS IN YOU.

Wednesday, August 14, 2024
St. Maximilian Kolbe

MORNING PRAYER————————

God, + come to my assistance.
—Lord, make haste to help me.

Glory to the Father, and to the Son,
    and to the Holy Spirit:
—as it was in the beginning, is now,
    and will be for ever. Amen. Alleluia.

Hymn   *Blessed Feasts of Blessed Martyrs, p. 682*

Psalmody   Ant. 1 **Give joy to your servant, Lord; to you I lift up my heart.**

Psalm 86   Turn your ear, O Lord, and give answer
for I am poor and needy.
Preserve my life, for I am faithful:
save the servant who trusts in you.

You are my God, have mercy on me, Lord,
for I cry to you all the day long.
Give joy to your servant, O Lord,
for to you I lift up my soul.

O Lord, you are good and forgiving,
full of love to all who call.
Give heed, O Lord, to my prayer
and attend to the sound of my voice.

In the day of distress I will call
and surely you will reply.
Among the gods there is none like you,
    O Lord;
nor work to compare with yours.

All the nations shall come to adore you
and glorify your name, O Lord:
for you are great and do marvelous deeds,
you who alone are God.

Show me, Lord, your way
so that I may walk in your truth.
Guide my heart to fear your name.

I will praise you, Lord my God,
    with all my heart
and glorify your name for ever;
for your love to me has been great:
you have saved me from the depths of
    the grave.

The proud have risen against me;
ruthless men seek my life:
to you they pay no heed.

But you, God of mercy and compassion,
slow to anger, O Lord,
abounding in love and truth,
turn and take pity on me.

O give your strength to your servant
and save your handmaid's son.
Show me a sign of your favor
that my foes may see to their shame
that you console me and give me your help.

Glory to the Father, and to the Son,
    and to the Holy Spirit:
—as it was in the beginning, is now,
and will be for ever. Amen.

Ant.   **Give joy to your servant, Lord; to you I lift
up my heart.**

Ant. 2   **Blessed is the upright man, who speaks
the truth.**

Canticle: Hear, you who are far off,
Isaiah 33:13–16   what I have done;
you who are near,
acknowledge my might.

On Zion sinners are in dread,
trembling grips the impious;
"Who of us can live with the consuming fire?
Who of us can live with the
    everlasting flames?"

He who practices virtue and speaks honestly,
who spurns what is gained by oppression,
brushing his hands
free of contact with a bribe,
stopping his ears lest he hear of bloodshed,
closing his eyes lest he look on evil.

He shall dwell on the heights,
his stronghold shall be the rocky fastness,
his food and drink
in steady supply.

Glory to the Father, and to the Son,
    and to the Holy Spirit:
—as it was in the beginning, is now,
and will be for ever. Amen.

Ant.   **Blessed is the upright man, who speaks
          the truth.**

Ant. 3   **Let us celebrate with joy in the presence of
          our Lord and King.**

Psalm 98 Sing a new song to the Lord
          for he has worked wonders.
          His right hand and his holy arm
          have brought salvation.

          The Lord has made known his salvation;
          has shown his justice to the nations.
          He has remembered his truth and love
          for the house of Israel.

          All the ends of the earth have seen
          the salvation of our God.
          Shout to the Lord, all the earth,
          ring out your joy.

          Sing psalms to the Lord with the harp
          with the sound of music.
          With trumpets and the sound of the horn
          acclaim the King, the Lord.

Let the sea and all within it thunder;
the world, and all its peoples.
Let the rivers clap their hands
and the hills ring out their joy.

Rejoice at the presence of the Lord,
for he comes to rule the earth.
He will rule the world with justice
and the peoples with fairness.

Glory to the Father, and to the Son,
     and to the Holy Spirit:
—as it was in the beginning, is now,
and will be for ever. Amen.

Ant.   **Let us celebrate with joy in the presence of
our Lord and King.**

Reading
2 Corinthians
1:3–5

Praised be God, the Father of our Lord Jesus
Christ, the Father of mercies, and the God
of all consolation! He comforts us in all our
afflictions and thus enables us to comfort
those who are in trouble, with the same
consolation we have received from him.
As we have shared much in the suffering
of Christ, so through Christ do we share
abundantly in his consolation.

Responsory The Lord is my strength, and I shall sing
     his praise.
—The Lord is my strength, and I shall sing
     his praise.

The Lord is my savior,
—and I shall sing his praise.

305

Glory to the Father, and to the Son,
  and to the Holy Spirit.
—The Lord is my strength, and I shall sing
  his praise.

**Gospel
Canticle**

Ant. **Christ will be exalted in me whether I
live or die. For to me to live is Christ and
to die is gain.**

*Canticle of
Zechariah
Luke 1:68–79*

Blessed + be the Lord, the God of Israel;
he has come to his people and set them free.

He has raised up for us a mighty savior,
born of the house of his servant David.

Through his holy prophets he
    promised of old
that he would save us from our enemies,
from the hands of all who hate us.

He promised to show mercy to our fathers
and to remember his holy covenant.

This was the oath he swore to our
    father Abraham:
to set us free from the hands of our enemies,
free to worship him without fear,
holy and righteous in his sight
    all the days of our life.

You, my child, shall be called the prophet of
    the Most High;
for you will go before the Lord to
    prepare his way,
to give his people knowledge of salvation
by the forgiveness of their sins.

In the tender compassion of our God
the dawn from on high shall break upon us,
to shine on those who dwell in darkness and
    the shadow of death,
and to guide our feet into the way of peace.

Glory to the Father, and to the Son,
    and to the Holy Spirit:
—as it was in the beginning, is now,
    and will be for ever. Amen.

Ant.   **Christ will be exalted in me whether I live
or die. For to me to live is Christ and to
die is gain.**

Intercessions   Our Savior's faithfulness is mirrored in the
fidelity of his witnesses who shed their
blood for the word of God. Let us praise
him in remembrance of them:
You redeemed us by your blood.

Your martyrs freely embraced death in
    bearing witness to the faith,
—give us the true freedom of the Spirit, O Lord.

Your martyrs professed their faith by
    shedding their blood,
—give us a faith, O Lord, that is constant and pure.

Your martyrs followed in your footsteps by
    carrying the cross,
—help us to endure courageously the
    misfortunes of life.

Your martyrs washed their garments in the
    blood of the Lamb,
—help us to avoid the weaknesses of the flesh
    and worldly allurements.

The Lord's
Prayer

Our Father, who art in heaven,
hallowed be thy name;
thy kingdom come,
thy will be done
on earth as it is in heaven.
Give us this day our daily bread,
and forgive us our trespasses,
as we forgive those who trespass against us;
and lead us not into temptation,
but deliver us from evil.

Pater noster, qui es in cælis:
sanctificetur nomen tuum;
adveniat regnum tuum;
fiat voluntas tua,
sicut in cælo, et in terra.
Panem nostrum cotidianum da nobis hodie;
et dimitte nobis debita nostra,
sicut et nos dimittimus debitoribus nostris;
et ne nos inducas in tentationem;
sed libera nos a malo.

Concluding Prayer

Gracious God,
you filled your priest and martyr,
Saint Maximilian Kolbe,
with zeal for your house
and love for his neighbor.
Through the prayers of this devoted servant
    of Mary Immaculate,
grant that in our efforts to serve others for
    your glory
we too may become like Christ your Son,
who loved his own in the world even
    to the end,
and now lives and reigns with you and
    the Holy Spirit,
God, for ever and ever.
—Amen.

Dismissal

If praying individually, or in a group without a priest or deacon:

May the Lord + bless us,
protect us from all evil
and bring us to everlasting life.
—Amen.

If praying with a priest or deacon, he dismisses the people:

The Lord be with you.
—And with your spirit.

May almighty God bless you,
the Father, and the Son, + and the Holy Spirit.
—Amen.

Go in peace.
—Thanks be to God.

EVENING PRAYER————————

BEGINS THE SOLEMNITY OF THE ASSUMPTION OF THE
BLESSED VIRGIN MARY

God, + come to my assistance.
—Lord, make haste to help me.

Glory to the Father, and to the Son,
    and to the Holy Spirit:
—as it was in the beginning, is now,
    and will be for ever. Amen. Alleluia.

Hymn	*The Saints of God!, p. 702*
Psalmody	Ant. 1 **Christ ascended into heaven and prepared an everlasting place for his immaculate Mother, alleluia.**
Psalm 113	

Praise, O servants of the Lord,
praise the name of the Lord!
May the name of the Lord be blessed
both now and for evermore!
From the rising of the sun to its setting
praised be the name of the Lord!

High above all nations is the Lord,
above the heavens his glory.
Who is like the Lord, our God,
who has risen on high to his throne
yet stoops from the heights to look down,
to look down upon heaven and earth?

From the dust he lifts up the lowly,
from his misery he raises the poor
to set him in the company of princes,
yes, with the princes of his people.
To the childless wife he gives a home
and gladdens her heart with children.

Glory to the Father, and to the Son,
    and to the Holy Spirit:
—as it was in the beginning, is now,
    and will be for ever. Amen.

Ant.   **Christ ascended into heaven and prepared
an everlasting place for his immaculate
Mother, alleluia.**

Ant. 2   **Through Eve the gates of heaven were
closed to all mankind; through the
Virgin Mother they were opened wide
again, alleluia.**

Psalm 147:12–20   O praise the Lord, Jerusalem!
Zion, praise your God!

He has strengthened the bars of your gates,
he has blessed the children within you.
He established peace on your borders,
he feeds you with finest wheat.

He sends out his word to the earth
and swiftly runs his command.
He showers down snow white as wool,
he scatters hoar-frost like ashes.

He hurls down hailstones like crumbs.
The waters are frozen at his touch;
he sends forth his word and it melts them:
at the breath of his mouth the waters flow.

He makes his word known to Jacob,
to Israel his laws and decrees.
He has not dealt thus with other nations;
he has not taught them his decrees.

Glory to the Father, and to the Son,
    and to the Holy Spirit:
—as it was in the beginning, is now,
and will be for ever. Amen.

Ant.

**Through Eve the gates of heaven were
closed to all mankind; through the
Virgin Mother they were opened wide
again, alleluia.**

Ant. 3

**The Virgin Mary has been exalted above
all the heavens; come, let all men glorify
Christ the King, whose kingdom will
endure for ever, alleluia.**

Canticle:
Ephesians
1:3–10

Praised be the God and Father
of our Lord Jesus Christ,
who has bestowed on us in Christ
every spiritual blessing in the heavens.

God chose us in him
before the world began,
to be holy
and blameless in his sight.

He predestined us
to be his adopted sons through Jesus Christ,
such was his will and pleasure,
that all might praise the glorious favor
he has bestowed on us in his beloved.

In him and through his blood, we have
        been redeemed,
and our sins forgiven,
so immeasurably generous
is God's favor to us.

God has given us the wisdom
to understand fully the mystery,
the plan he was pleased
to decree in Christ.

A plan to be carried out
in Christ, in the fullness of time,
to bring all things into one in him,
in the heavens and on earth.

Glory to the Father, and to the Son,
        and to the Holy Spirit:
—as it was in the beginning, is now,
and will be for ever. Amen.

Ant.   **The Virgin Mary has been exalted above
all the heavens; come, let all men glorify
Christ the King, whose kingdom will
endure for ever, alleluia.**

Reading
Romans 8:30

Those God predestined he likewise called;
those he called he also justified; and those he
justified he in turn glorified.

Responsory

As Mary is taken up to heaven,
   the angels of God rejoice.
—As Mary is taken up to heaven,
   the angels of God rejoice.

They worship the Lord and sing his praises.
—The angels of God rejoice.

Glory to the Father, and to the Son,
   and to the Holy Spirit.
—As Mary is taken up to heaven,
   the angels of God rejoice.

**Gospel
Canticle**

Ant. **All generations will call me blessed:
the Almighty has done great things for
me, alleluia.**

*Canticle of
Mary
Luke 1:46–55*

My + soul proclaims the greatness of the Lord,
my spirit rejoices in God my Savior
for he has looked with favor on his
      lowly servant.

From this day all generations will
      call me blessed:
the Almighty has done great things for me,
and holy is his Name.

He has mercy on those who fear him
in every generation.

He has shown the strength of his arm,
he has scattered the proud in their conceit.

He has cast down the mighty from
    their thrones,
and has lifted up the lowly.

He has filled the hungry with good things,
and the rich he has sent away empty.

He has come to the help of his servant Israel
for he has remembered his promise of mercy,
the promise he made to our fathers,
to Abraham and his children for ever.

Glory to the Father, and to the Son,
    and to the Holy Spirit:
—as it was in the beginning, is now,
and will be for ever. Amen.

Ant. **All generations will call me blessed:
the Almighty has done great things for
me, alleluia.**

Intercessions Let us praise God our almighty Father, who
    wished that Mary, his Son's mother, be
    celebrated by each generation. Now in
    need we ask:
Mary, full of grace, intercede for us.

O God, worker of miracles, you made the
    immaculate Virgin Mary share, body and
    soul, in your Son's glory in heaven,
—direct the hearts of your children to that
    same glory.

You made Mary our mother. Through
her intercession grant strength to the
weak, comfort to the sorrowing, pardon
to sinners,
—salvation and peace to all.

You made Mary full of grace,
—grant all men the joyful abundance of
your grace.

Make your Church of one mind and one
heart in love,
—and help all those who believe to be one in
prayer with Mary, the mother of Jesus.

You crowned Mary queen of heaven,
—may all the dead rejoice in your kingdom
with the saints for ever.

The Lord's
Prayer

Our Father, who art in heaven,
hallowed be thy name;
thy kingdom come,
thy will be done
on earth as it is in heaven.
Give us this day our daily bread,
and forgive us our trespasses,
as we forgive those who trespass against us;
and lead us not into temptation,
but deliver us from evil.

Pater noster, qui es in cælis:
sanctificetur nomen tuum;
adveniat regnum tuum;
fiat voluntas tua,
sicut in cælo, et in terra.
Panem nostrum cotidianum da nobis hodie;
et dimitte nobis debita nostra,
sicut et nos dimittimus debitoribus nostris;
et ne nos inducas in tentationem;
sed libera nos a malo.

Concluding Prayer

Almighty God,
you gave a humble virgin
the privilege of being the mother of your Son,
and crowned her with the glory of heaven.
May the prayers of the Virgin Mary
bring us to the salvation of Christ
and raise us up to eternal life.
We ask this through our Lord Jesus Christ,
    your Son,
who lives and reigns with you and
    the Holy Spirit,
God, for ever and ever.
—Amen.

Dismissal

If praying individually, or in a group without a priest or deacon:

May the Lord + bless us,
protect us from all evil
and bring us to everlasting life.
—Amen.

If praying with a priest or deacon, he dismisses the people:

The Lord be with you.
—And with your spirit.

May almighty God bless you,
the Father, and the Son, + and the Holy Spirit.
—Amen.

Go in peace.
—Thanks be to God.

NIGHT PRAYER———————————————

God, + come to my assistance.
—Lord, make haste to help me.

Glory to the Father, and to the Son,
and to the Holy Spirit:
—as it was in the beginning, is now,
and will be for ever. Amen. Alleluia.

Examen   *An optional brief examination of conscience may be made. Call to mind your*
sins and failings this day.

Hymn   *O Gladsome Light, p. 696*

Psalmody   Ant. 1 **Have mercy, Lord, and hear my prayer.**

Psalm 4   When I call, answer me, O God of justice;
from anguish you released me; have mercy
and hear me!

O men, how long will your hearts be closed,
will you love what is futile and seek
what is false?

It is the Lord who grants favors to those
whom he loves;
the Lord hears me whenever I call him.

Fear him; do not sin: ponder on your bed
and be still.
Make justice your sacrifice and trust
in the Lord.

"What can bring us happiness?" many say.
Let the light of your face shine on us, O Lord.

You have put into my heart a greater joy
than they have from abundance of corn
and new wine.

I will lie down in peace and sleep
comes at once
for you alone, Lord, make me dwell in safety.

Glory to the Father, and to the Son,
and to the Holy Spirit:
—as it was in the beginning, is now,
and will be for ever. Amen.

Ant. **Have mercy, Lord, and hear my prayer.**

Ant. 2 **In the silent hours of night, bless the Lord.**

Psalm 134 O come, bless the Lord,
all you who serve the Lord,
who stand in the house of the Lord,
in the courts of the house of our God.

Lift up your hands to the holy place
and bless the Lord through the night.

May the Lord bless you from Zion,
he who made both heaven and earth.

Glory to the Father, and to the Son,
   and to the Holy Spirit:
—as it was in the beginning, is now,
   and will be for ever. Amen.

Ant.   **In the silent hours of night, bless the Lord.**

Reading
Deuteronomy
6:4–7

Hear, O Israel! The Lord is our God, the Lord
alone! Therefore, you shall love the Lord,
your God, with all your heart, and with all
your soul, and with all your strength. Take
to heart these words which I enjoin on you
today. Drill them into your children. Speak
of them at home and abroad, whether you
are busy or at rest.

Responsory   Into your hands, Lord, I commend my spirit.
—Into your hands, Lord, I commend my spirit.

You have redeemed us, Lord God of truth.
—I commend my spirit.

Glory to the Father, and to the Son,
   and to the Holy Spirit.
—Into your hands, Lord, I commend my spirit.

Gospel
Canticle

Ant.   **Protect us, Lord, as we stay awake;
watch over us as we sleep, that awake, we
may keep watch with Christ, and asleep,
rest in his peace.**

Canticle of Simeon
Luke 2:29–32

Lord, + now you let your servant go in peace;
your word has been fulfilled:
my own eyes have seen the salvation
which you have prepared in the sight of
    every people:
a light to reveal you to the nations
and the glory of your people Israel.

Glory to the Father, and to the Son,
    and to the Holy Spirit:
—as it was in the beginning, is now,
and will be for ever. Amen.

Ant.

**Protect us, Lord, as we stay awake; watch
over us as we sleep, that awake, we may
keep watch with Christ, and asleep, rest in
his peace.**

Concluding Prayer

Let us pray.
Lord,
we beg you to visit this house
and banish from it
all the deadly power of the enemy.
May your holy angels dwell here
to keep us in peace,
and may your blessing be upon us always.
We ask this through Christ our Lord.
—Amen.

Blessing

May the all-powerful Lord
grant us a restful night
and a peaceful death.
—Amen.

Marian Antiphon

Sing the "Ave Regina Cælorum," found on p. 680, or pray a Hail Mary.

THURSDAY, AUGUST 15, 2024 THE SOLEMNITY of the ASSUMPTION of the BLESSED VIRGIN MARY

MORNING PRAYER ──────────

God, + come to my assistance.
—Lord, make haste to help me.

Glory to the Father, and to the Son,
    and to the Holy Spirit:
—as it was in the beginning, is now,
and will be for ever. Amen. Alleluia.

Hymn   *Hail, Holy Queen, p. 685*

Psalmody   Ant. 1 **Blessed are you, O Mary, for the
world's salvation came forth through
you; now in glory, you rejoice for ever
with the Lord.**

Psalm 63:2–9   O God, you are my God, for you I long;
for you my soul is thirsting.
My body pines for you
like a dry, weary land without water.
So I gaze on you in the sanctuary
to see your strength and your glory.

For your love is better than life,
my lips will speak your praise.
So I will bless you all my life,
in your name I will lift up my hands.
My soul shall be filled as with a banquet,
my mouth shall praise you with joy.

On my bed I remember you.
On you I muse through the night
for you have been my help;
in the shadow of your wings I rejoice.
My soul clings to you;
your right hand holds me fast.

Glory to the Father, and to the Son,
    and to the Holy Spirit:
—as it was in the beginning, is now,
and will be for ever. Amen.

Ant.   **Blessed are you, O Mary, for the world's
salvation came forth through you; now in
glory, you rejoice for ever with the Lord.**

Ant. 2   **The Virgin Mary is exalted above the choirs
of angels; let all believers rejoice and
bless the Lord.**

Canticle: Bless the Lord, all you works of the Lord.
Daniel   Praise and exalt him above all forever.
3:57–88, 56 Angels of the Lord, bless the Lord.
You heavens, bless the Lord.
All you waters above the heavens,
    bless the Lord.
All you hosts of the Lord, bless the Lord.
Sun and moon, bless the Lord.
Stars of heaven, bless the Lord.

Every shower and dew, bless the Lord.
All you winds, bless the Lord.
Fire and heat, bless the Lord.
Cold and chill, bless the Lord.
Dew and rain, bless the Lord.
Frost and chill, bless the Lord.
Ice and snow, bless the Lord.
Nights and days, bless the Lord.
Light and darkness, bless the Lord.
Lightnings and clouds, bless the Lord.

Let the earth bless the Lord.
Praise and exalt him above all forever.
Mountains and hills, bless the Lord.
Everything growing from the earth,
    bless the Lord.
You springs, bless the Lord.
Seas and rivers, bless the Lord.
You dolphins and all water creatures,
    bless the Lord.
All you birds of the air, bless the Lord.
All you beasts, wild and tame, bless the Lord.
You sons of men, bless the Lord.

O Israel, bless the Lord.
Praise and exalt him above all forever.
Priests of the Lord, bless the Lord.
Servants of the Lord, bless the Lord.
Spirits and souls of the just, bless the Lord.
Holy men of humble heart, bless the Lord.
Hananiah, Azariah, Mishael, bless the Lord.
Praise and exalt him above all forever.

Let us bless the Father, and the Son,
    and the Holy Spirit.
Let us praise and exalt him above all forever.
Blessed are you, Lord, in the firmament
    of heaven.
Praiseworthy and glorious and exalted above
    all forever.

Ant. **The Virgin Mary is exalted above the choirs
of angels; let all believers rejoice and
bless the Lord.**

Ant. 3   **The Lord has made you so glorious that**
         your praise will never cease to resound
         among men.

Psalm 149   Sing a new song to the Lord,
            his praise in the assembly of the faithful.
            Let Israel rejoice in its maker,
            let Zion's sons exult in their king.
            Let them praise his name with dancing
            and make music with timbrel and harp.

            For the Lord takes delight in his people.
            He crowns the poor with salvation.
            Let the faithful rejoice in their glory,
            shout for joy and take their rest.
            Let the praise of God be on their lips
            and a two-edged sword in their hand,

            to deal out vengeance to the nations
            and punishment on all the peoples;
            to bind their kings in chains
            and their nobles in fetters of iron;
            to carry out the sentence pre-ordained;
            this honor is for all his faithful.

            Glory to the Father, and to the Son,
                and to the Holy Spirit:
         —as it was in the beginning, is now,
            and will be for ever. Amen.

Ant.   **The Lord has made you so glorious that**
         your praise will never cease to resound
         among men.

Reading
See Isaiah 61:10

I rejoice heartily in the Lord,
    in my God is the joy of my soul;
For he has clothed me with a robe of salvation,
    and wrapped me in a mantle of justice,
    like a bride bedecked with her jewels.

Responsory

Today the Virgin Mary was taken up
    to heaven.
—Today the Virgin Mary was taken up
    to heaven.

For all eternity she shares the victory of Christ.
—The Virgin Mary was taken up to heaven.

Glory to the Father, and to the Son,
    and to the Holy Spirit.
—Today the Virgin Mary was taken up
    to heaven.

Gospel
Canticle

Ant. **This daughter of Jerusalem is lovely and beautiful as she ascends to heaven like the rising sun at daybreak.**

Canticle of Zechariah Luke 1:68–79

Blessed + be the Lord, the God of Israel;
he has come to his people and set them free.

He has raised up for us a mighty savior,
born of the house of his servant David.

Through his holy prophets he
    promised of old
that he would save us from our enemies,
from the hands of all who hate us.

He promised to show mercy to our fathers
and to remember his holy covenant.

This was the oath he swore to our
    father Abraham:
to set us free from the hands of our enemies,
free to worship him without fear,
holy and righteous in his sight
    all the days of our life.

You, my child, shall be called the prophet of
    the Most High;
for you will go before the Lord to
    prepare his way,
to give his people knowledge of salvation
by the forgiveness of their sins.

In the tender compassion of our God
the dawn from on high shall break upon us,
to shine on those who dwell in darkness and
    the shadow of death,
and to guide our feet into the way of peace.

Glory to the Father, and to the Son,
    and to the Holy Spirit:
—as it was in the beginning, is now,
    and will be for ever. Amen.

Ant.   **This daughter of Jerusalem is lovely and
beautiful as she ascends to heaven like the
rising sun at daybreak.**

Let us glorify our Savior, who chose
the Virgin Mary for his mother. Let
us ask him:
May your mother intercede for us, Lord.

Eternal Word, you chose Mary as the
uncorrupted ark of your dwelling place,
—free us from the corruption of sin.

You are our redeemer, who made the
immaculate Virgin Mary your purest
home and the sanctuary of the Holy Spirit,
—make us temples of your Spirit for ever.

King of kings, you lifted up your mother,
body and soul, into heaven,
—help us to fix our thoughts on things above.

Lord of heaven and earth, you crowned Mary
and set her at your right hand as queen,
—make us worthy to share this glory.

Our Father, who art in heaven,
hallowed be thy name;
thy kingdom come,
thy will be done
on earth as it is in heaven.
Give us this day our daily bread,
and forgive us our trespasses,
as we forgive those who trespass against us;
and lead us not into temptation,
but deliver us from evil.

Pater noster, qui es in cælis:
sanctificetur nomen tuum;
adveniat regnum tuum;
fiat voluntas tua,
sicut in cælo, et in terra.
Panem nostrum cotidianum da nobis hodie;
et dimitte nobis debita nostra,
sicut et nos dimittimus debitoribus nostris;
et ne nos inducas in tentationem;
sed libera nos a malo.

Concluding
Prayer

All-powerful and ever-living God,
you raised the sinless Virgin Mary,
mother of your Son,
body and soul to the glory of heaven.
May we see heaven as our final goal
and come to share her glory.
We ask this through our Lord Jesus Christ,
your Son,
who lives and reigns with you and
the Holy Spirit,
God, for ever and ever.
—Amen.

Dismissal   *If praying individually, or in a group without a priest or deacon:*

May the Lord + bless us,
protect us from all evil
and bring us to everlasting life.
—Amen.

If praying with a priest or deacon, he dismisses the people:

The Lord be with you.
—And with your spirit.

May almighty God bless you,
the Father, and the Son, + and the Holy Spirit.
—Amen.

Go in peace.
—Thanks be to God.

EVENING PRAYER

God, + come to my assistance.
—Lord, make haste to help me.

Glory to the Father, and to the Son,
and to the Holy Spirit:
—as it was in the beginning, is now,
and will be for ever. Amen. Alleluia.

Hymn   *The Saints of God!, p. 702*

Psalmody   Ant. 1 **Mary has been taken up to heaven; the angels rejoice. They bless the Lord and sing his praises.**

Psalm 122   I rejoiced when I heard them say:
"Let us go to God's house."
And now our feet are standing
within your gates, O Jerusalem.

Jerusalem is built as a city
strongly compact.
It is there that the tribes go up,
the tribes of the Lord.

For Israel's law it is,
there to praise the Lord's name.
There were set the thrones of judgment
of the house of David.

For the peace of Jerusalem pray:
"Peace be to your homes!
May peace reign in your walls,
in your palaces, peace!"

For love of my brethren and friends
I say: "Peace upon you!"
For love of the house of the Lord
I will ask for your good.

Glory to the Father, and to the Son,
    and to the Holy Spirit:
—as it was in the beginning, is now,
and will be for ever. Amen.

Ant.   **Mary has been taken up to heaven; the
angels rejoice. They bless the Lord and sing
his praises.**

Ant. 2   **The Virgin Mary was taken up to the
heavenly bridal chamber where the King of
kings is seated on a starry throne.**

Psalm 127

If the Lord does not build the house,
in vain do its builders labor;
if the Lord does not watch over the city,
in vain does the watchman keep vigil.

In vain is your earlier rising,
your going later to rest,
you who toil for the bread you eat:
when he pours gifts on his beloved while
    they slumber.

Truly sons are a gift from the Lord,
a blessing, the fruit of the womb.
Indeed the sons of youth
are like arrows in the hand of a warrior.

O the happiness of the man
who has filled his quiver with these arrows!
He will have no cause for shame
when he disputes with his foes in
    the gateways.

Glory to the Father, and to the Son,
    and to the Holy Spirit:
—as it was in the beginning, is now,
and will be for ever. Amen.

Ant. **The Virgin Mary was taken up to the heavenly bridal chamber where the King of kings is seated on a starry throne.**

Ant. 3 **We share the fruit of life through you, O daughter blessed by the Lord.**

Canticle:
Ephesians
1:3–10

Praised be the God and Father
of our Lord Jesus Christ,
who bestowed on us in Christ
every spiritual blessing in the heavens.

God chose us in him
before the world began,
to be holy
and blameless in his sight.

He predestined us
to be his adopted sons through Jesus Christ,
such was his will and pleasure,
that all might praise the glorious favor
he has bestowed on us in his beloved.

In him and through his blood,
    we have been redeemed,
and our sins forgiven,
so immeasurably generous
is God's favor to us.

God has given us the wisdom
to understand fully the mystery,
the plan he was pleased
to decree in Christ.

A plan to be carried out
in Christ, in the fullness of time,
to bring all things into one in him,
in the heavens and on earth.

Glory to the Father, and to the Son,
     and to the Holy Spirit:
—as it was in the beginning, is now,
     and will be for ever. Amen.

Ant. **We share the fruit of life through you,**
O daughter blessed by the Lord.

Reading
1 Corinthians
15:22–23

Just as in Adam all die, so in Christ all will
come to life again, but each one in proper
order: Christ the first fruits and then, at his
coming, all those who belong to him.

Responsory   The Virgin Mary is exalted above the choirs
                     of angels.
              —The Virgin Mary is exalted above the choirs
                     of angels.

Blessed is the Lord who has raised her up.
—Above the choirs of angels.

Glory to the Father, and to the Son,
     and to the Holy Spirit.
—The Virgin Mary is exalted above the choirs
     of angels.

Gospel
Canticle

Ant. **Today the Virgin Mary was taken up**
to heaven; rejoice, for she reigns with
Christ for ever.

Canticle of
Mary
Luke 1:46–55

My + soul proclaims the greatness of the Lord,
my spirit rejoices in God my Savior
for he has looked with favor on his
        lowly servant.

From this day all generations will
        call me blessed:
the Almighty has done great things for me,
and holy is his Name.

He has mercy on those who fear him
in every generation.

He has shown the strength of his arm,
he has scattered the proud in their conceit.

He has cast down the mighty from
        their thrones,
and has lifted up the lowly.

He has filled the hungry with good things,
and the rich he has sent away empty.

He has come to the help of his servant Israel
for he has remembered his promise of mercy,
the promise he made to our fathers,
to Abraham and his children for ever.

Glory to the Father, and to the Son,
        and to the Holy Spirit:
—as it was in the beginning, is now,
    and will be for ever. Amen.

Ant.   **Today the Virgin Mary was taken up
to heaven; rejoice, for she reigns with
Christ for ever.**

Intercessions   Let us praise God our almighty Father, who
wished that Mary, his Son's mother, be
celebrated by each generation. Now in
need we ask:
Mary, full of grace, intercede for us.

O God, worker of miracles, you made the
Immaculate Virgin Mary share, body and
soul, in your Son's glory in heaven,
—direct the hearts of your children to that
same glory.

You made Mary our mother. Through
her intercession grant strength to the
weak, comfort to the sorrowing, pardon
to sinners,
—salvation and peace to all.

You made Mary full of grace,
—grant all men the joyful abundance of
your grace.

Make your Church of one mind and one
heart in love,
—and help all those who believe to be one in
prayer with Mary, the mother of Jesus.

You crowned Mary queen of heaven,
—may all the dead rejoice in your kingdom
with the saints for ever.

The Lord's
Prayer

Our Father, who art in heaven,
hallowed be thy name;
thy kingdom come,
thy will be done
on earth as it is in heaven.
Give us this day our daily bread,
and forgive us our trespasses,
as we forgive those who trespass against us;
and lead us not into temptation,
but deliver us from evil.

Pater noster, qui es in cælis:
sanctificetur nomen tuum;
adveniat regnum tuum;
fiat voluntas tua,
sicut in cælo, et in terra.
Panem nostrum cotidianum da nobis hodie;
et dimitte nobis debita nostra,
sicut et nos dimittimus debitoribus nostris;
et ne nos inducas in tentationem;
sed libera nos a malo.

Concluding
Prayer

All-powerful and ever-living God,
you raised the sinless Virgin Mary,
mother of your Son,
body and soul to the glory of heaven.
May we see heaven as our final goal
and come to share her glory.
We ask this through our Lord Jesus Christ,
your Son,
who lives and reigns with you and
the Holy Spirit,
God, for ever and ever.
—Amen.

Dismissal   *If praying individually, or in a group without a priest or deacon:*

May the Lord + bless us,
protect us from all evil
and bring us to everlasting life.
—Amen.

If praying with a priest or deacon, he dismisses the people:

The Lord be with you.
—And with your spirit.

May almighty God bless you,
the Father, and the Son, + and the Holy Spirit.
—Amen.

Go in peace.
—Thanks be to God.

NIGHT PRAYER

God, + come to my assistance.
—Lord, make haste to help me.

Glory to the Father, and to the Son,
    and to the Holy Spirit:
—as it was in the beginning, is now,
and will be for ever. Amen. Alleluia.

Examen   *An optional brief examination of conscience may be made. Call to mind your sins and failings this day.*

Hymn   *O Gladsome Light, p. 696*

Psalmody   Ant. **Night holds no terrors for me sleeping under God's wings.**

Psalm 91

He who dwells in the shelter of the Most High
and abides in the shade of the Almighty
says to the Lord: "My refuge,
my stronghold, my God in whom I trust!"

It is he who will free you from the snare
of the fowler who seeks to destroy you;
he will conceal you with his pinions
and under his wings you will find refuge.

You will not fear the terror of the night
nor the arrow that flies by day,
nor the plague that prowls in the darkness
nor the scourge that lays waste at noon.

A thousand may fall at your side,
ten thousand fall at your right,
you, it will never approach;
his faithfulness is buckler and shield.

Your eyes have only to look
to see how the wicked are repaid,
you who have said: "Lord, my refuge!"
and have made the Most High your dwelling.

Upon you no evil shall fall,
no plague approach where you dwell.
For you has he commanded his angels,
to keep you in all your ways.

They shall bear you upon their hands
lest you strike your foot against a stone.
On the lion and the viper you will tread
and trample the young lion and the dragon.

Since he clings to me in love, I will free him;
protect him for he knows my name.
When he calls I shall answer: "I am with you."
I will save him in distress and give him glory.

With length of life I will content him;
I shall let him see my saving power.

Glory to the Father, and to the Son,
    and to the Holy Spirit:
—as it was in the beginning, is now,
and will be for ever. Amen.

Ant. **Night holds no terrors for me sleeping
under God's wings.**

Reading
Revelation
22:4–5

They shall see the Lord face to face and bear
his name on their foreheads. The night shall
be no more. They will need no light from
lamps or the sun, for the Lord God shall give
them light, and they shall reign forever.

Responsory

Into your hands, Lord, I commend my spirit.
—Into your hands, Lord, I commend my spirit.

You have redeemed us, Lord God of truth.
—I commend my spirit.

Glory to the Father, and to the Son,
    and to the Holy Spirit.
—Into your hands, Lord, I commend my spirit.

Gospel
Canticle

Ant. **Protect us, Lord, as we stay awake;
watch over us as we sleep, that awake, we
may keep watch with Christ, and asleep,
rest in his peace.**

Canticle of
Simeon
Luke 2:29–32

Lord, + now you let your servant go in peace;
your word has been fulfilled:
my own eyes have seen the salvation
which you have prepared in the sight of
     every people:
a light to reveal you to the nations
and the glory of your people Israel.

Glory to the Father, and to the Son,
     and to the Holy Spirit:
—as it was in the beginning, is now,
and will be for ever. Amen.

Ant.

**Protect us, Lord, as we stay awake; watch
over us as we sleep, that awake, we may
keep watch with Christ, and asleep, rest in
his peace.**

Concluding
Prayer

Let us pray.
Lord,
we beg you to visit this house
and banish from it
all the deadly power of the enemy.
May your holy angels dwell here
to keep us in peace,
and may your blessing be upon us always.
We ask this through Christ our Lord.
—Amen.

Blessing
May the all-powerful Lord
grant us a restful night
and a peaceful death.
—Amen.

Marian
Antiphon
Sing the "Ave Regina Cælorum," found on p. 680, or pray a Hail Mary.

Friday, August 16, 2024
Friday of the Nineteenth Week in Ordinary Time

MORNING PRAYER

God, + come to my assistance.
—Lord, make haste to help me.

Glory to the Father, and to the Son,
      and to the Holy Spirit:
—as it was in the beginning, is now,
      and will be for ever. Amen. Alleluia.

Hymn
Now That the Sun Is Gleaming Bright, p. 695

Psalmody
Ant. 1 **You alone I have grieved by my sin;
have pity on me, O Lord.**

Psalm 51
Have mercy on me, God, in your kindness.
In your compassion blot out my offense.
O wash me more and more from my guilt
and cleanse me from my sin.

My offenses truly I know them;
my sin is always before me.
Against you, you alone, have I sinned;
what is evil in your sight I have done.

That you may be justified when you
    give sentence
and be without reproach when you judge.
O see, in guilt I was born,
a sinner was I conceived.

Indeed you love truth in the heart;
then in the secret of my heart teach
    me wisdom.
O purify me, then I shall be clean;
O wash me, I shall be whiter than snow.

Make me hear rejoicing and gladness,
that the bones you have crushed may revive.
From my sins turn away your face
and blot out all my guilt.

A pure heart create for me, O God,
put a steadfast spirit within me.
Do not cast me away from your presence,
nor deprive me of your holy spirit.

Give me again the joy of your help;
with a spirit of fervor sustain me,
that I may teach transgressors your ways
and sinners may return to you.

O rescue me, God, my helper,
and my tongue shall ring out your goodness.
O Lord, open my lips
and my mouth shall declare your praise.

For in sacrifice you take no delight,
burnt offering from me you would refuse,
my sacrifice, a contrite spirit.
A humbled, contrite heart you will not spurn.

In your goodness, show favor to Zion:
rebuild the walls of Jerusalem.
Then you will be pleased with lawful sacrifice,
holocausts offered on your altar.

Glory to the Father, and to the Son,
    and to the Holy Spirit:
—as it was in the beginning, is now,
and will be for ever. Amen.

Ant. **You alone I have grieved by my sin; have
pity on me, O Lord.**

Ant. 2 **Truly we know our offenses, Lord, for we
have sinned against you.**

*Canticle:
Jeremiah
14:17–21*

Let my eyes stream with tears
day and night, without rest,
over the great destruction which overwhelms
the virgin daughter of my people,
over her incurable wound.

If I walk out into the field,
look! those slain by the sword;
if I enter the city,
look! those consumed by hunger.
Even the prophet and the priest
forage in a land they know not.

Have you cast Judah off completely?
Is Zion loathsome to you?
Why have you struck us a blow
that cannot be healed?

We wait for peace, to no avail;
for a time of healing, but terror
    comes instead.
We recognize, O Lord, our wickedness,
the guilt of our fathers;
that we have sinned against you.

For your name's sake spurn us not,
disgrace not the throne of your glory;
remember your covenant with us, and
    break it not.

Glory to the Father, and to the Son,
    and to the Holy Spirit:
—as it was in the beginning, is now,
and will be for ever. Amen.

Ant.   **Truly we know our offenses, Lord, for we
have sinned against you.**

Ant. 3   **The Lord is God; we are his people, the
flock he shepherds.**

Psalm 100

Cry out with joy to the Lord, all the earth.
Serve the Lord with gladness.
Come before him, singing for joy.

Know that he, the Lord, is God.
He made us, we belong to him,
we are his people, the sheep of his flock.

Go within his gates, giving thanks.
Enter his courts with songs of praise.
Give thanks to him and bless his name.

Indeed, how good is the Lord,
eternal his merciful love.
He is faithful from age to age.

Glory to the Father, and to the Son,
    and to the Holy Spirit:
—as it was in the beginning, is now,
and will be for ever. Amen.

Ant.

**The Lord is God; we are his people, the
flock he shepherds.**

Reading
2 Corinthians
12:9b–10

I willingly boast of my weakness, that
the power of Christ may rest upon me.
Therefore I am content with weakness,
with mistreatment, with distress, with
persecutions and difficulties for the sake of
Christ; for when I am powerless, it is then
that I am strong.

Responsory   At daybreak, be merciful to me.
              —At daybreak, be merciful to me.

              Make known to me the path that I
                  must walk.
              —Be merciful to me.

              Glory to the Father, and to the Son,
                  and to the Holy Spirit.
              —At daybreak, be merciful to me.

Gospel   Ant. **The Lord has come to his people and
Canticle   set them free.**

Canticle of   Blessed + be the Lord, the God of Israel;
Zechariah   he has come to his people and set them free.
Luke 1:68–79

              He has raised up for us a mighty savior,
              born of the house of his servant David.

              Through his holy prophets he
                  promised of old
              that he would save us from our enemies,
              from the hands of all who hate us.

              He promised to show mercy to our fathers
              and to remember his holy covenant.

              This was the oath he swore to our
                  father Abraham:
              to set us free from the hands of our enemies,
              free to worship him without fear,
              holy and righteous in his sight
                  all the days of our life.

You, my child, shall be called the prophet of
    the Most High;
for you will go before the Lord to
    prepare his way,
to give his people knowledge of salvation
by the forgiveness of their sins.

In the tender compassion of our God
the dawn from on high shall break upon us,
to shine on those who dwell in darkness and
    the shadow of death,
and to guide our feet into the way of peace.

Glory to the Father, and to the Son,
    and to the Holy Spirit:
—as it was in the beginning, is now,
and will be for ever. Amen.

Ant. **The Lord has come to his people and set
them free.**

Intercessions Raising our eyes to Christ, who was born
    and died and rose again for his people, let
    us cry out:
Save those you have redeemed by your blood, Lord.

Blessed are you, Jesus, redeemer of mankind;
    you did not hesitate to undergo your
    passion and death,
—to redeem us by your precious blood.

You promised that you would provide living
    water, the fountain of eternal life,
—pour forth your Spirit upon all men.

You send disciples to preach the Gospel to
    all nations,
—help them to extend the victory of your cross.

You have given the sick and the suffering a
    share in your cross,
—give them patience and strength.

The Lord's
Prayer

Our Father, who art in heaven,
hallowed be thy name;
thy kingdom come,
thy will be done
on earth as it is in heaven.
Give us this day our daily bread,
and forgive us our trespasses,
as we forgive those who trespass against us;
and lead us not into temptation,
but deliver us from evil.

Pater noster, qui es in cælis:
sanctificetur nomen tuum;
adveniat regnum tuum;
fiat voluntas tua,
sicut in cælo, et in terra.
Panem nostrum cotidianum da nobis hodie;
et dimitte nobis debita nostra,
sicut et nos dimittimus debitoribus nostris;
et ne nos inducas in tentationem;
sed libera nos a malo.

Concluding
Prayer

Father all-powerful,
let your radiance dawn in our lives,
that we may walk in the light of your law
with you as our leader.
We ask this through our Lord Jesus Christ,
     your Son,
who lives and reigns with you and
     the Holy Spirit,
God, for ever and ever.
—Amen.

Dismissal

If praying individually, or in a group without a priest or deacon:

May the Lord + bless us,
protect us from all evil
and bring us to everlasting life.
—Amen.

If praying with a priest or deacon, he dismisses the people:

The Lord be with you.
—And with your spirit.

May almighty God bless you,
the Father, and the Son, + and the Holy Spirit.
—Amen.

Go in peace.
—Thanks be to God.

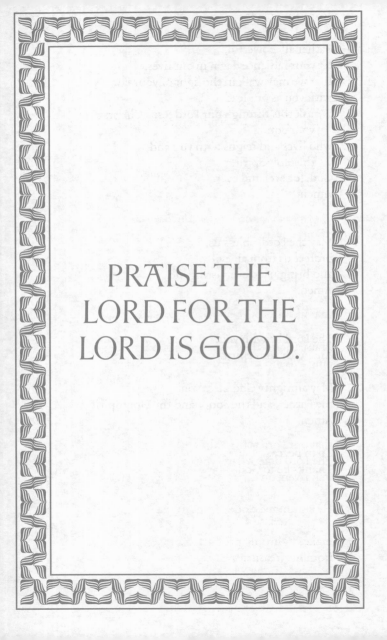

PRAISE THE
LORD FOR THE
LORD IS GOOD.

EVENING PRAYER———————————

God, + come to my assistance.
—Lord, make haste to help me.

Glory to the Father, and to the Son,
    and to the Holy Spirit:
—as it was in the beginning, is now,
    and will be for ever. Amen. Alleluia.

Hymn   *From All That Dwell Below the Skies, p. 684*

Psalmody   Ant. 1 **Great is the Lord, our God,
transcending all other gods.**

Psalm 135   Praise the name of the Lord,
            praise him, servants of the Lord,
            who stand in the house of the Lord
            in the courts of the house of our God.

            Praise the Lord for the Lord is good.
            Sing a psalm to his name for he is loving.
            For the Lord has chosen Jacob for himself
            and Israel for his own possession.

            For I know the Lord is great,
            that our Lord is high above all gods.
            The Lord does whatever he wills,
            in heaven, on earth, in the seas.

            He summons clouds from the ends of
                the earth;
            makes lightning produce the rain;
            from his treasuries he sends forth the wind.

The first-born of the Egyptians he smote,
of man and beast alike.
Signs and wonders he worked
in the midst of your land, O Egypt,
against Pharaoh and all his servants.

Nations in their greatness he struck
and kings in their splendor he slew.
Sihon, king of the Amorites,
Og, the king of Bashan,
and all the kingdoms of Canaan.
He let Israel inherit their land;
on his people their land he bestowed.

Glory to the Father, and to the Son,
    and to the Holy Spirit:
—as it was in the beginning, is now,
and will be for ever. Amen.

Ant.   **Great is the Lord, our God, transcending all
        other gods.**

Ant. 2 **House of Israel, bless the Lord! Sing psalms
        to him, for he is merciful.**

Psalm 135   Lord, your name stands for ever,
(continued) unforgotten from age to age:
        for the Lord does justice for his people;
        the Lord takes pity on his servants.

        Pagan idols are silver and gold,
        the work of human hands.
        They have mouths but they cannot speak;
        they have eyes but they cannot see.

They have ears but they cannot hear;
there is never a breath on their lips.
Their makers will come to be like them
and so will all who trust in them!

Sons of Israel, bless the Lord!
Sons of Aaron, bless the Lord!
Sons of Levi, bless the Lord!
You who fear him, bless the Lord!

From Zion may the Lord be blessed,
he who dwells in Jerusalem!

Glory to the Father, and to the Son,
    and to the Holy Spirit:
—as it was in the beginning, is now,
    and will be for ever. Amen.

Ant. **House of Israel, bless the Lord! Sing psalms
to him, for he is merciful.**

Ant. 3 **All nations will come and worship before
you, O Lord.**

Canticle:
Revelation
15:3-4

Mighty and wonderful are your works,
Lord God Almighty!
Righteous and true are your ways,
O King of the nations!

Who would dare refuse you honor,
or the glory due your name, O Lord?

Since you alone are holy,
all nations shall come
and worship in your presence.
Your mighty deeds are clearly seen.

Glory to the Father, and to the Son,
    and to the Holy Spirit:
—as it was in the beginning, is now,
    and will be for ever. Amen.

Ant. **All nations will come and worship before you, O Lord.**

Reading
James 1:2–4
My brothers, count it pure joy when you are involved in every sort of trial. Realize that when your faith is tested this makes for endurance. Let endurance come to its perfection so that you may be fully mature and lacking in nothing.

Responsory
Christ loved us and washed away our sins,
    in his own blood.
—Christ loved us and washed away our sins,
    in his own blood.

He made us a nation of kings and priests,
—in his own blood.

Glory to the Father, and to the Son,
    and to the Holy Spirit.
—Christ loved us and washed away our sins,
    in his own blood.

Gospel
Canticle

Ant. **The Lord has come to the help of his servants, for he has remembered his promise of mercy.**

Canticle of Mary
Luke 1:46–55

My + soul proclaims the greatness of the Lord,
my spirit rejoices in God my Savior
for he has looked with favor on his
    lowly servant.

From this day all generations will
    call me blessed:
the Almighty has done great things for me,
and holy is his Name.

He has mercy on those who fear him
in every generation.

He has shown the strength of his arm,
he has scattered the proud in their conceit.

He has cast down the mighty from
    their thrones,
and has lifted up the lowly.

He has filled the hungry with good things,
and the rich he has sent away empty.

He has come to the help of his servant Israel
for he has remembered his promise of mercy,
the promise he made to our fathers,
to Abraham and his children for ever.

Glory to the Father, and to the Son,
>and to the Holy Spirit:
—as it was in the beginning, is now,
and will be for ever. Amen.

Ant.   **The Lord has come to the help of his servants, for he has remembered his promise of mercy.**

Intercessions   Because of our sins the Father gave the Lord
Jesus up to death, and for our justification
he raised him up again. Let us pray:
Have mercy on your people, Lord.

Hear our prayers and spare us as we
confess our sins,
—grant us forgiveness and peace.

Your Apostle said: "Where sin abounds, grace
abounds all the more,"
—forgive us our transgressions.

Lord, we have sinned, yet we have also
acknowledged your infinite mercy,
—bring us to conversion.

Save your people from their sins, Lord,
—make them pleasing to you.

You opened Paradise to the thief who
believed in you,
—do not close the gates of heaven to the
faithful departed.

The Lord's
Prayer

Our Father, who art in heaven,
hallowed be thy name;
thy kingdom come,
thy will be done
on earth as it is in heaven.
Give us this day our daily bread,
and forgive us our trespasses,
as we forgive those who trespass against us;
and lead us not into temptation,
but deliver us from evil.

Pater noster, qui es in cælis:
sanctificetur nomen tuum;
adveniat regnum tuum;
fiat voluntas tua,
sicut in cælo, et in terra.
Panem nostrum cotidianum da nobis hodie;
et dimitte nobis debita nostra,
sicut et nos dimittimus debitoribus nostris;
et ne nos inducas in tentationem;
sed libera nos a malo.

Concluding
Prayer

Father,
in your loving plan
Christ your Son became the price of our
    salvation.
May we be united with him in his suffering
so that we may experience
the power of his resurrection
in the kingdom
where he lives and reigns with you and
    the Holy Spirit,
God, for ever and ever.
—Amen.

Dismissal   *If praying individually, or in a group without a priest or deacon:*

May the Lord + bless us,
protect us from all evil
and bring us to everlasting life.
—Amen.

If praying with a priest or deacon, he dismisses the people:

The Lord be with you.
—And with your spirit.

May almighty God bless you,
the Father, and the Son, + and the Holy Spirit.
—Amen.

Go in peace.
—Thanks be to God.

NIGHT PRAYER

God, + come to my assistance.
—Lord, make haste to help me.

Glory to the Father, and to the Son,
    and to the Holy Spirit:
—as it was in the beginning, is now,
and will be for ever. Amen. Alleluia.

Examen   *An optional brief examination of conscience may be made. Call to mind your sins and failings this day.*

Hymn   *O Gladsome Light, p. 696*

Psalmody   Ant. **Day and night I cry to you, my God.**

Psalm 88

Lord my God, I call for help by day;
I cry at night before you.
Let my prayer come into your presence.
O turn your ear to my cry.

For my soul is filled with evils;
my life is on the brink of the grave.
I am reckoned as one in the tomb:
I have reached the end of my strength,

like one alone among the dead;
like the slain lying in their graves;
like those you remember no more,
cut off, as they are, from your hand.

You have laid me in the depths of the tomb,
in places that are dark, in the depths.
Your anger weighs down upon me:
I am drowned beneath your waves.

You have taken away my friends
and made me hateful in their sight.
Imprisoned, I cannot escape;
my eyes are sunken with grief.

I call to you, Lord, all the day long;
to you I stretch out my hands.
Will you work your wonders for the dead?
Will the shades stand and praise you?

Will your love be told in the grave
or your faithfulness among the dead?
Will your wonders be known in the dark
or your justice in the land of oblivion?

As for me, Lord, I call to you for help:
in the morning my prayer comes before you.
Lord, why do you reject me?
Why do you hide your face?

Wretched, close to death from my youth,
I have borne your trials; I am numb.
Your fury has swept down upon me;
your terrors have utterly destroyed me.

They surround me all the day like a flood,
they assail me all together.
Friend and neighbor you have taken away:
my one companion is darkness.

Glory to the Father, and to the Son,
    and to the Holy Spirit:
—as it was in the beginning, is now,
    and will be for ever. Amen.

Ant. **Day and night I cry to you, my God.**

Reading
Jeremiah 14:9a

You are in our midst, O Lord,
    your name we bear:
        do not forsake us, O Lord, our God!

Responsory Into your hands, Lord, I commend my spirit.
—Into your hands, Lord, I commend my spirit.

You have redeemed us, Lord God of truth.
—I commend my spirit.

Glory to the Father, and to the Son,
    and to the Holy Spirit.
—Into your hands, Lord, I commend my spirit.

Gospel
Canticle

Ant. **Protect us, Lord, as we stay awake;
watch over us as we sleep, that awake, we
may keep watch with Christ, and asleep,
rest in his peace.**

Canticle of
Simeon
Luke 2:29–32

Lord, + now you let your servant go in peace;
your word has been fulfilled:
my own eyes have seen the salvation
which you have prepared in the sight of
    every people:
a light to reveal you to the nations
and the glory of your people Israel.

Glory to the Father, and to the Son,
    and to the Holy Spirit:
—as it was in the beginning, is now,
    and will be for ever. Amen.

Ant. **Protect us, Lord, as we stay awake; watch
over us as we sleep, that awake, we may
keep watch with Christ, and asleep, rest in
his peace.**

Concluding
Prayer

Let us pray.
All-powerful God,
keep us united with your Son
in his death and burial
so that we may rise to new life with him,
who lives and reigns for ever and ever.
—Amen.

Blessing   May the all-powerful Lord
             grant us a restful night
             and a peaceful death.
             —Amen.

Marian   *Sing the "Salve Regina," found on p. 700, or pray a Hail Mary.*
Antiphon

Saturday, August 17, 2024
Saturday of the Nineteenth Week
in Ordinary Time

MORNING PRAYER

God, + come to my assistance.
—Lord, make haste to help me.

Glory to the Father, and to the Son,
    and to the Holy Spirit:
—as it was in the beginning, is now,
and will be for ever. Amen. Alleluia.

Hymn   *Now That the Sun Is Gleaming Bright, p. 695*

Psalmody   Ant. 1 **Lord, you are near to us, and all your
             ways are true.**

Psalm   I call with all my heart; Lord, hear me,
119:145–152 I will keep your commands.
             I call upon you, save me
             and I will do your will.

I rise before dawn and cry for help,
I hope in your word.
My eyes watch through the night
to ponder your promise.

In your love hear my voice, O Lord;
give me life by your decrees.
Those who harm me unjustly draw near:
they are far from your law.

But you, O Lord, are close:
your commands are truth.
Long have I known that your will
is established for ever.

Glory to the Father, and to the Son,
    and to the Holy Spirit:
—as it was in the beginning, is now,
and will be for ever. Amen.

Ant.

**Lord, you are near to us, and all your
ways are true.**

Ant. 2

**Wisdom of God, be with me, always at
work in me.**

Canticle:
Wisdom 9:1–6,
9–11

God of my fathers, Lord of mercy,
you who have made all things by your word
and in your wisdom have established man
to rule the creatures produced by you,
to govern the world in holiness and justice,
and to render judgment in integrity of heart:

Give me Wisdom, the attendant at
    your throne,
and reject me not from among your children;
for I am your servant, the son of
    your handmaid,
a man weak and short-lived
and lacking in comprehension of judgment
    and of laws.

Indeed, though one be perfect among the
    sons of men,
if Wisdom, who comes from you, be
    not with him,
he shall be held in no esteem.

Now with you is Wisdom, who knows
    your works
and was present when you made the world;
who understands what is pleasing
    in your eyes
and what is conformable with your commands.

Send her forth from your holy heavens
and from your glorious throne dispatch her
that she may be with me and work with me,
that I may know what is your pleasure.

For she knows and understands all things,
and will guide me discreetly in my affairs
and safeguard me by her glory.

Glory to the Father, and to the Son,
    and to the Holy Spirit:
—as it was in the beginning, is now,
    and will be for ever. Amen.

Ant.   **Wisdom of God, be with me, always at work in me.**

Ant. 3   **The Lord remains faithful to his promise for ever.**

Psalm 117   O praise the Lord, all you nations,
            acclaim him, all you peoples!

            Strong is his love for us;
            he is faithful for ever.

            Glory to the Father, and to the Son,
                and to the Holy Spirit:
            —as it was in the beginning, is now,
                and will be for ever. Amen.

Ant.   **The Lord remains faithful to his promise for ever.**

Reading
Philippians
2:14–15
         In everything you do, act without grumbling
         or arguing; prove yourselves innocent and
         straightforward, children of God beyond
         reproach in the midst of a twisted and
         depraved generation—among whom you
         shine like the stars in the sky.

Responsory   I cry to you, O Lord, for you are my refuge.
             —I cry to you, O Lord, for you are my refuge.

             You are all I desire in the land of the living,
             —for you are my refuge.

Glory to the Father, and to the Son,
and to the Holy Spirit.
—I cry to you, O Lord, for you are my refuge.

**Gospel
Canticle**

Ant. **Lord, shine on those who dwell in
darkness and the shadow of death.**

*Canticle of
Zechariah
Luke 1:68–79*

Blessed + be the Lord, the God of Israel;
he has come to his people and set them free.

He has raised up for us a mighty savior,
born of the house of his servant David.

Through his holy prophets he
promised of old
that he would save us from our enemies,
from the hands of all who hate us.

He promised to show mercy to our fathers
and to remember his holy covenant.

This was the oath he swore to our
father Abraham:
to set us free from the hands of our enemies,
free to worship him without fear,
holy and righteous in his sight
all the days of our life.

You, my child, shall be called the prophet of
the Most High;
for you will go before the Lord to
prepare his way,
to give his people knowledge of salvation
by the forgiveness of their sins.

In the tender compassion of our God
the dawn from on high shall break upon us,
to shine on those who dwell in darkness and
    the shadow of death,
and to guide our feet into the way of peace.

Glory to the Father, and to the Son,
    and to the Holy Spirit:
—as it was in the beginning, is now,
and will be for ever. Amen.

Ant. **Lord, shine on those who dwell in darkness
and the shadow of death.**

Intercessions With confidence let us pray to the Father
    who willed that the Virgin Mary should
    surpass all creatures in heaven and earth:
    Look upon the Mother of your Son and hear our prayer.

We are grateful to you, Father of mercy, for
    you gave us Mary to be our mother and
    our model,
—through her intercession cleanse our hearts.

You inspired Mary to be attentive to your
    word and faithful in your service,
—through her intercession give us the gifts of
    the Holy Spirit.

You strengthened Mary at the foot of the
    cross and filled her with joy at the
    resurrection of your Son,
—through her intercession relieve our distress
    and strengthen our hope.

The Lord's
Prayer

Our Father, who art in heaven,
hallowed be thy name;
thy kingdom come,
thy will be done
on earth as it is in heaven.
Give us this day our daily bread,
and forgive us our trespasses,
as we forgive those who trespass against us;
and lead us not into temptation,
but deliver us from evil.

Pater noster, qui es in cælis:
sanctificetur nomen tuum;
adveniat regnum tuum;
fiat voluntas tua,
sicut in cælo, et in terra.
Panem nostrum cotidianum da nobis hodie;
et dimitte nobis debita nostra,
sicut et nos dimittimus debitoribus nostris;
et ne nos inducas in tentationem;
sed libera nos a malo.

Concluding
Prayer

God our Father,
fountain and source of our salvation,
may we proclaim your glory every day of
    our lives,
that we may sing your praise for ever
    in heaven.
We ask this through our Lord Jesus Christ,
    your Son,
who lives and reigns with you and
    the Holy Spirit,
God, for ever and ever.
—Amen.

Dismissal   *If praying individually, or in a group without a priest or deacon:*

May the Lord + bless us,
protect us from all evil
and bring us to everlasting life.
—Amen.

If praying with a priest or deacon, he dismisses the people:

The Lord be with you.
—And with your spirit.

May almighty God bless you,
the Father, and the Son, + and the Holy Spirit.
—Amen.

Go in peace.
—Thanks be to God.

EVENING PRAYER

BEGINS THE TWENTIETH SUNDAY IN ORDINARY TIME

God, + come to my assistance.
—Lord, make haste to help me.

Glory to the Father, and to the Son,
    and to the Holy Spirit:
—as it was in the beginning, is now,
and will be for ever. Amen. Alleluia.

Hymn   *From All That Dwell Below the Skies, p. 684*

Psalmody   Ant. 1 **Pray for the peace of Jerusalem.**

I rejoiced when I heard them say:
"Let us go to God's house."
And now our feet are standing
within your gates, O Jerusalem.

Jerusalem is built as a city
strongly compact.
It is there that the tribes go up,
the tribes of the Lord.

For Israel's law it is,
there to praise the Lord's name.
There were set the thrones of judgment
of the house of David.

For the peace of Jerusalem pray:
"Peace be to your homes!
May peace reign in your walls,
in your palaces, peace!"

For love of my brethren and friends
I say: "Peace upon you!"
For love of the house of the Lord
I will ask for your good.

Glory to the Father, and to the Son,
    and to the Holy Spirit:
—as it was in the beginning, is now,
and will be for ever. Amen.

Ant.   **Pray for the peace of Jerusalem.**

Ant. 2   **From the morning watch until night,
I have waited trustingly for the Lord.**

Psalm 130

Out of the depths I cry to you, O Lord,
Lord, hear my voice!
O let your ears be attentive
to the voice of my pleading.

If you, O Lord, should mark our guilt,
Lord, who would survive?
But with you is found forgiveness:
for this we revere you.

My soul is waiting for the Lord,
I count on his word.
My soul is longing for the Lord
more than watchman for daybreak.
Let the watchman count on daybreak
and Israel on the Lord.

Because with the Lord there is mercy
and fullness of redemption,
Israel indeed he will redeem
from all its iniquity.

Glory to the Father, and to the Son,
    and to the Holy Spirit:
—as it was in the beginning, is now,
and will be for ever. Amen.

Ant.

**From the morning watch until night, I
have waited trustingly for the Lord.**

Ant. 3

**Let everything in heaven and on earth bend
the knee at the name of Jesus.**

Canticle:
Philippians
2:6–11

Though he was in the form of God,
Jesus did not deem equality with God
something to be grasped at.

Rather, he emptied himself
and took the form of a slave,
being born in the likeness of men.

He was known to be of human estate,
and it was thus that he humbled himself,
obediently accepting even death,
death on a cross!

Because of this,
God highly exalted him
and bestowed on him the name
above every other name,

So that at Jesus' name
every knee must bend
in the heavens, on the earth,
and under the earth,
and every tongue proclaim
to the glory of God the Father:
JESUS CHRIST IS LORD!

Glory to the Father, and to the Son,
    and to the Holy Spirit:
—as it was in the beginning, is now,
and will be for ever. Amen.

Ant.   **Let everything in heaven and on earth bend
the knee at the name of Jesus.**

Reading
2 Peter 1:19–21

We possess the prophetic message as something altogether reliable. Keep your attention closely fixed on it, as you would on a lamp shining in a dark place until the first streaks of dawn appear and the morning star rises in your hearts. First you must understand this: there is no prophecy contained in Scripture which is a personal interpretation. Prophecy has never been put forward by man's willing it. It is rather that men impelled by the Holy Spirit have spoken under God's influence.

Responsory

From the rising of the sun to its setting, may the name of the Lord be praised.
—From the rising of the sun to its setting, may the name of the Lord be praised.

His splendor reaches far beyond the heavens;
—may the name of the Lord be praised.

Glory to the Father, and to the Son, and to the Holy Spirit.
—From the rising of the sun to its setting, may the name of the Lord be praised.

Gospel Canticle

Ant. **Woman, great is your faith; what you ask, I give to you.**

*Canticle of
Mary
Luke 1:46–55*

My + soul proclaims the greatness of the Lord,
my spirit rejoices in God my Savior
for he has looked with favor on his
    lowly servant.

From this day all generations will
    call me blessed:
the Almighty has done great things for me,
and holy is his Name.

He has mercy on those who fear him
in every generation.

He has shown the strength of his arm,
he has scattered the proud in their conceit.

He has cast down the mighty from
    their thrones,
and has lifted up the lowly.

He has filled the hungry with good things,
and the rich he has sent away empty.

He has come to the help of his servant Israel
for he has remembered his promise of mercy,
the promise he made to our fathers,
to Abraham and his children for ever.

Glory to the Father, and to the Son,
    and to the Holy Spirit:
—as it was in the beginning, is now,
    and will be for ever. Amen.

Ant.   **Woman, great is your faith; what you ask,
I give to you.**

Intercessions   Everyone who waits for the Lord finds joy.
Now we pray to him:
Look on us with favor, Lord, and hear us.

Faithful witness, firstborn of the dead, you
washed away our sins in your blood,
—make us always remember your
wonderful works.

You called men to be heralds of your
good news,
—make them strong and faithful messengers
of your kingdom.

King of peace, send your Spirit on the leaders
of the world,
—turn their eyes toward the poor and suffering.

Protect and defend those who are
discriminated against because of race,
color, class, language or religion,
—that they may be accorded the rights and
dignity which are theirs.

May all who died in your love share in your
happiness,
—with Mary, our mother, and all your
holy ones.

The Lord's
Prayer

Our Father, who art in heaven,
hallowed be thy name;
thy kingdom come,
thy will be done
on earth as it is in heaven.
Give us this day our daily bread,
and forgive us our trespasses,
as we forgive those who trespass against us;
and lead us not into temptation,
but deliver us from evil.

Pater noster, qui es in cælis:
sanctificetur nomen tuum;
adveniat regnum tuum;
fiat voluntas tua,
sicut in cælo, et in terra.
Panem nostrum cotidianum da nobis hodie;
et dimitte nobis debita nostra,
sicut et nos dimittimus debitoribus nostris;
et ne nos inducas in tentationem;
sed libera nos a malo.

Concluding
Prayer

God our Father,
may we love you in all things and above
      all things
and reach the joy you have prepared for us
beyond all our imagining.
We ask this through our Lord Jesus Christ,
      your Son,
who lives and reigns with you and
      the Holy Spirit,
God, for ever and ever.
—Amen.

Dismissal   *If praying individually, or in a group without a priest or deacon:*

May the Lord + bless us,
protect us from all evil
and bring us to everlasting life.
—Amen.

If praying with a priest or deacon, he dismisses the people:

The Lord be with you.
—And with your spirit.

May almighty God bless you,
the Father, and the Son, + and the Holy Spirit.
—Amen.

Go in peace.
—Thanks be to God.

NIGHT PRAYER

God, + come to my assistance.
—Lord, make haste to help me.

Glory to the Father, and to the Son,
    and to the Holy Spirit:
—as it was in the beginning, is now,
and will be for ever. Amen. Alleluia.

Examen   *An optional brief examination of conscience may be made. Call to mind your sins and failings this day.*

Hymn   *O Gladsome Light, p. 696*

Psalmody   Ant. 1 **Have mercy, Lord, and hear my prayer.**

Psalm 4

When I call, answer me, O God of justice;
from anguish you released me; have mercy
    and hear me!

O men, how long will your hearts be closed,
will you love what is futile and seek
    what is false?

It is the Lord who grants favors to those
    whom he loves;
the Lord hears me whenever I call him.

Fear him; do not sin: ponder on your bed
    and be still.
Make justice your sacrifice and trust
    in the Lord.

"What can bring us happiness?" many say.
Let the light of your face shine on us, O Lord.

You have put into my heart a greater joy
than they have from abundance of corn
    and new wine.

I will lie down in peace and sleep
    comes at once
for you alone, Lord, make me dwell in safety.

Glory to the Father, and to the Son,
    and to the Holy Spirit:
—as it was in the beginning, is now,
    and will be for ever. Amen.

Ant.   **Have mercy, Lord, and hear my prayer.**

Ant. 2   **In the silent hours of night, bless the Lord.**

Psalm 134   O come, bless the Lord,
all you who serve the Lord,
who stand in the house of the Lord,
in the courts of the house of our God.

Lift up your hands to the holy place
and bless the Lord through the night.

May the Lord bless you from Zion,
he who made both heaven and earth.

Glory to the Father, and to the Son,
   and to the Holy Spirit:
—as it was in the beginning, is now,
and will be for ever. Amen.

Ant.   **In the silent hours of night, bless the Lord.**

Reading   Hear, O Israel! The Lord is our God, the Lord
Deuteronomy   alone! Therefore, you shall love the Lord,
6:4–7   your God, with all your heart, and with all
your soul, and with all your strength. Take
to heart these words which I enjoin on you
today. Drill them into your children. Speak
of them at home and abroad, whether you
are busy or at rest.

Responsory   Into your hands, Lord, I commend my spirit.
—Into your hands, Lord, I commend my spirit.

You have redeemed us, Lord God of truth.
—I commend my spirit.

Glory to the Father, and to the Son,
　　and to the Holy Spirit.
—Into your hands, Lord, I commend my spirit.

Gospel
Canticle

Ant. **Protect us, Lord, as we stay awake;
watch over us as we sleep, that awake, we
may keep watch with Christ, and asleep,
rest in his peace.**

Canticle of
Simeon
Luke 2:29–32

Lord, + now you let your servant go in peace;
your word has been fulfilled:
my own eyes have seen the salvation
which you have prepared in the sight of
　　every people:
a light to reveal you to the nations
and the glory of your people Israel.

Glory to the Father, and to the Son,
　　and to the Holy Spirit:
—as it was in the beginning, is now,
　　and will be for ever. Amen.

Ant. **Protect us, Lord, as we stay awake; watch
over us as we sleep, that awake, we may
keep watch with Christ, and asleep, rest in
his peace.**

Concluding
Prayer

Let us pray.
Lord,
be with us throughout this night.
When day comes may we rise from sleep
to rejoice in the resurrection of your Christ,
who lives and reigns for ever and ever.
—Amen.

Blessing

May the all-powerful Lord
grant us a restful night
and a peaceful death.
—Amen.

Marian
Antiphon

Sing the "Salve Regina," found on p. 700, or pray a Hail Mary.

Sunday, August 18, 2024
Twentieth Sunday in Ordinary Time

MORNING PRAYER ——————————————————

God, + come to my assistance.
—Lord, make haste to help me.

Glory to the Father, and to the Son,
  and to the Holy Spirit:
—as it was in the beginning, is now,
  and will be for ever. Amen. Alleluia.

Hymn

Now That the Sun Is Gleaming Bright, p. 695

Psalmody

Ant. 1 **Praise the Lord, for his loving
kindness will never fail, alleluia.**

Psalm 118

Give thanks to the Lord for he is good,
  for his love endures forever.

Let the sons of Israel say:
"His love endures for ever."
Let the sons of Aaron say:
"His love endures for ever."
Let those who fear the Lord say:
"His love endures for ever."

I called to the Lord in my distress;
he answered and freed me.
The Lord is at my side; I do not fear.
What can man do against me?
The Lord is at my side as my helper:
I shall look down on my foes.

It is better to take refuge in the Lord
than to trust in men:
it is better to take refuge in the Lord
than to trust in princes.

The nations all encompassed me;
in the Lord's name I crushed them.
They compassed me, compassed me about;
in the Lord's name I crushed them.
They compassed me about like bees;
they blazed like a fire among thorns.
In the Lord's name I crushed them.

I was hard-pressed and was falling,
but the Lord came to help me.
The Lord is my strength and my song;
he is my savior.
There are shouts of joy and victory
in the tents of the just.

The Lord's right hand has triumphed;
his right hand raised me.
The Lord's right hand has triumphed;
I shall not die, I shall live
and recount his deeds.
I was punished, I was punished by the Lord,
but not doomed to die.

Open to me the gates of holiness:
I will enter and give thanks.
This is the Lord's own gate
where the just may enter.
I will thank you for you have answered
and you are my savior.

The stone which the builders rejected
has become the corner stone.
This is the work of the Lord,
a marvel in our eyes.
This day was made by the Lord;
we rejoice and are glad.

O Lord, grant us salvation;
O Lord, grant success.
Blessed in the name of the Lord
is he who comes.
We bless you from the house of the Lord;
the Lord God is our light.

Go forward in procession with branches
even to the altar.
You are my God, I thank you.
My God, I praise you.
Give thanks to the Lord for he is good;
for his love endures for ever.

Glory to the Father, and to the Son,
    and to the Holy Spirit:
—as it was in the beginning, is now,
    and will be for ever. Amen.

Ant.   **Praise the Lord, for his loving kindness will never fail, alleluia.**

Ant. 2   **Alleluia! Bless the Lord, all you works of the Lord, alleluia!**

Canticle:
Daniel
3:52–57

Blessed are you, O Lord, the God of our fathers,
praiseworthy and exalted above all forever.

And blessed is your holy and glorious name,
praiseworthy and exalted above all
    for all ages.

Blessed are you in the temple of your
    holy glory,
praiseworthy and glorious above all forever.

Blessed are you on the throne of
    your kingdom,
praiseworthy and exalted above all forever.

Blessed are you who look into the depths
from your throne upon the cherubim,
praiseworthy and exalted above all forever.

Blessed are you in the firmament of heaven,
praiseworthy and glorious forever.

Bless the Lord, all you works of the Lord,
praise and exalt him above all forever.

Glory to the Father, and to the Son,
    and to the Holy Spirit:
—as it was in the beginning, is now,
    and will be for ever. Amen.

Ant.   **Alleluia! Bless the Lord, all you works of the Lord, alleluia!**

Ant. 3   **Let everything that breathes give praise to the Lord, alleluia.**

Psalm 150 Praise God in his holy place,
           praise him in his mighty heavens.
           Praise him for his powerful deeds,
           praise his surpassing greatness.

           O praise him with sound of trumpet,
           praise him with lute and harp.
           Praise him with timbrel and dance,
           praise him with strings and pipes.

           O praise him with resounding cymbals,
           praise him with clashing of cymbals.
           Let everything that lives and that breathes
           give praise to the Lord.

           Glory to the Father, and to the Son,
               and to the Holy Spirit:
           —as it was in the beginning, is now,
           and will be for ever. Amen.

Ant.   **Let everything that breathes give praise to the Lord, alleluia.**

Reading
2 Timothy 2:8,
11–13

Remember that Jesus Christ, a descendant of David, was raised from the dead. You can depend on this:

> If we have died with him,
>> we shall also live with him;
> If we hold out to the end,
>> we shall also reign with him.

But if we deny him he will deny us. If we are unfaithful he will still remain faithful, for he cannot deny himself.

Responsory

We give thanks to you, O God,
  as we call upon your name.
—We give thanks to you, O God,
  as we call upon your name.

We cry aloud how marvelous you are,
—as we call upon your name.

Glory to the Father, and to the Son,
  and to the Holy Spirit.
—We give thanks to you, O God,
  as we call upon your name.

Gospel
Canticle

Ant. **I am the living bread come down from heaven. Anyone who eats this bread will live for ever, alleluia.**

Canticle of
Zechariah
Luke 1:68–79

Blessed + be the Lord, the God of Israel;
he has come to his people and set them free.

He has raised up for us a mighty savior,
born of the house of his servant David.

Through his holy prophets he
    promised of old
that he would save us from our enemies,
from the hands of all who hate us.

He promised to show mercy to our fathers
and to remember his holy covenant.

This was the oath he swore to our
    father Abraham:
to set us free from the hands of our enemies,
free to worship him without fear,
holy and righteous in his sight
    all the days of our life.

You, my child, shall be called the prophet of
    the Most High;
for you will go before the Lord to
    prepare his way,
to give his people knowledge of salvation
by the forgiveness of their sins.

In the tender compassion of our God
the dawn from on high shall break upon us,
to shine on those who dwell in darkness and
    the shadow of death,
and to guide our feet into the way of peace.

Glory to the Father, and to the Son,
    and to the Holy Spirit:
—as it was in the beginning, is now,
    and will be for ever. Amen.

Ant.   **I am the living bread come down from heaven. Anyone who eats this bread will live for ever, alleluia.**

Intercessions   Open your hearts to praise the God of power and goodness, for he loves us and knows our needs:
We praise you, Lord, and trust in you.

We bless you, almighty God, King of the universe, because you called us while we were yet sinners,
—to acknowledge your truth and to serve your majesty.

O God, you opened the gates of mercy for us,
—let us never turn aside from the path of life.

As we celebrate the resurrection of your beloved Son,
—help us to spend this day in the spirit of joy.

Give to your faithful, O Lord, a prayerful spirit of gratitude,
—that we may thank you for all your gifts.

The Lord's
Prayer

Our Father, who art in heaven,
hallowed be thy name;
thy kingdom come,
thy will be done
on earth as it is in heaven.
Give us this day our daily bread,
and forgive us our trespasses,
as we forgive those who trespass against us;
and lead us not into temptation,
but deliver us from evil.

Pater noster, qui es in cælis:
sanctificetur nomen tuum;
adveniat regnum tuum;
fiat voluntas tua,
sicut in cælo, et in terra.
Panem nostrum cotidianum da nobis hodie;
et dimitte nobis debita nostra,
sicut et nos dimittimus debitoribus nostris;
et ne nos inducas in tentationem;
sed libera nos a malo.

Concluding
Prayer

God our Father,
may we love you in all things and above
        all things
and reach the joy you have prepared for us
beyond all our imagining.
We ask this through our Lord Jesus Christ,
        your Son,
who lives and reigns with you and
        the Holy Spirit,
God, for ever and ever.
—Amen.

Dismissal   *If praying individually, or in a group without a priest or deacon:*

May the Lord + bless us,
protect us from all evil
and bring us to everlasting life.
—Amen.

If praying with a priest or deacon, he dismisses the people:

The Lord be with you.
—And with your spirit.

May almighty God bless you,
the Father, and the Son, + and the Holy Spirit.
—Amen.

Go in peace.
—Thanks be to God.

EVENING PRAYER ———————————

God, + come to my assistance.
—Lord, make haste to help me.

Glory to the Father, and to the Son,
    and to the Holy Spirit:
—as it was in the beginning, is now,
and will be for ever. Amen. Alleluia.

Hymn   *From All That Dwell Below the Skies, p. 684*

Psalmody   Ant. 1 **In eternal splendor, before the
dawn of light on earth, I have begotten
you, alleluia.**

Psalm 110:1–5, 7   The Lord's revelation to my Master:
                    "Sit on my right:
                    your foes I will put beneath your feet."

                    The Lord will wield from Zion
                    your scepter of power:
                    rule in the midst of all your foes.

                    A prince from the day of your birth
                    on the holy mountains;
                    from the womb before the dawn I begot you.

                    The Lord has sworn an oath he will
                        not change.
                    "You are a priest for ever,
                    a priest like Melchizedek of old."

                    The Master standing at your right hand
                    will shatter kings in the day of his
                        great wrath.

                    He shall drink from the stream by
                        the wayside
                    and therefore he shall lift up his head.

                    Glory to the Father, and to the Son,
                        and to the Holy Spirit:
                    —as it was in the beginning, is now,
                    and will be for ever. Amen.

Ant.   **In eternal splendor, before the dawn of
              light on earth, I have begotten you, alleluia.**

Ant. 2   **Blessed are they who hunger and thirst for
              holiness; they will be satisfied.**

Psalm 112

Happy the man who fears the Lord,
who takes delight in all his commands.
His sons will be powerful on earth;
the children of the upright are blessed.

Riches and wealth are in his house;
his justice stands firm for ever.
He is a light in the darkness for the upright:
he is generous, merciful and just.

The good man takes pity and lends,
he conducts his affairs with honor.
The just man will never waver:
he will be remembered for ever.

He has no fear of evil news;
with a firm heart he trusts in the Lord.
With a steadfast heart he will not fear;
he will see the downfall of his foes.

Open-handed, he gives to the poor;
his justice stands firm for ever.
His head will be raised in glory.

The wicked man sees and is angry,
grinds his teeth and fades away;
the desire of the wicked leads to doom.

Glory to the Father, and to the Son,
    and to the Holy Spirit:
—as it was in the beginning, is now,
and will be for ever. Amen.

Ant.   **Blessed are they who hunger and thirst for
holiness; they will be satisfied.**

Ant. 3 **Praise God, all you who serve him, both great and small, alleluia.**

Canticle: See
Revelation
19:1–7

Alleluia.
Salvation, glory, and power to our God:
his judgments are honest and true.
Alleluia.

Alleluia.
Sing praise to our God, all you his servants,
all who worship him reverently,
    great and small.
Alleluia.

Alleluia.
The Lord our all-powerful God is King;
let us rejoice, sing praise, and give him glory.
Alleluia.

Alleluia.
The wedding feast of the Lamb has begun,
and his bride is prepared to welcome him.
Alleluia.

Alleluia.
Glory to the Father, and to the Son,
and to the Holy Spirit:
Alleluia.

Alleluia.
as it was in the beginning, is now,
and will be for ever. Amen.
Alleluia.

Ant.   **Praise God, all you who serve him, both great and small, alleluia.**

Reading
Hebrews
12:22–24

You have drawn near to Mount Zion and the city of the living God, the heavenly Jerusalem, to myriads of angels in festal gathering, to the assembly of the first-born enrolled in heaven, to God the judge of all, to the spirits of just men made perfect, to Jesus, the mediator of a new covenant, and to the sprinkled blood which speaks more eloquently than that of Abel.

Responsory   Our Lord is great, mighty is his power.
—Our Lord is great, mighty is his power.

His wisdom is beyond compare,
—mighty is his power.

Glory to the Father, and to the Son,
    and to the Holy Spirit.
—Our Lord is great, mighty is his power.

Gospel
Canticle

Ant. **I have come to cast fire upon the earth; how I long to see the flame leap up!**

Canticle of
Mary
Luke 1:46–55

My + soul proclaims the greatness of the Lord,
my spirit rejoices in God my Savior
for he has looked with favor on his
    lowly servant.

From this day all generations will
    call me blessed:
the Almighty has done great things for me,
and holy is his Name.

He has mercy on those who fear him
in every generation.

He has shown the strength of his arm,
he has scattered the proud in their conceit.

He has cast down the mighty from
     their thrones,
and has lifted up the lowly.

He has filled the hungry with good things,
and the rich he has sent away empty.

He has come to the help of his servant Israel
for he has remembered his promise of mercy,
the promise he made to our fathers,
to Abraham and his children for ever.

Glory to the Father, and to the Son,
     and to the Holy Spirit:
—as it was in the beginning, is now,
     and will be for ever. Amen.

Ant.   **I have come to cast fire upon the earth; how
       I long to see the flame leap up!**

Intercessions   Rejoicing in the Lord, from whom all good
                    things come, let us pray:
                Lord, hear our prayer.

Father and Lord of all, you sent your Son
     into the world, that your name might be
     glorified in every place,
—strengthen the witness of your Church
     among the nations.

Make us obedient to the teachings of
your apostles,
—and bound to the truth of our faith.

As you love the innocent,
—render justice to those who are wronged.

Free those in bondage and give sight to
the blind,
—raise up the fallen and protect the stranger.

Fulfill your promise to those who already
sleep in your peace,
—through your Son grant them a blessed
resurrection.

The Lord's Prayer

Our Father, who art in heaven,
hallowed be thy name;
thy kingdom come,
thy will be done
on earth as it is in heaven.
Give us this day our daily bread,
and forgive us our trespasses,
as we forgive those who trespass against us;
and lead us not into temptation,
but deliver us from evil.

Pater noster, qui es in cælis:
sanctificetur nomen tuum;
adveniat regnum tuum;
fiat voluntas tua,
sicut in cælo, et in terra.
Panem nostrum cotidianum da nobis hodie;
et dimitte nobis debita nostra,
sicut et nos dimittimus debitoribus nostris;
et ne nos inducas in tentationem;
sed libera nos a malo.

Concluding Prayer

God our Father,
may we love you in all things and above
    all things
and reach the joy you have prepared for us
beyond all our imagining.
We ask this through our Lord Jesus Christ,
    your Son,
who lives and reigns with you and
    the Holy Spirit,
God, for ever and ever.
—Amen.

Dismissal

If praying individually, or in a group without a priest or deacon:

May the Lord + bless us,
protect us from all evil
and bring us to everlasting life.
—Amen.

If praying with a priest or deacon, he dismisses the people:

The Lord be with you.
—And with your spirit.

May almighty God bless you,
the Father, and the Son, + and the Holy Spirit.
—Amen.

Go in peace.
—Thanks be to God.

NIGHT PRAYER————————————————

God, + come to my assistance.
—Lord, make haste to help me.

Glory to the Father, and to the Son,
and to the Holy Spirit:
—as it was in the beginning, is now,
and will be for ever. Amen. Alleluia.

Examen   *An optional brief examination of conscience may be made. Call to mind your*
sins and failings this day.

Hymn   *O Gladsome Light, p. 696*

Psalmody   Ant. **Night holds no terrors for me sleeping
under God's wings.**

Psalm 91   He who dwells in the shelter of the Most High
and abides in the shade of the Almighty
says to the Lord: "My refuge,
my stronghold, my God in whom I trust!"

It is he who will free you from the snare
of the fowler who seeks to destroy you;
he will conceal you with his pinions
and under his wings you will find refuge.

You will not fear the terror of the night
nor the arrow that flies by day,
nor the plague that prowls in the darkness
nor the scourge that lays waste at noon.

A thousand may fall at your side,
ten thousand fall at your right,
you, it will never approach;
his faithfulness is buckler and shield.

Your eyes have only to look
to see how the wicked are repaid,
you who have said: "Lord, my refuge!"
and have made the Most High your dwelling.

Upon you no evil shall fall,
no plague approach where you dwell.
For you has he commanded his angels,
to keep you in all your ways.

They shall bear you upon their hands
lest you strike your foot against a stone.
On the lion and the viper you will tread
and trample the young lion and the dragon.

Since he clings to me in love, I will free him;
protect him for he knows my name.
When he calls I shall answer: "I am with you."
I will save him in distress and give him glory.

With length of life I will content him;
I shall let him see my saving power.

Glory to the Father, and to the Son,
    and to the Holy Spirit:
—as it was in the beginning, is now,
    and will be for ever. Amen.

Ant. **Night holds no terrors for me sleeping
under God's wings.**

Reading
Revelation
22:4–5

They shall see the Lord face to face and bear
his name on their foreheads. The night shall
be no more. They will need no light from
lamps or the sun, for the Lord God shall give
them light, and they shall reign forever.

Responsory

Into your hands, Lord, I commend my spirit.
—Into your hands, Lord, I commend my spirit.

You have redeemed us, Lord God of truth.
—I commend my spirit.

Glory to the Father, and to the Son,
    and to the Holy Spirit.
—Into your hands, Lord, I commend my spirit.

Gospel
Canticle

Ant. **Protect us, Lord, as we stay awake;
watch over us as we sleep, that awake, we
may keep watch with Christ, and asleep,
rest in his peace.**

Canticle of Simeon
Luke 2:29–32

Lord, + now you let your servant go in peace;
your word has been fulfilled:
my own eyes have seen the salvation
which you have prepared in the sight of
    every people:
a light to reveal you to the nations
and the glory of your people Israel.

Glory to the Father, and to the Son,
    and to the Holy Spirit:
—as it was in the beginning, is now,
and will be for ever. Amen.

Ant.

**Protect us, Lord, as we stay awake; watch
over us as we sleep, that awake, we may
keep watch with Christ, and asleep, rest in
his peace.**

Concluding
Prayer

Let us pray.
Lord,
we have celebrated today
the mystery of the rising of Christ to new life.
May we now rest in your peace,
safe from all that could harm us,
and rise again refreshed and joyful,
to praise you throughout another day.
We ask this through Christ our Lord.
—Amen.

Blessing

May the all-powerful Lord
grant us a restful night
and a peaceful death.
—Amen.

Marian
Antiphon

Sing the "Salve Regina," found on p. 700, or pray a Hail Mary.

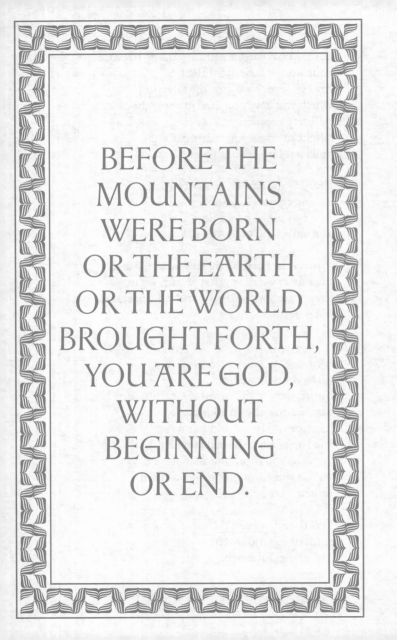

BEFORE THE
MOUNTAINS
WERE BORN
OR THE EARTH
OR THE WORLD
BROUGHT FORTH,
YOU ARE GOD,
WITHOUT
BEGINNING
OR END.

Monday, August 19, 2024
Monday of the Twentieth Week in Ordinary Time

MORNING PRAYER ─────────────────

God, + come to my assistance.
—Lord, make haste to help me.

Glory to the Father, and to the Son,
 and to the Holy Spirit:
—as it was in the beginning, is now,
and will be for ever. Amen. Alleluia.

Hymn *God Who Made Both Earth and Heaven, p. 688*

Psalmody Ant. 1 **Each morning, Lord, you fill us with your kindness.**

Psalm 90 O Lord, you have been our refuge
from one generation to the next.
Before the mountains were born
or the earth or the world brought forth,
you are God, without beginning or end.

You turn men back to dust
and say: "Go back, sons of men."
To your eyes a thousand years
are like yesterday, come and gone,
no more than a watch in the night.

You sweep men away like a dream,
like the grass which springs up in
 the morning.
In the morning it springs up and flowers:
by evening it withers and fades.

So we are destroyed in your anger,
struck with terror in your fury.
Our guilt lies open before you;
our secrets in the light of your face.

All our days pass away in your anger.
Our life is over like a sigh.
Our span is seventy years
or eighty for those who are strong.

And most of these are emptiness and pain.
They pass swiftly and we are gone.
Who understands the power of your anger
and fears the strength of your fury?

Make us know the shortness of our life
that we may gain wisdom of heart.
Lord, relent! Is your anger for ever?
Show pity to your servants.

In the morning, fill us with your love;
we shall exult and rejoice all our days.
Give us joy to balance our affliction
for the years when we knew misfortune.

Show forth your work to your servants;
let your glory shine on their children.
Let the favor of the Lord be upon us:
give success to the work of our hands,
give success to the work of our hands.

Glory to the Father, and to the Son,
    and to the Holy Spirit:
—as it was in the beginning, is now,
    and will be for ever. Amen.

Ant.   **Each morning, Lord, you fill us with your kindness.**

Ant. 2   **From the farthest bounds of earth, may God be praised!**

Canticle:
Isaiah 42:10–16

Sing to the Lord a new song,
his praise from the end of the earth:

Let the sea and what fills it resound,
the coastlands, and those who dwell in them.
Let the steppe and its cities cry out,
the villages where Kedar dwells;

let the inhabitants of Sela exult,
and shout from the top of the mountains.
Let them give glory to the Lord,
and utter his praise in the coastlands.

The Lord goes forth like a hero,
like a warrior he stirs up his ardor;
he shouts out his battle cry,
against his enemies he shows his might:

I have looked away, and kept silence,
I have said nothing, holding myself in;
but now, I cry out as a woman in labor,
gasping and panting.

I will lay waste mountains and hills,
all their herbage I will dry up;
I will turn the rivers into marshes,
and the marshes I will dry up.

I will lead the blind on their journey;
by paths unknown I will guide them.
I will turn darkness into light before them,
and make crooked ways straight.

Glory to the Father, and to the Son,
    and to the Holy Spirit:
—as it was in the beginning, is now,
and will be for ever. Amen.

Ant.   **From the farthest bounds of earth, may
God be praised!**

Ant. 3   **You who stand in his sanctuary, praise the
name of the Lord.**

Psalm 135:1–12   Praise the name of the Lord,
praise him, servants of the Lord,
who stand in the house of the Lord,
in the courts of the house of our God.

Praise the Lord for the Lord is good.
Sing a psalm to his name for he is loving.
For the Lord has chosen Jacob for himself
and Israel for his own possession.

For I know the Lord is great,
that our Lord is high above all gods.
The Lord does whatever he wills,
in heaven, on earth, in the seas.

He summons clouds from the ends of
    the earth;
makes lightning produce the rain;
from his treasuries he sends forth the wind.

The first-born of the Egyptians he smote,
of man and beast alike.
Signs and wonders he worked
in the midst of your land, O Egypt,
against Pharaoh and all his servants.

Nations in their greatness he struck
and kings in their splendor he slew.
Sihon, king of the Amorites,
Og, the king of Bashan,
and all the kingdoms of Canaan.
He let Israel inherit their land;
on his people their land he bestowed.

Glory to the Father, and to the Son,
    and to the Holy Spirit:
—as it was in the beginning, is now,
and will be for ever. Amen.

Ant.   **You who stand in his sanctuary, praise the
name of the Lord.**

Reading   We should be grateful to the Lord our
Judith 8:25–27   God, for putting us to the test, as he did
our forefathers. Recall how he dealt with
Abraham, and how he tried Isaac, and all that
happened to Jacob in Syrian Mesopotamia
while he was tending the flocks of Laban, his
mother's brother. Not for vengeance did the
Lord put them in the crucible to try their
hearts, nor has he done so with us. It is by
way of admonition that he chastises those
who are close to him.

Responsory   Sing for joy, God's chosen ones,
        give him the praise that is due.
—Sing for joy, God's chosen ones,
        give him the praise that is due.

Sing a new song to the Lord;
—give him the praise that is due.

Glory to the Father, and to the Son,
        and to the Holy Spirit.
—Sing for joy, God's chosen ones,
        give him the praise that is due.

Gospel
Canticle

Ant. **Blessed be the Lord, for he has come to his people and set them free.**

*Canticle of
Zechariah
Luke 1:68–79*

Blessed + be the Lord, the God of Israel;
he has come to his people and set them free.

He has raised up for us a mighty savior,
born of the house of his servant David.

Through his holy prophets he
    promised of old
that he would save us from our enemies,
from the hands of all who hate us.

He promised to show mercy to our fathers
and to remember his holy covenant.

This was the oath he swore to our
    father Abraham:
to set us free from the hands of our enemies,
free to worship him without fear,
holy and righteous in his sight
    all the days of our life.

You, my child, shall be called the prophet of
    the Most High;
for you will go before the Lord to
    prepare his way,
to give his people knowledge of salvation
by the forgiveness of their sins.

In the tender compassion of our God
the dawn from on high shall break upon us,
to shine on those who dwell in darkness and
    the shadow of death,
and to guide our feet into the way of peace.

Glory to the Father, and to the Son,
    and to the Holy Spirit:
—as it was in the beginning, is now,
    and will be for ever. Amen.

Ant.   **Blessed be the Lord, for he has come to his
people and set them free.**

Intercessions   Because Christ hears and saves those who
        hope in him, let us pray:
    We praise you, Lord, we hope in you.

    We thank you because you are rich in mercy,
    —and for the abundant love with which you
        have loved us.

With the Father you are always at work in
    the world,
—make all things new through the power of
    your Holy Spirit.

Open our eyes and the eyes of our brothers,
—to see your wonders this day.

You call us today to your service,
—make us stewards of your many gifts.

The Lord's
Prayer

Our Father, who art in heaven,
    hallowed be thy name;
    thy kingdom come,
    thy will be done
    on earth as it is in heaven.
    Give us this day our daily bread,
    and forgive us our trespasses,
    as we forgive those who trespass against us;
    and lead us not into temptation,
    but deliver us from evil.

Pater noster, qui es in cælis:
    sanctificetur nomen tuum;
    adveniat regnum tuum;
    fiat voluntas tua,
    sicut in cælo, et in terra.
    Panem nostrum cotidianum da nobis hodie;
    et dimitte nobis debita nostra,
    sicut et nos dimittimus debitoribus nostris;
    et ne nos inducas in tentationem;
    sed libera nos a malo.

Concluding
Prayer

God our creator,
you gave us the earth to cultivate
and the sun to serve our needs.
Help us to spend this day
for your glory and our neighbor's good.
We ask this through our Lord Jesus Christ,
        your Son,
who lives and reigns with you and
        the Holy Spirit,
God, for ever and ever.
—Amen.

Dismissal

If praying individually, or in a group without a priest or deacon:

May the Lord + bless us,
protect us from all evil
and bring us to everlasting life.
—Amen.

If praying with a priest or deacon, he dismisses the people:

The Lord be with you.
—And with your spirit.

May almighty God bless you,
the Father, and the Son, + and the Holy Spirit.
—Amen.

Go in peace.
—Thanks be to God.

EVENING PRAYER——————————

God, + come to my assistance.
—Lord, make haste to help me.

Glory to the Father, and to the Son,
    and to the Holy Spirit:
—as it was in the beginning, is now,
    and will be for ever. Amen. Alleluia.

Hymn   *Glorious Things of Thee Are Spoken, p. 686*

Psalmody   Ant. 1 **Give thanks to the Lord, for his great
            love is without end.**

Psalm 136   O give thanks to the Lord for he is good,
                for his love endures for ever.
            Give thanks to the God of gods,
                for his love endures for ever.
            Give thanks to the Lord of lords,
                for his love endures for ever;

            who alone has wrought marvelous works,
                for his love endures for ever;
            whose wisdom it was made the skies,
                for his love endures for ever;
            who fixed the earth firmly on the seas,
                for his love endures for ever.

            It was he who made the great lights,
                for his love endures for ever,
            the sun to rule in the day,
                for his love endures for ever,
            the moon and the stars in the night,
                for his love endures for ever.

Glory to the Father, and to the Son,
and to the Holy Spirit:
—as it was in the beginning, is now,
and will be for ever. Amen.

Ant.   **Give thanks to the Lord, for his great love
is without end.**

Ant. 2   **Great and wonderful are your deeds,
Lord God the Almighty.**

Psalm 136   The first-born of the Egyptians he smote,
(continued)   for his love endures for ever.
He brought Israel out from their midst,
for his love endures for ever;
arm outstretched, with power in his hand,
for his love endures for ever.

He divided the Red Sea in two,
for his love endures for ever;
he made Israel pass through the midst,
for his love endures for ever;
he flung Pharaoh and his force in the sea,
for his love endures for ever.

Through the desert his people he led,
for his love endures for ever.
Nations in their greatness he struck,
for his love endures for ever.
Kings in their splendor he slew,
for his love endures for ever.

Sihon, king of the Amorites,
for his love endures for ever;
and Og, the king of Bashan,
for his love endures for ever.

He let Israel inherit their land,
for his love endures for ever.
On his servant their land he bestowed,
for his love endures for ever.
He remembered us in our distress,
for his love endures for ever.

And he snatched us away from our foes,
for his love endures for ever.
He gives food to all living things,
for his love endures for ever.
To the God of heaven give thanks,
for his love endures for ever.

Glory to the Father, and to the Son,
    and to the Holy Spirit:
—as it was in the beginning, is now,
and will be for ever. Amen.

Ant.   **Great and wonderful are your deeds,
Lord God the Almighty.**

Ant. 3   **God planned in the fullness of time to
restore all things in Christ.**

Canticle: Praised be the God and Father
Ephesians   of our Lord Jesus Christ,
1:3–10   who has bestowed on us in Christ
every spiritual blessing in the heavens.

God chose us in him
before the world began,
to be holy
and blameless in his sight.

He predestined us
to be his adopted sons through Jesus Christ,
such was his will and pleasure,
that all might praise the glorious favor
he has bestowed on us in his beloved.

In him and through his blood,
    we have been redeemed,
and our sins forgiven,
so immeasurably generous
is God's favor to us.

God has given us the wisdom
to understand fully the mystery,
the plan he was pleased
to decree in Christ.

A plan to be carried out
in Christ, in the fullness of time,
to bring all things into one in him,
in the heavens and on earth.

Glory to the Father, and to the Son,
    and to the Holy Spirit:
—as it was in the beginning, is now,
and will be for ever. Amen.

Ant.   **God planned in the fullness of time to
restore all things in Christ.**

Reading
1 Thessalonians 3:12–13

May the Lord increase you and make you
overflow with love for one another and
for all, even as our love does for you. May
he strengthen your hearts, making them
blameless and holy before our God and
Father at the coming of our Lord Jesus Christ
with all his holy ones.

Responsory

Accept my prayer, O Lord,
    which rises up to you.
—Accept my prayer, O Lord,
    which rises up to you.

Like burning incense in your sight,
—which rises up to you.

Glory to the Father, and to the Son,
    and to the Holy Spirit.
—Accept my prayer, O Lord,
    which rises up to you.

Gospel Canticle

Ant. **For ever will my soul proclaim the greatness of the Lord.**

Canticle of Mary
Luke 1:46–55

My + soul proclaims the greatness of the Lord,
my spirit rejoices in God my Savior
for he has looked with favor on his
    lowly servant.

From this day all generations will
    call me blessed:
the Almighty has done great things for me,
and holy is his Name.

He has mercy on those who fear him
in every generation.

He has shown the strength of his arm,
he has scattered the proud in their conceit.

He has cast down the mighty from
    their thrones,
and has lifted up the lowly.

He has filled the hungry with good things,
and the rich he has sent away empty.

He has come to the help of his servant Israel
for he has remembered his promise of mercy,
the promise he made to our fathers,
to Abraham and his children for ever.

Glory to the Father, and to the Son,
    and to the Holy Spirit:
—as it was in the beginning, is now,
and will be for ever. Amen.

Ant.   **For ever will my soul proclaim the
greatness of the Lord.**

Intercessions   Jesus does not abandon those who hope in
            him; therefore, let us humbly ask him:
            Our Lord and our God, hear us.

            Christ our light, brighten your Church with
                your splendor,
        —so that it may be for the nations the great
                sacrament of your love.

Watch over the priests and ministers of
     your Church,
—so that after they have preached to others,
     they themselves may remain faithful in
     your service.

Through your blood you gave peace to
     the world,
—turn away the sin of strife, the scourge of war.

O Lord, help married couples with an
     abundance of your grace,
—so that they may better symbolize the
     mystery of your Church.

In your mercy forgive the sins of all the dead,
—that they may live with your saints.

The Lord's
Prayer

Our Father, who art in heaven,
hallowed be thy name;
thy kingdom come,
thy will be done
on earth as it is in heaven.
Give us this day our daily bread,
and forgive us our trespasses,
as we forgive those who trespass against us;
and lead us not into temptation,
but deliver us from evil.

Pater noster, qui es in cælis:
sanctificetur nomen tuum;
adveniat regnum tuum;
fiat voluntas tua,
sicut in cælo, et in terra.
Panem nostrum cotidianum da nobis hodie;
et dimitte nobis debita nostra,
sicut et nos dimittimus debitoribus nostris;
et ne nos inducas in tentationem;
sed libera nos a malo.

Concluding Prayer

Stay with us, Lord Jesus,
for evening draws near,
and be our companion on our way
to set our hearts on fire with new hope.
Help us to recognize your presence among us
in the Scriptures we read,
and in the breaking of bread,
for you live and reign with the Father and
    the Holy Spirit,
God, for ever and ever.
—Amen.

Dismissal

If praying individually, or in a group without a priest or deacon:

May the Lord + bless us,
protect us from all evil
and bring us to everlasting life.
—Amen.

If praying with a priest or deacon, he dismisses the people:

The Lord be with you.
—And with your spirit.

May almighty God bless you,
the Father, and the Son, + and the Holy Spirit.
—Amen.

Go in peace.
—Thanks be to God.

NIGHT PRAYER

God, + come to my assistance.
—Lord, make haste to help me.

Glory to the Father, and to the Son,
and to the Holy Spirit:
—as it was in the beginning, is now,
and will be for ever. Amen. Alleluia.

Examen   *An optional brief examination of conscience may be made. Call to mind your
sins and failings this day.*

Hymn   *O Gladsome Light, p. 696*

Psalmody   Ant. **O Lord, our God, unwearied is your
love for us.**

Psalm 86   Turn your ear, O Lord, and give answer
for I am poor and needy.
Preserve my life, for I am faithful:
save the servant who trusts in you.

You are my God; have mercy on me, Lord,
for I cry to you all the day long.
Give joy to your servant, O Lord,
for to you I lift up my soul.

O Lord, you are good and forgiving,
full of love to all who call.
Give heed, O Lord, to my prayer
and attend to the sound of my voice.

In the day of distress I will call
and surely you will reply.
Among the gods there is none like you,
    O Lord;
nor work to compare with yours.

All the nations shall come to adore you
and glorify your name, O Lord:
for you are great and do marvelous deeds,
you who alone are God.

Show me, Lord, your way
so that I may walk in your truth.
Guide my heart to fear your name.

I will praise you, Lord my God,
    with all my heart
and glorify your name for ever;
for your love to me has been great:
you have saved me from the depths of
    the grave.

The proud have risen against me;
ruthless men seek my life:
to you they pay no heed.

But you, God of mercy and compassion,
slow to anger, O Lord,
abounding in love and truth,
turn and take pity on me.

O give your strength to your servant
and save your handmaid's son.
Show me a sign of your favor
that my foes may see to their shame
that you console me and give me your help.

Glory to the Father, and to the Son,
    and to the Holy Spirit:
—as it was in the beginning, is now,
    and will be for ever. Amen.

Ant.   **O Lord, our God, unwearied is your
love for us.**

Reading
1 Thessalonians
5:9–10

God has destined us for acquiring salvation
through our Lord Jesus Christ. He died for
us, that all of us, whether awake or asleep,
together might live with him.

Responsory

Into your hands, Lord, I commend my spirit.
—Into your hands, Lord, I commend my spirit.

You have redeemed us, Lord God of truth.
—I commend my spirit.

Glory to the Father, and to the Son,
    and to the Holy Spirit.
—Into your hands, Lord, I commend my spirit.

Gospel
Canticle

Ant.   **Protect us, Lord, as we stay awake;
watch over us as we sleep, that awake, we
may keep watch with Christ, and asleep,
rest in his peace.**

Canticle of
Simeon
Luke 2:29–32

Lord, + now you let your servant go in peace;
your word has been fulfilled:
my own eyes have seen the salvation
which you have prepared in the sight of
    every people:
a light to reveal you to the nations
and the glory of your people Israel.

Glory to the Father, and to the Son,
    and to the Holy Spirit:
—as it was in the beginning, is now,
and will be for ever. Amen.

Ant.

**Protect us, Lord, as we stay awake; watch
over us as we sleep, that awake, we may
keep watch with Christ, and asleep, rest in
his peace.**

Concluding
Prayer

Let us pray.
Lord,
give our bodies restful sleep
and let the work we have done today
bear fruit in eternal life.
We ask this through Christ our Lord.
—Amen.

Blessing

May the all-powerful Lord
grant us a restful night
and a peaceful death.
—Amen.

Marian
Antiphon

Sing the "Salve Regina," found on p. 700, or pray a Hail Mary.

Tuesday, August 20, 2024
St. Bernard

MORNING PRAYER————————————————

God, + come to my assistance.
—Lord, make haste to help me.

Glory to the Father, and to the Son,
   and to the Holy Spirit:
—as it was in the beginning, is now,
   and will be for ever. Amen. Alleluia.

Hymn   *Jesus, Eternal Truth Sublime, p. 693*

Psalmody   Ant. 1 **I will sing to you, O Lord; I will learn from you the way of perfection.**

Psalm 101   My song is of mercy and justice;
I sing to you, O Lord.
I will walk in the way of perfection.
O when, Lord, will you come?

I will walk with blameless heart
within my house;
I will not set before my eyes
whatever is base.

I will hate the ways of the crooked;
they shall not be my friends.
The false-hearted must keep far away;
the wicked I disown.

The man who slanders his neighbor in secret
I will bring to silence.
The man of proud looks and haughty heart
I will never endure.

I look to the faithful in the land
that they may dwell with me.
He who walks in the way of perfection
shall be my friend.

No man who practices deceit
shall live within my house.
No man who utters lies shall stand
before my eyes.

Morning by morning I will silence
all the wicked in the land,
uprooting from the city of the Lord
all who do evil.

Glory to the Father, and to the Son,
    and to the Holy Spirit:
—as it was in the beginning, is now,
and will be for ever. Amen.

Ant.   **I will sing to you, O Lord; I will learn from you the way of perfection.**

Ant. 2   **Lord, do not withhold your compassion from us.**

Canticle:
Daniel 3:26, 27,
29, 34–41

Blessed are you, and praiseworthy,
O Lord, the God of our fathers,
and glorious forever is your name.

For you are just in all you have done;
all your deeds are faultless, all your
    ways right,
and all your judgments proper.

For we have sinned and transgressed
by departing from you,
and we have done every kind of evil.

For your name's sake, do not deliver us
    up forever,
or make void your covenant.

Do not take away your mercy from us,
for the sake of Abraham, your beloved,
Isaac your servant, and Israel your holy one,

to whom you promised to multiply
    their offspring
like the stars of heaven,
or the sand on the shore of the sea.

For we are reduced, O Lord, beyond any
    other nation,
brought low everywhere in the
    world this day
because of our sins.

We have in our day no prince, prophet,
    or leader,
no holocaust, sacrifice, oblation, or incense,
no place to offer first fruits, to find
    favor with you.

But with contrite heart and humble spirit
let us be received;
as though it were holocausts of rams
    and bullocks,
or thousands of fat lambs,
so let our sacrifice be in your presence today
as we follow you unreservedly;
for those who trust in you cannot be
    put to shame.

And now we follow you with our whole heart,
we fear you and we pray to you.

Glory to the Father, and to the Son,
    and to the Holy Spirit:
—as it was in the beginning, is now,
and will be for ever. Amen.

Ant.   **Lord, do not withhold your
            compassion from us.**

Ant. 3   **O God, I will sing to you a new song.**

Psalm 144:1–10

Blessed be the Lord, my rock,
who trains my arms for battle,
who prepares my hands for war.

He is my love, my fortress;
he is my stronghold, my savior,
my shield, my place of refuge.
He brings peoples under my rule.

Lord, what is man that you care for him,
mortal man, that you keep him in mind;
man, who is merely a breath,
whose life fades like a passing shadow?

Lower your heavens and come down;
touch the mountains; wreathe
    them in smoke.
Flash your lightnings; rout the foe,
shoot your arrows and put them to flight.

Reach down from heaven and save me;
draw me out from the mighty waters,
from the hands of alien foes
whose mouths are filled with lies,
whose hands are raised in perjury.

To you, O God, will I sing a new song;
I will play on the ten-stringed harp
to you who give kings their victory,
who set David your servant free.

Glory to the Father, and to the Son,
    and to the Holy Spirit:
—as it was in the beginning, is now,
and will be for ever. Amen.

Ant.   **O God, I will sing to you a new song.**

Reading
Wisdom 7:13–14

Simply I learned about Wisdom, and
    ungrudgingly do I share—
      her riches I do not hide away;
For to men she is an unfailing treasure;
    those who gain this treasure win the
      friendship of God,
      to whom the gifts they have from
      discipline commend them.

Responsory

Let the peoples proclaim the wisdom of
    the saints.
—Let the peoples proclaim the wisdom of
    the saints.

With joyful praise let the Church tell forth
—the wisdom of the saints.

Glory to the Father, and to the Son,
    and to the Holy Spirit.
—Let the peoples proclaim the wisdom of
    the saints.

Gospel
Canticle

Ant. **Blessed Bernard, your life, flooded by
the splendor of the divine Word, illumines
the Church with the light of true faith
and doctrine.**

Canticle of
Zechariah
Luke 1:68–79

Blessed + be the Lord, the God of Israel;
he has come to his people and set them free.

He has raised up for us a mighty savior,
born of the house of his servant David.

431

Through his holy prophets he
    promised of old
that he would save us from our enemies,
from the hands of all who hate us.

He promised to show mercy to our fathers
and to remember his holy covenant.

This was the oath he swore to our
    father Abraham:
to set us free from the hands of our enemies,
free to worship him without fear,
holy and righteous in his sight
    all the days of our life.

You, my child, shall be called the prophet of
    the Most High;
for you will go before the Lord to
    prepare his way,
to give his people knowledge of salvation
by the forgiveness of their sins.

In the tender compassion of our God
the dawn from on high shall break upon us,
to shine on those who dwell in darkness and
    the shadow of death,
and to guide our feet into the way of peace.

Glory to the Father, and to the Son,
    and to the Holy Spirit:
—as it was in the beginning, is now,
    and will be for ever. Amen.

Ant.   **Blessed Bernard, your life, flooded by the splendor of the divine Word, illumines the Church with the light of true faith and doctrine.**

Intercessions   Christ is the Good Shepherd who laid down his life for his sheep. Let us praise and thank him as we pray:
Nourish your people, Lord.

Christ, you decided to show your merciful love through your holy shepherds,
—let your mercy always reach us through them.

Through your vicars you continue to perform the ministry of shepherd of souls,
—direct us always through our leaders.

Through your holy ones, the leaders of your people, you served as physician of our bodies and our spirits,
—continue to fulfill your ministry of life and holiness in us.

You taught your flock through the prudence and love of your saints,
—grant us continual growth in holiness under the direction of our pastors.

The Lord's Prayer

Our Father, who art in heaven,
hallowed be thy name;
thy kingdom come,
thy will be done
on earth as it is in heaven.
Give us this day our daily bread,
and forgive us our trespasses,
as we forgive those who trespass against us;
and lead us not into temptation,
but deliver us from evil.

Pater noster, qui es in cælis:
sanctificetur nomen tuum;
adveniat regnum tuum;
fiat voluntas tua,
sicut in cælo, et in terra.
Panem nostrum cotidianum da nobis hodie;
et dimitte nobis debita nostra,
sicut et nos dimittimus debitoribus nostris;
et ne nos inducas in tentationem;
sed libera nos a malo.

Concluding Prayer

Heavenly Father,
Saint Bernard was filled with zeal for
    your house
and was a radiant light in your Church.
By his prayers
may we be filled with this spirit of zeal
and walk always as children of light.
We ask this through our Lord Jesus Christ,
    your Son,
who lives and reigns with you and
    the Holy Spirit,
God, for ever and ever.
—Amen.

Dismissal   *If praying individually, or in a group without a priest or deacon:*

May the Lord + bless us,
protect us from all evil
and bring us to everlasting life.
—Amen.

If praying with a priest or deacon, he dismisses the people:

The Lord be with you.
—And with your spirit.

May almighty God bless you,
the Father, and the Son, + and the Holy Spirit.
—Amen.

Go in peace.
—Thanks be to God.

EVENING PRAYER

God, + come to my assistance.
—Lord, make haste to help me.

Glory to the Father, and to the Son,
    and to the Holy Spirit:
—as it was in the beginning, is now,
and will be for ever. Amen. Alleluia.

Hymn   *The Saints of God!, p. 702*

Psalmody   Ant. 1 **If I forget you, Jerusalem, let my right hand wither.**

Psalm 137:1–6

By the rivers of Babylon
there we sat and wept,
remembering Zion;
on the poplars that grew there
we hung up our harps.

For it was there that they asked us,
our captors, for songs,
our oppressors, for joy.
"Sing to us," they said,
"one of Zion's songs."

O how could we sing
the song of the Lord
on alien soil?
If I forget you, Jerusalem,
let my right hand wither!

O let my tongue
cleave to my mouth
if I remember you not,
if I prize not Jerusalem
above all my joys!

Glory to the Father, and to the Son,
    and to the Holy Spirit:
—as it was in the beginning, is now,
and will be for ever. Amen.

Ant.

**If I forget you, Jerusalem, let my right
hand wither.**

Ant. 2

**In the presence of the angels I will sing to
you, my God.**

Psalm 138

I thank you, Lord, with all my heart,
you have heard the words of my mouth.
In the presence of the angels I will bless you.
I will adore before your holy temple.

I thank you for your faithfulness and love
which excel all we ever knew of you.
On the day I called, you answered;
you increased the strength of my soul.

All earth's kings shall thank you
when they hear the words of your mouth.
They shall sing of the Lord's ways:
"How great is the glory of the Lord!"

The Lord is high yet he looks on the lowly
and the haughty he knows from afar.
Though I walk in the midst of affliction
you give me life and frustrate my foes.

You stretch out your hand and save me,
your hand will do all things for me.
Your love, O Lord, is eternal,
discard not the work of your hands.

Glory to the Father, and to the Son,
    and to the Holy Spirit:
—as it was in the beginning, is now,
and will be for ever. Amen.

Ant.   **In the presence of the angels I will sing to
you, my God.**

Ant. 3   **Adoration and glory belong by right to the Lamb who was slain.**

Canticle:
Revelation 4:11;
5:9, 10, 12

O Lord our God, you are worthy
to receive glory and honor and power.

For you have created all things;
by your will they came to be and were made.

Worthy are you, O Lord,
to receive the scroll and break open its seals.

For you were slain;
with your blood you purchased for God
men of every race and tongue,
of every people and nation.

You made of them a kingdom,
and priests to serve our God,
and they shall reign on the earth.

Worthy is the Lamb that was slain
to receive power and riches,
wisdom and strength,
honor and glory and praise.

Glory to the Father, and to the Son,
    and to the Holy Spirit:
—as it was in the beginning, is now,
    and will be for ever. Amen.

Ant.   **Adoration and glory belong by right to the Lamb who was slain.**

Reading
James 3:17–18

Wisdom from above is first of all innocent. It is also peaceable, lenient, docile, rich in sympathy and the kindly deeds that are its fruits, impartial and sincere. The harvest of justice is sown in peace for those who cultivate peace.

Responsory   In the midst of the Church he spoke with
                  eloquence.
              —In the midst of the Church he spoke with
                  eloquence.

              The Lord filled him with the spirit of
                  wisdom and understanding.
              —He spoke with eloquence.

              Glory to the Father, and to the Son,
                  and to the Holy Spirit.
              —In the midst of the Church he spoke with
                  eloquence.

Gospel
Canticle

Ant. **Bernard, eloquent doctor of the Church, friend of Christ the Bridegroom, eminent preacher of the Virgin Mother's glory, at Clairvaux you became the illustrious shepherd of your followers.**

*Canticle of
Mary
Luke 1:46–55*

My + soul proclaims the greatness of the Lord,
my spirit rejoices in God my Savior
for he has looked with favor on his
    lowly servant.

From this day all generations will
    call me blessed:
the Almighty has done great things for me,
and holy is his Name.

He has mercy on those who fear him
in every generation.

He has shown the strength of his arm,
he has scattered the proud in their conceit.

He has cast down the mighty from
    their thrones,
and has lifted up the lowly.

He has filled the hungry with good things,
and the rich he has sent away empty.

He has come to the help of his servant Israel
for he has remembered his promise of mercy,
the promise he made to our fathers,
to Abraham and his children for ever.

Glory to the Father, and to the Son,
    and to the Holy Spirit:
—as it was in the beginning, is now,
and will be for ever. Amen.

Ant.   **Bernard, eloquent doctor of the Church,
       friend of Christ the Bridegroom, eminent
       preacher of the Virgin Mother's glory,
       at Clairvaux you became the illustrious
       shepherd of your followers.**

Intercessions   Jesus Christ is worthy of all praise, for he was
       appointed high priest among men and
       their representative before God. We honor
       him and in our weakness we pray:
       Bring salvation to your people, Lord.

       You marvelously illuminated your Church
       through distinguished leaders and holy
       men and women,
       —let Christians rejoice always in such splendor.

       You forgave the sins of your people when
       their holy leaders like Moses sought your
       compassion,
       —through their intercession continue to purify
       and sanctify your holy people.

       In the midst of their brothers and sisters you
       anointed your holy ones and filled them
       with the Holy Spirit,
       —fill all the leaders of your people with the
       same Spirit.

       You yourself are the only visible possession of
       our holy pastors,
       —let none of them, won at the price of your
       blood, remain far from you.

The shepherds of your Church keep your
    flock from being snatched out of your
    hand. Through them you give your flock
    eternal life,
—save those who have died, those for whom
    you gave up your life.

The Lord's
Prayer

Our Father, who art in heaven,
hallowed be thy name;
thy kingdom come,
thy will be done
on earth as it is in heaven.
Give us this day our daily bread,
and forgive us our trespasses,
as we forgive those who trespass against us;
and lead us not into temptation,
but deliver us from evil.

Pater noster, qui es in cælis:
sanctificetur nomen tuum;
adveniat regnum tuum;
fiat voluntas tua,
sicut in cælo, et in terra.
Panem nostrum cotidianum da nobis hodie;
et dimitte nobis debita nostra,
sicut et nos dimittimus debitoribus nostris;
et ne nos inducas in tentationem;
sed libera nos a malo.

Concluding
Prayer

Heavenly Father,
Saint Bernard was filled with zeal for
      your house
and was a radiant light in your Church.
By his prayers
may we be filled with this spirit of zeal
and walk always as children of light.
We ask this through our Lord Jesus Christ,
      your Son,
who lives and reigns with you and
      the Holy Spirit,
God, for ever and ever.
—Amen.

Dismissal

If praying individually, or in a group without a priest or deacon:

May the Lord + bless us,
protect us from all evil
and bring us to everlasting life.
—Amen.

If praying with a priest or deacon, he dismisses the people:

The Lord be with you.
—And with your spirit.

May almighty God bless you,
the Father, and the Son, + and the Holy Spirit.
—Amen.

Go in peace.
—Thanks be to God.

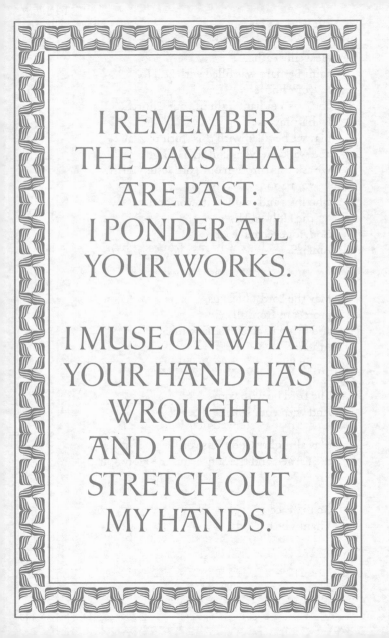

I REMEMBER
THE DAYS THAT
ARE PAST:
I PONDER ALL
YOUR WORKS.

I MUSE ON WHAT
YOUR HAND HAS
WROUGHT
AND TO YOU I
STRETCH OUT
MY HANDS.

NIGHT PRAYER———————————

God, + come to my assistance.
—Lord, make haste to help me.

Glory to the Father, and to the Son,
    and to the Holy Spirit:
—as it was in the beginning, is now,
    and will be for ever. Amen. Alleluia.

Examen *An optional brief examination of conscience may be made. Call to mind your sins and failings this day.*

Hymn *O Gladsome Light, p. 696*

Psalmody Ant. **Do not hide your face from me; in you I put my trust.**

Psalm 143:1–11 Lord, listen to my prayer:
turn your ear to my appeal.
You are faithful, you are just; give answer.
Do not call your servant to judgment
for no one is just in your sight.

The enemy pursues my soul;
he has crushed my life to the ground;
he has made me dwell in darkness
like the dead, long forgotten.
Therefore my spirit fails;
my heart is numb within me.

I remember the days that are past:
I ponder all your works.
I muse on what your hand has wrought
and to you I stretch out my hands.
Like a parched land my soul thirsts for you.

Lord, make haste and answer;
for my spirit fails within me.
Do not hide your face
lest I become like those in the grave.

In the morning let me know your love
for I put my trust in you.
Make me know the way I should walk:
to you I lift up my soul.

Rescue me, Lord, from my enemies;
I have fled to you for refuge.
Teach me to do your will
for you, O Lord, are my God.
Let your good spirit guide me
in ways that are level and smooth.

For your name's sake, Lord, save my life;
in your justice save my soul from distress.

Glory to the Father, and to the Son,
    and to the Holy Spirit:
—as it was in the beginning, is now,
and will be for ever. Amen.

Ant. **Do not hide your face from me; in you I
put my trust.**

Reading
1 Peter 5:8–9a
Stay sober and alert. Your opponent the
devil is prowling like a roaring lion looking
for someone to devour. Resist him, solid in
your faith.

Responsory   Into your hands, Lord, I commend my spirit.
—Into your hands, Lord, I commend my spirit.

You have redeemed us, Lord God of truth.
—I commend my spirit.

Glory to the Father, and to the Son,
    and to the Holy Spirit.
—Into your hands, Lord, I commend my spirit.

Gospel   Ant. **Protect us, Lord, as we stay awake;**
Canticle   **watch over us as we sleep, that awake, we**
                may keep watch with Christ, and asleep,
                rest in his peace.

Canticle of   Lord, + now you let your servant go in peace;
Simeon   your word has been fulfilled:
Luke 2:29–32 my own eyes have seen the salvation
                which you have prepared in the sight of
                    every people:
                a light to reveal you to the nations
                and the glory of your people Israel.

Glory to the Father, and to the Son,
    and to the Holy Spirit:
—as it was in the beginning, is now,
    and will be for ever. Amen.

Ant.   **Protect us, Lord, as we stay awake; watch**
                over us as we sleep, that awake, we may
                keep watch with Christ, and asleep, rest in
                his peace.

Concluding
Prayer

Let us pray.
Lord,
fill this night with your radiance.
May we sleep in peace and rise with joy
to welcome the light of a new day in
    your name.
We ask this through Christ our Lord.
—Amen.

Blessing

May the all-powerful Lord
grant us a restful night
and a peaceful death.
—Amen.

Marian
Antiphon

Sing the "Salve Regina," found on p. 700, or pray a Hail Mary.

Wednesday, August 21, 2024
St. Pius X

MORNING PRAYER————————————

God, + come to my assistance.
—Lord, make haste to help me.

Glory to the Father, and to the Son,
    and to the Holy Spirit:
—as it was in the beginning, is now,
    and will be for ever. Amen. Alleluia.

Hymn

Jesus, Eternal Truth Sublime, p. 693

Psalmody

Ant. 1 **My heart is ready, O God, my
heart is ready.**

Psalm 108

My heart is ready, O God;
I will sing, sing your praise.
Awake, my soul;
awake, lyre and harp.
I will awake the dawn.

I will thank you, Lord, among the peoples,
among the nations I will praise you,
for your love reaches to the heavens
and your truth to the skies.
O God, arise above the heavens;
may your glory shine on earth!

O come and deliver your friends;
help with your right hand and reply.
From his holy place God has made
this promise:
"I will triumph and divide the land
of Shechem;
I will measure out the valley of Succoth.

Gilead is mine and Manasseh.
Ephraim I take for my helmet,
Judah for my commander's staff.
Moab I will use for my washbowl,
on Edom I will plant my shoe.
Over the Philistines I will shout in triumph."

But who will lead me to conquer the fortress?
Who will bring me face to face with Edom?
Will you utterly reject us, O God,
and no longer march with our armies?

Give us help against the foe:
for the help of man is vain.
With God we shall do bravely
and he will trample down our foes.

Glory to the Father, and to the Son,
    and to the Holy Spirit:
—as it was in the beginning, is now,
and will be for ever. Amen.

Ant.   **My heart is ready, O God, my heart is ready.**

Ant. 2   **The Lord has robed me with grace and
          salvation.**

Canticle:
Isaiah
61:10–62:5

I rejoice heartily in the Lord,
in my God is the joy of my soul;
for he has clothed me with a robe of salvation,
and wrapped me in a mantle of justice,
like a bridegroom adorned with a diadem,
like a bride bedecked with her jewels.

As the earth brings forth its plants,
and a garden makes its growth spring up,
so will the Lord God make justice and praise
spring up before all the nations.

For Zion's sake I will not be silent,
for Jerusalem's sake I will not be quiet,
until her vindication shines forth
    like the dawn
and her victory like a burning torch.

Nations shall behold your vindication,
and all kings your glory;
you shall be called by a new name
pronounced by the mouth of the Lord.
You shall be a glorious crown in the hand
  of the Lord,
a royal diadem held by your God.

No more shall men call you "Forsaken,"
or your land "Desolate,"
but you shall be called "My delight,"
and your land "Espoused."
For the Lord delights in you,
and makes your land his spouse.

As a young man marries a virgin,
your Builder shall marry you;
and as a bridegroom rejoices in his bride
so shall your God rejoice in you.

Glory to the Father, and to the Son,
  and to the Holy Spirit:
—as it was in the beginning, is now,
and will be for ever. Amen.

Ant.   **The Lord has robed me with grace and
salvation.**

Ant. 3   **I will praise my God all the days of my life.**

Psalm 146

My soul, give praise to the Lord;
I will praise the Lord all my days,
make music to my God while I live.

Put no trust in princes,
in mortal men in whom there is no help.
Take their breath, they return to clay
and their plans that day come to nothing.

He is happy who is helped by Jacob's God,
whose hope is in the Lord his God,
who alone made heaven and earth,
the seas and all they contain.

It is he who keeps faith for ever,
who is just to those who are oppressed.
It is he who gives bread to the hungry,
the Lord, who sets prisoners free,

the Lord who gives sight to the blind,
who raises up those who are bowed down,
the Lord, who protects the stranger
and upholds the widow and orphan.

It is the Lord who loves the just
but thwarts the path of the wicked.
The Lord will reign for ever,
Zion's God, from age to age.

Glory to the Father, and to the Son,
    and to the Holy Spirit:
—as it was in the beginning, is now,
    and will be for ever. Amen.

Ant. **I will praise my God all the days of my life.**

Reading
Hebrews
13:7–9a

Remember your leaders who spoke the
word of God to you; consider how their
lives ended, and imitate their faith. Jesus
Christ is the same yesterday, today, and
forever. Do not be carried away by all kinds
of strange teaching.

Responsory

On your walls, Jerusalem, I have set my
    watchmen to guard you.
—On your walls, Jerusalem, I have set my
    watchmen to guard you.

Day or night, they will not cease to proclaim
    the name of the Lord.
—I have set my watchmen to guard you.

Glory to the Father, and to the Son,
    and to the Holy Spirit.
—On your walls, Jerusalem, I have set my
    watchmen to guard you.

Gospel
Canticle

Ant. **What you say of me does not come
from yourselves; it is the Spirit of my
Father speaking in you.**

Canticle of
Zechariah
Luke 1:68–79

Blessed + be the Lord, the God of Israel;
he has come to his people and set them free.

He has raised up for us a mighty savior,
born of the house of his servant David.

Through his holy prophets he
        promised of old
that he would save us from our enemies,
from the hands of all who hate us.

He promised to show mercy to our fathers
and to remember his holy covenant.

This was the oath he swore to our
        father Abraham:
to set us free from the hands of our enemies,
free to worship him without fear,
holy and righteous in his sight
        all the days of our life.

You, my child, shall be called the prophet of
        the Most High;
for you will go before the Lord to
        prepare his way,
to give his people knowledge of salvation
by the forgiveness of their sins.

In the tender compassion of our God
the dawn from on high shall break upon us,
to shine on those who dwell in darkness and
        the shadow of death,
and to guide our feet into the way of peace.

Glory to the Father, and to the Son,
        and to the Holy Spirit:
—as it was in the beginning, is now,
        and will be for ever. Amen.

Ant. **What you say of me does not come from yourselves; it is the Spirit of my Father speaking in you.**

Intercessions Christ is the Good Shepherd who laid down his life for his sheep. Let us praise and thank him as we pray:
Nourish your people, Lord.

Christ, you decided to show your merciful love through your holy shepherds,
—let your mercy always reach us through them.

Through your vicars you continue to perform the ministry of shepherd of souls,
—direct us always through our leaders.

Through your holy ones, the leaders of your people, you served as physician of our bodies and our spirits,
—continue to fulfill your ministry of life and holiness in us.

You taught your flock through the prudence and love of your saints,
—grant us continual growth in holiness under the direction of our pastors.

The Lord's
Prayer

Our Father, who art in heaven,
hallowed be thy name;
thy kingdom come,
thy will be done
on earth as it is in heaven.
Give us this day our daily bread,
and forgive us our trespasses,
as we forgive those who trespass against us;
and lead us not into temptation,
but deliver us from evil.

Pater noster, qui es in cælis:
sanctificetur nomen tuum;
adveniat regnum tuum;
fiat voluntas tua,
sicut in cælo, et in terra.
Panem nostrum cotidianum da nobis hodie;
et dimitte nobis debita nostra,
sicut et nos dimittimus debitoribus nostris;
et ne nos inducas in tentationem;
sed libera nos a malo.

Concluding
Prayer

Father,
to defend the Catholic faith
and to make all things new in Christ,
you filled Saint Pius X
with heavenly wisdom and apostolic courage.
May his example and teaching
lead us to the reward of eternal life.
Grant this through our Lord Jesus Christ,
    your Son,
who lives and reigns with you and
    the Holy Spirit,
God, for ever and ever.
—Amen.

Dismissal   *If praying individually, or in a group without a priest or deacon:*

May the Lord + bless us,
protect us from all evil
and bring us to everlasting life.
—Amen.

If praying with a priest or deacon, he dismisses the people:

The Lord be with you.
—And with your spirit.

May almighty God bless you,
the Father, and the Son, + and the Holy Spirit.
—Amen.

Go in peace.
—Thanks be to God.

EVENING PRAYER

God, + come to my assistance.
—Lord, make haste to help me.

Glory to the Father, and to the Son,
    and to the Holy Spirit:
—as it was in the beginning, is now,
and will be for ever. Amen. Alleluia.

Hymn   *The Saints of God!, p. 702*

Psalmody   Ant. 1 **Lord, how wonderful is your wisdom,
so far beyond my understanding.**

Psalm 139

O Lord, you search me and you know me,
you know my resting and my rising,
you discern my purpose from afar.
You mark when I walk or lie down,
all my ways lie open to you.

Before ever a word is on my tongue
you know it, O Lord, through and through.
Behind and before you besiege me,
your hand ever laid upon me.
Too wonderful for me, this knowledge,
too high, beyond my reach.

O where can I go from your spirit,
or where can I flee from your face?
If I climb the heavens, you are there.
If I lie in the grave, you are there.

If I take the wings of the dawn
and dwell at the sea's furthest end,
even there your hand would lead me,
your right hand would hold me fast.

If I say: "Let the darkness hide me
and the light around me be night,"
even darkness is not dark for you
and the night is as clear as the day.

Glory to the Father, and to the Son,
    and to the Holy Spirit:
—as it was in the beginning, is now,
and will be for ever. Amen.

Ant.   **Lord, how wonderful is your wisdom, so far
beyond my understanding.**

Ant. 2   **I am the Lord: I search the mind and
probe the heart; I give to each one as his
deeds deserve.**

Psalm 139   For it was you who created my being,
(continued)   knit me together in my mother's womb.
I thank you for the wonder of my being,
for the wonders of all your creation.

Already you knew my soul,
my body held no secret from you
when I was being fashioned in secret
and molded in the depths of the earth.

Your eyes saw all my actions,
they were all of them written in your book;
every one of my days was decreed
before one of them came into being.

To me, how mysterious your thoughts,
the sum of them not to be numbered!
If I count them, they are more than the sand;
to finish, I must be eternal, like you.

O search me, God, and know my heart.
O test me and know my thoughts.
See that I follow not the wrong path
and lead me in the path of life eternal.

Glory to the Father, and to the Son,
    and to the Holy Spirit:
—as it was in the beginning, is now,
    and will be for ever. Amen.

Ant.   **I am the Lord: I search the mind and
    probe the heart; I give to each one as his
    deeds deserve.**

Ant. 3   **Through him all things were made; he
    holds all creation together in himself.**

Canticle: Let us give thanks to the Father
Colossians   for having made you worthy
1:12–20   to share the lot of the saints
    in light.

He rescued us
from the power of darkness
and brought us
into the kingdom of his beloved Son.
Through him we have redemption,
the forgiveness of our sins.

He is the image of the invisible God,
the first-born of all creatures.
In him everything in heaven and on earth
    was created,
things visible and invisible.

All were created through him;
all were created for him.
He is before all else that is.
In him everything continues in being.

It is he who is head of the body, the church!
he who is the beginning,
the first-born of the dead,
so that primacy may be his in everything.

It pleased God to make absolute fullness
      reside in him
and, by means of him, to reconcile
      everything in his person,
both on earth and in the heavens,
making peace through the blood of his cross.

Glory to the Father, and to the Son,
      and to the Holy Spirit:
—as it was in the beginning, is now,
and will be for ever. Amen.

Ant.   **Through him all things were made; he
holds all creation together in himself.**

Reading
1 Peter 5:1–4

To the elders among you I, a fellow elder, a
witness of Christ's sufferings and sharer in
the glory that is to be revealed, make this
appeal. God's flock is in your midst; give it
a shepherd's care. Watch over it willingly
as God would have you do, not under
constraint; and not for shameful profit
either, but generously. Be examples to the
flock, not lording it over those assigned to
you, so that when the chief Shepherd appears
you will win for yourselves the unfading
crown of glory.

This is a man who loved his brethren and
         ever prayed for them.
—This is a man who loved his brethren and
         ever prayed for them.

He spent himself in their service,
—and ever prayed for them.

Glory to the Father, and to the Son,
         and to the Holy Spirit.
—This is a man who loved his brethren and
         ever prayed for them.

*Gospel
Canticle*

Ant. **This is a faithful and wise steward: the
Lord entrusted the care of his household
to him, so that he might give them their
portion of food at the proper season.**

*Canticle of
Mary
Luke 1:46–55*

My + soul proclaims the greatness of the Lord,
my spirit rejoices in God my Savior
for he has looked with favor on his
         lowly servant.

From this day all generations will
         call me blessed:
the Almighty has done great things for me,
and holy is his Name.

He has mercy on those who fear him
in every generation.

He has shown the strength of his arm,
he has scattered the proud in their conceit.

He has cast down the mighty from
    their thrones,
and has lifted up the lowly.

He has filled the hungry with good things,
and the rich he has sent away empty.

He has come to the help of his servant Israel
for he has remembered his promise of mercy,
the promise he made to our fathers,
to Abraham and his children for ever.

Glory to the Father, and to the Son,
    and to the Holy Spirit:
—as it was in the beginning, is now,
and will be for ever. Amen.

Ant. **This is a faithful and wise steward: the
Lord entrusted the care of his household
to him, so that he might give them their
portion of food at the proper season.**

Intercessions Jesus Christ is worthy of all praise, for he was
    appointed high priest among men and
    their representative before God. We honor
    him and in our weakness we pray:
    Bring salvation to your people, Lord.

You marvelously illuminated your Church
    through distinguished leaders and holy
    men and women,
—let Christians rejoice always in such splendor.

You forgave the sins of your people when
their holy leaders like Moses sought your
compassion,
—through their intercession continue to purify
and sanctify your holy people.

In the midst of their brothers and sisters you
anointed your holy ones and filled them
with the Holy Spirit,
—fill all the leaders of your people with the
same Spirit.

You yourself are the only visible possession of
our holy pastors,
—let none of them, won at the price of your
blood, remain far from you.

The shepherds of your Church keep your
flock from being snatched out of your
hand. Through them you give your flock
eternal life,
—save those who have died, those for whom
you gave up your life.

The Lord's Prayer

Our Father, who art in heaven,
hallowed be thy name;
thy kingdom come,
thy will be done
on earth as it is in heaven.
Give us this day our daily bread,
and forgive us our trespasses,
as we forgive those who trespass against us;
and lead us not into temptation,
but deliver us from evil.

Pater noster, qui es in cælis:
sanctificetur nomen tuum;
adveniat regnum tuum;
fiat voluntas tua,
sicut in cælo, et in terra.
Panem nostrum cotidianum da nobis hodie;
et dimitte nobis debita nostra,
sicut et nos dimittimus debitoribus nostris;
et ne nos inducas in tentationem;
sed libera nos a malo.

Concluding Prayer

Father,
to defend the Catholic faith
and to make all things new in Christ,
you filled Saint Pius X
with heavenly wisdom and apostolic courage.
May his example and teaching
lead us to the reward of eternal life.
Grant this through our Lord Jesus Christ,
    your Son,
who lives and reigns with you and
    the Holy Spirit,
God, for ever and ever.
—Amen.

Dismissal

If praying individually, or in a group without a priest or deacon:

May the Lord + bless us,
protect us from all evil
and bring us to everlasting life.
—Amen.

If praying with a priest or deacon, he dismisses the people:

The Lord be with you.
—And with your spirit.

May almighty God bless you,
the Father, and the Son, + and the Holy Spirit.
—Amen.

Go in peace.
—Thanks be to God.

NIGHT PRAYER

God, + come to my assistance.
—Lord, make haste to help me.

Glory to the Father, and to the Son,
and to the Holy Spirit:
—as it was in the beginning, is now,
and will be for ever. Amen. Alleluia.

Examen   *An optional brief examination of conscience may be made. Call to mind your sins and failings this day.*

Hymn   *O Gladsome Light, p. 696*

Psalmody   Ant. 1 **Lord God, be my refuge and my strength.**

Psalm 31:1–6   In you, O Lord, I take refuge.
Let me never be put to shame.
In your justice, set me free,
hear me and speedily rescue me.

Be a rock of refuge for me,
a mighty stronghold to save me,
for you are my rock, my stronghold.
For your name's sake, lead me and guide me.

Release me from the snares they have hidden
for you are my refuge, Lord.
Into your hands I commend my spirit.
It is you who will redeem me, Lord.

Glory to the Father, and to the Son,
    and to the Holy Spirit:
—as it was in the beginning, is now,
and will be for ever. Amen.

Ant. **Lord God, be my refuge and my strength.**

Ant. 2 **Out of the depths I cry to you, Lord.**

Psalm 130 Out of the depths I cry to you, O Lord,
Lord, hear my voice!
O let your ears be attentive
to the voice of my pleading.

If you, O Lord, should mark our guilt,
Lord, who would survive?
But with you is found forgiveness:
for this we revere you.

My soul is waiting for the Lord,
I count on his word.
My soul is longing for the Lord
more than watchman for daybreak.
Let the watchman count on daybreak
and Israel on the Lord.

Because with the Lord there is mercy
and fullness of redemption,
Israel indeed he will redeem
from all its iniquity.

Glory to the Father, and to the Son,
and to the Holy Spirit:
—as it was in the beginning, is now,
and will be for ever. Amen.

Ant.   **Out of the depths I cry to you, Lord.**

Reading
Ephesians
4:26–27

If you are angry, let it be without sin. The
sun must not go down on your wrath; do not
give the devil a chance to work on you.

Responsory

Into your hands, Lord, I commend my spirit.
—Into your hands, Lord, I commend my spirit.

You have redeemed us, Lord God of truth.
—I commend my spirit.

Glory to the Father, and to the Son,
and to the Holy Spirit.
—Into your hands, Lord, I commend my spirit.

Gospel
Canticle

Ant. **Protect us, Lord, as we stay awake;
watch over us as we sleep, that awake, we
may keep watch with Christ, and asleep,
rest in his peace.**

Canticle of
Simeon
Luke 2:29–32

Lord, + now you let your servant go in peace;
your word has been fulfilled:
my own eyes have seen the salvation
which you have prepared in the sight of
every people:
a light to reveal you to the nations
and the glory of your people Israel.

Glory to the Father, and to the Son,
    and to the Holy Spirit:
—as it was in the beginning, is now,
and will be for ever. Amen.

Ant. **Protect us, Lord, as we stay awake; watch over us as we sleep, that awake, we may keep watch with Christ, and asleep, rest in his peace.**

Concluding Prayer

Let us pray.
Lord Jesus Christ,
you have given your followers
an example of gentleness and humility,
a task that is easy, a burden that is light.
Accept the prayers and work of this day,
and give us the rest that will strengthen us
to render more faithful service to you
who live and reign for ever and ever.
—Amen.

Blessing

May the all-powerful Lord
grant us a restful night
and a peaceful death.
—Amen.

Marian Antiphon

Sing the "Salve Regina," found on p. 700, or pray a Hail Mary.

Thursday, August 22, 2024
Queenship of the Blessed Virgin Mary

MORNING PRAYER

God, + come to my assistance.
—Lord, make haste to help me.

Glory to the Father, and to the Son,
  and to the Holy Spirit:
—as it was in the beginning, is now,
  and will be for ever. Amen. Alleluia.

Hymn   *Hail, Holy Queen, p. 685*

Psalmody   Ant. 1 **At daybreak, be merciful to me, O Lord.**

Psalm 143:1–11
Lord, listen to my prayer:
turn your ear to my appeal.
You are faithful, you are just; give answer.
Do not call your servant to judgment
for no one is just in your sight.

The enemy pursues my soul;
he has crushed my life to the ground;
he has made me dwell in darkness
like the dead, long forgotten.
Therefore my spirit fails;
my heart is numb within me.

I remember the days that are past:
I ponder all your works.
I muse on what your hand has wrought
and to you I stretch out my hands.
Like a parched land my soul thirsts for you.

Lord, make haste and answer,
for my spirit fails within me.
Do not hide your face
lest I become like those in the grave.

In the morning let me know your love
for I put my trust in you.
Make me know the way I should walk:
to you I lift up my soul.

Rescue me, Lord, from my enemies;
I have fled to you for refuge.
Teach me to do your will
for you, O Lord, are my God.
Let your good spirit guide me
in ways that are level and smooth.

For your name's sake, Lord, save my life;
in your justice save my soul from distress.

Glory to the Father, and to the Son,
    and to the Holy Spirit:
—as it was in the beginning, is now,
and will be for ever. Amen.

Ant. **At daybreak, be merciful to me, O Lord.**

Ant. 2 **The Lord will make a river of peace flow
through Jerusalem.**

Canticle:
Isaiah
66:10–14a

Rejoice with Jerusalem and be glad
    because of her,
all you who love her;
exult, exult with her,
all you who were mourning over her!

Oh, that you may suck fully
of the milk of her comfort,
that you may nurse with delight
at her abundant breasts!

For thus says the Lord:
Lo, I will spread prosperity over her
    like a river,
and the wealth of the nations like an
    overflowing torrent.

As nurslings, you shall be carried in her arms,
and fondled in her lap;
as a mother comforts her son,
so will I comfort you;
in Jerusalem you shall find your comfort.

When you see this, your heart shall rejoice,
and your bodies flourish like the grass.

Glory to the Father, and to the Son,
    and to the Holy Spirit:
—as it was in the beginning, is now,
and will be for ever. Amen.

Ant.

**The Lord will make a river of peace flow
through Jerusalem.**

Ant. 3   **Let us joyfully praise the Lord our God.**

Psalm 147:1–11   Praise the Lord for he is good;
          sing to our God for he is loving:
          to him our praise is due.

          The Lord builds up Jerusalem
          and brings back Israel's exiles,
          he heals the broken-hearted,
          he binds up all their wounds.
          He fixes the number of the stars;
          he calls each one by its name.

          Our Lord is great and almighty;
          his wisdom can never be measured.
          The Lord raises the lowly;
          he humbles the wicked to the dust.
          O sing to the Lord, giving thanks;
          sing psalms to our God with the harp.

          He covers the heavens with clouds;
          he prepares the rain for the earth,
          making mountains sprout with grass
          and with plants to serve man's needs.
          He provides the beasts with their food
          and young ravens that call upon him.

          His delight is not in horses
          nor his pleasure in warriors' strength.
          The Lord delights in those who revere him,
          in those who wait for his love.

Glory to the Father, and to the Son,
    and to the Holy Spirit:
—as it was in the beginning, is now,
    and will be for ever. Amen.

Ant.   **Let us joyfully praise the Lord our God.**

Reading
See Isaiah 61:10

I rejoice heartily in the Lord,
    in my God is the joy of my soul;
For he has clothed me with a robe of salvation,
    and wrapped me in a mantle of justice,
    like a bride bedecked with her jewels.

Responsory

The Lord has chosen her,
    his loved one from the beginning.
—The Lord has chosen her,
    his loved one from the beginning.

He has taken her to live with him,
—his loved one from the beginning.

Glory to the Father, and to the Son,
    and to the Holy Spirit.
—The Lord has chosen her,
    his loved one from the beginning.

Gospel
Canticle

Ant. **Mary, ever-virgin, most honored
Queen of the world, you gave birth to our
Savior, Christ the Lord.**

Canticle of
Zechariah
Luke 1:68–79

Blessed + be the Lord, the God of Israel;
he has come to his people and set them free.

He has raised up for us a mighty savior,
born of the house of his servant David.

Through his holy prophets he
    promised of old
that he would save us from our enemies,
from the hands of all who hate us.

He promised to show mercy to our fathers
and to remember his holy covenant.

This was the oath he swore to our
    father Abraham:
to set us free from the hands of our enemies,
free to worship him without fear,
holy and righteous in his sight
    all the days of our life.

You, my child, shall be called the prophet of
    the Most High;
for you will go before the Lord to
    prepare his way,
to give his people knowledge of salvation
by the forgiveness of their sins.

In the tender compassion of our God
the dawn from on high shall break upon us,
to shine on those who dwell in darkness and
    the shadow of death,
and to guide our feet into the way of peace.

Glory to the Father, and to the Son,
  and to the Holy Spirit:
—as it was in the beginning, is now,
  and will be for ever. Amen.

Ant. **Mary, ever-virgin, most honored Queen
of the world, you gave birth to our Savior,
Christ the Lord.**

Intercessions Let us glorify our Savior, who chose
  the Virgin Mary for his mother. Let
  us ask him:
May your mother intercede for us, Lord.

Sun of Justice, the immaculate Virgin was
  the white dawn announcing your rising,
—grant that we may always live in the light of
  your coming.

Eternal Word, you chose Mary as the
  uncorrupted ark of your dwelling place,
—free us from the corruption of sin.

Savior of mankind, your mother stood at the
  foot of your cross,
—grant, through her intercession, that we may
  rejoice to share in your passion.

With ultimate generosity and love, you gave
  Mary as a mother to your beloved disciple,
—help us to live as worthy sons of so
  noble a mother.

The Lord's
Prayer

Our Father, who art in heaven,
hallowed be thy name;
thy kingdom come,
thy will be done
on earth as it is in heaven.
Give us this day our daily bread,
and forgive us our trespasses,
as we forgive those who trespass against us;
and lead us not into temptation,
but deliver us from evil.

Pater noster, qui es in cælis:
sanctificetur nomen tuum;
adveniat regnum tuum;
fiat voluntas tua,
sicut in cælo, et in terra.
Panem nostrum cotidianum da nobis hodie;
et dimitte nobis debita nostra,
sicut et nos dimittimus debitoribus nostris;
et ne nos inducas in tentationem;
sed libera nos a malo.

Concluding
Prayer

Father,
you have given us the mother of your Son
to be our queen and mother.
With the support of her prayers
may we come to share the glory of
    your children
in the kingdom of heaven.
We ask this through our Lord Jesus Christ,
    your Son,
who lives and reigns with you and
    the Holy Spirit,
God, for ever and ever.
—Amen.

Dismissal   *If praying individually, or in a group without a priest or deacon:*

May the Lord + bless us,
protect us from all evil
and bring us to everlasting life.
—Amen.

If praying with a priest or deacon, he dismisses the people:

The Lord be with you.
—And with your spirit.

May almighty God bless you,
the Father, and the Son, + and the Holy Spirit.
—Amen.

Go in peace.
—Thanks be to God.

EVENING PRAYER

God, + come to my assistance.
—Lord, make haste to help me.

Glory to the Father, and to the Son,
    and to the Holy Spirit:
—as it was in the beginning, is now,
and will be for ever. Amen. Alleluia.

Hymn   *The Saints of God!, p. 702*

Psalmody   Ant. 1 **He is my comfort and my refuge. In him I put my trust.**

Psalm 144

Blessed be the Lord, my rock
who trains my arms for battle,
who prepares my hands for war.

He is my love, my fortress;
he is my stronghold, my savior,
my shield, my place of refuge.
He brings peoples under my rule.

Lord, what is man that you care for him,
mortal man, that you keep him in mind;
man, who is merely a breath,
whose life fades like a shadow?

Lower your heavens and come down;
touch the mountains; wreathe
    them in smoke.
Flash your lightnings; rout the foe,
shoot your arrows and put them to flight.

Reach down from heaven and save me;
draw me out from the mighty waters,
from the hands of alien foes
whose mouths are filled with lies,
whose hands are raised in perjury.

Glory to the Father, and to the Son,
    and to the Holy Spirit:
—as it was in the beginning, is now,
and will be for ever. Amen.

Ant. **He is my comfort and my refuge. In him I
put my trust.**

Ant. 2   **Blessed are the people whose God
is the Lord.**

Psalm 144   To you, O God, will I sing a new song;
(continued)   I will play on the ten-stringed harp
to you who give kings their victory,
who set David your servant free.

You set him free from the evil sword;
you rescued him from alien foes
whose mouths were filled with lies,
whose hands were raised in perjury.

Let our sons then flourish like saplings
grown tall and strong from their youth:
our daughters graceful as columns,
adorned as though for a palace.

Let our barns be filled to overflowing
with crops of every kind;
our sheep increasing by thousands,
myriads of sheep in our fields,
our cattle heavy with young,

no ruined wall, no exile,
no sound of weeping in our streets.
Happy the people with such blessings;
happy the people whose God is the Lord.

Glory to the Father, and to the Son,
    and to the Holy Spirit:
—as it was in the beginning, is now,
and will be for ever. Amen.

Ant.
Blessed are the people whose God is the Lord.

Ant. 3
Now the victorious reign of our God has begun.

Canticle:
Revelation
11:17–18;
12:10b–12a

We praise you, the Lord God Almighty,
who is and who was.
You have assumed your great power,
you have begun your reign.

The nations have raged in anger,
but then came your day of wrath
and the moment to judge the dead:
the time to reward your servants
    the prophets
and the holy ones who revere you,
the great and the small alike.

Now have salvation and power come,
The reign of our God and the authority
of his Anointed One.
For the accuser of our brothers is cast out,
who night and day accused them before God.

They defeated him by the blood of the Lamb
and by the word of their testimony;
love for life did not deter them from death.
So rejoice, you heavens,
and you that dwell therein!

Glory to the Father, and to the Son,
    and to the Holy Spirit:
—as it was in the beginning, is now,
and will be for ever. Amen.

Ant. **Now the victorious reign of our God has begun.**

Reading
Galatians
4:4–5

When the designated time had come, God sent forth his Son born of a woman, born under the law, to deliver from the law those who were subjected to it, so that we might receive our status as adopted sons.

Responsory

Hail, Mary, full of grace, the Lord is with you.
—Hail, Mary, full of grace, the Lord is with you.

Blessed are you among women and blessed is
    the fruit of your womb.
—The Lord is with you.

Glory to the Father, and to the Son,
    and to the Holy Spirit.
—Hail, Mary, full of grace, the Lord is with you.

Gospel
Canticle

Ant. **Blessed are you, Virgin Mary, because you believed that the Lord's words to you would be fulfilled; now you reign with Christ for ever.**

Canticle of
Mary
Luke 1:46–55

My + soul proclaims the greatness of the Lord,
my spirit rejoices in God my Savior
for he has looked with favor on his
        lowly servant.

From this day all generations will
        call me blessed:
the Almighty has done great things for me,
and holy is his Name.

He has mercy on those who fear him
in every generation.

He has shown the strength of his arm,
he has scattered the proud in their conceit.

He has cast down the mighty from
    their thrones,
and has lifted up the lowly.

He has filled the hungry with good things,
and the rich he has sent away empty.

He has come to the help of his servant Israel
for he has remembered his promise of mercy,
the promise he made to our fathers,
to Abraham and his children for ever.

Glory to the Father, and to the Son,
    and to the Holy Spirit:
—as it was in the beginning, is now,
    and will be for ever. Amen.

Ant. **Blessed are you, Virgin Mary, because
you believed that the Lord's words to you
would be fulfilled; now you reign with
Christ for ever.**

Intercessions Let us praise God our almighty Father, who
    wished that Mary, his Son's mother, be
    celebrated by each generation. Now in
    need we ask:
    Mary, full of grace, intercede for us.

O God, worker of miracles, you made the
    Immaculate Virgin Mary share body and
    soul in your Son's glory in heaven,
—direct the hearts of your children to that
    same glory.

You made Mary our mother. Through
    her intercession grant strength to the
    weak, comfort to the sorrowing, pardon
    to sinners,
—salvation and peace to all.

You made Mary full of grace,
—grant all men the joyful abundance of
    your grace.

Make your Church of one mind and one
    heart in love,
—and help all those who believe to be one in
    prayer with Mary, the mother of Jesus.

You crowned Mary queen of heaven,
—may all the dead rejoice in your kingdom
    with the saints for ever.

The Lord's
Prayer

Our Father, who art in heaven,
    hallowed be thy name;
    thy kingdom come,
    thy will be done
    on earth as it is in heaven.
Give us this day our daily bread,
    and forgive us our trespasses,
    as we forgive those who trespass against us;
    and lead us not into temptation,
    but deliver us from evil.

Pater noster, qui es in cælis:
sanctificetur nomen tuum;
adveniat regnum tuum;
fiat voluntas tua,
sicut in cælo, et in terra.
Panem nostrum cotidianum da nobis hodie;
et dimitte nobis debita nostra,
sicut et nos dimittimus debitoribus nostris;
et ne nos inducas in tentationem;
sed libera nos a malo.

Concluding Prayer

Father,
you have given us the mother of your Son
to be our queen and mother.
With the support of her prayers
may we come to share the glory of
     your children
in the kingdom of heaven.
We ask this through our Lord Jesus Christ,
     your Son,
who lives and reigns with you and
     the Holy Spirit,
God, for ever and ever.
—Amen.

Dismissal

If praying individually, or in a group without a priest or deacon:

May the Lord + bless us,
protect us from all evil
and bring us to everlasting life.
—Amen.

If praying with a priest or deacon, he dismisses the people:

The Lord be with you.
—And with your spirit.

May almighty God bless you,
the Father, and the Son, + and the Holy Spirit.
—Amen.

Go in peace.
—Thanks be to God.

NIGHT PRAYER

God, + come to my assistance.
—Lord, make haste to help me.

Glory to the Father, and to the Son,
and to the Holy Spirit:
—as it was in the beginning, is now,
and will be for ever. Amen. Alleluia.

Examen   *An optional brief examination of conscience may be made. Call to mind your sins and failings this day.*

Hymn   *O Gladsome Light, p. 696*

Psalmody   Ant. **In you, my God, my body will rest in hope.**

Psalm 16   Preserve me, God, I take refuge in you.
I say to the Lord: "You are my God.
My happiness lies in you alone."

He has put into my heart a marvelous love
for the faithful ones who dwell in his land.
Those who choose other gods increase
their sorrows.
Never will I offer their offerings of blood.
Never will I take their name upon my lips.

O Lord, it is you who are my portion and cup;
it is you yourself who are my prize.
The lot marked out for me is my delight:
welcome indeed the heritage that falls to me!

I will bless the Lord who gives me counsel,
who even at night directs my heart.
I keep the Lord ever in my sight:
since he is at my right hand,
    I shall stand firm.

And so my heart rejoices, my soul is glad;
even my body shall rest in safety.
For you will not leave my soul
    among the dead,
nor let your beloved know decay.

You will show me the path of life,
the fullness of joy in your presence,
at your right hand happiness for ever.

Glory to the Father, and to the Son,
    and to the Holy Spirit:
—as it was in the beginning, is now,
and will be for ever. Amen.

Ant.   **In you, my God, my body will rest in hope.**

Reading
1 Thessalonians
5:23
May the God of peace make you perfect in
holiness. May he preserve you whole and
entire, spirit, soul, and body, irreproachable
at the coming of our Lord Jesus Christ.

Responsory Into your hands, Lord, I commend my spirit.
—Into your hands, Lord, I commend my spirit.

You have redeemed us, Lord God of truth.
—I commend my spirit.

Glory to the Father, and to the Son,
   and to the Holy Spirit.
—Into your hands, Lord, I commend my spirit.

Gospel Canticle Ant. **Protect us, Lord, as we stay awake; watch over us as we sleep, that awake, we may keep watch with Christ, and asleep, rest in his peace.**

Canticle of Simeon Luke 2:29–32 Lord, + now you let your servant go in peace;
your word has been fulfilled:
my own eyes have seen the salvation
which you have prepared in the sight of
   every people:
a light to reveal you to the nations
and the glory of your people Israel.

Glory to the Father, and to the Son,
   and to the Holy Spirit:
—as it was in the beginning, is now,
   and will be for ever. Amen.

Ant. **Protect us, Lord, as we stay awake; watch over us as we sleep, that awake, we may keep watch with Christ, and asleep, rest in his peace.**

Concluding
Prayer

Let us pray.
Lord God,
send peaceful sleep
to refresh our tired bodies.
May your help always renew us
and keep us strong in your service.
We ask this through Christ our Lord.
—Amen.

Blessing

May the all-powerful Lord
grant us a restful night
and a peaceful death.
—Amen.

Marian
Antiphon

Sing the "Ave Regina Cælorum," found on p. 680, or pray a Hail Mary.

Friday, August 23, 2024
Friday of the Twentieth Week in Ordinary Time

MORNING PRAYER ————————————

God, + come to my assistance.
—Lord, make haste to help me.

Glory to the Father, and to the Son,
    and to the Holy Spirit:
—as it was in the beginning, is now,
    and will be for ever. Amen. Alleluia.

Hymn   *God Who Made Both Earth and Heaven, p. 688*

Psalmody   Ant. 1 **Create a clean heart in me, O God; renew in me a steadfast spirit.**

Psalm 51   Have mercy on me, God, in your kindness.
In your compassion blot out my offense.
O wash me more and more from my guilt
and cleanse me from my sin.

My offenses truly I know them;
my sin is always before me.
Against you, you alone, have I sinned;
what is evil in your sight I have done.

That you may be justified when you
    give sentence
and be without reproach when you judge.
O see, in guilt I was born,
a sinner was I conceived.

Indeed you love truth in the heart;
then in the secret of my heart teach
   me wisdom.
O purify me, then I shall be clean;
O wash me, I shall be whiter than snow.

Make me hear rejoicing and gladness,
that the bones you have crushed may revive.
From my sins turn away your face
and blot out all my guilt.

A pure heart create for me, O God,
put a steadfast spirit within me.
Do not cast me away from your presence,
nor deprive me of your holy spirit.

Give me again the joy of your help;
with a spirit of fervor sustain me,
that I may teach transgressors your ways
and sinners may return to you.

O rescue me, God, my helper,
and my tongue shall ring out your goodness.
O Lord, open my lips
and my mouth shall declare your praise.

For in sacrifice you take no delight,
burnt offering from me you would refuse,
my sacrifice, a contrite spirit.
A humbled, contrite heart you will not spurn.

In your goodness, show favor to Zion:
rebuild the walls of Jerusalem.
Then you will be pleased with lawful sacrifice,
holocausts offered on your altar.

Glory to the Father, and to the Son,
    and to the Holy Spirit:
—as it was in the beginning, is now,
    and will be for ever. Amen.

Ant.   **Create a clean heart in me, O God; renew in
me a steadfast spirit.**

Ant. 2   **Rejoice, Jerusalem, for through you all men
will be gathered to the Lord.**

Canticle: Let all men speak of the Lord's majesty,
Tobit 13:8–11,   and sing his praises in Jerusalem.
13–15

O Jerusalem, holy city,
he scourged you for the works of your hands,
but will again pity the children of the
    righteous.

Praise the Lord for his goodness,
and bless the King of the ages,
so that his tent may be rebuilt in
    you with joy.

May he gladden within you all who
    were captives;
all who were ravaged may he cherish
    within you
for all generations to come.

A bright light will shine to all parts of
    the earth;
many nations shall come to you from afar,
and the inhabitants of all the limits of
    the earth,
drawn to you by the name of the Lord God,
bearing in their hands their gifts for the King
    of heaven.

Every generation shall give joyful
    praise in you,
and shall call you the chosen one,
through all ages forever.

Go, then, rejoice over the children of the
    righteous,
who shall all be gathered together
and shall bless the Lord of the ages.

Happy are those who love you,
and happy those who rejoice in your
    prosperity.

Happy are all the men who shall
    grieve over you,
over all your chastisements,

for they shall rejoice in you
as they behold all your joy forever.

My spirit blesses the Lord, the great King.

Glory to the Father, and to the Son,
   and to the Holy Spirit:
—as it was in the beginning, is now,
and will be for ever. Amen.

Ant.

**Rejoice, Jerusalem, for through you all men
will be gathered to the Lord.**

Ant. 3

**Zion, praise your God, who sent his Word
to renew the earth.**

Psalm 147:12–20

O praise the Lord, Jerusalem!
Zion, praise your God!

He has strengthened the bars of your gates,
he has blessed the children within you.
He established peace on your borders,
he feeds you with finest wheat.

He sends out his word to the earth
and swiftly runs his command.
He showers down snow white as wool,
he scatters hoar-frost like ashes.

He hurls down hailstones like crumbs.
The waters are frozen at his touch;
he sends forth his word and it melts them:
at the breath of his mouth the waters flow.

He makes his word known to Jacob,
to Israel his laws and decrees.
He has not dealt thus with other nations;
he has not taught them his decrees.

Glory to the Father, and to the Son,
 and to the Holy Spirit:
—as it was in the beginning, is now,
 and will be for ever. Amen.

Ant. **Zion, praise your God, who sent his Word
to renew the earth.**

Reading
*Galatians
2:19b–20*
I have been crucified with Christ, and the life
I live now is not my own; Christ is living in
me. I still live my human life, but it is a life
of faith in the Son of God, who loved me and
gave himself for me.

Responsory
The Lord, the Most High, has done good
 things for me.
In need I shall cry out to him.
—The Lord, the Most High, has done good
 things for me.
In need I shall cry out to him.

May he send his strength to rescue me.
—In need I shall cry out to him.

Glory to the Father, and to the Son,
 and to the Holy Spirit.
—The Lord, the Most High, has done good
 things for me.
In need I shall cry out to him.

Gospel
Canticle
Ant. **Through the tender compassion of
our God the dawn from on high shall
break upon us.**

*Canticle of
Zechariah
Luke 1:68–79*

Blessed + be the Lord, the God of Israel;
he has come to his people and set them free.

He has raised up for us a mighty savior,
born of the house of his servant David.

Through his holy prophets he
        promised of old
that he would save us from our enemies,
from the hands of all who hate us.

He promised to show mercy to our fathers
and to remember his holy covenant.

This was the oath he swore to our
        father Abraham:
to set us free from the hands of our enemies,
free to worship him without fear,
holy and righteous in his sight
        all the days of our life.

You, my child, shall be called the prophet of
        the Most High;
for you will go before the Lord to
        prepare his way,
to give his people knowledge of salvation
by the forgiveness of their sins.

In the tender compassion of our God
the dawn from on high shall break upon us,
to shine on those who dwell in darkness and
        the shadow of death,
and to guide our feet into the way of peace.

Glory to the Father, and to the Son,
    and to the Holy Spirit:
—as it was in the beginning, is now,
    and will be for ever. Amen.

Ant.   **Through the tender compassion of
our God the dawn from on high shall
break upon us.**

Intercessions   We trust in God's concern for every person
        he has created and redeemed through
        his Son. Let us, therefore, renew our
        prayer to him:
    Fulfill the good work you have begun in us, Lord.

O God of mercy, guide us toward
    spiritual growth,
—fill our minds with thoughts of truth,
    justice and love.

For your name's sake, do not abandon
    us for ever,
—and do not annul your covenant.

Accept us, for our hearts are humble and our
    spirits contrite,
—and those who trust in you shall not be
    put to shame.

You have called us to a prophetic vocation
    in Christ,
—help us proclaim your mighty deeds.

The Lord's
Prayer

Our Father, who art in heaven,
hallowed be thy name;
thy kingdom come,
thy will be done
on earth as it is in heaven.
Give us this day our daily bread,
and forgive us our trespasses,
as we forgive those who trespass against us;
and lead us not into temptation,
but deliver us from evil.

Pater noster, qui es in cælis:
sanctificetur nomen tuum;
adveniat regnum tuum;
fiat voluntas tua,
sicut in cælo, et in terra.
Panem nostrum cotidianum da nobis hodie;
et dimitte nobis debita nostra,
sicut et nos dimittimus debitoribus nostris;
et ne nos inducas in tentationem;
sed libera nos a malo.

Concluding
Prayer

Lord,
fill our hearts with your love
as morning fills the sky.
By living your law may we have
your peace in this life
and endless joy in the life to come.
We ask this through our Lord Jesus Christ,
        your Son,
who lives and reigns with you and
        the Holy Spirit,
God, for ever and ever.
—Amen.

Dismissal   *If praying individually, or in a group without a priest or deacon:*

May the Lord + bless us,
protect us from all evil
and bring us to everlasting life.
—Amen.

If praying with a priest or deacon, he dismisses the people:

The Lord be with you.
—And with your spirit.

May almighty God bless you,
the Father, and the Son, + and the Holy Spirit.
—Amen.

Go in peace.
—Thanks be to God.

EVENING PRAYER —————————————

God, + come to my assistance.
—Lord, make haste to help me.

Glory to the Father, and to the Son,
    and to the Holy Spirit:
—as it was in the beginning, is now,
and will be for ever. Amen. Alleluia.

Hymn   *Glorious Things of Thee Are Spoken, p. 686*

Psalmody   Ant. 1 **Day after day I will bless you, Lord; I
will tell of your marvelous deeds.**

Psalm 145

I will give you glory, O God my King,
I will bless your name for ever.

I will bless you day after day
and praise your name for ever.
The Lord is great, highly to be praised,
his greatness cannot be measured.

Age to age shall proclaim your works,
shall declare your mighty deeds,
shall speak of your splendor and glory,
tell the tale of your wonderful works.

They will speak of your terrible deeds,
recount your greatness and might.
They will recall your abundant goodness;
age to age shall ring out your justice.

The Lord is kind and full of compassion,
slow to anger, abounding in love.
How good is the Lord to all,
compassionate to all his creatures.

All your creatures shall thank you, O Lord,
and your friends shall repeat their blessing.
They shall speak of the glory of your reign
and declare your might, O God,

to make known to men your mighty deeds
and the glorious splendor of your reign.
Yours is an everlasting kingdom;
your rule lasts from age to age.

Glory to the Father, and to the Son,
    and to the Holy Spirit:
—as it was in the beginning, is now,
    and will be for ever. Amen.

Ant.   **Day after day I will bless you, Lord; I will
           tell of your marvelous deeds.**

Ant. 2   **To you alone, Lord, we look with
           confidence; you are ever close to those who
           call upon you.**

Psalm 145   The Lord is faithful in all his words
(continued) and loving in all his deeds.
            The Lord supports all who fall
            and raises all who are bowed down.

            The eyes of all creatures look to you
            and you give them their food in due time.
            You open wide your hand,
            grant the desires of all who live.

            The Lord is just in all his ways
            and loving in all his deeds.
            He is close to all who call him,
            who call on him from their hearts.

            He grants the desires of those who fear him,
            he hears their cry and he saves them.
            The Lord protects all who love him;
            but the wicked he will utterly destroy.

            Let me speak the praise of the Lord,
            let all mankind bless his holy name
            for ever, for ages unending.

Glory to the Father, and to the Son,
    and to the Holy Spirit:
—as it was in the beginning, is now,
and will be for ever. Amen.

Ant.   **To you alone, Lord, we look with
confidence; you are ever close to those who
call upon you.**

Ant. 3   **King of all the ages, your ways are
perfect and true.**

Canticle: Mighty and wonderful are your works,
Revelation   Lord God Almighty!
15:3–4   Righteous and true are your ways,
O King of the nations!

Who would dare refuse you honor,
or the glory due your name, O Lord?

Since you alone are holy,
all nations shall come
and worship in your presence.
Your mighty deeds are clearly seen.

Glory to the Father, and to the Son,
    and to the Holy Spirit:
—as it was in the beginning, is now,
and will be for ever. Amen.

Ant.   **King of all the ages, your ways are
perfect and true.**

Reading
Romans 8:1–2

There is no condemnation now for those who are in Christ Jesus. The law of the spirit, the spirit of life in Christ Jesus, has freed you from the law of sin and death.

Responsory

Christ died for our sins to make of us an offering to God.
—Christ died for our sins to make of us an offering to God.

He died to this world of sin, and rose in the power of the Spirit,
—to make of us an offering to God.

Glory to the Father, and to the Son, and to the Holy Spirit.
—Christ died for our sins to make of us an offering to God.

Gospel Canticle

Ant. **Remember your mercy, Lord, the promise of mercy you made to our fathers.**

Canticle of Mary
Luke 1:46–55

My + soul proclaims the greatness of the Lord, my spirit rejoices in God my Savior for he has looked with favor on his lowly servant.

From this day all generations will call me blessed:
the Almighty has done great things for me, and holy is his Name.

He has mercy on those who fear him in every generation.

He has shown the strength of his arm,
he has scattered the proud in their conceit.

He has cast down the mighty from
    their thrones,
and has lifted up the lowly.

He has filled the hungry with good things,
and the rich he has sent away empty.

He has come to the help of his servant Israel
for he has remembered his promise of mercy,
the promise he made to our fathers,
to Abraham and his children for ever.

Glory to the Father, and to the Son,
    and to the Holy Spirit:
—as it was in the beginning, is now,
and will be for ever. Amen.

Ant.   **Remember your mercy, Lord, the promise
of mercy you made to our fathers.**

Intercessions   Let us pray to Christ, the source of hope for
    all who know his name:
Lord, have mercy.

Christ, our frail humanity is prone to fall,
—strengthen us through your help.

Left to itself, our nature is inclined to sin,
—let your love always restore it to grace.

Lord, sin offends you, repentance pleases you,
—do not punish us in your wrath even when
    we have sinned.

You forgave the penitent woman, and placed
    the wandering sheep on your shoulders,
—do not deprive us of your mercy.

By your death on the cross you opened the
    gates of heaven,
—admit into your kingdom all who
    hoped in you.

The Lord's Prayer

Our Father, who art in heaven,
hallowed be thy name;
thy kingdom come,
thy will be done
on earth as it is in heaven.
Give us this day our daily bread,
and forgive us our trespasses,
as we forgive those who trespass against us;
and lead us not into temptation,
but deliver us from evil.

Pater noster, qui es in cælis:
sanctificetur nomen tuum;
adveniat regnum tuum;
fiat voluntas tua,
sicut in cælo, et in terra.
Panem nostrum cotidianum da nobis hodie;
et dimitte nobis debita nostra,
sicut et nos dimittimus debitoribus nostris;
et ne nos inducas in tentationem;
sed libera nos a malo.

505

Concluding
Prayer

God our Father,
you brought salvation to all mankind
through the suffering of Christ your Son.
May your people strive to offer themselves to
    you as a living sacrifice
and be filled with the abundance of your love.
We ask this through our Lord Jesus Christ,
    your Son,
who lives and reigns with you and
    the Holy Spirit,
God, for ever and ever.
—Amen.

Dismissal   *If praying individually, or in a group without a priest or deacon:*

May the Lord + bless us,
protect us from all evil
and bring us to everlasting life.
—Amen.

If praying with a priest or deacon, he dismisses the people:

The Lord be with you.
—And with your spirit.

May almighty God bless you,
the Father, and the Son, + and the Holy Spirit.
—Amen.

Go in peace.
—Thanks be to God.

HE HAS CAST
DOWN THE
MIGHTY FROM
THEIR THRONES,
AND HAS LIFTED
UP THE LOWLY.

NIGHT PRAYER————————————————

God, + come to my assistance.
—Lord, make haste to help me.

Glory to the Father, and to the Son,
    and to the Holy Spirit:
—as it was in the beginning, is now,
    and will be for ever. Amen. Alleluia.

Examen   *An optional brief examination of conscience may be made. Call to mind your*
            sins and failings this day.

Hymn   *O Gladsome Light, p. 696*

Psalmody   Ant. **Day and night I cry to you, my God.**

Psalm 88   Lord my God, I call for help by day;
            I cry at night before you.
            Let my prayer come into your presence.
            O turn your ear to my cry.

            For my soul is filled with evils;
            my life is on the brink of the grave.
            I am reckoned as one in the tomb:
            I have reached the end of my strength,

            like one alone among the dead;
            like the slain lying in their graves;
            like those you remember no more,
            cut off, as they are, from your hand.

            You have laid me in the depths of the tomb,
            in places that are dark, in the depths.
            Your anger weighs down upon me:
            I am drowned beneath your waves.

You have taken away my friends
and made me hateful in their sight.
Imprisoned, I cannot escape;
my eyes are sunken with grief.

I call to you, Lord, all the day long;
to you I stretch out my hands.
Will you work your wonders for the dead?
Will the shades stand and praise you?

Will your love be told in the grave
or your faithfulness among the dead?
Will your wonders be known in the dark
or your justice in the land of oblivion?

As for me, Lord, I call to you for help:
in the morning my prayer comes before you.
Lord, why do you reject me?
Why do you hide your face?

Wretched, close to death from my youth,
I have borne your trials; I am numb.
Your fury has swept down upon me;
your terrors have utterly destroyed me.

They surround me all the day like a flood,
they assail me all together.
Friend and neighbor you have taken away:
my one companion is darkness.

Glory to the Father, and to the Son,
    and to the Holy Spirit:
—as it was in the beginning, is now,
and will be for ever. Amen.

Ant.   **Day and night I cry to you, my God.**

Reading
Jeremiah 14:9a

You are in our midst, O Lord,
 your name we bear:
 do not forsake us, O Lord, our God!

Responsory

Into your hands, Lord, I commend my spirit.
—Into your hands, Lord, I commend my spirit.

You have redeemed us, Lord God of truth.
—I commend my spirit.

Glory to the Father, and to the Son,
 and to the Holy Spirit.
—Into your hands, Lord, I commend my spirit.

Gospel
Canticle

Ant. **Protect us, Lord, as we stay awake;
watch over us as we sleep, that awake, we
may keep watch with Christ, and asleep,
rest in his peace.**

Canticle of
Simeon
Luke 2:29–32

Lord, + now you let your servant go in peace;
your word has been fulfilled:
my own eyes have seen the salvation
which you have prepared in the sight of
 every people:
a light to reveal you to the nations
and the glory of your people Israel.

Glory to the Father, and to the Son,
 and to the Holy Spirit:
—as it was in the beginning, is now,
 and will be for ever. Amen.

Ant.   **Protect us, Lord, as we stay awake; watch
over us as we sleep, that awake, we may
keep watch with Christ, and asleep, rest in
his peace.**

Concluding   Let us pray.
Prayer   All-powerful God,
keep us united with your Son
in his death and burial
so that we may rise to new life with him,
who lives and reigns for ever and ever.
—Amen.

Blessing   May the all-powerful Lord
grant us a restful night
and a peaceful death.
—Amen.

Marian   *Sing the "Salve Regina," found on p. 700, or pray a Hail Mary.*
Antiphon

Saturday, August 24, 2024
St. Bartholomew

MORNING PRAYER————————————————

God, + come to my assistance.
—Lord, make haste to help me.

Glory to the Father, and to the Son,
    and to the Holy Spirit:
—as it was in the beginning, is now,
and will be for ever. Amen. Alleluia.

Hymn   *Let All on Earth Their Voices Raise, p. 694*

Psalmody   Ant. 1 **My commandment is this: love one another as I have loved you.**

Psalm 63:2–9   O God, you are my God, for you I long;
for you my soul is thirsting.
My body pines for you
like a dry, weary land without water.
So I gaze on you in the sanctuary
to see your strength and your glory.

For your love is better than life,
my lips will speak your praise.
So I will bless you all my life,
in your name I will lift up my hands.
My soul shall be filled as with a banquet,
my mouth shall praise you with joy.

On my bed I remember you.
On you I muse through the night
for you have been my help;
in the shadow of your wings I rejoice.
My soul clings to you;
your right hand holds me fast.

Glory to the Father, and to the Son,
    and to the Holy Spirit:
—as it was in the beginning, is now,
and will be for ever. Amen.

Ant.   **My commandment is this: love one
another as I have loved you.**

Ant. 2   **There is no greater love than to lay down
your life for your friends.**

Canticle:
Daniel
3:57–88, 56

Bless the Lord, all you works of the Lord.
Praise and exalt him above all forever.
Angels of the Lord, bless the Lord.
You heavens, bless the Lord.
All you waters above the heavens,
    bless the Lord.
All you hosts of the Lord, bless the Lord.
Sun and moon, bless the Lord.
Stars of heaven, bless the Lord.

Every shower and dew, bless the Lord.
All you winds, bless the Lord.
Fire and heat, bless the Lord.
Cold and chill, bless the Lord.
Dew and rain, bless the Lord.
Frost and chill, bless the Lord.
Ice and snow, bless the Lord.
Nights and days, bless the Lord.
Light and darkness, bless the Lord.
Lightnings and clouds, bless the Lord.

Let the earth bless the Lord.
Praise and exalt him above all forever.
Mountains and hills, bless the Lord.
Everything growing from the earth,
    bless the Lord.
You springs, bless the Lord.
Seas and rivers, bless the Lord.
You dolphins and all water creatures,
    bless the Lord.
All you birds of the air, bless the Lord.
All you beasts, wild and tame, bless the Lord.
You sons of men, bless the Lord.

O Israel, bless the Lord.
Praise and exalt him above all forever.
Priests of the Lord, bless the Lord.
Servants of the Lord, bless the Lord.
Spirits and souls of the just, bless the Lord.
Holy men of humble heart, bless the Lord.
Hananiah, Azariah, Mishael, bless the Lord.
Praise and exalt him above all forever.

Let us bless the Father, and the Son, and the
   Holy Spirit.
Let us praise and exalt him above all forever.
Blessed are you, Lord, in the firmament
   of heaven.
Praiseworthy and glorious and exalted above
   all forever.

Ant. **There is no greater love than to lay down
your life for your friends.**

Ant. 3 **You are my friends, says the Lord, if you do
what I command you.**

Psalm 149 Sing a new song to the Lord,
his praise in the assembly of the faithful.
Let Israel rejoice in its maker,
let Zion's sons exult in their king.
Let them praise his name with dancing
and make music with timbrel and harp.

For the Lord takes delight in his people.
He crowns the poor with salvation.
Let the faithful rejoice in their glory,
shout for joy and take their rest.
Let the praise of God be on their lips
and a two-edged sword in their hand,

to deal out vengeance to the nations
and punishment on all the peoples;
to bind their kings in chains
and their nobles in fetters of iron;
to carry out the sentence pre-ordained;
this honor is for all his faithful.

Glory to the Father, and to the Son,
    and to the Holy Spirit:
—as it was in the beginning, is now,
    and will be for ever. Amen.

Ant. **You are my friends, says the Lord, if you do
what I command you.**

Reading
Ephesians
2:19–22

You are strangers and aliens no longer. No,
you are fellow citizens of the saints and
members of the household of God. You form
a building which rises on the foundation
of the apostles and prophets, with Christ
Jesus himself as the capstone. Through him
the whole structure is fitted together and
takes shape as a holy temple in the Lord; in
him you are being built into this temple, to
become a dwelling place for God in the Spirit.

Responsory

You have made them rulers over all the earth.
—You have made them rulers over all the earth.

They will always remember your
    name, O Lord,
—over all the earth.

Glory to the Father, and to the Son,
    and to the Holy Spirit.
—You have made them rulers over all the earth.

Gospel
Canticle

Ant. **On the foundation stones of the
heavenly Jerusalem, the names of the
twelve apostles of the Lamb are written;
the Lamb of God is the light of that
holy city.**

Canticle of
Zechariah
Luke 1:68–79

Blessed + be the Lord, the God of Israel;
he has come to his people and set them free.

He has raised up for us a mighty savior,
born of the house of his servant David.

Through his holy prophets he
        promised of old
that he would save us from our enemies,
from the hands of all who hate us.

He promised to show mercy to our fathers
and to remember his holy covenant.

This was the oath he swore to our
        father Abraham:
to set us free from the hands of our enemies,
free to worship him without fear,
holy and righteous in his sight
        all the days of our life.

You, my child, shall be called the prophet of
        the Most High;
for you will go before the Lord to
        prepare his way,
to give his people knowledge of salvation
by the forgiveness of their sins.

In the tender compassion of our God
the dawn from on high shall break upon us,
to shine on those who dwell in darkness and
        the shadow of death,
and to guide our feet into the way of peace.

Glory to the Father, and to the Son,
    and to the Holy Spirit:
—as it was in the beginning, is now,
    and will be for ever. Amen.

Ant.   **On the foundation stones of the heavenly
Jerusalem, the names of the twelve apostles
of the Lamb are written; the Lamb of God
is the light of that holy city.**

Intercessions   Beloved friends, we have inherited heaven
    along with the apostles. Let us give
    thanks to the Father for all his gifts:
The company of apostles praises you, O Lord.

Praise be to you, Lord, for the banquet of
    Christ's body and blood given us through
    the apostles,
—which refreshes us and gives us life.

Praise be to you, Lord, for the feast of your
    word prepared for us by the apostles,
—giving us light and joy.

Praise be to you, Lord, for your holy Church,
    founded on the apostles,
—where we are gathered together into your
    community.

Praise be to you, Lord, for the cleansing
    power of baptism and penance that you
    have entrusted to your apostles,
—through which we are cleansed of our sins.

The Lord's
Prayer

Our Father, who art in heaven,
hallowed be thy name;
thy kingdom come,
thy will be done
on earth as it is in heaven.
Give us this day our daily bread,
and forgive us our trespasses,
as we forgive those who trespass against us;
and lead us not into temptation,
but deliver us from evil.

Pater noster, qui es in cælis:
sanctificetur nomen tuum;
adveniat regnum tuum;
fiat voluntas tua,
sicut in cælo, et in terra.
Panem nostrum cotidianum da nobis hodie;
et dimitte nobis debita nostra,
sicut et nos dimittimus debitoribus nostris;
et ne nos inducas in tentationem;
sed libera nos a malo.

Concluding
Prayer

Lord,
sustain within us the faith
which made Saint Bartholomew ever loyal
    to Christ.
Let your Church be the sign of salvation
for all the nations of the world.
We ask this through our Lord Jesus Christ,
    your Son,
who lives and reigns with you and
    the Holy Spirit,
God, for ever and ever.
—Amen.

Dismissal *If praying individually, or in a group without a priest or deacon:*

May the Lord + bless us,
protect us from all evil
and bring us to everlasting life.
—Amen.

If praying with a priest or deacon, he dismisses the people:

The Lord be with you.
—And with your spirit.

May almighty God bless you,
the Father, and the Son, + and the Holy Spirit.
—Amen.

Go in peace.
—Thanks be to God.

EVENING PRAYER

BEGINS THE TWENTY-FIRST SUNDAY IN ORDINARY TIME

God, + come to my assistance.
—Lord, make haste to help me.

Glory to the Father, and to the Son,
    and to the Holy Spirit:
—as it was in the beginning, is now,
and will be for ever. Amen. Alleluia.

Hymn *Blessed Feasts of Blessed Martyrs, p. 682*

Psalmody Ant. 1 **Like burning incense, Lord, let my prayer rise up to you.**

Psalm 141:1–9   I have called to you, Lord; hasten to help me!
Hear my voice when I cry to you.
Let my prayer arise before you like incense,
the raising of my hands like an
        evening oblation.

Set, O Lord, a guard over my mouth;
keep watch at the door of my lips!
Do not turn my heart to things that
        are wrong,
to evil deeds with men who are sinners.

Never allow me to share in their feasting.
If a good man strikes or reproves me it
        is kindness;
but let the oil of the wicked not
        anoint my head.
Let my prayer be ever against their malice.

Their princes were thrown down by the side
        of the rock:
then they understood that my words
        were kind.
As a millstone is shattered to pieces on
        the ground,
so their bones were strewn at the mouth of
        the grave.

To you, Lord God, my eyes are turned:
in you I take refuge; spare my soul!
From the trap they have laid for me
        keep me safe:
keep me from the snares of those who do evil.

Glory to the Father, and to the Son,
    and to the Holy Spirit:
—as it was in the beginning, is now,
and will be for ever. Amen.

Ant.   **Like burning incense, Lord, let my prayer rise up to you.**

Ant. 2   **You are my refuge, Lord; you are all that I desire in life.**

Psalm 142   With all my voice I cry to the Lord,
with all my voice I entreat the Lord.
I pour out my trouble before him;
I tell him all my distress
while my spirit faints within me.
But you, O Lord, know my path.

On the way where I shall walk
they have hidden a snare to entrap me.
Look on my right and see:
there is not one who takes my part.
I have no means of escape,
not one who cares for my soul.

I cry to you, O Lord.
I have said: "You are my refuge,
all I have left in the land of the living."
Listen then to my cry
for I am in the depths of distress.

Rescue me from those who pursue me
for they are stronger than I.
Bring my soul out of this prison
and then I shall praise your name.
Around me the just will assemble
because of your goodness to me.

Glory to the Father, and to the Son,
    and to the Holy Spirit:
—as it was in the beginning, is now,
and will be for ever. Amen.

Ant.   **You are my refuge, Lord; you are all that I desire in life.**

Ant. 3   **The Lord Jesus humbled himself, and God exalted him for ever.**

Canticle: Philippians 2:6–11

Though he was in the form of God,
Jesus did not deem equality with God
something to be grasped at.

Rather, he emptied himself
and took the form of a slave,
being born in the likeness of men.

He was known to be of human estate,
and it was thus that he humbled himself,
obediently accepting even death,
death on a cross!

Because of this,
God highly exalted him
and bestowed on him the name
above every other name,

So that at Jesus' name
every knee must bend
in the heavens, on the earth,
and under the earth,
and every tongue proclaim
to the glory of God the Father:
JESUS CHRIST IS LORD!

Glory to the Father, and to the Son,
    and to the Holy Spirit:
—as it was in the beginning, is now,
and will be for ever. Amen.

Ant.   **The Lord Jesus humbled himself, and God
exalted him for ever.**

Reading
Romans
11:33–36

How deep are the riches and the wisdom and
the knowledge of God! How inscrutable his
judgments, how unsearchable his ways! For
"who has known the mind of the Lord? Or
who has been his counselor? Who has given
him anything so as to deserve return?" For
from him and through him and for him all
things are. To him be glory forever. Amen.

Responsory   Our hearts are filled with wonder as we
            contemplate your works, O Lord.
—Our hearts are filled with wonder as we
            contemplate your works, O Lord.

We praise the wisdom which
    wrought them all,
—as we contemplate your works, O Lord.

Glory to the Father, and to the Son,
and to the Holy Spirit.
—Our hearts are filled with wonder as we
contemplate your works, O Lord.

Gospel
Canticle

Ant. **You are Christ, the Son of the living
God. Blessed are you, Simon, son of John.**

*Canticle of
Mary
Luke 1:46–55*

My + soul proclaims the greatness of the Lord,
my spirit rejoices in God my Savior
for he has looked with favor on his
lowly servant.

From this day all generations will
call me blessed:
the Almighty has done great things for me,
and holy is his Name.

He has mercy on those who fear him
in every generation.

He has shown the strength of his arm,
he has scattered the proud in their conceit.

He has cast down the mighty from
their thrones,
and has lifted up the lowly.

He has filled the hungry with good things,
and the rich he has sent away empty.

He has come to the help of his servant Israel
for he has remembered his promise of mercy,
the promise he made to our fathers,
to Abraham and his children for ever.

525

Glory to the Father, and to the Son,
and to the Holy Spirit:
—as it was in the beginning, is now,
and will be for ever. Amen.

Ant.   **You are Christ, the Son of the living God.
Blessed are you, Simon, son of John.**

Intercessions We give glory to the one God—Father,
Son and Holy Spirit—and in our
weakness we pray:
Lord, be with your people.

Holy Lord, Father all-powerful, let justice
spring up on the earth,
—then your people will dwell in the
beauty of peace.

Let every nation come into your kingdom,
—so that all peoples will be saved.

Let married couples live in your peace,
—and grow in mutual love.

Reward all who have done good to us, Lord,
—and grant them eternal life.

Look with compassion on victims of
hatred and war,
—grant them heavenly peace.

The Lord's
Prayer

Our Father, who art in heaven,
hallowed be thy name;
thy kingdom come,
thy will be done
on earth as it is in heaven.
Give us this day our daily bread,
and forgive us our trespasses,
as we forgive those who trespass against us;
and lead us not into temptation,
but deliver us from evil.

Pater noster, qui es in cælis:
sanctificetur nomen tuum;
adveniat regnum tuum;
fiat voluntas tua,
sicut in cælo, et in terra.
Panem nostrum cotidianum da nobis hodie;
et dimitte nobis debita nostra,
sicut et nos dimittimus debitoribus nostris;
et ne nos inducas in tentationem;
sed libera nos a malo.

Concluding
Prayer

Father,
help us to seek the values
that will bring us lasting joy in this
        changing world.
In our desire for what you promise
make us one in mind and heart.
Grant this through our Lord Jesus Christ,
        your Son,
who lives and reigns with you and
        the Holy Spirit,
God, for ever and ever.
—Amen.

Dismissal   *If praying individually, or in a group without a priest or deacon:*

May the Lord + bless us,
protect us from all evil
and bring us to everlasting life.
—Amen.

If praying with a priest or deacon, he dismisses the people:

The Lord be with you.
—And with your spirit.

May almighty God bless you,
the Father, and the Son, + and the Holy Spirit.
—Amen.

Go in peace.
—Thanks be to God.

NIGHT PRAYER————————————————

God, + come to my assistance.
—Lord, make haste to help me.

Glory to the Father, and to the Son,
    and to the Holy Spirit:
—as it was in the beginning, is now,
and will be for ever. Amen. Alleluia.

Examen   *An optional brief examination of conscience may be made. Call to mind your
sins and failings this day.*

Hymn   *O Gladsome Light, p. 696*

Psalmody   Ant. 1 **Have mercy, Lord, and hear my prayer.**

Psalm 4

When I call, answer me, O God of justice;
from anguish you released me; have mercy
    and hear me!

O men, how long will your hearts be closed,
will you love what is futile and seek
    what is false?

It is the Lord who grants favors to those
    whom he loves;
the Lord hears me whenever I call him.

Fear him; do not sin: ponder on your bed
    and be still.
Make justice your sacrifice and trust
    in the Lord.

"What can bring us happiness?" many say.
Let the light of your face shine on us, O Lord.

You have put into my heart a greater joy
than they have from abundance of corn
    and new wine.

I will lie down in peace and sleep
    comes at once
for you alone, Lord, make me dwell in safety.

Glory to the Father, and to the Son,
    and to the Holy Spirit:
—as it was in the beginning, is now,
and will be for ever. Amen.

Ant.   **Have mercy, Lord, and hear my prayer.**

Ant. 2   **In the silent hours of night, bless the Lord.**

Psalm 134

O come, bless the Lord,
all you who serve the Lord,
who stand in the house of the Lord,
in the courts of the house of our God.

Lift up your hands to the holy place
and bless the Lord through the night.

May the Lord bless you from Zion,
he who made both heaven and earth.

Glory to the Father, and to the Son,
   and to the Holy Spirit:
—as it was in the beginning, is now,
and will be for ever. Amen.

Ant.   **In the silent hours of night, bless the Lord.**

Reading
*Deuteronomy
6:4-7*

Hear, O Israel! The Lord is our God, the Lord
alone! Therefore, you shall love the Lord,
your God, with all your heart, and with all
your soul, and with all your strength. Take
to heart these words which I enjoin on you
today. Drill them into your children. Speak
of them at home and abroad, whether you
are busy or at rest.

Responsory   Into your hands, Lord, I commend my spirit.
—Into your hands, Lord, I commend my spirit.

You have redeemed us, Lord God of truth.
—I commend my spirit.

Glory to the Father, and to the Son,
    and to the Holy Spirit.
—Into your hands, Lord, I commend my spirit.

Gospel Canticle

Ant. **Protect us, Lord, as we stay awake; watch over us as we sleep, that awake, we may keep watch with Christ, and asleep, rest in his peace.**

Canticle of Simeon Luke 2:29–32

Lord, + now you let your servant go in peace;
your word has been fulfilled:
my own eyes have seen the salvation
which you have prepared in the sight of
    every people:
a light to reveal you to the nations
and the glory of your people Israel.

Glory to the Father, and to the Son,
    and to the Holy Spirit:
—as it was in the beginning, is now,
    and will be for ever. Amen.

Ant. **Protect us, Lord, as we stay awake; watch over us as we sleep, that awake, we may keep watch with Christ, and asleep, rest in his peace.**

Concluding Prayer

Let us pray.
Lord,
be with us throughout this night.
When day comes may we rise from sleep
to rejoice in the resurrection of your Christ,
who lives and reigns for ever and ever.
—Amen.

Blessing   May the all-powerful Lord
grant us a restful night
and a peaceful death.
—Amen.

Marian   *Sing the "Salve Regina," found on p. 700, or pray a Hail Mary.*
Antiphon

Sunday, August 25, 2024
Twenty-First Sunday in Ordinary Time

MORNING PRAYER————————————

God, + come to my assistance.
—Lord, make haste to help me.

Glory to the Father, and to the Son,
and to the Holy Spirit:
—as it was in the beginning, is now,
and will be for ever. Amen. Alleluia.

Hymn   *God Who Made Both Earth and Heaven, p. 688*

Psalmody   Ant. 1 **As morning breaks I look to you, O
God, to be my strength this day, alleluia.**

Psalm 63:2–9   O God, you are my God, for you I long;
for you my soul is thirsting.
My body pines for you
like a dry, weary land without water.
So I gaze on you in the sanctuary
to see your strength and your glory.

For your love is better than life,
my lips will speak your praise.
So I will bless you all my life,
in your name I will lift up my hands.
My soul shall be filled as with a banquet,
my mouth shall praise you with joy.

On my bed I remember you.
On you I muse through the night
for you have been my help;
in the shadow of your wings I rejoice.
My soul clings to you;
your right hand holds me fast.

Glory to the Father, and to the Son,
    and to the Holy Spirit:
—as it was in the beginning, is now,
and will be for ever. Amen.

Ant.   **As morning breaks I look to you, O God, to
be my strength this day, alleluia.**

Ant. 2   **From the midst of the flames the three
young men cried out with one voice:
Blessed be God, alleluia.**

Canticle:
Daniel
3:57–88, 56

Bless the Lord, all you works of the Lord.
Praise and exalt him above all forever.
Angels of the Lord, bless the Lord.
You heavens, bless the Lord.
All you waters above the heavens,
    bless the Lord.
All you hosts of the Lord, bless the Lord.
Sun and moon, bless the Lord.
Stars of heaven, bless the Lord.

Every shower and dew, bless the Lord.
All you winds, bless the Lord.
Fire and heat, bless the Lord.
Cold and chill, bless the Lord.
Dew and rain, bless the Lord.
Frost and chill, bless the Lord.
Ice and snow, bless the Lord.
Nights and days, bless the Lord.
Light and darkness, bless the Lord.
Lightnings and clouds, bless the Lord.

Let the earth bless the Lord.
Praise and exalt him above all forever.
Mountains and hills, bless the Lord.
Everything growing from the earth,
     bless the Lord.
You springs, bless the Lord.
Seas and rivers, bless the Lord.
You dolphins and all water creatures,
     bless the Lord.
All you birds of the air, bless the Lord.
All you beasts, wild and tame, bless the Lord.
You sons of men, bless the Lord.

O Israel, bless the Lord.
Praise and exalt him above all forever.
Priests of the Lord, bless the Lord.
Servants of the Lord, bless the Lord.
Spirits and souls of the just, bless the Lord.
Holy men of humble heart, bless the Lord.
Hananiah, Azariah, Mishael, bless the Lord.
Praise and exalt him above all forever.

Let us bless the Father, and the Son, and the
    Holy Spirit.
Let us praise and exalt him above all forever.
Blessed are you, Lord, in the firmament
    of heaven.
Praiseworthy and glorious and exalted above
    all forever.

Ant.   **From the midst of the flames the three
young men cried out with one voice:
Blessed be God, alleluia.**

Ant. 3   **Let the people of Zion rejoice in their
King, alleluia.**

Psalm 149   Sing a new song to the Lord,
    his praise in the assembly of the faithful.
Let Israel rejoice in its maker,
    let Zion's sons exult in their king.
Let them praise his name with dancing
    and make music with timbrel and harp.

For the Lord takes delight in his people.
He crowns the poor with salvation.
Let the faithful rejoice in their glory,
    shout for joy and take their rest.
Let the praise of God be on their lips
    and a two-edged sword in their hand,

to deal out vengeance to the nations
    and punishment on all the peoples;
to bind their kings in chains
    and their nobles in fetters of iron;
to carry out the sentence pre-ordained;
    this honor is for all his faithful.

Glory to the Father, and to the Son,
and to the Holy Spirit:
—as it was in the beginning, is now,
and will be for ever. Amen.

Ant.   **Let the people of Zion rejoice in their
King, alleluia.**

Reading
*Revelation
7:10, 12*

Salvation is from our God, who is seated on
the throne, and from the Lamb! Praise and
glory, wisdom and thanksgiving and honor,
power and might, to our God forever and
ever. Amen!

Responsory

Christ, Son of the living God,
have mercy on us.
—Christ, Son of the living God,
have mercy on us.

You are seated at the right hand of the Father,
—have mercy on us.

Glory to the Father, and to the Son,
and to the Holy Spirit.
—Christ, Son of the living God,
have mercy on us.

Gospel
Canticle

Ant. **Lord, to whom shall we go? You have
the words of eternal life. We believe and
we are convinced that you are Christ, the
Son of God, alleluia.**

Canticle of
Zechariah
Luke 1:68–79

Blessed + be the Lord, the God of Israel;
he has come to his people and set them free.

He has raised up for us a mighty savior,
born of the house of his servant David.

Through his holy prophets he
    promised of old
that he would save us from our enemies,
from the hands of all who hate us.

He promised to show mercy to our fathers
and to remember his holy covenant.

This was the oath he swore to our
    father Abraham:
to set us free from the hands of our enemies,
free to worship him without fear,
holy and righteous in his sight
    all the days of our life.

You, my child, shall be called the prophet of
    the Most High;
for you will go before the Lord to
    prepare his way,
to give his people knowledge of salvation
by the forgiveness of their sins.

In the tender compassion of our God
the dawn from on high shall break upon us,
to shine on those who dwell in darkness and
    the shadow of death,
and to guide our feet into the way of peace.

Glory to the Father, and to the Son,
    and to the Holy Spirit:
—as it was in the beginning, is now,
    and will be for ever. Amen.

Ant.   **Lord, to whom shall we go? You have the
words of eternal life. We believe and we are
convinced that you are Christ, the Son of
God, alleluia.**

Intercessions   Christ is the sun that never sets, the true
    light that shines on every man. Let us call
    out to him in praise:
    Lord, you are our life and our salvation.

Creator of the stars, we thank you for your
    gift, the first rays of the dawn,
—and we commemorate your resurrection.

May your Holy Spirit teach us to do your
    will today,
—and may your Wisdom guide us always.

Each Sunday give us the joy of gathering as
    your people,
—around the table of your Word and
    your Body.

From our hearts we thank you,
—for your countless blessings.

The Lord's
Prayer

Our Father, who art in heaven,
hallowed be thy name;
thy kingdom come,
thy will be done
on earth as it is in heaven.
Give us this day our daily bread,
and forgive us our trespasses,
as we forgive those who trespass against us;
and lead us not into temptation,
but deliver us from evil.

Pater noster, qui es in cælis:
sanctificetur nomen tuum;
adveniat regnum tuum;
fiat voluntas tua,
sicut in cælo, et in terra.
Panem nostrum cotidianum da nobis hodie;
et dimitte nobis debita nostra,
sicut et nos dimittimus debitoribus nostris;
et ne nos inducas in tentationem;
sed libera nos a malo.

Concluding
Prayer

Father,
help us to seek the values
that will bring us lasting joy in this
        changing world.
In our desire for what you promise
make us one in mind and heart.
Grant this through our Lord Jesus Christ,
        your Son,
who lives and reigns with you and
        the Holy Spirit,
God, for ever and ever.
—Amen.

Dismissal   *If praying individually, or in a group without a priest or deacon:*

May the Lord + bless us,
protect us from all evil
and bring us to everlasting life.
—Amen.

If praying with a priest or deacon, he dismisses the people:

The Lord be with you.
—And with your spirit.

May almighty God bless you,
the Father, and the Son, + and the Holy Spirit.
—Amen.

Go in peace.
—Thanks be to God.

EVENING PRAYER

God, + come to my assistance.
—Lord, make haste to help me.

Glory to the Father, and to the Son,
     and to the Holy Spirit:
—as it was in the beginning, is now,
and will be for ever. Amen. Alleluia.

Hymn   *Glorious Things of Thee Are Spoken, p. 686*

Psalmody   Ant. 1 **The Lord will stretch forth his mighty
scepter from Zion, and he will reign for
ever, alleluia.**

Psalm 110:1–5, 7   The Lord's revelation to my Master:
"Sit on my right:
your foes I will put beneath your feet."

The Lord will wield from Zion
your scepter of power:
rule in the midst of all your foes.

A prince from the day of your birth
on the holy mountains;
from the womb before the dawn I begot you.

The Lord has sworn an oath he will
not change.
"You are a priest for ever,
a priest like Melchizedek of old."

The Master standing at your right hand
will shatter kings in the day of his
great wrath.

He shall drink from the stream by
the wayside
and therefore he shall lift up his head.

Glory to the Father, and to the Son,
and to the Holy Spirit:
—as it was in the beginning, is now,
and will be for ever. Amen.

Ant.   **The Lord will stretch forth his mighty
scepter from Zion, and he will reign for
ever, alleluia.**

Ant. 2   **The earth is shaken to its depths before the glory of your face.**

Psalm 114   When Israel came forth from Egypt,
Jacob's sons from an alien people,
Judah became the Lord's temple,
Israel became his kingdom.

The sea fled at the sight:
the Jordan turned back on its course,
the mountains leapt like rams
and the hills like yearling sheep.

Why was it, sea, that you fled,
that you turned back, Jordan, on
    your course?
Mountains, that you leapt like rams,
hills, like yearling sheep?

Tremble, O earth, before the Lord,
in the presence of the God of Jacob,
who turns the rock into a pool
and flint into a spring of water.

Glory to the Father, and to the Son,
    and to the Holy Spirit:
—as it was in the beginning, is now,
and will be for ever. Amen.

Ant.   **The earth is shaken to its depths before the glory of your face.**

Ant. 3   **All power is yours, Lord God, our mighty King, alleluia.**

Canticle: See Revelation 19:1–7

Alleluia.
Salvation, glory, and power to our God:
his judgments are honest and true.
Alleluia.

Alleluia.
Sing praise to our God, all you his servants,
all who worship him reverently, great
    and small.
Alleluia.

Alleluia.
The Lord our all-powerful God is King;
let us rejoice, sing praise, and give him glory.
Alleluia.

Alleluia.
The wedding feast of the Lamb has begun,
and his bride is prepared to welcome him.
Alleluia.

Alleluia.
Glory to the Father, and to the Son,
and to the Holy Spirit:
Alleluia.

Alleluia.
as it was in the beginning, is now,
and will be for ever. Amen.
Alleluia.

Ant.   **All power is yours, Lord God, our mighty
King, alleluia.**

Reading
2 Corinthians
1:3–4

Praised be God, the Father of our Lord Jesus Christ, the Father of mercies and the God of all consolation! He comforts us in all our afflictions and thus enables us to comfort those who are in trouble, with the same consolation we have received from him.

Responsory

The whole creation proclaims the greatness
   of your glory.
—The whole creation proclaims the greatness
   of your glory.

Eternal ages praise
—the greatness of your glory.

Glory to the Father, and to the Son,
   and to the Holy Spirit.
—The whole creation proclaims the greatness
   of your glory.

Gospel
Canticle

Ant. **Many shall come from the east and the west, and they shall sit down with Abraham and Isaac and Jacob in the kingdom of heaven.**

Canticle of
Mary
Luke 1:46–55

My + soul proclaims the greatness of the Lord,
my spirit rejoices in God my Savior
for he has looked with favor on his
   lowly servant.

From this day all generations will
   call me blessed:
the Almighty has done great things for me,
and holy is his Name.

He has mercy on those who fear him
in every generation.

He has shown the strength of his arm,
he has scattered the proud in their conceit.

He has cast down the mighty from
    their thrones,
and has lifted up the lowly.

He has filled the hungry with good things,
and the rich he has sent away empty.

He has come to the help of his servant Israel
for he has remembered his promise of mercy,
the promise he made to our fathers,
to Abraham and his children for ever.

Glory to the Father, and to the Son,
    and to the Holy Spirit:
—as it was in the beginning, is now,
and will be for ever. Amen.

Ant.   **Many shall come from the east and
the west, and they shall sit down with
Abraham and Isaac and Jacob in the
kingdom of heaven.**

Intercessions   Christ the Lord is our head; we are his
                   members. In joy let us call out to him:
                Lord, may your kingdom come.

                Christ our Savior, make your Church a more
                   vivid symbol of the unity of all mankind,
                —make it more effectively the sacrament of
                   salvation for all peoples.

                Through your presence, guide the college of
                   bishops in union with the Pope,
                —give them the gifts of unity, love and peace.

                Bind all Christians more closely to yourself,
                   their divine Head,
                —lead them to proclaim your kingdom by the
                   witness of their lives.

                Grant peace to the world,
                —let every land flourish in justice and security.

                Grant to the dead the glory of resurrection,
                —and give us a share in their happiness.

The Lord's   Our Father, who art in heaven,
Prayer   hallowed be thy name;
                   thy kingdom come,
                   thy will be done
                   on earth as it is in heaven.
                   Give us this day our daily bread,
                   and forgive us our trespasses,
                   as we forgive those who trespass against us;
                   and lead us not into temptation,
                   but deliver us from evil.

Pater noster, qui es in cælis:
sanctificetur nomen tuum;
adveniat regnum tuum;
fiat voluntas tua,
sicut in cælo, et in terra.
Panem nostrum cotidianum da nobis hodie;
et dimitte nobis debita nostra,
sicut et nos dimittimus debitoribus nostris;
et ne nos inducas in tentationem;
sed libera nos a malo.

Concluding Prayer

Father,
help us to seek the values
that will bring us lasting joy in this
       changing world.
In our desire for what you promise
make us one in mind and heart.
Grant this through our Lord Jesus Christ,
       your Son,
who lives and reigns with you and
       the Holy Spirit,
God, for ever and ever.
—Amen.

Dismissal

If praying individually, or in a group without a priest or deacon:

May the Lord + bless us,
protect us from all evil
and bring us to everlasting life.
—Amen.

If praying with a priest or deacon, he dismisses the people:

The Lord be with you.
—And with your spirit.

May almighty God bless you,
the Father, and the Son, + and the Holy Spirit.
—Amen.

Go in peace.
—Thanks be to God.

NIGHT PRAYER

God, + come to my assistance.
—Lord, make haste to help me.

Glory to the Father, and to the Son,
    and to the Holy Spirit:
—as it was in the beginning, is now,
    and will be for ever. Amen. Alleluia.

Examen   *An optional brief examination of conscience may be made. Call to mind your sins and failings this day.*

Hymn   *O Gladsome Light, p. 696*

Psalmody   Ant. **Night holds no terrors for me sleeping under God's wings.**

Psalm 91   He who dwells in the shelter of the Most High
and abides in the shade of the Almighty
says to the Lord: "My refuge,
my stronghold, my God in whom I trust!"

It is he who will free you from the snare
of the fowler who seeks to destroy you;
he will conceal you with his pinions
and under his wings you will find refuge.

You will not fear the terror of the night
nor the arrow that flies by day,
nor the plague that prowls in the darkness
nor the scourge that lays waste at noon.

A thousand may fall at your side,
ten thousand fall at your right,
you, it will never approach;
his faithfulness is buckler and shield.

Your eyes have only to look
to see how the wicked are repaid,
you who have said: "Lord, my refuge!"
and have made the Most High your dwelling.

Upon you no evil shall fall,
no plague approach where you dwell.
For you has he commanded his angels,
to keep you in all your ways.

They shall bear you upon their hands
lest you strike your foot against a stone.
On the lion and the viper you will tread
and trample the young lion and the dragon.

Since he clings to me in love, I will free him;
protect him for he knows my name.
When he calls I shall answer: "I am with you."
I will save him in distress and give him glory.

With length of life I will content him;
I shall let him see my saving power.

Glory to the Father, and to the Son,
and to the Holy Spirit:
—as it was in the beginning, is now,
and will be for ever. Amen.

Ant. **Night holds no terrors for me sleeping under God's wings.**

Reading
Revelation 22:4–5

They shall see the Lord face to face and bear his name on their foreheads. The night shall be no more. They will need no light from lamps or the sun, for the Lord God shall give them light, and they shall reign forever.

Responsory

Into your hands, Lord, I commend my spirit.
—Into your hands, Lord, I commend my spirit.

You have redeemed us, Lord God of truth.
—I commend my spirit.

Glory to the Father, and to the Son,
and to the Holy Spirit.
—Into your hands, Lord, I commend my spirit.

Gospel
Canticle

Ant. **Protect us, Lord, as we stay awake; watch over us as we sleep, that awake, we may keep watch with Christ, and asleep, rest in his peace.**

Canticle of
Simeon
Luke 2:29–32

Lord, + now you let your servant go in peace;
your word has been fulfilled:
my own eyes have seen the salvation
which you have prepared in the sight of
    every people:
a light to reveal you to the nations
and the glory of your people Israel.

Glory to the Father, and to the Son,
    and to the Holy Spirit:
—as it was in the beginning, is now,
and will be for ever. Amen.

Ant.

**Protect us, Lord, as we stay awake; watch
over us as we sleep, that awake, we may
keep watch with Christ, and asleep, rest in
his peace.**

Concluding
Prayer

Let us pray.
Lord,
we have celebrated today
the mystery of the rising of Christ to new life.
May we now rest in your peace,
safe from all that could harm us,
and rise again refreshed and joyful,
to praise you throughout another day.
We ask this through Christ our Lord.
—Amen.

Blessing

May the all-powerful Lord
grant us a restful night
and a peaceful death.
—Amen.

Marian
Antiphon

Sing the "Salve Regina," found on p. 700, or pray a Hail Mary.

IT IS YOU WHOM I
INVOKE, O LORD.
IN THE MORNING
YOU HEAR ME;
IN THE MORNING
I OFFER YOU
MY PRAYER,
WATCHING AND
WAITING.

Monday, August 26, 2024
Monday of the Twenty-First Week in Ordinary Time

MORNING PRAYER————————————————

God, + come to my assistance.
—Lord, make haste to help me.

Glory to the Father, and to the Son,
    and to the Holy Spirit:
—as it was in the beginning, is now,
    and will be for ever. Amen. Alleluia.

Hymn   *God Who Made Both Earth and Heaven, p. 688*

Psalmody   Ant. 1 **I lift up my heart to you, O Lord, and
you will hear my morning prayer.**

Psalm 5:2–10,
12–13

To my words give ear, O Lord,
    give heed to my groaning.
Attend to the sound of my cries,
    my King and my God.

It is you whom I invoke, O Lord.
In the morning you hear me;
in the morning I offer you my prayer,
    watching and waiting.

You are no God who loves evil;
no sinner is your guest.
The boastful shall not stand their ground
before your face.

You hate all who do evil;
you destroy all who lie.
The deceitful and bloodthirsty man
the Lord detests.

But I through the greatness of your love
have access to your house.
I bow down before your holy temple,
filled with awe.

Lead me, Lord, in your justice,
because of those who lie in wait;
make clear your way before me.

No truth can be found in their mouths,
their heart is all mischief,
their throat a wide-open grave,
all honey their speech.

All those you protect shall be glad
and ring out their joy.
You shelter them; in you they rejoice,
those who love your name.

It is you who bless the just man, Lord:
you surround him with favor as with a shield.

Glory to the Father, and to the Son,
    and to the Holy Spirit:
—as it was in the beginning, is now,
    and will be for ever. Amen.

Ant.   **I lift up my heart to you, O Lord, and you
will hear my morning prayer.**

Ant. 2   **We praise your glorious name, O Lord, our God.**

Canticle: Blessed may you be, O Lord,
1 Chronicles God of Israel our father,
29:10–13   from eternity to eternity.

              Yours, O Lord, are grandeur and power,
              majesty, splendor, and glory.

              For all in heaven and on earth is yours;
              yours, O Lord, is the sovereignty:
              you are exalted as head over all.

              Riches and honor are from you,
              and you have dominion over all.
              In your hand are power and might;
              it is yours to give grandeur and
                  strength to all.

              Therefore, our God, we give you thanks
              and we praise the majesty of your name.

              Glory to the Father, and to the Son,
                  and to the Holy Spirit:
              —as it was in the beginning, is now,
              and will be for ever. Amen.

Ant.   **We praise your glorious name, O Lord, our God.**

Ant. 3   **Adore the Lord in his holy court.**

Psalm 29

O give the Lord, you sons of God,
   give the Lord glory and power;
   give the Lord the glory of his name.
   Adore the Lord in his holy court.

The Lord's voice resounding on the waters,
   the Lord on the immensity of waters;
   the voice of the Lord, full of power,
   the voice of the Lord, full of splendor.

The Lord's voice shattering the cedars,
   the Lord shatters the cedars of Lebanon;
   he makes Lebanon leap like a calf
   and Sirion like a young wild-ox.

The Lord's voice flashes flames of fire.

The Lord's voice shaking the wilderness,
   the Lord shakes the wilderness of Kadesh;
   the Lord's voice rending the oak tree
   and stripping the forest bare.

The God of glory thunders.
   In his temple they all cry: "Glory!"
   The Lord sat enthroned over the flood;
   the Lord sits as king for ever.

The Lord will give strength to his people,
   the Lord will bless his people with peace.

Glory to the Father, and to the Son,
      and to the Holy Spirit:
—as it was in the beginning, is now,
   and will be for ever. Amen.

Ant. **Adore the Lord in his holy court.**

Reading
*2 Thessalonians
3:10b–13*

Anyone who would not work should not eat. We hear that some of you are unruly, not keeping busy but acting like busy-bodies. We enjoin all such, and we urge them strongly in the Lord Jesus Christ, to earn the food they eat by working quietly. You must never grow weary of doing what is right, brothers.

Responsory

Blessed be the Lord our God,
  blessed from age to age.
—Blessed be the Lord our God,
  blessed from age to age.

His marvelous works are beyond compare,
—blessed from age to age.

Glory to the Father, and to the Son,
    and to the Holy Spirit.
—Blessed be the Lord our God,
  blessed from age to age.

**Gospel
Canticle**

Ant. **Blessed be the Lord our God.**

*Canticle of
Zechariah
Luke 1:68–79*

Blessed + be the Lord, the God of Israel;
he has come to his people and set them free.

He has raised up for us a mighty savior,
born of the house of his servant David.

Through his holy prophets he
    promised of old
that he would save us from our enemies,
from the hands of all who hate us.

He promised to show mercy to our fathers
and to remember his holy covenant.

This was the oath he swore to our
        father Abraham:
to set us free from the hands of our enemies,
free to worship him without fear,
holy and righteous in his sight
        all the days of our life.

You, my child, shall be called the prophet of
        the Most High;
for you will go before the Lord to
        prepare his way,
to give his people knowledge of salvation
by the forgiveness of their sins.

In the tender compassion of our God
the dawn from on high shall break upon us,
to shine on those who dwell in darkness and
        the shadow of death,
and to guide our feet into the way of peace.

Glory to the Father, and to the Son,
        and to the Holy Spirit:
—as it was in the beginning, is now,
and will be for ever. Amen.

Ant.   **Blessed be the Lord our God.**

Intercessions We esteem Christ above all men, for he was
                  filled with grace and the Holy Spirit. In
                  faith let us implore him:
                  Give us your Spirit, Lord.

               Grant us a peaceful day,
               —when evening comes we will praise you with
                  joy and purity of heart.

               Let your splendor rest upon us today,
               —direct the work of our hands.

               May your face shine upon us and keep
                  us in peace,
               —may your strong arm protect us.

               Look kindly on all who put their trust in
                  our prayers,
               —fill them with every bodily and
                  spiritual grace.

The Lord's   Our Father, who art in heaven,
Prayer   hallowed be thy name;
               thy kingdom come,
               thy will be done
               on earth as it is in heaven.
               Give us this day our daily bread,
               and forgive us our trespasses,
               as we forgive those who trespass against us;
               and lead us not into temptation,
               but deliver us from evil.

Pater noster, qui es in cælis:
sanctificetur nomen tuum;
adveniat regnum tuum;
fiat voluntas tua,
sicut in cælo, et in terra.
Panem nostrum cotidianum da nobis hodie;
et dimitte nobis debita nostra,
sicut et nos dimittimus debitoribus nostris;
et ne nos inducas in tentationem;
sed libera nos a malo.

Concluding Prayer

Father,
may everything we do
begin with your inspiration
and continue with your saving help.
Let our work always find its origin in you
and through you reach completion.
We ask this through our Lord Jesus Christ,
     your Son,
who lives and reigns with you and
     the Holy Spirit,
God, for ever and ever.
—Amen.

Dismissal

If praying individually, or in a group without a priest or deacon:

May the Lord + bless us,
protect us from all evil
and bring us to everlasting life.
—Amen.

If praying with a priest or deacon, he dismisses the people:

The Lord be with you.
—And with your spirit.

May almighty God bless you,
the Father, and the Son, + and the Holy Spirit.
—Amen.

Go in peace.
—Thanks be to God.

EVENING PRAYER ————————————

God, + come to my assistance.
—Lord, make haste to help me.

Glory to the Father, and to the Son,
and to the Holy Spirit:
—as it was in the beginning, is now,
and will be for ever. Amen. Alleluia.

Hymn   *Glorious Things of Thee Are Spoken, p. 686*

Psalmody   Ant. 1 **The Lord looks tenderly on those
                who are poor.**

Psalm 11   In the Lord I have taken my refuge.
                How can you say to my soul:
                "Fly like a bird to its mountain.

                See the wicked bracing their bow;
                they are fixing their arrows on the string
                to shoot upright men in the dark.
                Foundations once destroyed, what can
                    the just do?"

                The Lord is in his holy temple,
                the Lord, whose throne is in heaven.
                His eyes look down on the world;
                his gaze tests mortal men.

The Lord tests the just and the wicked:
the lover of violence he hates.
He sends fire and brimstone on the wicked;
he sends a scorching wind as their lot.

The Lord is just and loves justice:
the upright shall see his face.

Glory to the Father, and to the Son,
    and to the Holy Spirit:
—as it was in the beginning, is now,
and will be for ever. Amen.

Ant.
**The Lord looks tenderly on those
who are poor.**

Ant. 2
**Blessed are the pure of heart, for they
shall see God.**

Psalm 15
Lord, who shall be admitted to your tent
and dwell on your holy mountain?

He who walks without fault;
he who acts with justice
and speaks the truth from his heart;
he who does not slander with his tongue;

he who does no wrong to his brother,
who casts no slur on his neighbor,
who holds the godless in disdain,
but honors those who fear the Lord;

he who keeps his pledge, come what may;
who takes no interest on a loan
and accepts no bribes against the innocent.
Such a man will stand firm for ever.

Glory to the Father, and to the Son,
   and to the Holy Spirit:
—as it was in the beginning, is now,
and will be for ever. Amen.

Ant.   **Blessed are the pure of heart, for they shall see God.**

Ant. 3   **God chose us in his Son to be his adopted children.**

Canticle:
Ephesians
1:3–10

Praised be the God and Father
of our Lord Jesus Christ,
who has bestowed on us in Christ
every spiritual blessing in the heavens.

God chose us in him
before the world began,
to be holy
and blameless in his sight.

He predestined us
to be his adopted sons through Jesus Christ,
such was his will and pleasure,
that all might praise the glorious favor
he has bestowed on us in his beloved.

In him and through his blood, we have
    been redeemed,
and our sins forgiven,
so immeasurably generous
is God's favor to us.

God has given us the wisdom
to understand fully the mystery,
the plan he was pleased
to decree in Christ.

A plan to be carried out
in Christ, in the fullness of time,
to bring all things into one in him,
in the heavens and on earth.

Glory to the Father, and to the Son,
    and to the Holy Spirit:
—as it was in the beginning, is now,
and will be for ever. Amen.

Ant.   **God chose us in his Son to be his
adopted children.**

Reading
*Colossians
1:9b–11*
    May you attain full knowledge of God's
will through perfect wisdom and spiritual
insight. Then you will lead a life worthy of
the Lord and pleasing to him in every way.
You will multiply good works of every sort
and grow in the knowledge of God. By the
might of his glory you will be endowed with
the strength needed to stand fast, even to
endure joyfully whatever may come.

Responsory

Lord, you alone can heal me,
    for I have grieved you by my sins.
—Lord, you alone can heal me,
    for I have grieved you by my sins.

Once more I say: O Lord, have mercy on me,
—for I have grieved you by my sins.

Glory to the Father, and to the Son,
    and to the Holy Spirit.
—Lord, you alone can heal me,
    for I have grieved you by my sins.

Gospel Canticle

Ant. **My soul proclaims the greatness of the Lord, for he has looked with favor on his lowly servant.**

Canticle of Mary
Luke 1:46–55

My + soul proclaims the greatness of the Lord,
my spirit rejoices in God my Savior
for he has looked with favor on his
    lowly servant.

From this day all generations will
    call me blessed:
the Almighty has done great things for me,
and holy is his Name.

He has mercy on those who fear him
in every generation.

He has shown the strength of his arm,
he has scattered the proud in their conceit.

He has cast down the mighty from
    their thrones,
and has lifted up the lowly.

He has filled the hungry with good things,
and the rich he has sent away empty.

He has come to the help of his servant Israel
for he has remembered his promise of mercy,
the promise he made to our fathers,
to Abraham and his children for ever.

Glory to the Father, and to the Son,
    and to the Holy Spirit:
—as it was in the beginning, is now,
and will be for ever. Amen.

Ant.   **My soul proclaims the greatness of the
Lord, for he has looked with favor on his
lowly servant.**

Intercessions   God has made an everlasting covenant
            with his people, and he never ceases to
            bless them. Grateful for these gifts, we
            confidently direct our prayer to him:
            Lord, bless your people.

        Save your people, Lord,
    —and bless your inheritance.

        Gather into one body all who bear the name
            of Christian,
    —that the world may believe in Christ whom
            you have sent.

Give our friends and our loved ones a share
    in divine life,
—let them be symbols of Christ before men.

Show your love to those who are suffering,
—open their eyes to the vision of your
    revelation.

Be compassionate to those who have died,
—welcome them into the company of the
    faithful departed.

The Lord's Prayer

Our Father, who art in heaven,
hallowed be thy name;
thy kingdom come,
thy will be done
on earth as it is in heaven.
Give us this day our daily bread,
and forgive us our trespasses,
as we forgive those who trespass against us;
and lead us not into temptation,
but deliver us from evil.

Pater noster, qui es in cælis:
sanctificetur nomen tuum;
adveniat regnum tuum;
fiat voluntas tua,
sicut in cælo, et in terra.
Panem nostrum cotidianum da nobis hodie;
et dimitte nobis debita nostra,
sicut et nos dimittimus debitoribus nostris;
et ne nos inducas in tentationem;
sed libera nos a malo.

Concluding
Prayer

Father,
may this evening pledge of our service to you
bring you glory and praise.
For our salvation you looked with favor
on the lowliness of the Virgin Mary;
lead us to the fullness of the salvation
you have prepared for us.
We ask this through our Lord Jesus Christ,
        your Son,
who lives and reigns with you and
        the Holy Spirit,
God, for ever and ever.
—Amen.

Dismissal   *If praying individually, or in a group without a priest or deacon:*

May the Lord + bless us,
protect us from all evil
and bring us to everlasting life.
—Amen.

If praying with a priest or deacon, he dismisses the people:

The Lord be with you.
—And with your spirit.

May almighty God bless you,
the Father, and the Son, + and the Holy Spirit.
—Amen.

Go in peace.
—Thanks be to God.

NIGHT PRAYER————————————

God, + come to my assistance.
—Lord, make haste to help me.

Glory to the Father, and to the Son,
    and to the Holy Spirit:
—as it was in the beginning, is now,
    and will be for ever. Amen. Alleluia.

Examen   *An optional brief examination of conscience may be made. Call to mind your
sins and failings this day.*

Hymn   *O Gladsome Light, p. 696*

Psalmody   Ant. **O Lord, our God, unwearied is your
love for us.**

Psalm 86   Turn your ear, O Lord, and give answer
for I am poor and needy.
Preserve my life, for I am faithful:
save the servant who trusts in you.

You are my God; have mercy on me, Lord,
for I cry to you all the day long.
Give joy to your servant, O Lord,
for to you I lift up my soul.

O Lord, you are good and forgiving,
full of love to all who call.
Give heed, O Lord, to my prayer
and attend to the sound of my voice.

In the day of distress I will call
and surely you will reply.
Among the gods there is none like you,
    O Lord;
nor work to compare with yours.

All the nations shall come to adore you
and glorify your name, O Lord:
for you are great and do marvelous deeds,
you who alone are God.

Show me, Lord, your way
so that I may walk in your truth.
Guide my heart to fear your name.

I will praise you, Lord my God,
    with all my heart
and glorify your name for ever;
for your love to me has been great:
you have saved me from the depths of
    the grave.

The proud have risen against me;
ruthless men seek my life:
to you they pay no heed.

But you, God of mercy and compassion,
slow to anger, O Lord,
abounding in love and truth,
turn and take pity on me.

O give your strength to your servant
and save your handmaid's son.
Show me a sign of your favor
that my foes may see to their shame
that you console me and give me your help.

Glory to the Father, and to the Son,
    and to the Holy Spirit:
—as it was in the beginning, is now,
    and will be for ever. Amen.

Ant.   **O Lord, our God, unwearied is your
love for us.**

Reading
1 *Thessalonians*
5:9–10

God has destined us for acquiring salvation
through our Lord Jesus Christ. He died for
us, that all of us, whether awake or asleep,
together might live with him.

Responsory

Into your hands, Lord, I commend my spirit.
—Into your hands, Lord, I commend my spirit.

You have redeemed us, Lord God of truth.
—I commend my spirit.

Glory to the Father, and to the Son,
      and to the Holy Spirit.
—Into your hands, Lord, I commend my spirit.

Gospel
Canticle

Ant. **Protect us, Lord, as we stay awake;
watch over us as we sleep, that awake, we
may keep watch with Christ, and asleep,
rest in his peace.**

Canticle of
Simeon
Luke 2:29–32

Lord, + now you let your servant go in peace;
your word has been fulfilled:
my own eyes have seen the salvation
which you have prepared in the sight of
      every people:
a light to reveal you to the nations
and the glory of your people Israel.

Glory to the Father, and to the Son,
      and to the Holy Spirit:
—as it was in the beginning, is now,
and will be for ever. Amen.

Ant. **Protect us, Lord, as we stay awake; watch
over us as we sleep, that awake, we may
keep watch with Christ, and asleep, rest in
his peace.**

Concluding   *Let us pray.*
Prayer
Lord,
give our bodies restful sleep
and let the work we have done today
bear fruit in eternal life.
We ask this through Christ our Lord.
—Amen.

Blessing   May the all-powerful Lord
grant us a restful night
and a peaceful death.
—Amen.

Marian   *Sing the "Salve Regina," found on p. 700, or pray a Hail Mary.*
Antiphon

Tuesday, August 27, 2024
St. Monica

God, + come to my assistance.
—Lord, make haste to help me.

Glory to the Father, and to the Son,
    and to the Holy Spirit:
—as it was in the beginning, is now,
    and will be for ever. Amen. Alleluia.

Hymn   *High Let Us All Our Voices Raise, p. 692*

Psalmody   Ant. 1 **The man whose deeds are blameless and whose heart is pure will climb the mountain of the Lord.**

Psalm 24   The Lord's is the earth and its fullness,
the world and all its peoples.
It is he who set it on the seas;
on the waters he made it firm.

Who shall climb the mountain of the Lord?
Who shall stand in his holy place?
The man with clean hands and pure heart,
who desires not worthless things,
who has not sworn so as to deceive
    his neighbor.

He shall receive blessings from the Lord
and reward from the God who saves him.
Such are the men who seek him,
seek the face of the God of Jacob.

O gates, lift high your heads;
grow higher, ancient doors.
Let him enter, the king of glory!

Who is the king of glory?
The Lord, the mighty, the valiant,
the Lord, the valiant in war.

O gates, lift high your heads;
grow higher, ancient doors.
Let him enter, the king of glory!

Who is he, the king of glory?
He, the Lord of armies,
he is the king of glory.

Glory to the Father, and to the Son,
    and to the Holy Spirit:
—as it was in the beginning, is now,
and will be for ever. Amen.

Ant.   **The man whose deeds are blameless
and whose heart is pure will climb the
mountain of the Lord.**

Ant. 2   **Praise the eternal King in all your deeds.**

Canticle: Blessed be God who lives forever,
Tobit 13:1–8   because his kingdom lasts for all ages.

For he scourges and then has mercy;
he casts down to the depths of the
    nether world,
and he brings up from the great abyss.
No one can escape his hand.

Praise him, you Israelites, before the Gentiles,
for though he has scattered you among them,
he has shown you his greatness even there.

Exalt him before every living being,
because he is the Lord our God,
our Father and God forever.

He scourged you for your iniquities,
but will again have mercy on you all.
He will gather you from all the Gentiles
among whom you have been scattered.

When you turn back to him with all
    your heart,
to do what is right before him,
then he will turn back to you,
and no longer hide his face from you.

So now consider what he has done for you,
and praise him with full voice.
Bless the Lord of righteousness,
and exalt the King of the ages.

In the land of my exile I praise him,
and show his power and majesty to a
    sinful nation.
"Turn back, you sinners! do the right
    before him:
perhaps he may look with favor upon you
and show you mercy.

"As for me, I exalt my God,
and my spirit rejoices in the King of heaven.
Let all people speak of his majesty,
and sing his praises in Jerusalem."

Glory to the Father, and to the Son,
and to the Holy Spirit:
—as it was in the beginning, is now,
and will be for ever. Amen.

Ant. **Praise the eternal King in all your deeds.**

Ant. 3 **The loyal heart must praise the Lord.**

Psalm 33

Ring out your joy to the Lord, O you just;
for praise is fitting for loyal hearts.

Give thanks to the Lord upon the harp,
with a ten-stringed lute sing him songs.
O sing him a song that is new,
play loudly, with all your skill.

For the word of the Lord is faithful
and all his works to be trusted.
The Lord loves justice and right
and fills the earth with his love.

By his word the heavens were made,
by the breath of his mouth all the stars.
He collects the waves of the ocean;
he stores up the depths of the sea.

Let all the earth fear the Lord,
all who live in the world revere him.
He spoke; and it came to be.
He commanded; it sprang into being.

He frustrates the designs of the nations,
he defeats the plans of the peoples.
His own designs shall stand for ever,
the plans of his heart from age to age.

They are happy, whose God is the Lord,
the people he has chosen as his own.
From the heavens the Lord looks forth,
he sees all the children of men.

From the place where he dwells he gazes
on all the dwellers on the earth,
he who shapes the hearts of them all
and considers all their deeds.

A king is not saved by his army,
nor a warrior preserved by his strength.
A vain hope for safety is the horse;
despite its power it cannot save.

The Lord looks on those who revere him,
on those who hope in his love,
to rescue their souls from death,
to keep them alive in famine.

Our soul is waiting for the Lord.
The Lord is our help and our shield.
In him do our hearts find joy.
We trust in his holy name.

May your love be upon us, O Lord,
as we place all our hope in you.

Glory to the Father, and to the Son,
and to the Holy Spirit:
—as it was in the beginning, is now,
and will be for ever. Amen.

Ant.   **The loyal heart must praise the Lord.**

Reading
Romans 12:1–2

Brothers, I beg you through the mercy of
God to offer your bodies as a living sacrifice
holy and acceptable to God, your spiritual
worship. Do not conform yourselves to this
age but be transformed by the renewal of
your mind, so that you may judge what is
God's will, what is good, pleasing and perfect.

Responsory

The Lord will help her; his loving presence
will be with her.
—The Lord will help her; his loving presence
will be with her.

He dwells in her; she will not falter.
—His loving presence will be with her.

Glory to the Father, and to the Son,
and to the Holy Spirit.
—The Lord will help her; his loving presence
will be with her.

Gospel
Canticle

Ant. **You answered her prayer, O Lord, you
did not disregard her tears which fell upon
the earth wherever she prayed.**

Canticle of
Zechariah
Luke 1:68–79

Blessed + be the Lord, the God of Israel;
he has come to his people and set them free.

He has raised up for us a mighty savior,
born of the house of his servant David.

Through his holy prophets he
    promised of old
that he would save us from our enemies,
from the hands of all who hate us.

He promised to show mercy to our fathers
and to remember his holy covenant.

This was the oath he swore to our
    father Abraham:
to set us free from the hands of our enemies,
free to worship him without fear,
holy and righteous in his sight
    all the days of our life.

You, my child, shall be called the prophet of
    the Most High;
for you will go before the Lord to
    prepare his way,
to give his people knowledge of salvation
by the forgiveness of their sins.

In the tender compassion of our God
the dawn from on high shall break upon us,
to shine on those who dwell in darkness and
    the shadow of death,
and to guide our feet into the way of peace.

Glory to the Father, and to the Son,
   and to the Holy Spirit:
—as it was in the beginning, is now,
   and will be for ever. Amen.

Ant.   **You answered her prayer, O Lord, you did
not disregard her tears which fell upon the
earth wherever she prayed.**

Intercessions   My brothers, with all the holy women, let
   us profess our faith in our Savior and
   call upon him:
   Come, Lord Jesus.

Lord Jesus, you forgave the sinful woman
   because she loved much,
—forgive us who have sinned much.

Lord Jesus, the holy women ministered to
   your needs during your journeys,
—help us to follow your footsteps.

Lord Jesus, master, Mary listened to your
   words while Martha served your needs,
—help us to serve you with love and devotion.

Lord Jesus, you call everyone who does your
   will your brother, sister and mother,
—help us to do what is pleasing to you in word
   and action.

The Lord's Prayer

Our Father, who art in heaven,
hallowed be thy name;
thy kingdom come,
thy will be done
on earth as it is in heaven.
Give us this day our daily bread,
and forgive us our trespasses,
as we forgive those who trespass against us;
and lead us not into temptation,
but deliver us from evil.

Pater noster, qui es in cælis:
sanctificetur nomen tuum;
adveniat regnum tuum;
fiat voluntas tua,
sicut in cælo, et in terra.
Panem nostrum cotidianum da nobis hodie;
et dimitte nobis debita nostra,
sicut et nos dimittimus debitoribus nostris;
et ne nos inducas in tentationem;
sed libera nos a malo.

Concluding Prayer

God of mercy,
comfort of those in sorrow,
the tears of Saint Monica moved you
to convert her son Saint Augustine to the
    faith of Christ.
By their prayers, help us to turn from our sins
and to find your loving forgiveness.
Grant this through our Lord Jesus Christ,
    your Son,
who lives and reigns with you and
    the Holy Spirit,
God, for ever and ever.
—Amen.

Dismissal   *If praying individually, or in a group without a priest or deacon:*

May the Lord + bless us,
protect us from all evil
and bring us to everlasting life.
—Amen.

If praying with a priest or deacon, he dismisses the people:

The Lord be with you.
—And with your spirit.

May almighty God bless you,
the Father, and the Son, + and the Holy Spirit.
—Amen.

Go in peace.
—Thanks be to God.

EVENING PRAYER—————————————

God, + come to my assistance.
—Lord, make haste to help me.

Glory to the Father, and to the Son,
    and to the Holy Spirit:
—as it was in the beginning, is now,
    and will be for ever. Amen. Alleluia.

Hymn   *The Saints of God!, p. 702*

Psalmody   Ant. 1 **God has crowned his Christ
with victory.**

Psalm 20

May the Lord answer in time of trial;
may the name of Jacob's God protect you.

May he send you help from his shrine
and give you support from Zion.
May he remember all your offerings
and receive your sacrifice with favor.

May he give you your heart's desire
and fulfill every one of your plans.
May we ring out our joy at your victory
and rejoice in the name of our God.
May the Lord grant all your prayers.

I am sure now that the Lord
will give victory to his anointed,
will reply from his holy heaven
with the mighty victory of his hand.

Some trust in chariots or horses,
but we in the name of the Lord.
They will collapse and fall,
but we shall hold and stand firm.

Give victory to the king, O Lord,
give answer on the day we call.

Glory to the Father, and to the Son,
    and to the Holy Spirit:
—as it was in the beginning, is now,
and will be for ever. Amen.

Ant.   **God has crowned his Christ with victory.**

Ant. 2 **We celebrate your mighty works with songs of praise, O Lord.**

Psalm 21:2–8, 14   O Lord, your strength gives joy to the king;
how your saving help makes him glad!
You have granted him his heart's desire;
you have not refused the prayer of his lips.

You came to meet him with the blessings
of success,
you have set on his head a crown of pure gold.
He asked you for life and this you have given,
days that will last from age to age.

Your saving help has given him glory.
You have laid upon him majesty and splendor,
you have granted your blessings to
him for ever.
You have made him rejoice with the joy of
your presence.

The king has put his trust in the Lord:
through the mercy of the Most High he shall
stand firm.
O Lord, arise in your strength;
we shall sing and praise your power.

Glory to the Father, and to the Son,
and to the Holy Spirit:
—as it was in the beginning, is now,
and will be for ever. Amen.

Ant. **We celebrate your mighty works with songs of praise, O Lord.**

Ant. 3 **Lord, you have made us a kingdom and priests for God our Father.**

Canticle:
Revelation 4:11;
5:9, 10, 12

O Lord, our God, you are worthy
to receive glory and honor and power.

For you have created all things;
by your will they came to be and were made.

Worthy are you, O Lord,
to receive the scroll and break open its seals.

For you were slain;
with your blood you purchased for God
men of every race and tongue,
of every people and nation.

You made of them a kingdom,
and priests to serve our God,
and they shall reign on the earth.

Worthy is the Lamb that was slain
to receive power and riches,
wisdom and strength,
honor and glory and praise.

Glory to the Father, and to the Son,
and to the Holy Spirit:
—as it was in the beginning, is now,
and will be for ever. Amen.

Ant. **Lord, you have made us a kingdom and priests for God our Father.**

Reading
Romans 8:28–30
We know that God makes all things work together for the good of those who have been called according to his decree. Those whom he foreknew he predestined to share the image of his Son, that the Son might be the first-born of many brothers. Those he predestined he likewise called; those he called he also justified; and those he justified he in turn glorified.

Responsory

The Lord has chosen her, his loved one from the beginning.
—The Lord has chosen her, his loved one from the beginning.

He has taken her to live with him,
—his loved one from the beginning.

Glory to the Father, and to the Son, and to the Holy Spirit.
—The Lord has chosen her, his loved one from the beginning.

Gospel Canticle

Ant. **While in this world, Monica lived in Christ; the goodness of her life was so evident that the name of the Lord was praised in her faith and in her works.**

Canticle of Mary
Luke 1:46–55
My + soul proclaims the greatness of the Lord, my spirit rejoices in God my Savior for he has looked with favor on his lowly servant.

From this day all generations will
     call me blessed:
the Almighty has done great things for me,
and holy is his Name.

He has mercy on those who fear him
in every generation.

He has shown the strength of his arm,
he has scattered the proud in their conceit.

He has cast down the mighty from
     their thrones,
and has lifted up the lowly.

He has filled the hungry with good things,
and the rich he has sent away empty.

He has come to the help of his servant Israel
for he has remembered his promise of mercy,
the promise he made to our fathers,
to Abraham and his children for ever.

Glory to the Father, and to the Son,
     and to the Holy Spirit:
—as it was in the beginning, is now,
and will be for ever. Amen.

Ant.   **While in this world, Monica lived in Christ;
the goodness of her life was so evident that
the name of the Lord was praised in her
faith and in her works.**

Intercessions Through the intercession of holy women let
us pray for the Church in these words:
Be mindful of your Church, Lord.

Through all the women martyrs who
conquered bodily death by their courage,
—strengthen your Church in the hour of trial.

Through married women who have advanced
in grace by holy matrimony,
—make the apostolic mission of your
Church fruitful.

Through widows who eased their loneliness
and sanctified it by prayer and hospitality,
—help your Church reveal the mystery of your
love to the world.

Through mothers who have borne children
for the kingdom of God and the human
community,
—help your Church bring all men and women
to a rebirth in life and salvation.

Through all your holy women who have
been worthy to contemplate the light of
your countenance,
—let the deceased members of your Church
exult in that same vision forever.

The Lord's
Prayer

Our Father, who art in heaven,
hallowed be thy name;
thy kingdom come,
thy will be done
on earth as it is in heaven.
Give us this day our daily bread,
and forgive us our trespasses,
as we forgive those who trespass against us;
and lead us not into temptation,
but deliver us from evil.

Pater noster, qui es in cælis:
sanctificetur nomen tuum;
adveniat regnum tuum;
fiat voluntas tua,
sicut in cælo, et in terra.
Panem nostrum cotidianum da nobis hodie;
et dimitte nobis debita nostra,
sicut et nos dimittimus debitoribus nostris;
et ne nos inducas in tentationem;
sed libera nos a malo.

Concluding
Prayer

God of mercy,
comfort of those in sorrow,
the tears of Saint Monica moved you
to convert her son Saint Augustine to the
    faith of Christ.
By their prayers, help us to turn from our sins
and to find your loving forgiveness.
Grant this through our Lord Jesus Christ,
    your Son,
who lives and reigns with you and
    the Holy Spirit,
God, for ever and ever.
—Amen.

Dismissal   *If praying individually, or in a group without a priest or deacon:*

May the Lord + bless us,
protect us from all evil
and bring us to everlasting life.
—Amen.

If praying with a priest or deacon, he dismisses the people:

The Lord be with you.
—And with your spirit.

May almighty God bless you,
the Father, and the Son, + and the Holy Spirit.
—Amen.

Go in peace.
—Thanks be to God.

NIGHT PRAYER

God, + come to my assistance.
—Lord, make haste to help me.

Glory to the Father, and to the Son,
    and to the Holy Spirit:
—as it was in the beginning, is now,
and will be for ever. Amen. Alleluia.

Examen   *An optional brief examination of conscience may be made. Call to mind your sins and failings this day.*

Hymn   *O Gladsome Light, p. 696*

Psalmody   Ant. **Do not hide your face from me; in you I put my trust.**

Psalm 143:1–11

Lord, listen to my prayer:
turn your ear to my appeal.
You are faithful, you are just; give answer.
Do not call your servant to judgment
for no one is just in your sight.

The enemy pursues my soul;
he has crushed my life to the ground;
he has made me dwell in darkness
like the dead, long forgotten.
Therefore my spirit fails;
my heart is numb within me.

I remember the days that are past:
I ponder all your works.
I muse on what your hand has wrought
and to you I stretch out my hands.
Like a parched land my soul thirsts for you.

Lord, make haste and answer;
for my spirit fails within me.
Do not hide your face
lest I become like those in the grave.

In the morning let me know your love
for I put my trust in you.
Make me know the way I should walk:
to you I lift up my soul.

Rescue me, Lord, from my enemies;
I have fled to you for refuge.
Teach me to do your will
for you, O Lord, are my God.
Let your good spirit guide me
in ways that are level and smooth.

For your name's sake, Lord, save my life;
in your justice save my soul from distress.

Glory to the Father, and to the Son,
    and to the Holy Spirit:
—as it was in the beginning, is now,
and will be for ever. Amen.

Ant.   **Do not hide your face from me; in you I
put my trust.**

Reading   Stay sober and alert. Your opponent the
1 Peter 5:8–9a devil is prowling like a roaring lion looking
for someone to devour. Resist him, solid in
your faith.

Responsory   Into your hands, Lord, I commend my spirit.
—Into your hands, Lord, I commend my spirit.

You have redeemed us, Lord God of truth.
—I commend my spirit.

Glory to the Father, and to the Son,
    and to the Holy Spirit.
—Into your hands, Lord, I commend my spirit.

Gospel   Ant. **Protect us, Lord, as we stay awake;
Canticle   watch over us as we sleep, that awake, we
may keep watch with Christ, and asleep,
rest in his peace.**

*Canticle of
Simeon
Luke 2:29–32*

Lord, + now you let your servant go in peace;
your word has been fulfilled:
my own eyes have seen the salvation
which you have prepared in the sight of
    every people:
a light to reveal you to the nations
and the glory of your people Israel.

Glory to the Father, and to the Son,
    and to the Holy Spirit:
—as it was in the beginning, is now,
and will be for ever. Amen.

Ant.

**Protect us, Lord, as we stay awake; watch
over us as we sleep, that awake, we may
keep watch with Christ, and asleep, rest in
his peace.**

Concluding
Prayer

Let us pray.
Lord,
fill this night with your radiance.
May we sleep in peace and rise with joy
to welcome the light of a new day in
    your name.
We ask this through Christ our Lord.
—Amen.

Blessing

May the all-powerful Lord
grant us a restful night
and a peaceful death.
—Amen.

Marian
Antiphon

Sing the "Salve Regina," found on p. 700, or pray a Hail Mary.

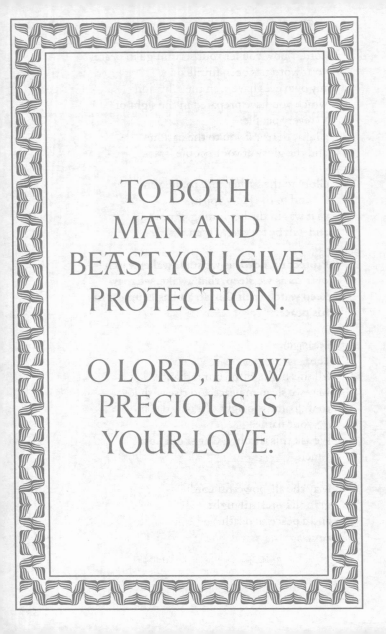

TO BOTH
MAN AND
BEAST YOU GIVE
PROTECTION.

O LORD, HOW
PRECIOUS IS
YOUR LOVE.

Wednesday, August 28, 2024
St. Augustine

MORNING PRAYER——————————————

God, + come to my assistance.
—Lord, make haste to help me.

Glory to the Father, and to the Son,
　　and to the Holy Spirit:
—as it was in the beginning, is now,
　　and will be for ever. Amen. Alleluia.

Hymn　　*Jesus, Eternal Truth Sublime, p. 693*

Psalmody　　Ant. 1　**O Lord, in your light we see light itself.**

Psalm 36　　Sin speaks to the sinner
in the depths of his heart.
There is no fear of God
before his eyes.

He so flatters himself in his mind
that he knows not his guilt.
In his mouth are mischief and deceit.
All wisdom is gone.

He plots the defeat of goodness
as he lies on his bed.
He has set his foot on evil ways,
he clings to what is evil.

Your love, Lord, reaches to heaven;
your truth to the skies.
Your justice is like God's mountain,
your judgments like the deep.

To both man and beast you give protection.
O Lord, how precious is your love.
My God, the sons of men
find refuge in the shelter of your wings.

They feast on the riches of your house;
they drink from the stream of your delight.
In you is the source of life
and in your light we see light.

Keep on loving those who know you,
doing justice for upright hearts.
Let the foot of the proud not crush me
nor the hand of the wicked cast me out.

See how the evil-doers fall!
Flung down, they shall never arise.

Glory to the Father, and to the Son,
    and to the Holy Spirit:
—as it was in the beginning, is now,
and will be for ever. Amen.

Ant.   **O Lord, in your light we see light itself.**

Ant. 2   **O God, you are great and glorious; we
marvel at your power.**

Canticle:
Judith 16:2–3a,
13–15

Strike up the instruments,
    a song to my God with timbrels,
    chant to the Lord with cymbals.
Sing to him a new song,
    exalt and acclaim his name.

A new hymn I will sing to my God.
O Lord, great are you and glorious,
    wonderful in power and unsurpassable.

Let your every creature serve you;
    for you spoke, and they were made,
    you sent forth your spirit, and they
        were created;
    no one can resist your word.

The mountains to their bases, and the seas,
        are shaken;
    the rocks, like wax, melt before your glance.
But to those who fear you,
    you are very merciful.

Glory to the Father, and to the Son,
        and to the Holy Spirit:
—as it was in the beginning, is now,
    and will be for ever. Amen.

Ant.   **O God, you are great and glorious; we
marvel at your power.**

Ant. 3   **Exult in God's presence with hymns
of praise.**

Psalm 47

All peoples, clap your hands,
cry to God with shouts of joy!
For the Lord, the Most High, we must fear,
great king over all the earth.

He subdues peoples under us
and nations under our feet.
Our inheritance, our glory, is from him,
given to Jacob out of love.

God goes up with shouts of joy;
the Lord goes up with trumpet blast.
Sing praise for God, sing praise,
sing praise to our king, sing praise.

God is king of all the earth.
Sing praise with all your skill.
God is king over the nations;
God reigns on his holy throne.

The princes of the peoples are assembled
with the people of Abraham's God.
The rulers of the earth belong to God,
to God who reigns over all.

Glory to the Father, and to the Son,
    and to the Holy Spirit:
—as it was in the beginning, is now,
and will be for ever. Amen.

Ant.   **Exult in God's presence with hymns
of praise.**

Reading
Wisdom 7:13–14

Simply I learned about Wisdom, and
  ungrudgingly do I share—
    her riches I do not hide away;
For to men she is an unfailing treasure;
  those who gain this treasure win the
    friendship of God,
    to whom the gifts they have from
      discipline commend them.

Responsory

Let the peoples proclaim the wisdom of
  the saints.
—Let the peoples proclaim the wisdom of
  the saints.

With joyful praise let the Church tell forth
—the wisdom of the saints.

Glory to the Father, and to the Son,
  and to the Holy Spirit.
—Let the peoples proclaim the wisdom of
  the saints.

Gospel
Canticle

Ant. **You inspire us, O Lord, to delight in
praising you, because you made us for
yourself; our hearts are restless until they
rest in you.**

*Canticle of
Zechariah
Luke 1:68–79*

Blessed + be the Lord, the God of Israel;
he has come to his people and set them free.

He has raised up for us a mighty savior,
born of the house of his servant David.

Through his holy prophets he
    promised of old
that he would save us from our enemies,
from the hands of all who hate us.

He promised to show mercy to our fathers
and to remember his holy covenant.

This was the oath he swore to our
    father Abraham:
to set us free from the hands of our enemies,
free to worship him without fear,
holy and righteous in his sight
    all the days of our life.

You, my child, shall be called the prophet of
    the Most High;
for you will go before the Lord to
    prepare his way,
to give his people knowledge of salvation
by the forgiveness of their sins.

In the tender compassion of our God
the dawn from on high shall break upon us,
to shine on those who dwell in darkness and
    the shadow of death,
and to guide our feet into the way of peace.

Glory to the Father, and to the Son,
    and to the Holy Spirit:
—as it was in the beginning, is now,
    and will be for ever. Amen.

Ant.   **You inspire us, O Lord, to delight in praising you, because you made us for yourself; our hearts are restless until they rest in you.**

Intercessions   Christ is the Good Shepherd who laid down his life for his sheep. Let us praise and thank him as we pray:
Nourish your people, Lord.

Christ, you decided to show your merciful love through your holy shepherds,
—let your mercy always reach us through them.

Through your vicars you continue to perform the ministry of shepherd of souls,
—direct us always through our leaders.

Through your holy ones, the leaders of your people, you served as physician of our bodies and our spirits,
—continue to fulfill your ministry of life and holiness in us.

You taught your flock through the prudence and love of your saints,
—grant us continual growth in holiness under the direction of our pastors.

The Lord's Prayer

Our Father, who art in heaven,
hallowed be thy name;
thy kingdom come,
thy will be done
on earth as it is in heaven.
Give us this day our daily bread,
and forgive us our trespasses,
as we forgive those who trespass against us;
and lead us not into temptation,
but deliver us from evil.

Pater noster, qui es in cælis:
sanctificetur nomen tuum;
adveniat regnum tuum;
fiat voluntas tua,
sicut in cælo, et in terra.
Panem nostrum cotidianum da nobis hodie;
et dimitte nobis debita nostra,
sicut et nos dimittimus debitoribus nostris;
et ne nos inducas in tentationem;
sed libera nos a malo.

Concluding Prayer

Lord,
renew in your Church
the spirit you gave Saint Augustine.
Filled with this spirit,
may we thirst for you alone as the
    fountain of wisdom
and seek you as the source of eternal love.
We ask this through our Lord Jesus Christ,
    your Son,
who lives and reigns with you and
    the Holy Spirit,
God, for ever and ever.
—Amen.

Dismissal   *If praying individually, or in a group without a priest or deacon:*

May the Lord + bless us,
protect us from all evil
and bring us to everlasting life.
—Amen.

If praying with a priest or deacon, he dismisses the people:

The Lord be with you.
—And with your spirit.

May almighty God bless you,
the Father, and the Son, + and the Holy Spirit.
—Amen.

Go in peace.
—Thanks be to God.

EVENING PRAYER

God, + come to my assistance.
—Lord, make haste to help me.

Glory to the Father, and to the Son,
   and to the Holy Spirit:
—as it was in the beginning, is now,
and will be for ever. Amen. Alleluia.

Hymn   *The Saints of God!, p. 702*

Psalmody   Ant. 1 **The Lord is my light and my help; whom shall I fear?**

Psalm 27

The Lord is my light and my help;
whom shall I fear?
The Lord is the stronghold of my life;
before whom shall I shrink?

When evil-doers draw near
to devour my flesh,
it is they, my enemies and foes,
who stumble and fall.

Though an army encamp against me
my heart would not fear.
Though war break out against me
even then would I trust.

There is one thing I ask of the Lord,
for this I long,
to live in the house of the Lord,
all the days of my life,
to savor the sweetness of the Lord,
to behold his temple.

For there he keeps me safe in his tent
in the day of evil.
He hides me in the shelter of his tent,
on a rock he sets me safe.

And now my head shall be raised
above my foes who surround me,
and I shall offer within his tent
a sacrifice of joy.

I will sing and make music for the Lord.

Glory to the Father, and to the Son,
and to the Holy Spirit:
—as it was in the beginning, is now,
and will be for ever. Amen.

Ant.   **The Lord is my light and my help; whom shall I fear?**

Ant. 2   **I long to look on you, O Lord; do not turn your face from me.**

Psalm 27
(continued)

O Lord, hear my voice when I call;
have mercy and answer.
Of you my heart has spoken:
"Seek his face."

It is your face, O Lord, that I seek;
hide not your face.
Dismiss not your servant in anger;
you have been my help.

Do not abandon or forsake me,
O God my help!
Though father and mother forsake me,
the Lord will receive me.

Instruct me, Lord, in your way;
on an even path lead me.
When they lie in ambush, protect me
from my enemy's greed.
False witnesses rise against me,
breathing out fury.

I am sure I shall see the Lord's goodness
in the land of the living.
Hope in him, hold firm and take heart.
Hope in the Lord!

Glory to the Father, and to the Son,
     and to the Holy Spirit:
—as it was in the beginning, is now,
     and will be for ever. Amen.

Ant.   **I long to look on you, O Lord; do not turn
your face from me.**

Ant. 3   **He is the first-born of all creation; in every
way the primacy is his.**

Canticle: Let us give thanks to the Father
Colossians   for having made you worthy
1:12–20   to share the lot of the saints
     in light.

He rescued us
from the power of darkness
and brought us
into the kingdom of his beloved Son.
Through him we have redemption,
the forgiveness of our sins.

He is the image of the invisible God,
the first-born of all creatures.
In him everything in heaven and on earth
     was created,
things visible and invisible.

All were created through him;
all were created for him.
He is before all else that is.
In him everything continues in being.

It is he who is head of the body, the church!
he who is the beginning,
the first-born of the dead,
so that primacy may be his in everything.

It pleased God to make absolute fullness
    reside in him
and, by means of him, to reconcile
    everything in his person,
both on earth and in the heavens,
making peace through the blood of his cross.

Glory to the Father, and to the Son,
    and to the Holy Spirit:
—as it was in the beginning, is now,
and will be for ever. Amen.

Ant.   **He is the first-born of all creation; in every way the primacy is his.**

Reading   Wisdom from above is first of all innocent.
James 3:17–18   It is also peaceable, lenient, docile, rich in
sympathy and the kindly deeds that are its
fruits, impartial and sincere. The harvest
of justice is sown in peace for those who
cultivate peace.

Responsory

In the midst of the Church he spoke with
        eloquence.
—In the midst of the Church he spoke with
        eloquence.

The Lord filled him with the spirit of
        wisdom and understanding.
—He spoke with eloquence.

Glory to the Father, and to the Son,
        and to the Holy Spirit.
—In the midst of the Church he spoke with
        eloquence.

Gospel
Canticle

Ant. **Late have I loved you, O Beauty ever
ancient, ever new, late have I loved you.
You called, you shouted and you shattered
my deafness.**

Canticle of
Mary
Luke 1:46–55

My + soul proclaims the greatness of the Lord,
my spirit rejoices in God my Savior
for he has looked with favor on his
        lowly servant.

From this day all generations will
        call me blessed:
the Almighty has done great things for me,
and holy is his Name.

He has mercy on those who fear him
in every generation.

He has shown the strength of his arm,
he has scattered the proud in their conceit.

He has cast down the mighty from
    their thrones,
and has lifted up the lowly.

He has filled the hungry with good things,
and the rich he has sent away empty.

He has come to the help of his servant Israel
for he has remembered his promise of mercy,
the promise he made to our fathers,
to Abraham and his children for ever.

Glory to the Father, and to the Son,
    and to the Holy Spirit:
—as it was in the beginning, is now,
and will be for ever. Amen.

Ant.   **Late have I loved you, O Beauty ever
         ancient, ever new, late have I loved you.
         You called, you shouted and you shattered
         my deafness.**

Intercessions   Jesus Christ is worthy of all praise, for he was
                  appointed high priest among men and
                  their representative before God. We honor
                  him and in our weakness we pray:
                  Bring salvation to your people, Lord.

         You marvelously illuminated your Church
             through distinguished leaders and holy
             men and women,
         —let Christians rejoice always in such splendor.

You forgave the sins of your people when
their holy leaders like Moses sought your
compassion,
—through their intercession continue to purify
and sanctify your holy people.

In the midst of their brothers and sisters you
anointed your holy ones and filled them
with the Holy Spirit,
—fill all the leaders of your people with the
same Spirit.

You yourself are the only visible possession of
our holy pastors,
—let none of them, won at the price of your
blood, remain far from you.

The shepherds of your Church keep your
flock from being snatched out of your
hand. Through them you give your flock
eternal life,
—save those who have died, those for whom
you gave up your life.

The Lord's
Prayer

Our Father, who art in heaven,
hallowed be thy name;
thy kingdom come,
thy will be done
on earth as it is in heaven.
Give us this day our daily bread,
and forgive us our trespasses,
as we forgive those who trespass against us;
and lead us not into temptation,
but deliver us from evil.

Pater noster, qui es in cælis:
sanctificetur nomen tuum;
adveniat regnum tuum;
fiat voluntas tua,
sicut in cælo, et in terra.
Panem nostrum cotidianum da nobis hodie;
et dimitte nobis debita nostra,
sicut et nos dimittimus debitoribus nostris;
et ne nos inducas in tentationem;
sed libera nos a malo.

Concluding Prayer

Lord,
renew in your Church
the spirit you gave Saint Augustine.
Filled with this spirit,
may we thirst for you alone as the
    fountain of wisdom
and seek you as the source of eternal love.
We ask this through our Lord Jesus Christ,
    your Son,
who lives and reigns with you and
    the Holy Spirit,
God, for ever and ever.
—Amen.

Dismissal

If praying individually, or in a group without a priest or deacon:

May the Lord + bless us,
protect us from all evil
and bring us to everlasting life.
—Amen.

If praying with a priest or deacon, he dismisses the people:

The Lord be with you.
—And with your spirit.

May almighty God bless you,
the Father, and the Son, + and the Holy Spirit.
—Amen.

Go in peace.
—Thanks be to God.

NIGHT PRAYER

God, + come to my assistance.
—Lord, make haste to help me.

Glory to the Father, and to the Son,
and to the Holy Spirit:
—as it was in the beginning, is now,
and will be for ever. Amen. Alleluia.

Examen   *An optional brief examination of conscience may be made. Call to mind your sins and failings this day.*

Hymn   *O Gladsome Light, p. 696*

Psalmody   Ant. 1 **Lord God, be my refuge and my strength.**

Psalm 31:1–6   In you, O Lord, I take refuge.
Let me never be put to shame.
In your justice, set me free,
hear me and speedily rescue me.

Be a rock of refuge for me,
a mighty stronghold to save me,
for you are my rock, my stronghold.
For your name's sake, lead me and guide me.

Release me from the snares they have hidden
for you are my refuge, Lord.
Into your hands I commend my spirit.
It is you who will redeem me, Lord.

Glory to the Father, and to the Son,
    and to the Holy Spirit:
—as it was in the beginning, is now,
and will be for ever. Amen.

Ant. **Lord God, be my refuge and my strength.**

Ant. 2 **Out of the depths I cry to you, Lord.**

Psalm 130

Out of the depths I cry to you, O Lord,
Lord, hear my voice!
O let your ears be attentive
to the voice of my pleading.

If you, O Lord, should mark our guilt,
Lord, who would survive?
But with you is found forgiveness:
for this we revere you.

My soul is waiting for the Lord,
I count on his word.
My soul is longing for the Lord
more than watchman for daybreak.
Let the watchman count on daybreak
and Israel on the Lord.

Because with the Lord there is mercy
and fullness of redemption,
Israel indeed he will redeem
from all its iniquity.

Glory to the Father, and to the Son,
　　and to the Holy Spirit:
—as it was in the beginning, is now,
　and will be for ever. Amen.

Ant.　**Out of the depths I cry to you, Lord.**

Reading
*Ephesians
4:26–27*

If you are angry, let it be without sin. The
sun must not go down on your wrath; do not
give the devil a chance to work on you.

Responsory

Into your hands, Lord, I commend my spirit.
—Into your hands, Lord, I commend my spirit.

You have redeemed us, Lord God of truth.
—I commend my spirit.

Glory to the Father, and to the Son,
　　and to the Holy Spirit.
—Into your hands, Lord, I commend my spirit.

Gospel
Canticle

Ant.　**Protect us, Lord, as we stay awake;
watch over us as we sleep, that awake, we
may keep watch with Christ, and asleep,
rest in his peace.**

*Canticle of
Simeon
Luke 2:29–32*

Lord, + now you let your servant go in peace;
your word has been fulfilled:
my own eyes have seen the salvation
which you have prepared in the sight of
　　every people:
a light to reveal you to the nations
and the glory of your people Israel.

Glory to the Father, and to the Son,
    and to the Holy Spirit:
—as it was in the beginning, is now,
    and will be for ever. Amen.

Ant.   **Protect us, Lord, as we stay awake; watch over us as we sleep, that awake, we may keep watch with Christ, and asleep, rest in his peace.**

Concluding Prayer

Let us pray.
Lord Jesus Christ,
you have given your followers
an example of gentleness and humility,
a task that is easy, a burden that is light.
Accept the prayers and work of this day,
and give us the rest that will strengthen us
to render more faithful service to you
who live and reign for ever and ever.
—Amen.

Blessing

May the all-powerful Lord
grant us a restful night
and a peaceful death.
—Amen.

Marian Antiphon

Sing the "Salve Regina," found on p. 700, or pray a Hail Mary.

Thursday, August 29, 2024
Passion of St. John the Baptist

God, + come to my assistance.
—Lord, make haste to help me.

Glory to the Father, and to the Son,
    and to the Holy Spirit:
—as it was in the beginning, is now,
    and will be for ever. Amen. Alleluia.

Hymn   *Blessed Feasts of Blessed Martyrs, p. 682*

Psalmody   Ant. 1 **The Lord extended his hand and
touched my lips; he ordered me to
prophesy to the nations.**

Psalm 63:2–9   O God, you are my God, for you I long;
    for you my soul is thirsting.
My body pines for you
    like a dry, weary land without water.
So I gaze on you in the sanctuary
    to see your strength and your glory.

For your love is better than life,
    my lips will speak your praise.
So I will bless you all my life,
    in your name I will lift up my hands.
My soul shall be filled as with a banquet,
    my mouth shall praise you with joy.

On my bed I remember you.
On you I muse through the night
for you have been my help;
in the shadow of your wings I rejoice.
My soul clings to you;
your right hand holds me fast.

Glory to the Father, and to the Son,
    and to the Holy Spirit:
as it was in the beginning, is now,
and will be for ever. Amen.

Ant. **The Lord extended his hand and touched my lips; he ordered me to prophesy to the nations.**

Ant. 2 **Herod feared John, knowing him to be a good and holy man, and guarded him carefully.**

Canticle:
Daniel
3:57–88, 56

Bless the Lord, all you works of the Lord.
Praise and exalt him above all forever.
Angels of the Lord, bless the Lord.
You heavens, bless the Lord.
All you waters above the heavens,
    bless the Lord.
All you hosts of the Lord, bless the Lord.
Sun and moon, bless the Lord.
Stars of heaven, bless the Lord.

Every shower and dew, bless the Lord.
All you winds, bless the Lord.
Fire and heat, bless the Lord.
Cold and chill, bless the Lord.
Dew and rain, bless the Lord.
Frost and chill, bless the Lord.
Ice and snow, bless the Lord.
Nights and days, bless the Lord.
Light and darkness, bless the Lord.
Lightnings and clouds, bless the Lord.

Let the earth bless the Lord.
Praise and exalt him above all forever.
Mountains and hills, bless the Lord.
Everything growing from the earth,
    bless the Lord.
You springs, bless the Lord.
Seas and rivers, bless the Lord.
You dolphins and all water creatures,
    bless the Lord.
All you birds of the air, bless the Lord.
All you beasts, wild and tame, bless the Lord.
You sons of men, bless the Lord.

O Israel, bless the Lord.
Praise and exalt him above all forever.
Priests of the Lord, bless the Lord.
Servants of the Lord, bless the Lord.
Spirits and souls of the just, bless the Lord.
Holy men of humble heart, bless the Lord.
Hananiah, Azariah, Mishael, bless the Lord.
Praise and exalt him above all forever.

Let us bless the Father, and the Son,
    and the Holy Spirit.
Let us praise and exalt him above all forever.
Blessed are you, Lord, in the firmament
    of heaven.
Praiseworthy and glorious and exalted above
    all forever.

Ant.   **Herod feared John, knowing him to be
a good and holy man, and guarded him
carefully.**

Ant. 3   **Although John's words disturbed him
greatly, Herod enjoyed listening to John.**

Psalm 149   Sing a new song to the Lord,
his praise in the assembly of the faithful.
Let Israel rejoice in its maker,
let Zion's sons exult in their king.
Let them praise his name with dancing
and make music with timbrel and harp.

For the Lord takes delight in his people.
He crowns the poor with salvation.
Let the faithful rejoice in their glory,
shout for joy and take their rest.
Let the praise of God be on their lips
and a two-edged sword in their hand,

to deal out vengeance to the nations
and punishment on all the peoples;
to bind their kings in chains
and their nobles in fetters of iron;
to carry out the sentence pre-ordained;
this honor is for all his faithful.

Glory to the Father, and to the Son,
    and to the Holy Spirit:
—as it was in the beginning, is now,
    and will be for ever. Amen.

Ant.   **Although John's words disturbed him greatly, Herod enjoyed listening to John.**

Reading
Isaiah 49:1b–2

The Lord called me from birth,
    from my mother's womb he gave
        me my name.
He made me a sharp-edged sword
    and concealed me in the shadow
        of his arm.
He made me a polished arrow,
    in his quiver he hid me.

Responsory   You sent your disciples to John,
    and he gave witness to the truth.
—You sent your disciples to John,
    and he gave witness to the truth.

He was like a brightly shining light.
—And he gave witness to the truth.

Glory to the Father, and to the Son,
    and to the Holy Spirit.
—You sent your disciples to John,
    and he gave witness to the truth.

Gospel
Canticle

Ant. **The friend of the bridegroom, who waits and listens for his return, rejoices when he hears his voice: so now my joy is complete.**

*Canticle of
Zechariah
Luke 1:68–79*

Blessed + be the Lord, the God of Israel;
he has come to his people and set them free.

He has raised up for us a mighty savior,
born of the house of his servant David.

Through his holy prophets he
    promised of old
that he would save us from our enemies,
from the hands of all who hate us.

He promised to show mercy to our fathers
and to remember his holy covenant.

This was the oath he swore to our
    father Abraham:
to set us free from the hands of our enemies,
free to worship him without fear,
holy and righteous in his sight
    all the days of our life.

You, my child, shall be called the prophet of
    the Most High;
for you will go before the Lord to
    prepare his way,
to give his people knowledge of salvation
by the forgiveness of their sins.

In the tender compassion of our God
the dawn from on high shall break upon us,
to shine on those who dwell in darkness and
    the shadow of death,
and to guide our feet into the way of peace.

Glory to the Father, and to the Son,
  and to the Holy Spirit:
—as it was in the beginning, is now,
  and will be for ever. Amen.

Ant.   **The friend of the bridegroom, who waits
and listens for his return, rejoices when he
hears his voice: so now my joy is complete.**

Intercessions   In faith let us call upon Christ who sent John
         to prepare for his coming:
         Dawn from on high, break upon us.

Your coming caused John the Baptist to leap
   for joy in his mother's womb,
—help us to rejoice at your coming among us.

Through the life and preaching of the Baptist
   you showed us the way to repentance,
—turn our hearts to follow the
   commandments of your kingdom.

You willed that your coming among men
   should be announced by John the Baptist,
—send new heralds to proclaim you
   throughout the world.

You wished to be baptized by John
   in the Jordan to fulfill all that the
   Father required,
—help us to do the Father's will.

The Lord's
Prayer

Our Father, who art in heaven,
hallowed be thy name;
thy kingdom come,
thy will be done
on earth as it is in heaven.
Give us this day our daily bread,
and forgive us our trespasses,
as we forgive those who trespass against us;
and lead us not into temptation,
but deliver us from evil.

Pater noster, qui es in cælis:
sanctificetur nomen tuum;
adveniat regnum tuum;
fiat voluntas tua,
sicut in cælo, et in terra.
Panem nostrum cotidianum da nobis hodie;
et dimitte nobis debita nostra,
sicut et nos dimittimus debitoribus nostris;
et ne nos inducas in tentationem;
sed libera nos a malo.

Concluding
Prayer

God our Father,
you called John the Baptist
to be the herald of your Son's birth and death.
As he gave his life in witness to truth
    and justice,
so may we strive to profess our faith in
    your gospel.
Grant this through our Lord Jesus Christ,
    your Son,
who lives and reigns with you and
    the Holy Spirit,
God, for ever and ever.
—Amen.

Dismissal   *If praying individually, or in a group without a priest or deacon:*

May the Lord + bless us,
protect us from all evil
and bring us to everlasting life.
—Amen.

If praying with a priest or deacon, he dismisses the people:

The Lord be with you.
—And with your spirit.

May almighty God bless you,
the Father, and the Son, + and the Holy Spirit.
—Amen.

Go in peace.
—Thanks be to God.

EVENING PRAYER

God, + come to my assistance.
—Lord, make haste to help me.

Glory to the Father, and to the Son,
   and to the Holy Spirit:
—as it was in the beginning, is now,
and will be for ever. Amen. Alleluia.

Hymn   *You Sought the Solitude of Caves, p. 704*

Psalmody   Ant. 1 **Do not be afraid to face them, for I am with you, says the Lord.**

Psalm 116:1–9

I love the Lord for he has heard
the cry of my appeal;
for he turned his ear to me
in the day when I called him.

They surrounded me, the snares of death,
with the anguish of the tomb;
they caught me, sorrow and distress.
I called on the Lord's name.

O Lord, my God, deliver me!

How gracious is the Lord, and just;
our God has compassion.
The Lord protects the simple hearts;
I was helpless so he saved me.

Turn back, my soul, to your rest
for the Lord has been good;
he has kept my soul from death,
my eyes from tears
and my feet from stumbling.

I will walk in the presence of the Lord
in the land of the living.

Glory to the Father, and to the Son,
    and to the Holy Spirit:
—as it was in the beginning, is now,
and will be for ever. Amen.

Ant.

Do not be afraid to face them, for I am with you, says the Lord.

Ant. 2   **He sent an executioner to behead John who was in prison.**

Psalm 116:10–19   I trusted, even when I said:
"I am sorely afflicted,"
 and when I said in my alarm:
"No man can be trusted."

How can I repay the Lord
for his goodness to me?
The cup of salvation I will raise;
I will call on the Lord's name.

My vows to the Lord I will fulfill
before all his people.
O precious in the eyes of the Lord
is the death of his faithful.

Your servant, Lord, your servant am I;
you have loosened my bonds.
A thanksgiving sacrifice I make:
I will call on the Lord's name.

My vows to the Lord I will fulfill
before all his people,
in the courts of the house of the Lord,
in your midst, O Jerusalem.

Glory to the Father, and to the Son,
    and to the Holy Spirit:
—as it was in the beginning, is now,
and will be for ever. Amen.

Ant.   **He sent an executioner to behead John who was in prison.**

Ant. 3 **The disciples of John came and took his
body and laid it in a tomb.**

Canticle:
Revelation 4:11;
5:9, 10, 12

O Lord, our God, you are worthy
to receive glory and honor and power.
For you have created all things;
by your will they came to be and were made.

Worthy are you, O Lord,
to receive the scroll and break open its seals.

For you were slain.
With your blood you purchased for God
men of every race and tongue,
of every people and nation.

You made of them a kingdom,
and priests to serve our God,
and they shall reign on the earth.

Worthy is the Lamb that was slain
to receive power and riches,
wisdom and strength,
honor and glory and praise.

Glory to the Father, and to the Son,
    and to the Holy Spirit:
—as it was in the beginning, is now,
and will be for ever. Amen.

Ant. **The disciples of John came and took his
body and laid it in a tomb.**

Reading
Acts 13:23–25

According to his promise, God has brought
forth from David's descendants Jesus, a savior
for Israel. John heralded the coming of Jesus
by proclaiming a baptism of repentance to
all the people of Israel. As John's career was
coming to an end, he would say, "What you
suppose me to be I am not. Rather, look for
the one who comes after me. I am not worthy
to unfasten the sandals on his feet."

Responsory

The friend of the bridegroom rejoices
upon hearing the bridegroom's voice.
—The friend of the bridegroom rejoices
upon hearing the bridegroom's voice.

Now my joy is complete
—upon hearing the bridegroom's voice.

Glory to the Father, and to the Son,
and to the Holy Spirit.
—The friend of the bridegroom rejoices
upon hearing the bridegroom's voice.

**Gospel
Canticle**

Ant. **I am not the Christ; I have been sent
before him to prepare his way. He must
increase, and I must decrease.**

*Canticle of
Mary
Luke 1:46–55*

My + soul proclaims the greatness of the Lord,
my spirit rejoices in God my Savior
for he has looked with favor on his
lowly servant.

From this day all generations will
    call me blessed:
the Almighty has done great things for me,
and holy is his Name.

He has mercy on those who fear him
in every generation.

He has shown the strength of his arm,
he has scattered the proud in their conceit.

He has cast down the mighty from
    their thrones,
and has lifted up the lowly.

He has filled the hungry with good things,
and the rich he has sent away empty.

He has come to the help of his servant Israel
for he has remembered his promise of mercy,
the promise he made to our fathers,
to Abraham and his children for ever.

Glory to the Father, and to the Son,
    and to the Holy Spirit:
—as it was in the beginning, is now,
and will be for ever. Amen.

Ant.   **I am not the Christ; I have been sent before
him to prepare his way. He must increase,
and I must decrease.**

Intercessions   Let us pray joyfully to God our Father who
                called John the Baptist to proclaim the
                coming of the kingdom of Christ:
                O Lord, guide our feet into the way of peace.

                You called John the Baptist from his mother's
                    womb to prepare the way of your Son,
                —help us to follow in that path which the
                    Baptist opened before the Lord Jesus.

                May your Church, in imitation of the Baptist,
                    fearlessly point out the Lamb of God,
                —so that people in every age may acknowledge
                    that the Lord comes to them.

                John the Baptist did not exalt himself but
                    acknowledged his role as forerunner of
                    the Christ,
                —teach us to acknowledge that you are the
                    giver of all our good gifts and that we
                    must use them in your service.

                You called John the Baptist to give testimony
                    to you by his life and even by his death,
                —help us to imitate his unceasing witness to
                    your truth.

                Remember those who have died,
                —give them a place of light, happiness,
                    and peace.

The Lord's Prayer

Our Father, who art in heaven,
hallowed be thy name;
thy kingdom come,
thy will be done
on earth as it is in heaven.
Give us this day our daily bread,
and forgive us our trespasses,
as we forgive those who trespass against us;
and lead us not into temptation,
but deliver us from evil.

Pater noster, qui es in cælis:
sanctificetur nomen tuum;
adveniat regnum tuum;
fiat voluntas tua,
sicut in cælo, et in terra.
Panem nostrum cotidianum da nobis hodie;
et dimitte nobis debita nostra,
sicut et nos dimittimus debitoribus nostris;
et ne nos inducas in tentationem;
sed libera nos a malo.

Concluding Prayer

God our Father,
you called John the Baptist
to be the herald of your Son's birth and death.
As he gave his life in witness to truth
    and justice,
so may we strive to profess our faith in
    your gospel.
Grant this through our Lord Jesus Christ,
    your Son,
who lives and reigns with you and
    the Holy Spirit,
God, for ever and ever.
—Amen.

Dismissal   *If praying individually, or in a group without a priest or deacon:*

May the Lord + bless us,
protect us from all evil
and bring us to everlasting life.
—Amen.

If praying with a priest or deacon, he dismisses the people:

The Lord be with you.
—And with your spirit.

May almighty God bless you,
the Father, and the Son, + and the Holy Spirit.
—Amen.

Go in peace.
—Thanks be to God.

NIGHT PRAYER

God, + come to my assistance.
—Lord, make haste to help me.

Glory to the Father, and to the Son,
    and to the Holy Spirit:
—as it was in the beginning, is now,
and will be for ever. Amen. Alleluia.

Examen   *An optional brief examination of conscience may be made. Call to mind your*
          sins and failings this day.

Hymn   *O Gladsome Light, p. 696*

Psalmody   Ant. **In you, my God, my body will**
            rest in hope.

Psalm 16   Preserve me, God, I take refuge in you.
I say to the Lord: "You are my God.
My happiness lies in you alone."

He has put into my heart a marvelous love
for the faithful ones who dwell in his land.
Those who choose other gods increase
     their sorrows.
Never will I offer their offerings of blood.
Never will I take their name upon my lips.

O Lord, it is you who are my portion and cup;
it is you yourself who are my prize.
The lot marked out for me is my delight:
welcome indeed the heritage that falls to me!

I will bless the Lord who gives me counsel,
who even at night directs my heart.
I keep the Lord ever in my sight:
since he is at my right hand,
     I shall stand firm.

And so my heart rejoices, my soul is glad;
even my body shall rest in safety.
For you will not leave my soul
     among the dead,
nor let your beloved know decay.

You will show me the path of life,
the fullness of joy in your presence,
at your right hand happiness for ever.

Glory to the Father, and to the Son,
    and to the Holy Spirit:
—as it was in the beginning, is now,
    and will be for ever. Amen.

Ant. **In you, my God, my body will rest in hope.**

Reading
*1 Thessalonians
5:23*

May the God of peace make you perfect in
holiness. May he preserve you whole and
entire, spirit, soul, and body, irreproachable
at the coming of our Lord Jesus Christ.

Responsory   Into your hands, Lord, I commend my spirit.
—Into your hands, Lord, I commend my spirit.

You have redeemed us, Lord God of truth.
—I commend my spirit.

Glory to the Father, and to the Son,
    and to the Holy Spirit.
—Into your hands, Lord, I commend my spirit.

Gospel
Canticle

Ant. **Protect us, Lord, as we stay awake;
watch over us as we sleep, that awake, we
may keep watch with Christ, and asleep,
rest in his peace.**

Canticle of
Simeon
Luke 2:29–32

Lord, + now you let your servant go in peace;
    your word has been fulfilled:
my own eyes have seen the salvation
which you have prepared in the sight of
        every people:
a light to reveal you to the nations
and the glory of your people Israel.

Glory to the Father, and to the Son,
and to the Holy Spirit:
—as it was in the beginning, is now,
and will be for ever. Amen.

Ant.   **Protect us, Lord, as we stay awake; watch over us as we sleep, that awake, we may keep watch with Christ, and asleep, rest in his peace.**

Concluding Prayer   *Let us pray.*
Lord God,
send peaceful sleep
to refresh our tired bodies.
May your help always renew us
and keep us strong in your service.
We ask this through Christ our Lord.
—Amen.

Blessing   May the all-powerful Lord
grant us a restful night
and a peaceful death.
—Amen.

Marian Antiphon   *Sing the "Salve Regina," found on p. 700, or pray a Hail Mary.*

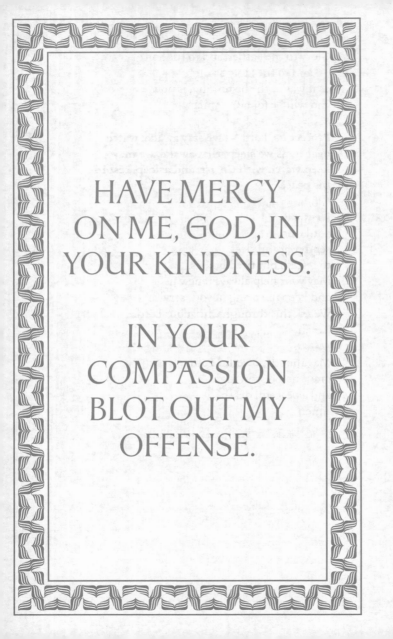

HAVE MERCY
ON ME, GOD, IN
YOUR KINDNESS.

IN YOUR
COMPASSION
BLOT OUT MY
OFFENSE.

Friday, August 30, 2024
Friday of the Twenty-First Week in Ordinary Time

MORNING PRAYER————————————————

God, + come to my assistance.
—Lord, make haste to help me.

Glory to the Father, and to the Son,
    and to the Holy Spirit:
—as it was in the beginning, is now,
    and will be for ever. Amen. Alleluia.

Hymn   *God Who Made Both Earth and Heaven, p. 688*

Psalmody   Ant. 1 **Lord, you will accept the true sacrifice offered on your altar.**

Psalm 51   Have mercy on me, God, in your kindness.
In your compassion blot out my offense.
O wash me more and more from my guilt
and cleanse me from my sin.

My offenses truly I know them;
my sin is always before me.
Against you, you alone, have I sinned;
what is evil in your sight I have done.

That you may be justified when you
    give sentence
and be without reproach when you judge.
O see, in guilt I was born,
a sinner was I conceived.

Indeed you love truth in the heart;
then in the secret of my heart teach
   me wisdom.
O purify me, then I shall be clean;
O wash me, I shall be whiter than snow.

Make me hear rejoicing and gladness,
that the bones you have crushed may revive.
From my sins turn away your face
and blot out all my guilt.

A pure heart create for me, O God,
put a steadfast spirit within me.
Do not cast me away from your presence,
nor deprive me of your holy spirit.

Give me again the joy of your help;
with a spirit of fervor sustain me,
that I may teach transgressors your ways
and sinners may return to you.

O rescue me, God, my helper,
and my tongue shall ring out your goodness.
O Lord, open my lips
and my mouth shall declare your praise.

For in sacrifice you take no delight,
burnt offering from me you would refuse,
my sacrifice, a contrite spirit.
A humbled, contrite heart you will not spurn.

In your goodness, show favor to Zion:
rebuild the walls of Jerusalem.
Then you will be pleased with lawful sacrifice,
holocausts offered on your altar.

Glory to the Father, and to the Son,
    and to the Holy Spirit:
—as it was in the beginning, is now,
    and will be for ever. Amen.

Ant.   **Lord, you will accept the true sacrifice
        offered on your altar.**

Ant. 2   **All the descendants of Israel will glory in
        the Lord's gift of victory.**

Canticle: Truly with you God is hidden,
Isaiah 45:15–25   the God of Israel, the savior!
        Those are put to shame and disgrace
        who vent their anger against him.
        Those go in disgrace
        who carve images.

        Israel, you are saved by the Lord,
            saved forever!
        You shall never be put to shame or disgrace
        in future ages.

        For thus says the Lord,
        the creator of the heavens,
        who is God,
        the designer and maker of the earth
        who established it,
        not creating it to be a waste,
        but designing it to be lived in:

I am the Lord, and there is no other.
I have not spoken from hiding
nor from some dark place of the earth.
And I have not said to the
    descendants of Jacob,
"Look for me in an empty waste."
I, the Lord, promise justice,
I foretell what is right.

Come and assemble, gather together,
you fugitives from among the Gentiles!
They are without knowledge who bear
    wooden idols
and pray to gods that cannot save.

Come here and declare
in counsel together:
Who announced this from the beginning
and foretold it from of old?
Was it not I, the Lord,
besides whom there is no other God?
There is no just and saving God but me.

Turn to me and be safe,
all you ends of the earth,
for I am God; there is no other!

By myself I swear,
uttering my just decree
and my unalterable word:

To me every knee shall bend;
by me every tongue shall swear,
saying, "Only in the Lord
are just deeds and power.

Before him in shame shall come
all who vent their anger against him.
In the Lord shall be the vindication
    and the glory
of all the descendants of Israel."

Glory to the Father, and to the Son,
    and to the Holy Spirit:
—as it was in the beginning, is now,
and will be for ever. Amen.

Ant.
**All the descendants of Israel will glory in
the Lord's gift of victory.**

Ant. 3
Let us go into God's presence singing for joy.

Psalm 100
Cry out with joy to the Lord, all the earth.
Serve the Lord with gladness.
Come before him, singing for joy.

Know that he, the Lord, is God.
He made us, we belong to him,
we are his people, the sheep of his flock.

Go within his gates, giving thanks.
Enter his courts with songs of praise.
Give thanks to him and bless his name.

Indeed, how good is the Lord,
eternal his merciful love.
He is faithful from age to age.

641

Glory to the Father, and to the Son,
    and to the Holy Spirit:
—as it was in the beginning, is now,
    and will be for ever. Amen.

Ant.   **Let us go into God's presence singing for joy.**

Reading
*Ephesians
4:29–32*

Never let evil talk pass your lips; say only the good things men need to hear, things that will really help them. Do nothing that will sadden the Holy Spirit with whom you were sealed against the day of redemption. Get rid of all bitterness, all passion and anger, harsh words, slander, and malice of every kind. In place of these, be kind to one another, compassionate, and mutually forgiving, just as God has forgiven you in Christ.

Responsory   At daybreak, be merciful to me.
—At daybreak, be merciful to me.

Make known to me the path that I
    must walk.
—Be merciful to me.

Glory to the Father, and to the Son,
    and to the Holy Spirit.
—At daybreak, be merciful to me.

Gospel
Canticle

Ant. **The Lord has come to his people and set them free.**

*Canticle of
Zechariah
Luke 1:68–79*

Blessed + be the Lord, the God of Israel;
he has come to his people and set them free.

He has raised up for us a mighty savior,
born of the house of his servant David.

Through his holy prophets he
    promised of old
that he would save us from our enemies,
from the hands of all who hate us.

He promised to show mercy to our fathers
and to remember his holy covenant.

This was the oath he swore to our
    father Abraham:
to set us free from the hands of our enemies,
free to worship him without fear,
holy and righteous in his sight
    all the days of our life.

You, my child, shall be called the prophet of
    the Most High;
for you will go before the Lord to
    prepare his way,
to give his people knowledge of salvation
by the forgiveness of their sins.

In the tender compassion of our God
the dawn from on high shall break upon us,
to shine on those who dwell in darkness and
    the shadow of death,
and to guide our feet into the way of peace.

Glory to the Father, and to the Son,
    and to the Holy Spirit:
—as it was in the beginning, is now,
and will be for ever. Amen.

Ant.   **The Lord has come to his people and set them free.**

Intercessions   Through his cross the Lord Jesus brought salvation to the human race. We adore him and in faith we call out to him:
Lord, pour out your mercy upon us.

Christ, Rising Sun, warm us with your rays,
—and restrain us from every evil impulse.

Keep guard over our thoughts, words and actions,
—and make us pleasing in your sight this day.

Turn your gaze from our sinfulness,
—and cleanse us from our iniquities.

Through your cross and resurrection,
—fill us with the consolation of the Spirit.

The Lord's Prayer   Our Father, who art in heaven,
hallowed be thy name;
thy kingdom come,
thy will be done
on earth as it is in heaven.
Give us this day our daily bread,
and forgive us our trespasses,
as we forgive those who trespass against us;
and lead us not into temptation,
but deliver us from evil.

Pater noster, qui es in cælis:
sanctificetur nomen tuum;
adveniat regnum tuum;
fiat voluntas tua,
sicut in cælo, et in terra.
Panem nostrum cotidianum da nobis hodie;
et dimitte nobis debita nostra,
sicut et nos dimittimus debitoribus nostris;
et ne nos inducas in tentationem;
sed libera nos a malo.

Concluding Prayer

God our Father,
you conquer the darkness of ignorance
by the light of your Word.
Strengthen within our hearts
the faith you have given us;
let not temptation ever quench the fire
that your love has kindled within us.
We ask this through our Lord Jesus Christ,
    your Son,
who lives and reigns with you and
    the Holy Spirit,
God, for ever and ever.
—Amen.

Dismissal

If praying individually, or in a group without a priest or deacon:

May the Lord + bless us,
protect us from all evil
and bring us to everlasting life.
—Amen.

If praying with a priest or deacon, he dismisses the people:

The Lord be with you.
—And with your spirit.

May almighty God bless you,
the Father, and the Son, + and the Holy Spirit.
—Amen.

Go in peace.
—Thanks be to God.

EVENING PRAYER————————————————

God, + come to my assistance.
—Lord, make haste to help me.

Glory to the Father, and to the Son,
and to the Holy Spirit:
—as it was in the beginning, is now,
and will be for ever. Amen. Alleluia.

Hymn   *Glorious Things of Thee Are Spoken, p. 686*

Psalmody   Ant. 1 **Lord, lay your healing hand upon me,
for I have sinned.**

Psalm 41   Happy the man who considers the poor
and the weak.
The Lord will save him in the day of evil,
will guard him, give him life, make him
happy in the land
and will not give him up to the will
of his foes.
The Lord will help him on his bed of pain,
he will bring him back from sickness
to health.

As for me, I said: "Lord, have mercy on me,
heal my soul for I have sinned against you."
My foes are speaking evil against me.
"How long before he dies and his name be
    forgotten?"
They come to visit me and speak
    empty words,
their hearts full of malice, they spread
    it abroad.

My enemies whisper together against me.
They all weigh up the evil which is on me:
"Some deadly thing has fastened upon him,
he will not rise again from where he lies."
Thus even my friend, in whom I trusted,
who ate my bread, has turned against me.

But you, O Lord, have mercy on me.
Let me rise once more and I will repay them.
By this I shall know that you are my friend,
if my foes do not shout in triumph over me.
If you uphold me I shall be unharmed
and set in your presence for evermore.

Blessed be the Lord, the God of Israel
from age to age. Amen. Amen.

Glory to the Father, and to the Son,
    and to the Holy Spirit:
—as it was in the beginning, is now,
and will be for ever. Amen.

Ant.   **Lord, lay your healing hand upon me,
for I have sinned.**

Ant. 2   **The mighty Lord is with us; the God of Jacob is our stronghold.**

Psalm 46   God is for us a refuge and strength,
a helper close at hand, in time of distress:
so we shall not fear though the earth
    should rock,
though the mountains fall into the depths
    of the sea,
even though its waters rage and foam,
even though the mountains be shaken by
    its waves.

The Lord of hosts is with us:
the God of Jacob is our stronghold.

The waters of a river give joy to God's city,
the holy place where the Most High dwells.
God is within, it cannot be shaken;
God will help it at the dawning of the day.
Nations are in tumult, kingdoms are shaken:
he lifts his voice, the earth shrinks away.

The Lord of hosts is with us:
the God of Jacob is our stronghold.

Come, consider the works of the Lord,
the redoubtable deeds he has done on
    the earth.
He puts an end to wars over all the earth;
the bow he breaks, the spear he snaps.
He burns the shields with fire.
"Be still and know that I am God,
supreme among the nations, supreme on
    the earth!"

The Lord of hosts is with us:
the God of Jacob is our stronghold.

Glory to the Father, and to the Son,
    and to the Holy Spirit:
—as it was in the beginning, is now,
and will be for ever. Amen.

Ant.   **The mighty Lord is with us; the God of
Jacob is our stronghold.**

Ant. 3   **All nations will come and worship before
you, O Lord.**

Canticle:
Revelation
15:3–4

Mighty and wonderful are your works,
Lord God Almighty!
Righteous and true are your ways,
O King of the nations!

Who would dare refuse you honor,
or the glory due your name, O Lord?

Since you alone are holy,
all nations shall come
and worship in your presence.
Your mighty deeds are clearly seen.

Glory to the Father, and to the Son,
    and to the Holy Spirit:
—as it was in the beginning, is now,
and will be for ever. Amen.

Ant.   **All nations will come and worship before you, O Lord.**

Reading
Romans 15:1–3

We who are strong in faith should be patient with the scruples of those whose faith is weak; we must not be selfish. Each should please his neighbor so as to do him good by building up his spirit. Thus, in accord with Scripture, Christ did not please himself: "The reproaches they uttered against you fell on me."

Responsory

Christ loved us and washed away our sins,
    in his own blood.
—Christ loved us and washed away our sins,
    in his own blood.

He made us a nation of kings and priests,
—in his own blood.

Glory to the Father, and to the Son,
    and to the Holy Spirit.
—Christ loved us and washed away our sins,
    in his own blood.

Gospel
Canticle

Ant. **The Lord has come to the help of his servants, for he has remembered his promise of mercy.**

Canticle of
Mary
Luke 1:46–55

My + soul proclaims the greatness of the Lord,
my spirit rejoices in God my Savior
for he has looked with favor on his
    lowly servant.

From this day all generations will
    call me blessed:
the Almighty has done great things for me,
and holy is his Name.

He has mercy on those who fear him
in every generation.

He has shown the strength of his arm,
he has scattered the proud in their conceit.

He has cast down the mighty from
    their thrones,
and has lifted up the lowly.

He has filled the hungry with good things,
and the rich he has sent away empty.

He has come to the help of his servant Israel
for he has remembered his promise of mercy,
the promise he made to our fathers,
to Abraham and his children for ever.

Glory to the Father, and to the Son,
    and to the Holy Spirit:
—as it was in the beginning, is now,
and will be for ever. Amen.

Ant.   **The Lord has come to the help of his
servants, for he has remembered his
promise of mercy.**

Intercessions Blessed be God, who hears the prayers of the
needy, and fills the hungry with good
things. Let us pray to him in confidence:
Lord, show us your mercy.

Merciful Father, upon the cross Jesus offered
you the perfect evening sacrifice,
—we pray now for all the suffering members of
his Church.

Release those in bondage, give sight to
the blind,
—shelter the widow and the orphan.

Clothe your faithful people in the armor of
salvation,
—and shield them from the deceptions of
the devil.

Let your merciful presence be with us, Lord,
at the hour of our death,
—may we be found faithful and leave this
world in your peace.

Lead the departed into the light of your
dwelling place,
—that they may gaze upon you for all eternity.

The Lord's
Prayer

Our Father, who art in heaven,
hallowed be thy name;
thy kingdom come,
thy will be done
on earth as it is in heaven.
Give us this day our daily bread,
and forgive us our trespasses,
as we forgive those who trespass against us;
and lead us not into temptation,
but deliver us from evil.

Pater noster, qui es in cælis:
sanctificetur nomen tuum;
adveniat regnum tuum;
fiat voluntas tua,
sicut in cælo, et in terra.
Panem nostrum cotidianum da nobis hodie;
et dimitte nobis debita nostra,
sicut et nos dimittimus debitoribus nostris;
et ne nos inducas in tentationem;
sed libera nos a malo.

Concluding
Prayer

God our Father,
help us to follow the example
of your Son's patience in suffering.
By sharing the burden he carries,
may we come to share his glory
in the kingdom where he lives with you and
        the Holy Spirit,
God, for ever and ever.
—Amen.

Dismissal   *If praying individually, or in a group without a priest or deacon:*

May the Lord + bless us,
protect us from all evil
and bring us to everlasting life.
—Amen.

If praying with a priest or deacon, he dismisses the people:

The Lord be with you.
—And with your spirit.

May almighty God bless you,
the Father, and the Son, + and the Holy Spirit.
—Amen.

Go in peace.
—Thanks be to God.

NIGHT PRAYER

God, + come to my assistance.
—Lord, make haste to help me.

Glory to the Father, and to the Son,
    and to the Holy Spirit:
—as it was in the beginning, is now,
and will be for ever. Amen. Alleluia.

Examen   *An optional brief examination of conscience may be made. Call to mind your sins and failings this day.*

Hymn   *O Gladsome Light, p. 696*

Psalmody   Ant. **Day and night I cry to you, my God.**

Psalm 88   Lord my God, I call for help by day;
I cry at night before you.
Let my prayer come into your presence.
O turn your ear to my cry.

For my soul is filled with evils;
my life is on the brink of the grave.
I am reckoned as one in the tomb:
I have reached the end of my strength,

like one alone among the dead;
like the slain lying in their graves;
like those you remember no more,
cut off, as they are, from your hand.

You have laid me in the depths of the tomb,
in places that are dark, in the depths.
Your anger weighs down upon me:
I am drowned beneath your waves.

You have taken away my friends
and made me hateful in their sight.
Imprisoned, I cannot escape;
my eyes are sunken with grief.

I call to you, Lord, all the day long;
to you I stretch out my hands.
Will you work your wonders for the dead?
Will the shades stand and praise you?

Will your love be told in the grave
or your faithfulness among the dead?
Will your wonders be known in the dark
or your justice in the land of oblivion?

As for me, Lord, I call to you for help:
in the morning my prayer comes before you.
Lord, why do you reject me?
Why do you hide your face?

Wretched, close to death from my youth,
I have borne your trials; I am numb.
Your fury has swept down upon me;
your terrors have utterly destroyed me.

They surround me all the day like a flood,
they assail me all together.
Friend and neighbor you have taken away:
my one companion is darkness.

Glory to the Father, and to the Son,
    and to the Holy Spirit:
—as it was in the beginning, is now,
and will be for ever. Amen.

Ant.   **Day and night I cry to you, my God.**

Reading   You are in our midst, O Lord,
Jeremiah 14:9a   your name we bear:
                do not forsake us, O Lord, our God!

Responsory   Into your hands, Lord, I commend my spirit.
—Into your hands, Lord, I commend my spirit.

You have redeemed us, Lord God of truth.
—I commend my spirit.

Glory to the Father, and to the Son,
and to the Holy Spirit.
—Into your hands, Lord, I commend my spirit.

Gospel Canticle

Ant. **Protect us, Lord, as we stay awake;
watch over us as we sleep, that awake, we
may keep watch with Christ, and asleep,
rest in his peace.**

Canticle of Simeon
Luke 2:29–32

Lord, + now you let your servant go in peace;
your word has been fulfilled:
my own eyes have seen the salvation
which you have prepared in the sight of
every people:
a light to reveal you to the nations
and the glory of your people Israel.

Glory to the Father, and to the Son,
and to the Holy Spirit:
—as it was in the beginning, is now,
and will be for ever. Amen.

Ant. **Protect us, Lord, as we stay awake; watch
over us as we sleep, that awake, we may
keep watch with Christ, and asleep, rest in
his peace.**

Concluding Prayer

Let us pray.
All-powerful God,
keep us united with your Son
in his death and burial
so that we may rise to new life with him,
who lives and reigns for ever and ever.
—Amen.

Blessing   May the all-powerful Lord
            grant us a restful night
            and a peaceful death.
            —Amen.

Marian   *Sing the "Salve Regina," found on p. 700, or pray a Hail Mary.*
Antiphon

Saturday, August 31, 2024
Saturday of the Twenty-First Week in Ordinary Time

MORNING PRAYER————————————

God, + come to my assistance.
—Lord, make haste to help me.

Glory to the Father, and to the Son,
    and to the Holy Spirit:
—as it was in the beginning, is now,
and will be for ever. Amen. Alleluia.

Hymn   *God Who Made Both Earth and Heaven, p. 688*

Psalmody   Ant. 1 **Dawn finds me ready to welcome
            you, my God.**

Psalm   I call with all my heart; Lord, hear me,
119:145–152 I will keep your commands.
            I call upon you, save me
            and I will do your will.

I rise before dawn and cry for help,
I hope in your word.
My eyes watch through the night
to ponder your promise.

In your love hear my voice, O Lord;
give me life by your decrees.
Those who harm me unjustly draw near:
they are far from your law.

But you, O Lord, are close:
your commands are truth.
Long have I known that your will
is established for ever.

Glory to the Father, and to the Son,
    and to the Holy Spirit:
—as it was in the beginning, is now,
and will be for ever. Amen.

Ant.   **Dawn finds me ready to welcome you,
my God.**

Ant. 2   **The Lord is my strength, and I shall sing
his praise, for he has become my Savior.**

Canticle:
Exodus 15:1–4a,
8–13, 17–18

I will sing to the Lord, for he is gloriously
    triumphant;
horse and chariot he has cast into the sea.

My strength and my courage is the Lord,
and he has been my savior.
He is my God, I praise him;
the God of my father, I extol him.

The Lord is a warrior,
Lord is his name!
Pharaoh's chariots and army he hurled
    into the sea.
At a breath of your anger the waters piled up,
the flowing waters stood like a mound,
the flood waters congealed in the midst
    of the sea.

The enemy boasted, "I will pursue and
    overtake them;
I will divide the spoils and have my
    fill of them;
I will draw my sword; my hand shall
    despoil them!"
When your wind blew, the sea covered them;
like lead they sank in the mighty waters.

Who is like to you among the gods, O Lord?
Who is like to you, magnificent in holiness?
O terrible in renown, worker of wonders,
when you stretched out your right hand, the
    earth swallowed them!

In your mercy you led the people
    you redeemed;
in your strength you guided them to your
    holy dwelling.

And you brought them in and planted them
    on the mountain of your inheritance—
the place where you made your seat, O Lord,
the sanctuary, O Lord, which your hands
    established.
The Lord shall reign forever and ever.

Glory to the Father, and to the Son,
    and to the Holy Spirit:
—as it was in the beginning, is now,
    and will be for ever. Amen.

Ant.   **The Lord is my strength, and I shall sing
his praise, for he has become my Savior.**

Ant. 3   **O praise the Lord, all you nations.**

Psalm 117   O praise the Lord, all you nations,
acclaim him, all you peoples!

Strong is his love for us;
he is faithful for ever.

Glory to the Father, and to the Son,
    and to the Holy Spirit:
—as it was in the beginning, is now,
    and will be for ever. Amen.

Ant.   **O praise the Lord, all you nations.**

Reading
2 Peter 1:10–11   Be solicitous to make your call and election
permanent, brothers; surely those who do so
will never be lost. On the contrary, your entry
into the everlasting kingdom of our Lord and
Savior Jesus Christ will be richly provided for.

Responsory   I cry to you, O Lord, for you are my refuge.
—I cry to you, O Lord, for you are my refuge.

You are all I desire in the land of the living;
—for you are my refuge.

Glory to the Father, and to the Son,
    and to the Holy Spirit.
—I cry to you, O Lord, for you are my refuge.

Gospel
Canticle

Ant. **Lord, shine on those who dwell in darkness and the shadow of death.**

Canticle of
Zechariah
Luke 1:68–79

Blessed + be the Lord, the God of Israel;
he has come to his people and set them free.

He has raised up for us a mighty savior,
born of the house of his servant David.

Through his holy prophets he
    promised of old
that he would save us from our enemies,
from the hands of all who hate us.

He promised to show mercy to our fathers
and to remember his holy covenant.

This was the oath he swore to our
    father Abraham:
to set us free from the hands of our enemies,
free to worship him without fear,
holy and righteous in his sight
    all the days of our life.

You, my child, shall be called the prophet of
    the Most High;
for you will go before the Lord to
    prepare his way,
to give his people knowledge of salvation
by the forgiveness of their sins.

In the tender compassion of our God
the dawn from on high shall break upon us,
to shine on those who dwell in darkness and
    the shadow of death,
and to guide our feet into the way of peace.

Glory to the Father, and to the Son,
    and to the Holy Spirit:
—as it was in the beginning, is now,
and will be for ever. Amen.

Ant. **Lord, shine on those who dwell in darkness
and the shadow of death.**

Intercessions Let us all praise Christ. In order to become
    our faithful and merciful high priest
    before the Father's throne, he chose to
    become one of us, a brother in all things.
    In prayer we ask of him:
Lord, share with us the treasure of your love.

Sun of Justice, you filled us with light at
    our baptism,
—we dedicate this day to you.

At every hour of the day, we give you glory,
—in all our deeds, we offer you praise.

Mary, your mother, was obedient to
    your word,
—direct our lives in accordance with that word.

Our lives are surrounded with passing
    things; set our hearts on things of heaven,
—so that through faith, hope and charity
    we may come to enjoy the vision of
    your glory.

The Lord's Prayer

Our Father, who art in heaven,
hallowed be thy name;
thy kingdom come,
thy will be done
on earth as it is in heaven.
Give us this day our daily bread,
and forgive us our trespasses,
as we forgive those who trespass against us;
and lead us not into temptation,
but deliver us from evil.

Pater noster, qui es in cælis:
sanctificetur nomen tuum;
adveniat regnum tuum;
fiat voluntas tua,
sicut in cælo, et in terra.
Panem nostrum cotidianum da nobis hodie;
et dimitte nobis debita nostra,
sicut et nos dimittimus debitoribus nostris;
et ne nos inducas in tentationem;
sed libera nos a malo.

Concluding
Prayer

Lord,
free us from the dark night of death.
Let the light of resurrection
dawn within our hearts
to bring us to the radiance of eternal life.
We ask this through our Lord Jesus Christ,
    your Son,
who lives and reigns with you and
    the Holy Spirit,
God, for ever and ever.
—Amen.

Dismissal   *If praying individually, or in a group without a priest or deacon:*

May the Lord + bless us,
protect us from all evil
and bring us to everlasting life.
—Amen.

If praying with a priest or deacon, he dismisses the people:

The Lord be with you.
—And with your spirit.

May almighty God bless you,
the Father, and the Son, + and the Holy Spirit.
—Amen.

Go in peace.
—Thanks be to God.

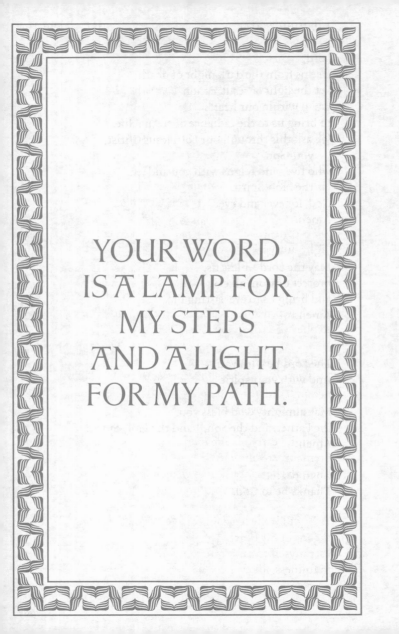

YOUR WORD
IS A LAMP FOR
MY STEPS
AND A LIGHT
FOR MY PATH.

EVENING PRAYER————————————
BEGINS THE TWENTY-SECOND SUNDAY IN ORDINARY TIME

God, + come to my assistance.
—Lord, make haste to help me.

Glory to the Father, and to the Son,
    and to the Holy Spirit:
—as it was in the beginning, is now,
    and will be for ever. Amen. Alleluia.

Hymn   *Glorious Things of Thee Are Spoken, p. 686*

Psalmody   Ant. 1 **Your word, O Lord, is the lantern to
              light our way, alleluia.**

Psalm   Your word is a lamp for my steps
119:105–112   and a light for my path.
              I have sworn and have made up my mind
              to obey your decrees.

              Lord, I am deeply afflicted:
              by your word give me life.
              Accept, Lord, the homage of my lips
              and teach me your decrees.

              Though I carry my life in my hands,
              I remember your law.
              Though the wicked try to ensnare me
              I do not stray from your precepts.

              Your will is my heritage for ever,
              the joy of my heart.
              I set myself to carry out your will
              in fullness, for ever.

Glory to the Father, and to the Son,
   and to the Holy Spirit:
—as it was in the beginning, is now,
   and will be for ever. Amen.

Ant.   **Your word, O Lord, is the lantern to light our way, alleluia.**

Ant. 2   **When I see your face, O Lord, I shall know the fullness of joy, alleluia.**

Psalm 16   Preserve me, God, I take refuge in you.
I say to the Lord: "You are my God.
My happiness lies in you alone."

He has put into my heart a marvelous love
for the faithful ones who dwell in his land.
Those who choose other gods increase
   their sorrows.
Never will I offer their offerings of blood.
Never will I take their name upon my lips.

O Lord, it is you who are my portion and cup;
it is you yourself who are my prize.
The lot marked out for me is my delight:
welcome indeed the heritage that falls to me!

I will bless the Lord who gives me counsel,
who even at night directs my heart.
I keep the Lord ever in my sight:
since he is at my right hand,
   I shall stand firm.

And so my heart rejoices, my soul is glad;
even my body shall rest in safety.
For you will not leave my soul
    among the dead,
nor let your beloved know decay.

You will show me the path of life,
the fullness of joy in your presence,
at your right hand happiness for ever.

Glory to the Father, and to the Son,
    and to the Holy Spirit:
—as it was in the beginning, is now,
and will be for ever. Amen.

Ant.   **When I see your face, O Lord, I shall know
the fullness of joy, alleluia.**

Ant. 3   **Let everything in heaven and on earth bend
the knee at the name of Jesus, alleluia.**

Canticle:
Philippians
2:6–11

Though he was in the form of God,
Jesus did not deem equality with God
something to be grasped at.

Rather, he emptied himself
and took the form of a slave,
being born in the likeness of men.

He was known to be of human estate,
and it was thus that he humbled himself,
obediently accepting even death,
death on a cross!

Because of this,
God highly exalted him
and bestowed on him the name
above every other name,

So that at Jesus' name
every knee must bend
in the heavens, on the earth,
and under the earth,
and every tongue proclaim
to the glory of God the Father:
JESUS CHRIST IS LORD!

Glory to the Father, and to the Son,
    and to the Holy Spirit:
—as it was in the beginning, is now,
and will be for ever. Amen.

Ant.   **Let everything in heaven and on earth bend
the knee at the name of Jesus, alleluia.**

Reading
Colossians
1:2b–6a

May God our Father give you grace and peace.
We always give thanks to God, the Father
of our Lord Jesus Christ, in our prayers for
you because we have heard of your faith in
Christ Jesus and the love you bear toward all
the saints—moved as you are by the hope
held in store for you in heaven. You heard of
this hope through the message of truth, the
gospel, which has come to you, has borne
fruit, and has continued to grow in your
midst, as it has everywhere in the world.

Responsory

From the rising of the sun to its setting,
may the name of the Lord be praised.
—From the rising of the sun to its setting,
may the name of the Lord be praised.

His splendor reaches far beyond the heavens;
—may the name of the Lord be praised.

Glory to the Father, and to the Son,
    and to the Holy Spirit.
—From the rising of the sun to its setting,
may the name of the Lord be praised.

Gospel
Canticle

Ant. **Of what use is it to a man to gain the whole world, if he pays for it by losing his soul?**

Canticle of Mary
Luke 1:46–55

My + soul proclaims the greatness of the Lord,
my spirit rejoices in God my Savior
for he has looked with favor on his
    lowly servant.

From this day all generations will
    call me blessed:
the Almighty has done great things for me,
and holy is his Name.

He has mercy on those who fear him
in every generation.

He has shown the strength of his arm,
he has scattered the proud in their conceit.

He has cast down the mighty from
    their thrones,
and has lifted up the lowly.

He has filled the hungry with good things,
and the rich he has sent away empty.

He has come to the help of his servant Israel
for he has remembered his promise of mercy,
the promise he made to our fathers,
to Abraham and his children for ever.

Glory to the Father, and to the Son,
    and to the Holy Spirit:
—as it was in the beginning, is now,
and will be for ever. Amen.

Ant.　**Of what use is it to a man to gain the whole
world, if he pays for it by losing his soul?**

Intercessions　God aids and protects the people he has
      chosen for his inheritance. Let us give
      thanks to him and proclaim his goodness:
Lord, we trust in you.

We pray for N., our Pope, and N., our bishop,
—protect them and in your goodness make
    them holy.

May the sick feel their companionship with
    the suffering Christ,
—and know that they will enjoy his eternal
    consolation.

In your goodness have compassion on
    the homeless,
—help them to find proper housing.

In your goodness give and preserve the fruits
    of the earth,
—so that each day there may be bread
      enough for all.

Lord, you attend the dying with great mercy,
—grant them an eternal dwelling.

The Lord's Prayer

Our Father, who art in heaven,
hallowed be thy name;
thy kingdom come,
thy will be done
on earth as it is in heaven.
Give us this day our daily bread,
and forgive us our trespasses,
as we forgive those who trespass against us;
and lead us not into temptation,
but deliver us from evil.

Pater noster, qui es in cælis:
sanctificetur nomen tuum;
adveniat regnum tuum;
fiat voluntas tua,
sicut in cælo, et in terra.
Panem nostrum cotidianum da nobis hodie;
et dimitte nobis debita nostra,
sicut et nos dimittimus debitoribus nostris;
et ne nos inducas in tentationem;
sed libera nos a malo.

Concluding Prayer

Almighty God,
every good thing comes from you.
Fill our hearts with love for you,
increase our faith,
and by your constant care
protect the good you have given us.
We ask this through our Lord Jesus Christ,
    your Son,
who lives and reigns with you and
    the Holy Spirit,
God, for ever and ever.
—Amen.

Dismissal

If praying individually, or in a group without a priest or deacon:

May the Lord + bless us,
protect us from all evil
and bring us to everlasting life.
—Amen.

If praying with a priest or deacon, he dismisses the people:

The Lord be with you.
—And with your spirit.

May almighty God bless you,
the Father, and the Son, + and the Holy Spirit.
—Amen.

Go in peace.
—Thanks be to God.

NIGHT PRAYER————————————————

God, + come to my assistance.
—Lord, make haste to help me.

Glory to the Father, and to the Son,
    and to the Holy Spirit:
—as it was in the beginning, is now,
    and will be for ever. Amen. Alleluia.

Examen *An optional brief examination of conscience may be made. Call to mind your*
sins and failings this day.

Hymn *O Gladsome Light, p. 696*

Psalmody Ant. 1 **Have mercy, Lord, and hear my prayer.**

Psalm 4 When I call, answer me, O God of justice;
from anguish you released me; have mercy
    and hear me!

O men, how long will your hearts be closed,
will you love what is futile and seek
    what is false?

It is the Lord who grants favors to those
    whom he loves;
the Lord hears me whenever I call him.

Fear him; do not sin: ponder on your bed
    and be still.
Make justice your sacrifice and trust
    in the Lord.

"What can bring us happiness?" many say.
Let the light of your face shine on us, O Lord.

You have put into my heart a greater joy
than they have from abundance of corn
    and new wine.

I will lie down in peace and sleep
    comes at once
for you alone, Lord, make me dwell in safety.

Glory to the Father, and to the Son,
    and to the Holy Spirit:
—as it was in the beginning, is now,
and will be for ever. Amen.

Ant.   **Have mercy, Lord, and hear my prayer.**

Ant. 2   **In the silent hours of night, bless the Lord.**

Psalm 134   O come, bless the Lord,
all you who serve the Lord,
who stand in the house of the Lord,
in the courts of the house of our God.

Lift up your hands to the holy place
and bless the Lord through the night.

May the Lord bless you from Zion,
he who made both heaven and earth.

Glory to the Father, and to the Son,
    and to the Holy Spirit:
—as it was in the beginning, is now,
and will be for ever. Amen.

Ant.   **In the silent hours of night, bless the Lord.**

Reading
Deuteronomy 6:4–7

Hear, O Israel! The Lord is our God, the Lord alone! Therefore, you shall love the Lord, your God, with all your heart, and with all your soul, and with all your strength. Take to heart these words which I enjoin on you today. Drill them into your children. Speak of them at home and abroad, whether you are busy or at rest.

Responsory

Into your hands, Lord, I commend my spirit.
—Into your hands, Lord, I commend my spirit.

You have redeemed us, Lord God of truth.
—I commend my spirit.

Glory to the Father, and to the Son,
    and to the Holy Spirit.
—Into your hands, Lord, I commend my spirit.

Gospel Canticle

Ant. **Protect us, Lord, as we stay awake; watch over us as we sleep, that awake, we may keep watch with Christ, and asleep, rest in his peace.**

Canticle of Simeon
Luke 2:29–32

Lord, + now you let your servant go in peace;
your word has been fulfilled:
my own eyes have seen the salvation
which you have prepared in the sight of
    every people:
a light to reveal you to the nations
and the glory of your people Israel.

Glory to the Father, and to the Son,
and to the Holy Spirit:
—as it was in the beginning, is now,
and will be for ever. Amen.

Ant. **Protect us, Lord, as we stay awake; watch over us as we sleep, that awake, we may keep watch with Christ, and asleep, rest in his peace.**

Concluding Prayer

Let us pray.
Lord,
be with us throughout this night.
When day comes may we rise from sleep
to rejoice in the resurrection of your Christ,
who lives and reigns for ever and ever.
—Amen.

Blessing

May the all-powerful Lord
grant us a restful night
and a peaceful death.
—Amen.

Marian Antiphon

Sing the "Salve Regina," found on p. 700, or pray a Hail Mary.

Hymns

Ave Regina Cælorum

A – ve, Re – gi – na cæ – lo – rum.

A – ve, Do – mi – na an – ge – lo – rum:

Sal – ve, ra – dix, sal – ve, por – ta.

Ex qua mun – do lux est or – ta:

Gau - de Vir - go glo - ri - o - sa,

Su - per om - nes spe - ci - o - sa:

Va - le, O val - de de - co - ra,

Et pro no - bis Chris-tum ex - o - ra.

Text: Latin, 12th century
Tune: AVE REGINA CAELORUM
Irregular meter

Blessed Feasts of Blessed Martyrs

Bless - ed   feasts   of   bless - ed   mar - tyrs,
Faith   and   hope   and   love   un - daunt - ed
Where - fore   made   co - heirs   of   glo - ry,

Saint - ly   wom - en,   saint - ly   men,
Filled   the   sure   and   sin - gle   heart.
Ye   that   sit   with   Christ   on   high,

With   af - fec - tion's   rec - ol - lec - tions
Thus   they,   glo - rious   and   vic - to - rious,
Join   our   plead - ing,   in - ter - ced - ing,

Greet   we   your   re - turn   a - gain.
Brave - ly   bore   the   mar - tyr's   part.
As   for   grace   and   peace   we   cry,

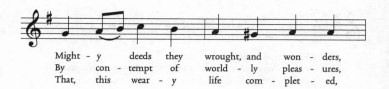

Might - y   deeds   they   wrought, and   won - ders,
By   con - tempt   of   world - ly   pleas - ures,
That,   this   wear - y   life   com - plet - ed,

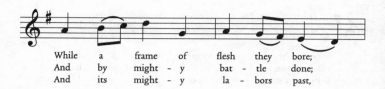

While   a   frame   of   flesh   they   bore;
And   by   might - y   bat - tle   done;
And   its   might - y   la - bors   past,

We   with   meet - est   praise   and   sweet - est
Have   they   mer - it - ed   with   an - gels
We   may   mer - it   to   be   seat - ed

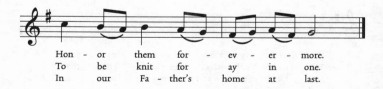

Hon - or   them   for - ev - er - more.
To   be   knit   for   ay   in   one.
In   our   Fa - ther's   home   at   last.

Text: *O beata beatorum*, translated by J.M. Neale
Tune: IN BABILONE, from *Oude en Nieuwe Hollantse Boerenlities en Contradanseu*
8.7.8.7 D

From All That Dwell Below the Skies

From all that dwell be - low the skies
E - ter - nal are your mer - cies, Lord;
Your loft - y themes, blest mor - tals, bring;
In ev - ery land be - gin the song;

Let the Cre - a - tor's praise a - rise;
E - ter - nal truth at - tends your Word.
In songs of praise di - vine - ly sing;
To ev - ery land the strains be - long;

Let the Re - deem - er's name be sung
Your praise shall sound from shore to shore,
The great sal - va - tion loud pro - claim,
In cheer - ful sounds all voic - es raise,

Through ev - ery land by ev - ery tongue.
Till suns shall rise and set no more.
And shout for joy the Sav - ior's name.
And fill the world with loud - est praise.

Text: Isaac Watts
Tune: DUKE STREET, John Hatton
Long Meter, 8.8.8.8

Hail, Holy Queen

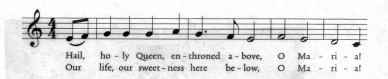

Hail, ho - ly Queen, en - throned a - bove, O Ma - ri - a!
Our life, our sweet - ness here be - low, O Ma - ri - a!

Hail, moth-er of mer-cy and of love, O Ma - ri - a!
Our hope in sor-row and in woe, O Ma - ri - a!

Tri - umph, all ye cher - u - bim, Sing with us, ye

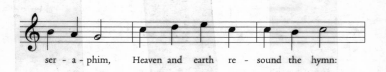

ser - a - phim, Heaven and earth re - sound the hymn:

Sal - ve, sal - ve, sal - ve, Re - gi - na!

Text: *Salve Regina coelitum*, anonymous translator
Tune: SALVE REGINA COELITUM, German melody
8.4.8.4.7.7.7.4.5

685

Glorious Things of Thee Are Spoken

Glo - rious things of thee are spo - ken,
See! the streams of liv - ing wa - ters,
Round each hab - i - ta - tion hov - ering,
Sav - ior, if of Zi - on's cit - y

Zi - on, cit - y of our God!
Spring - ing from e - ter - nal love,
See the cloud and fire ap - pear!
I through grace a mem - ber am,

He whose word can - not be bro - ken
Well sup - ply thy sons and daugh - ters,
For a glo - ry and a cov - ering
Let the world de - ride or pit - y,

Formed thee for his own a - bode.
And all fear of want re - move:
Show - ing that the Lord is near.
I will glo - ry in thy name:

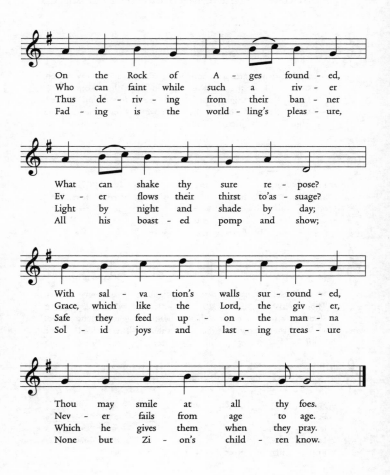

On the Rock of A - ges found - ed,
Who can faint while such a riv - er
Thus de - riv - ing from their ban - ner
Fad - ing is the world - ling's pleas - ure,

What can shake thy sure re - pose?
Ev - er flows their thirst to'as - suage?
Light by night and shade by day;
All his boast - ed pomp and show;

With sal - va - tion's walls sur - round - ed,
Grace, which like the Lord, the giv - er,
Safe they feed up - on the man - na
Sol - id joys and last - ing treas - ure

Thou may smile at all thy foes.
Nev - er fails from age to age.
Which he gives them when they pray.
None but Zi - on's child - ren know.

Text: John Newton
Tune: HYMN TO JOY, arranged from Ludwig van Beethoven
8.7.8.7 D

God Who Made Both Earth and Heaven

God who made both earth and heav - en,
God, I thank thee: in thy keep - ing
Let the night of sin that shroud - ed
O my God, I now com - mend me
Thus a - fresh with each new morn - ing

Fa - ther, Son, and Ho - ly Ghost,
Safe - ly have I slum - bered here;
Form - er days with this de - part;
Whol - ly to thy might - y hand:
Save me from the power of sin;

Who the day and night have giv - en,
Thou hast guard - ed me while sleep - ing
Shine on me with beams un - cloud - ed:
All the powers that thou dost lend me
Hour - ly let me feel thy warn - ing

Sun and moon and star - ry host,
From all dan - ger, pain, and fear,
Je - sus, in thy lov - ing heart
Let me use at thy com - mand;
Rul - ing, prompt - ing all with - in,

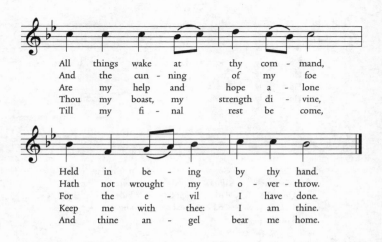

All things wake at thy com - mand,
And the cun - ning of my foe
Are my help and hope a - lone
Thou my boast, my strength di - vine,
Till my fi - nal rest be come,

Held in be - ing by thy hand.
Hath not wrought my o - ver - throw.
For the e - vil I have done.
Keep me with thee: I am thine.
And thine an - gel bear me home.

Text: *Gott des Himmels und der Erden*, Heinrich Albert, translated
by Catherine Winkworth
Tune: ZEUCH MICH, ZEUCH MICH, from *Geistreiches Gesangbuch*
8.7.8.7

Holy, Holy, Holy

Ho - ly, ho - ly, ho - ly,
Ho - ly, ho - ly, ho - ly,
Ho - ly, ho - ly, ho - ly,
Ho - ly, ho - ly, ho - ly,

Lord_____ God al - might - y,
all the saints a - dore thee,
though the dark - ness hide thee,
Lord_____ God al - might - y,

Ear - ly in the morn___ - ing our
Cast - ing down their gold - en crowns a -
Though the eye of sin - ful man thy
All thy works shall praise thy name in

song shall rise to thee.
round the glass - y sea.
glo - ry may not see,
earth and sky and sea.

Holy, holy, ho—ly,
Cher—u—bim and ser—a—phim
On—ly thou are ho—ly;
Holy, holy, ho—ly,

mer—ci—ful and might—y,
fall—ing down be—fore thee,
there is none be—side thee:
mer—ci—ful and might—y,

God in three Per—sons,
Who were, and are, and
Per—fect in power, in
God in three Per—sons,

bless—ed Trin—i—ty.
ev—er—more shall be.
love and pur—i—ty.
bless—ed Trin—i—ty.

Text: Reginald Heber
Tune: NICAEA, John B. Dykes
11.12.12.10

691

High Let Us All Our Voices Raise

High let us all our voices raise
Filled with a pure celestial glow,
O Christ, the strength of all the strong,
To God the Father, with the Son,

In that heroic woman's praise
She spurned false love of things below,
To whom our holiest deeds belong,
And Holy Spirit, Three in One,

Whose name with saintly glory bright
And heedless here on earth to stay,
Through her prevailing prayers on high
Be glory while the ages flow

Bedecks the starry realms of light.
She climbed to heaven her toilsome way.
In mercy hear your people's cry.
From all above and all below.

Text: *Fortem virili pectore*, Silvio Antoniano, translated by Edward Caswall
Tune: OLD HUNDREDTH, Louis Bourgeois
Long Meter, 8.8.8.8

Jesus, Eternal Truth Sublime

Je - sus, e - ter - nal Truth sub - lime,
A - gain re - turns the sa - cred day
You, Je - sus, his all - gra - cious Lord,
In ho - ly deeds of faith and love,

Through end - less years the same!
With heaven - ly glo - ry bright
Con - fess - ing to the last,
In fast - ings and in prayers,

O Crown of those who through all time
Which saw your saint go on his way
He trod be - neath him Sa - tan's fraud,
His days were spent, and now a - bove

Con - fess your ho - ly name!
In - to the realms of light.
And stood for - ev - er fast.
Your heaven - ly Feast he shares.

Text: *Iesu, Corona celsior,* translated by Edward Caswall
Tune: LAND OF REST, American folk melody
Common Meter, 8.6.8.6

Let All on Earth Their Voices Raise

Let all on earth their voic - es raise,
Lord, at whose word they bore the light
Lord, at whose will to them was given
Lord, in whose might they spoke the word
And when the thrones are set on high,

Re - ech - oing heaven's tri - um - phant praise
Of gos - pel truth o'er heath - en night,
To bind and loose in earth and heaven,
That cured dis - ease and health re - stored,
And judg - ment's aw - ful hour draws nigh,

To him who gave th'a - pos - tles grace
To us that heaven - ly light im - part
Our chains un - bind, our sins un - do,
To us its heal - ing power pro - long;
Then, Lord, with them pro - nounce us blest,

To run on earth their glo - rious race.
To glad our eyes and cheer our heart.
And in our hearts your grace re - new.
Sup - port the weak, con - firm the strong.
And take us to your end - less rest.

Text: *Exsultet cælum laudibus*, translated by Richard Mant
Tune: TALLIS' CANON, Thomas Tallis
Long Meter, 8.8.8.8

Now That the Sun Is Gleaming Bright

Now that the sun is gleaming bright,
No sin - ful word, nor deed of wrong,
And while the hours in or - der flow,
And grant that to your hon - or, Lord,

Im - plore we, bend - ing low,
Nor thoughts that id - ly rove,
O Christ, se - cure - ly fence
Our dai - ly toil may tend:

That he, the un - cre - at - ed Light
But sim - ple truth be on our tongue,
Our gates, be - lea - guered by the foe:
That we be - gin it at your word,

May guide us as we go.
And in our hearts be love.
The gate of ev - ery sense.
And in your fa - vor end.

Text: *Iam lucis orto sidere*, translated by St. John Henry Newman
Tune: NEW BRITAIN, from *Virginia Harmony*
Common Meter, 8.6.8.6

695

O Gladsome Light

O glad-some Light, O grace of God the
As fades the day's last light we see the
To you of right be-longs all praise of

Fa - ther's face, The e - ter - nal splen-dor wear - ing;
lamps of night, Our com-mon hymn out-pour - ing,
ho - ly songs, O Son of God, Life - giv - er.

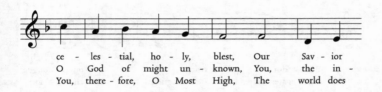

ce - les - tial, ho - ly, blest, Our Sav - ior
O God of might un - known, You, the in -
You, there - fore, O Most High, The world does

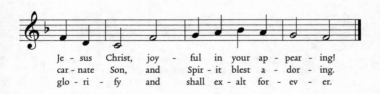

Je - sus Christ, joy - ful in your ap - pear - ing!
car - nate Son, and Spir - it blest a - dor - ing.
glo - ri - fy and shall ex - alt for - ev - er.

Text: Φῶς Ἱλαρόν, translated by Robert Bridges
Tune: NUNC DIMITTIS, Genevan Psalter

6.6.7 D

O God, Creator of All Things

O God, Cre - a - tor of all things,
We hymn you thanks for this done day,
To you our deep - est hearts re - sound,
And when the dark - ness is pro - found,
O Christ and Fa - ther, we re - quest,

Who o'er the fir - ma - ment are King,
And for the ris - ing night we pray
To you our voic - es' tune - ful sound;
And day lies in dark's pris - on bound,
From you and from your Spir - it blest,

Who clothe the day with gild - ing light,
That you will has - ten to our aid,
To you a - ris - es high a - bove,
May faith know not the want of light,
That you who gov - ern with one might

And with the grace of sleep the night,
To help us fill the vows we made.
From so - ber minds, our pur - est love.
But light the ver - y dark of night.
May care for us through - out the night.

Text: *Deus Creator omnium*, St. Ambrose, translated by Kathleen Pluth
Tune: JESU DULCIS MEMORIA, Latin hymn tune
Long Meter, 8.8.8.8

O Light of Light, by Love Inclined

O Light of Light, by love in - clined,
More bright by day your face did show,
The heavens a - bove your glo - ry named:
May all who seek your praise a - right
E - ter - nal God, to you we raise,

Je - sus, Re - deem - er of man - kind,
Your cloth - ing whit - er than the snow,
The Fa - ther's voice the Son pro - claimed,
Through pur - er lives show forth your light,
O King of kings, our hymn of praise,

With lov - ing - kind - ness grant to hear
When on the mount to mor - tals blest
To whom, the King of glo - ry now,
So to the bright - ness of the skies
Who, Three in One and One in Three,

From sup - pliant voic - es praise and prayer.
Our Mak - er you were man - i - fest.
All faith - ful hearts a - dor - ing bow.
By ho - ly deeds our hearts shall rise.
Do live and reign e - ter - nal - ly.

Text: *O nata Lux de Lumine*, translated by Laurence Housman
Tune: DUKE STREET, John Hatton
Long Meter, 8.8.8.8

O Wondrous Type! O Vision Fair

O won - drous type! O vi - sion fair
The Law and proph - ets there have place,
With shin - ing face and bright ar - ray
And faith - ful hearts are raised on high

Of glo - ry that the Church shall share
Two cho - sen wit - ness - es of grace;
Christ deigns to man - i - fest that day
By this great vi - sion's mys - ter - y

Which Christ up - on the moun - tain shows,
The Fa - ther's voice from out the cloud
What glo - ry shall be theirs a - bove
For which in joy - ful strains we raise

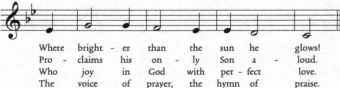

Where bright - er than the sun he glows!
Pro - claims his on - ly Son a - loud.
Who joy in God with per - fect love.
The voice of prayer, the hymn of praise.

Text: *Cælestis formam gloriæ*, translated by J.M. Neale
Tune: DEO GRACIAS, English ballad melody
Long Meter, 8.8.8.8

699

Salve Regina

Sal - ve, Re - gi - na, Ma - ter mi - se - ri - cor - di - æ,

vit - a, dul - ce - do, et spes no - stra, sal - ve.

Ad te cla - ma - mus, ex - su - les fi - li - i He - væ.

Ad te sus - pi - ra - mus, ge - men - tes et flen - tes

in hac la - cri - ma - rum val - le. Ei - a er - go, ad - vo - ca - ta nos - tra,

il - los tu - os mi - se - ri - cor-des o - cu - los ad nos con - ver - te.

Et Je - sum, be - ne - di-ctum fru-ctum ven-tris tu - i,

no - bis post hoc ex - si - li - um o - sten - de.

O_____ cle - mens, O_____ pi - a,

O_____ dul - cis Vir - go Ma - ri - a.

Text: Latin, 11th century
Tune: SALVE REGINA
Irregular meter

The Saints of God!

The saints of God! Their con - flict past,
The saints of God! Life's voy - age o'er,
The saints of God their vig - il keep,
Fa - ther of saints! To you we cry;

And life's long bat - tle won at last,
Safe land - ed on that bliss - ful shore,
While yet their mor - tal bod - ies sleep,
O Sav - ior! Plead for us on high;

No more they need the shield or sword,
No storm - y tem - pests now they dread,
Till from the dust they too shall rise
O Ho - ly Ghost! Our guide and friend,

They cast them down be - fore their Lord:
No roar - ing bil - lows lift their head.
And soar tri - um - phant to the skies:
Grant us your grace till life shall end,

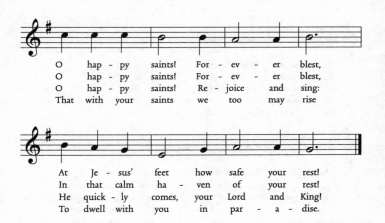

O hap - py saints! For - ev - er blest,
O hap - py saints! For - ev - er blest,
O hap - py saints! Re - joice and sing:
That with your saints we too may rise

At Je - sus' feet how safe your rest!
In that calm ha - ven of your rest!
He quick - ly comes, your Lord and King!
To dwell with you in par - a - dise.

Text: William Dalrymple Maclagan
Tune: ST. CATHERINE, Henry F. Hemy
8.8.8.8.8.8.8

You Sought the Solitude of Caves

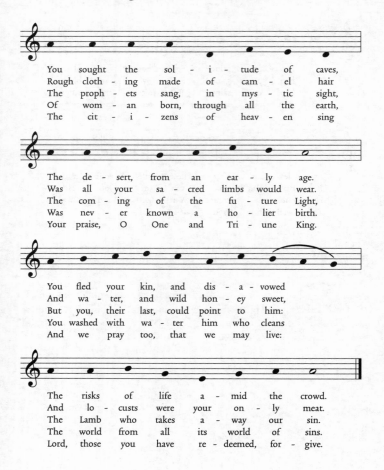

You sought the sol - i - tude of caves,
Rough cloth - ing made of cam - el hair
The proph - ets sang, in mys - tic sight,
Of wom - an born, through all the earth,
The cit - i - zens of heav - en sing

The de - sert, from an ear - ly age.
Was all your sa - cred limbs would wear.
The com - ing of the fu - ture Light,
Was nev - er known a ho - lier birth.
Your praise, O One and Tri - une King.

You fled your kin, and dis - a - vowed
And wa - ter, and wild hon - ey sweet,
But you, their last, could point to him:
You washed with wa - ter him who cleans
And we pray too, that we may live:

The risks of life a - mid the crowd.
And lo - custs were your on - ly meat.
The Lamb who takes a - way our sin.
The world from all its world of sins.
Lord, those you have re - deemed, for - give.

Text: *Antra deserti*, attributed to Paul the Deacon,
translated by Kathleen Pluth
Tune: JESU DULCIS MEMORIA, Latin hymn tune
Long Meter, 8.8.8.8

Ave Regina Cælorum (p. 680)
This melody is one of a kind and does not have an alternative. The text may be recited, or a Hail Mary may be said.

Blessed Feasts of Blessed Martyrs (p. 682)
This melody is also sung with the text "There's a Wideness in God's Mercy." **Alternate melodies:** God, We Praise You; Joyful, Joyful, We Adore Thee; Love Divine, All Loves Excelling; Praise the Lord, Ye Heavens, Adore Him; Sing with All the Saints in Glory

From All That Dwell Below the Skies (p. 684)
This melody is also sung with the texts "Jesus Shall Reign" and "I Know That My Redeemer Lives." **Alternate melodies:** All Hail, Adored Trinity; All People That on Earth Do Dwell; Creator of the Stars of Night; From All That Dwell Below the Skies; Lift Up Your Heads; O Radiant Light; O Salutaris Hostia (O Saving Victim); Take Up Your Cross; The God Whom Earth and Sea and Sky; To Thee Before the Close of Day (Before the Final Light of Day); When I Survey the Wondrous Cross

Glorious Things of Thee Are Spoken (p. 686)
This melody is also sung with the text "Joyful, Joyful, We Adore Thee." **Alternate melodies:** God, We Praise You; Love Divine, All Loves Excelling; Praise the Lord, Ye Heavens, Adore Him; There's a Wideness in God's Mercy

God Who Made Both Earth and Heaven (p. 688)
Alternate melody: Light Serene of Holy Glory

Hail, Holy Queen (p. 685)
This melody is one of a kind and does not have an alternative. The text may be recited, or another Marian hymn may be sung.

Holy, Holy, Holy (p. 690)
This hymn is in an unusual meter. The text may be recited, or another hymn may be sung instead.

High Let Us All Our Voices Raise (p. 692)
This melody is also sung with the texts "All Hail, Adored Trinity" and "All People That on Earth Do Dwell." **Alternate melodies:** Creator of the Stars of Night; From All That Dwell Below the Skies; I Know That My Redeemer Lives; Jesus Shall Reign; Lift Up Your Heads; O Radiant Light; O Salutaris Hostia (O Saving Victim); Take Up Your Cross; The God Whom Earth and Sea and Sky; To Thee Before the Close of Day (Before the Final Light of Day); When I Survey the Wondrous Cross

Jesus, Eternal Truth Sublime (p. 693)
This melody is also sung with the text "Jerusalem, My Happy Home." **Alternate melodies:** Amazing Grace; Praise to the Holiest in the Height; The Head That Once Was Crowned with Thorns; The King of Love My Shepherd Is; The King Shall Come When Morning Dawns; We Walk by Faith

Let All on Earth Their Voices Raise (p. 694)

This melody is also sung with the text "All Praise to Thee, My God, This Night."

Alternate melodies: All Hail, Adored Trinity; All People That on Earth Do Dwell; Creator of the Stars of Night; From All That Dwell Below the Skies; I Know That My Redeemer Lives; Jesus Shall Reign; Lift Up Your Heads; O Radiant Light; O Salutaris Hostia (O Saving Victim); Take Up Your Cross; The God Whom Earth and Sea and Sky; To Thee Before the Close of Day (Before the Final Light of Day); When I Survey the Wondrous Cross

Now That the Sun Is Gleaming Bright (p. 695)

This melody is also sung with the text "Amazing Grace."

Alternate melodies: Jerusalem, My Happy Home; Praise to the Holiest in the Height; The Head That Once Was Crowned with Thorns; The King of Love My Shepherd Is; The King Shall Come When Morning Dawns; We Walk by Faith

O Gladsome Light (p. 696)

This melody is one of a kind and does not have an alternative. The text may be recited, or another hymn may be sung.

O God, Creator of All Things (p. 697)

This melody is also sung with the text "O Radiant Light."

Alternate melodies: All Hail, Adored Trinity; All People That on Earth Do Dwell; Creator of the Stars of Night; From All That Dwell Below the Skies; I Know That My Redeemer Lives; Jesus Shall Reign; Lift Up Your Heads; O Salutaris Hostia (O Saving Victim); Take Up Your Cross; The God Whom Earth and Sea and Sky; To Thee Before the Close of Day (Before the Final Light of Day); When I Survey the Wondrous Cross

O Light of Light, by Love Inclined (p. 698)

This melody is also sung with the texts "From All That Dwell Below the Skies," "Jesus Shall Reign," and "I Know That My Redeemer Lives."

Alternate melodies: All Hail, Adored Trinity; All People That on Earth Do Dwell; Creator of the Stars of Night; Lift Up Your Heads; O Radiant Light; O Salutaris Hostia (O Saving Victim); Take Up Your Cross; The God Whom Earth and Sea and Sky; To Thee Before the Close of Day (Before the Final Light of Day); When I Survey the Wondrous Cross

O Wondrous Type! O Vision Fair
(p. 699)
Alternate melodies: All Hail, Adored
Trinity; All People That on Earth Do
Dwell; Creator of the Stars of Night;
From All That Dwell Below the Skies;
I Know That My Redeemer Lives; Jesus
Shall Reign; Lift Up Your Heads; O
Radiant Light; O Salutaris Hostia (O
Saving Victim); Take Up Your Cross;
The God Whom Earth and Sea and
Sky; To Thee Before the Close of Day
(Before the Final Light of Day); When
I Survey the Wondrous Cross

Salve Regina (p. 700)
This melody is one of a kind and does
not have an alternative. The text may
be recited, or a Hail Mary may be said.

The Saints of God! (p. 702)
This melody is also sung with the text
"Faith of Our Fathers."
Alternate melodies: Eternal
Father, Strong to Save; O Come, O
Come, Emmanuel

You Sought the Solitude of Caves
(p. 704)
This melody is also sung with the text
"O Radiant Light."
Alternate melodies: All Hail, Adored
Trinity; All People That on Earth Do
Dwell; Creator of the Stars of Night;
From All That Dwell Below the Skies;
I Know That My Redeemer Lives;
Jesus Shall Reign; Lift Up Your Heads;
O Salutaris Hostia (O Saving Victim);
Take Up Your Cross; The God Whom
Earth and Sea and Sky; To Thee Before
the Close of Day (Before the Final
Light of Day); When I Survey the
Wondrous Cross

Pray with the Church.

Subscribe at wordonfire.org/pray
and receive a new Liturgy of the Hours
booklet each month.

To update your address or modify your account,
simply go to account.wordonfire.org/loth

The Liturgy of the Hours (ISSN 2771-1285) is published monthly by
Word on Fire Catholic Ministries, 25 Northwest Point Blvd,
Suite 1025, Elk Grove Village, IL 60007. Periodicals Postage Paid at
Elk Grove Village, IL, and at additional mailing offices.

POSTMASTER: Send address changes to The Liturgy of the Hours,
PO Box 97330, Washington, DC 20090-7330.

Issue 27

AUGUST 2024   2771-1285

7   93888   60467   3